GLOBAL POLITICAL ECONOMY

A Critique of Contemporary Capitalism

Edited by

V. Upadhyay and Paramjit Singh

Global Political Economy: A Critique of Contemporary Capitalism
Edited by V. Upadhyay and Paramjit Singh

First Published 2021
Reprinted 2023

ISBN 978-93-5002-697-7 (Pb)

Published by
AAKAR BOOKS
28 E Pocket IV, Mayur Vihar Phase I
Delhi 110 091 India
aakarbooks@gmail.com

Laser Typeset at
Arpit Printographers, Delhi

Printed at
D.K. Fine Art, Delhi

Contents

Preface

The present volume is an attempt to make students and researchers familiar with contemporary issues in global political economy with a focus on the working of global capitalism in the last four to five decades. This volume will be useful for universities and colleges which are already conducting political economy courses. They can update their curriculum to cover the emergent global issues in detail along with providing minimum necessary coverage of historical issues/debates. As per our experience, students of political economy often find it difficult to get a range of topics from a single book as they generally get in case of other subjects. The Indian Political Economy Association has been constantly getting demands from students, researchers and teachers to publish a volume which can cover new issues of global political economy relevant for students and researchers.

Keeping all this in mind, the Indian Political Economy Association has decided to publish a volume that attempts to cover a wide range of topics of historical and contemporary relevance. This project was undertaken by the association a year ago. Both of us have had the privilege to accomplish this task. We held a few meetings with scholars and professors of political economy from various parts of the country to shortlist the topics. We also had a workshop on contemporary questions of global political economy in 2019. After all the discussions and debates, we have shortlisted some important issues for this volume. We have contacted leading political economists in India and abroad for contributions. We are confident that this volume will play a pivotal role in enhancing the understanding of the young political economists regarding issues of global relevance.

Many scholars who are associated with the Indian Political Economy Association have given their insightful suggestions for the completion of this work. We would like to thank the journals who gave us permission to reprint some papers for the benefit of scholars of political economy. We wish to thank the editors of *Social Scientist, Monthly Review* and *Agrarian South: Journal of Political Economy* who permitted us to reprint their papers in this volume. We would also like to extend our gratitude to the members of the Indian Political Economy Association who reposed trust in us to complete this task. At the end we would like to thank Aakar Books for accepting our proposal and agreed to publish this volume. We sincerely hope that this volume will open up many dimensions for political economy researchers for further exploration.

Introduction

V. Upadhyay and Paramjit Singh

Political economy is a field of study that deals with the interaction between political and economic forces. The issues of political economy have transformed greatly after the ascendancy of neoliberal capitalism during the 1970s. The modern phase of capitalism is characterised as the phase of globalisation, liberalisation and financialisation. Global political economy is a relatively new discipline that aims at developing an understanding of patterns of interaction and change in the globalised world by looking at both international politics and economics in an integrated manner. The purpose of this volume is to make students and researchers familiar with theoretical concepts and recent developments in global capitalism. It is an attempt to present an alternative paradigm on contemporary issues in global political economy with a focus on the working of global capitalism in the last four to five decades.

The present volume is an attempt to provide an integrated understanding of subjects covering historical debates, conceptual framework and contemporary challenges produced by neoliberal capitalism. There are various approaches to global political economy which elucidate the contemporary challenges posed by economic globalisation. These approaches range from liberal mainstream approaches to Marxist approaches. The mainstream approaches have a serious drawback because of their ahistorical approach as they take the capitalist system as given and do not consider the global political economic problems as an outcome of the accumulation logic of capitalism. On the other hand, the Marxian approach has a merit that it understands the national and global economic and political problems as structural to accumulation logic of capitalism.

The focus of Marxist analysis is, however, more on historical subjects, such as early industrial development in Europe, and inter-war colonial period, as a result of which new existential crises—the environmental crisis, the growing threat of a nuclear war, and threats of new dangerous technologies—are not given adequate and urgent attention they deserve. The conventional wisdom that has been developed by the neoliberal politicians and intellectuals of the Global North about the advantages of neoliberal policies came under severe criticism after the outbreak of the global financial crisis in 2008. The ideology of neoliberlaism propagated by the supporters of this ideology posits that the only hope for prosperity for people in developing nations of the Global South lies in opening all the markets (and even the social and cultural spaces that have traditionally not been part of the market) for capital, domestic as well as foreign. The deregulation of capital in the name of free market and freedom for capital has given birth to multiple threats in developed as well as developing countries that have not been the subject matter of mainstream economics. The failure of neoliberal capitalism and the growing economic and power imbalances in world economy suggest that it is time for pro-people intellectuals to build a consensus and rethink political economy of globalisation.

In the present volume, a historical perspective is adopted to bridge the gap between theoretical advances and real world problems produced by contemporary neoliberal capitalism. It has been realised that in order to understand and analyse contemporary capitalism, it is extremely important to understand its historical nature and the interrelation between economics, politics and the environment. Therefore, in response to the recent economic and political developments, this volume will provide a historically-grounded account to understand the current challenges posed by global capitalism. It traces the evolution of the global political economy on theoretical grounds which are rooted in Marxian historical materialism and analysis of capitalism followed by the investigation of current challenges. It explores in detail the dynamics of global political economy in the 21st century, providing systematic coverage of the key spheres of activity—such as production, finance, labour, imperialism, new forms of capitalist accumulation, and the environment.

A detailed understanding of major recent challenges that have brought the failures of world capitalism to the surface is necessary for seeking mechanisms for addressing these challenges. In the following sections we will try to cover some of the recent threats posed by global capitalism and their implications for the world economy and politics. The first part examines the long-term effects of the COVID-19 pandemic. As the chapters in this volume were written before the beginning of the global health crisis and, therefore, do not take into account the effects of the crisis, it was felt necessary to provide an overview of the possible long-term consequences of the pandemic in the introduction section itself. The second part examines the question of distribution—one of the central questions of our time—through understanding the question of income and wealth inequality. The third part discusses the persistence of hunger and food insecurity in the Global South and the failure of capitalism to counter these problems. The last part provides the summary of a range of topics covered in the present volume.

PART I

The Long-Term Global Effects of the COVID-19 Crisis

Coronavirus (COVID-19) that started in China in early December spread to the entire world within a span of a few months. This is a reflection of how globalised the world is now. The main cause of the fast transmission of this novel virus has been the high volume of international travel. This virus has infected about 20 million people around the world and there have been close to one million deaths caused by the virus. The effects of the pandemic go much beyond the world-wide health crisis created by it.

There have been many pandemics in the past. During the last hundred years or so, the world has seen pandemics such as Spanish flu, Asian flu, HIV SARS, Swine flu, MERS, and Ebola, that led to millions of deaths worldwide. It is estimated that about 50 million people died due to Spanish flu during 1918-19. But never before has the world's reaction to a pandemic been such as this time: The worldwide panic reaction to COVID-19 has no parallel in history.

Every country has responded to this health crisis with measures that have paralysed life continuously for many months. Many nations imposed curfew-like lockdowns which completely constrained all aspects of life bringing economic, social and political activities to a virtual standstill.

In this section we will focus on the economic and political effects of prolonged lockdowns and the methods to enforce them.

Fast Descent into Depression

Panic reaction to the health crisis led to governments almost everywhere to impose restrictions on people's movement. People were asked not to venture out of houses for months and maintain social distancing. In many countries, these restrictions were very swift and draconian. As a result, economic activities there collapsed completely within a space of a few days. In the US, for example, a near full-employment economy in the early months of 2020, ground to a halt in a matter of a few weeks rendering more than 40 million workers jobless. The rate of unemployment reached the 1930s Depression level of about 25 per cent. There are forecasts of 10 to 15 per cent decline in GDP in 2020. Many countries in Europe, Latin America, Asia and Africa face a similar situation of massive unemployment and loss of income and livelihood.

The burden of the lockdown-induced economic downfall has fallen mostly on the poorer sections of the society. It is mostly the poor people, low-wage earners who have seen their jobs disappearing and their lives shattered overnight. Millions of people across nations have been pushed into extreme poverty due to lockdowns.

Uncertain Path of Recovery

The path of economic recovery[1] depends on many factors. Even after the lockdowns are lifted, the economy may take several years to reach the pre-COVID levels. In some respects, the economic effects of the health crisis are likely to continue over a very long period. There are many sectors in the economy such as air travel, tourism, hotels and restaurants, major entertainment and sports events, that may never see a full recovery. In that sense, some parts of the economy might be lost permanently.

This health crisis combined with the unprecedented panic-stricken reaction is also likely to alter people's consumption and saving behaviour. Excessive consumption on the part of people is an essential requirement for the functioning of the present capitalist system. But the psychological effects caused by the fearful experience of the health crisis are certain to make people much more risk-averse in the future. This is certain to dampen the pace of capital accumulation, and in turn, reduce the capitalist economies' growth potential.

Impact of Stimulus Measures

Different countries have adopted varying measures to ameliorate the downside effects of lockdowns on the economy. The US, Canada, and many European countries have announced huge fiscal stimulus packages with the aim to lessen the sufferings of people and businesses hurt due to prolonged lockdowns. The purpose of the rescue measures is also to put the economy back on a path of revival and growth.

Many countries have made extensive use of expansive monetary policies. Central banks in many countries have reduced key interest rates to near zero and in some countries benchmark interest rates have moved into negative zone. Implications of these easy money policies go far beyond the immediate effects on the revival path of the economies. The unprecedentedly liberal use of money expansion puts a question mark on integrity and soundness of fiat money in many Western capitalist countries. Excessive increase in money supply can lead to inflationary outcomes in case the growth in real economy remains very sluggish. This can erode the value of money rapidly. But more importantly, it needs to be understood that infusion of large quantities of money in the economy is hardly ever distributionally neutral. The experience of Western economies in recent decades clearly shows that large money infusion works primarily to enhance wealth of the richer sections in the society.

The US government has launched $2 trillion worth stimulus

package and there are plans to borrow additional $3 trillion to foot the bill for its economic rescue measures. The Federal Reserve has taken its quantitative easing policies to new heights. It has undertaken unprecedented measures to support the economy. The Fed promises to buy any amount of treasury bonds issued by the US government for the purpose of financing its stimulus plans. It is de facto monetisation of fiscal deficit. This method, guided by insights of the modern monetary theory, and referred to as 'printing of money' is now being used on a large scale. The Federal Reserve has extended its bond buying activity much beyond treasury bonds and mortgage backed securities which have been its traditional areas of operation. The Fed has shown willingness to buy corporate bonds, including junk bonds.

The main beneficiaries of the US assistance programmes have been large corporations, especially the blue chip companies. The stimulus schemes have worked largely to prop up financial markets, including the stock markets. The quantitative easing policies pursued by the Federal Reserve have significantly increased wealth inequalities in the US.

The poorer sections of the society across all nations have borne the brunt of the lockdowns imposed by state order. According to the ILO, 1.6 billion people in informal sector, which is nearly half of the global workforce, were at risk of losing income due to the lockdowns. The ILO also estimates that 305 million full-time jobs were at risk of being lost. According to the report published by UNU-WIDER, the economic fallout from lockdowns could plunge about 400 million people worldwide into extreme poverty.

Legitimacy of Fiat Money

Is there a limit to the printing of money? What is the significance of the soundness and integrity of money in the functioning of modern capitalist system? It is quite likely that at some stage people will lose faith in fiat money if money supply growth loses connection with the pace of growth of real economy. This is a phenomenon that occurs quite often in developing countries. The advanced capitalist countries with hard currencies have so far been able to avoid this fate in the post-war period. But in the aftermath of depression caused by COVID-19, even the advanced capitalist economies cannot be immune from the dangers of stagflation, or of runaway inflation.

The loss of faith in fiat currencies in the advanced capitalist countries will have both domestic as well as international repercussions. As discussed above, the massive infusion of money in the economy by large-scale printing of fiat money has distributional consequences. In the US, the additional money so created has largely gone to the rich. It obviously raises a question in the minds of common people that if money can be created so easily and be given to the rich, then why do they have to pay taxes, or why can't money created from thin air be given to them. The recent 'Black Lives Matter' (BLM) protests in the US and elsewhere have witnessed unprecedented levels of intensity and anger. Certainly one important factor behind it has been the realisation on the part of the common people how unjust and iniquitous the ruling classes' response to the COVID-19 crisis has been.

Impact on Dollar Hegemony

It is a subject of debate now that the current stance of the US monetary policy of excessive quantitative easing may cause severe damage to the dollar's status as the world's reserve currency.

For seventy-five years since the end of the Second World War, the status of the US dollar as the primary global reserve currency has continued virtually uncontested. About 60 per cent of the world's currency reserves are in dollars and the vast majority of global trade and investment takes place in dollars. In comparison, about 20 per cent of global currency reserves are in euros.

The US has been running consistent trade and current account deficits with the rest of the world over the past four decades. The dollar's world reserve currency status allows the U.S. to borrow from the rest of the world large sums of money. The United States has the largest external debt in the world. In 2018, foreigners owned $6.2 trillion of US debt. Excessive printing of money by the Federal Reserve as a response to the COVID-19 crisis is likely to instil fear among the United States' foreign lenders. This is because excessive increase in supply of money could lead to high inflation causing a sharp decline in the value of the dollar. The US government's stimulus package running into trillions of dollars is largely being financed from borrowings from the Federal Reserve. This is an indication of the changes in foreign perceptions of the United States' strength which over time will cause erosion in the dollar's hegemonic status.

Of course, there are other geopolitical developments happening at the same time that are also contributing to this phenomenon of the declining power of the US dollar. The developing cold-war between the US and China is a major factor among them.

In recent years, America has been very aggressive in using its currency's power to impose sanctions on countries with whom it has any disagreement or dispute. It is forcing not only its rivals but also its allies to explore other options. It is true that replacement of the dollar by some other currency as the world reserve currency does not appear likely in the near future. The TINA argument is not without merit. But there are other ways in which the domination of the dollar is coming under challenge.

In the past few years, many countries, including China and Russia, are making attempts towards de-dollarisation[2] of their economies. These countries are diversifying their foreign exchange reserves and conducting trade transactions in other reserve currencies (such as euro) or in their own national currencies. This trend towards de-dollarisation that has been underway for many years now is likely to accelerate because of the large-scale use of quantitative easing policies by the Federal Reserve in response to the COVID-19 crisis. Compared to the US, the post-COVID economic recovery in China is likely to be much stronger, leading to a significant reduction in the GDP-gap between the two countries. The shift in balance in favour of China is likely to hasten or accelerate the process of de-dollarisation.

These fast-pace changes will instil fear in the US, a declining power fearing loss of hegemonic control over the world. As acts of desperation, the US is likely to take urgent steps to check China's rise. These steps could include enhanced trade war, alliance formation, and military moves.

Implications of Decline in US Hegemony for the Emerging Multipolarity in the World Order

There is a growing general consensus that the 200 years long period of Western domination of the world is coming to an end and a new world order is emerging. How does the COVID-19 crisis affect the world order or the pace of change? The important question today is: Will the pandemic push the world towards bipolarity[3]? Or, will it strengthen the present trend the world is witnessing towards emergence of a multipolar[4] world order?

Bipolarity, in today's context, means that the world gets divided into two warring groups: One led by the US and the other by China. This does not appear to be a realistic possibility in today's circumstances. Why this is so?

There are two major powers today: The US and China. But there are also other powerful nations/blocks such as Russia, Europe, Japan, and India, who stand to lose their independence if the world turns bipolar.

Like the Soviet Union during the Cold War era, Russia today is able to provide a counterbalance to the US and other Western powers in military terms. Despite very close strategic alliance with China, Russia is the main proponent of multipolarity in world relations. Russia has acted very forcefully and decisively against Western designs in many places, such as Syria. There are many countries, such as Iran, Venezuela, and North Korea, who are victims of US aggression in the forms of economic sanctions and even threat of direct military action. These countries invariably turn to Russia for support not only at the United Nations Security Council but also in forms of direct material assistance.

Europe and Japan enjoy close economic relations with China which are mutually beneficial to all of them. Europe and Japan will, therefore, be wary of aligning too closely with the US in its attempt at containing China. America's alliance with Western Europe is no longer as strong as it once was.

India's prestige in the global community has somewhat diminished in the past few years. The main reason for this has been a significant decline in its economic strength. The government's few missteps—demonetisation and GST—led to considerable slowdown in India's GDP growth. But the panic reaction to the novel virus in terms of severe lockdowns has created conditions of depression pushing the economy back by several years. Despite these setbacks, India continues to maintain a significant position on the world stage. This is largely due to its potential to become a major global player some day in the future.

India's declared foreign policy position is of 'strategic autonomy'. India's foreign policy stance has, however, undergone a discernible change in recent years. Increasing military purchases from the US and membership of the 'Quad' are an indication of a pro-US shift in India's foreign policy. There is a growing perception in many capitals that India has not been able to maintain its independent status as it is not able to stand up to US pressure.

India's stand in geo-political affairs is of high significance. If India moves very close to the US camp, it pushes the world towards a dangerous situation of bipolarity. It is therefore very important to pay close attention to India's foreign policy moves.

Both the US and China may not be very enthusiastic about being the poles. By being a pole, a country derives many benefits by virtue of its dominant position. But it also has associated costs. The Soviet Union could not bear the burden of being a pole for very long and disintegrated due to internal pressures. The Trump administration probably sees the costs of being a pole outweighing the benefits. The situation, however, may change if Trump loses the election and Joe Biden becomes the next President. China too is not prepared to take on a leadership role. It still lacks strength to take up its position as a second pole.

Rescue Measures Aim to Strengthen Capitalism

As discussed above, most of the benefits of the governments' stimulus measures in the advanced capitalist countries are going to the richer sections of the society. But, to an extent, the poor and working people are also receiving assistance in the form of income support, enhanced unemployment benefits, and increased access to healthcare. Some political thinkers argue that these governments' interventions are heralding a new era of socialism in the advanced capitalist countries. This interpretation of the recent policy changes is, however, completely unwarranted. These measures should be seen as desperate attempts by the ruling classes in these countries to save capitalist structures from complete collapse. These are very temporary in nature. Their basic purpose is to safeguard the long-term interests of the ruling corporate and financial elite.

Totalitarian Surveillance

The response to the COVID-19 crisis has been in the form of lockdowns across most countries. In many places, the state resorted to prison-like restrictions on people's freedom of movement, assembly and expression that brought civil life, and political and economic activities to a virtual standstill. The state used unprecedentedly authoritarian methods to control and dictate people's behaviour in the name of securing health safety. But quite often, it was evident that governments used the corona crisis as a cover to seize new powers that had not much to do with the health emergency. New dangerous surveillance technologies such as technologies to track were pressed onto service to monitor people's movements as well as to manipulate their behaviour. The dictatorial tendencies developed during the coronavirus crisis are likely to persist even after the health crisis is over.[5]

Reduction in Ecological Footprints and Lessons for the Future

The panic reaction to the novel virus menace has led to devastating social and economic consequences worldwide. The income and employment losses have reached depression levels. The economic downturns have, however, produced some positive outcomes as far as the environmental dimension is concerned. The projected fall in global economic output is certain to curtail greenhouse gas emissions for at least a few years helping humanity in its fight against global warming.

Even if it happened under duress, people refrained from consumption of non-essentials for several months during the prolonged lockdowns. Is it possible to adopt this mode of low consumption if a climate crisis warrants it? Several categories of consumption, such as international tourism, are of significance here. As is widely predicted, several activities that are responsible for large gas emissions, especially activities related to travel and tourism, may not recover to pre-COVID levels for many years. This brings some hope that the emission targets set in the Paris Agreement may be possible to meet.

The coronavirus crisis has exposed profound flaws in the working of the present socio-economic system. The modern capitalist system driven by corporate monopoly and financial interests has proven utterly dysfunctional in the face of the challenge posed by the new virus. The whole system that appeared very robust and sound not so long ago, turned out to be very fragile. If the capitalist structures built over decades have proven incapable to deal with a health emergency, how can these be expected to deal with larger existential threats facing humanity today? As Chomsky points out:

> The coronavirus is serious enough, but it is worth recalling that there are two much greater threats approaching, far worse than anything that is happening in human history: one is the growing threat of a nuclear war and the other of course is the growing threat of global warming. Coronavirus is horrible and can have terrifying consequences, but there will be recovery. While the others won't be recovered, it's finished.[6]

We can hope for a better future, a more equitable and sustainable world, if human society shows willingness to use lessons learnt in the fight against the coronavirus crisis to deal with the existential threats of our times.

PART II

Income and Wealth Inequality

From the beginning of the Industrial Revolution to the end of the 1840s, questions related to distribution were central in the political economy discourse in the Western societies. During the early period, the most important political economy issue related to distribution of income, wealth and power between landowners and capitalists (the bourgeoisie). Adam Smith's *An Inquiry into the Nature and Causes of the Wealth of Nations* appeared during this period.

With growth of industrialisation, the working class emerged as a new important social class and focus of debates (including in economic theory) shifted to distribution of income between rent, wages and profits as reflected in Ricardo's work. By 1830, the industrial bourgeoisie assumed power in England and France with the help of the proletariat and their struggle with landowners had abated. Therefore, the bourgeoisie's class struggle with the proletariat became more important. The 1830s and 1840s were highly turbulent years across Europe. Popular uprisings and workers' struggles (notably in France in 1848) came close to toppling the existing social order. This was also the period that produced many contending socialist theories with enormous influence on the civil society.

By the end of the 1840s, most of it had calmed down. The period after 1848 is referred to as the period of social peace (the Age of Capital). (The peace, of course, did not last very long. The struggle for colonies that ensued culminated in two world wars.) With disappearance of dissent that at one time had become very threatening, a period of social and political tranquillity followed which emphasised social harmony and progress. Mainstream ideology that advanced rationale in support of the existing social order acquired dominance to the extent that did not leave much space for the contending ideologies. This was especially true in the field of economics. Mainstream economic theory's focus almost completely shifted towards understanding the working of the market system. All numerous currents of socialist thought lost their potency. From a position of challenging the capitalist system, they shifted to a position content with modifications in the system, to accommodate the concerns of the working class. Their efforts in these directions led to establishment of the welfare state in European nations.

With the decline of revolutionary left ideology in the West, the questions related to distribution got extremely marginalised. In mainstream economics, discussion of distribution was confined to the new field of Welfare Economics. Utilitarianism had initially allowed for redistributive measures if they had the effects of increasing total utility (happiness or welfare) of the society as a whole. But later when arguments that did not allow inter-personal comparison of utilities had won the field, and when Pareto and Arrow criteria were assigned supreme place in the theory, possibilities of redistributive measures even when they increased society's total welfare were not permitted within the theoretical framework of Welfare Economics. The subject was trivialised as it in essence became a field for futile puzzle-solving by academicians. John Rawls' contribution which sought to provide justification for an egalitarian society failed to bring the focus back on distribution as his argument rested on the premise of an imaginary rather than real society. Critiquing Rawls' theory of justice, Sen states: 'Indeed, the theory of justice, as formulated under the current dominant transcendental institutionalism, reduces many of the most relevant issues of justice into empty—even if acknowledged to be "well-meaning"—rhetoric.'[7]

There is a great deal of new literature that deals with the relationship of economic growth with income and wealth distribution and poverty reduction. Some important questions raised in this context are: What generally is the impact of economic growth on distribution of income and wealth? Does economic growth worsen distribution (make it more uneven) or improves it (i.e. it reduces disparity)? Does the impact of economic growth on distribution depend on initial conditions? Does it depend on the nature of growth? What roles do balance of class power, nature of regime, governance factor and policy framework play in this? We explore these issues in the following section below.

After the Second World War, i.e. from the 1950s to the 1970s, the dominant view, known as 'the inverted-U hypothesis,' held that in the early period of economic growth, distribution tends to worsen; and only after achieving a certain economic level, one can expect improvement in distribution. This hypothesis was propounded by Simon Kuznets in his 1955 paper that contained an empirical investigation of the relationship between per capita income and inequality in a cross section of countries.

There was an earlier discernible similarity between Kuznets' empirical results and prediction of Lewis' 1954 labour supply model. Lewis' model focused on structural change in a dual economy setting, in which labour was shifted from a labour surplus traditional agricultural sector to a modern industrial sector. This process of labour transfer continued till the labour supply was exhausted. The Kuznets' hypothesis suggested a trade-off between equality and growth. For a short while, in the 1970s, a trend in literature emerged that downplayed the trade-off arguments and advocated that to alleviate poverty in many developing countries, redistribution measures should be identified that do not hamper growth.[8]

The enthusiasm for 'growth with justice,' however, did not last long. The focus of literature shifted with the rise of neoliberalism and market fundamentalism in the early 1980s. During this neoliberal phase, questions related to distribution and poverty were set aside in favour of growth. It was argued that growth itself would curtail poverty through 'trickle down' mechanisms. There was, however, not much discussion about the processes through which trickle-down would work.

There are broadly two opposing strands found in the literature on the subject of distribution. At one end of the spectrum are those who argue that a free market-based system and liberal economic policies raise incomes of all, the rich and poor, proportionately. This 'growth is distribution-neutral' stance translates into a stance that 'growth is good for the poor.' It is stated that as incomes of the poor also rise with the incomes of the rest in society, there is a reduction in poverty as measured by some fixed income levels.

At the other end of the spectrum is the argument that economic growth, especially during the last four decades, has been associated with an increase in inequality. This has prevented benefits of economic growth reaching the poor.

During the last 40 years, income inequality has risen considerably in all Western economies and more so in the USA. Thomas Piketty's magnum opus published in 2014 *Capital in the Twenty-First Century* (referred to as C_{21}) deals with the issues of long-term trends in inequality of wealth and income in such great details and so thoroughly as not seen for a long time. Piketty's book focuses in particular on the increasing disparity between the upper centile of the income and wealth distribution and the rest. Before the publication of C_{21} as well as Piketty's earlier works with his co-author, Emmanuel Saez, 'most discussions of economic disparity more or less ignored the very rich.'

For several decades after the Second World War, the dominant mainstream view, known as the Kuznets' fact was that 'all or nearly all economies had been through or would go through an industrial age in which inequality rises and then a social-democratic mass-consumption age in which inequality falls and then stabilises. It..... turns out not to be a fact—-merely transient historical contingency.'[9]

As Krugman writes:

> In America in particular the share of national income going to the top one per cent has followed a great U-shaped arc. Before World War I, the one per cent received around a fifth of total income in both Britain and the United States. By 1950 that share had been cut by more than half. But since 1980 the one per cent has seen its income share surge again—and in the United States it's back to what it was a century ago.[10]

Based on a systematic analysis of long-term statistics on inequality and growth, Piketty shows that wealth concentration in the United States and Europe has just now returned to the high levels observed earlier about one hundred years ago. He also records that inequality in capital income in the Western capitalist economies has been rising rapidly since the beginning of the 21st century. According to Krugman, 'The big idea of *Capital in the Twenty-First Century* is that we haven't just gone back to 19th century levels of income inequality, we're also on a path back to "patrimonial capitalism," in which the commanding heights of the economy are controlled not by talented individuals but by family dynasties.'[11]

One major contribution of Piketty's work has been to show clearly that the role of inheritance flows in the dynamics of capital accumulation in the advanced capitalist economies is too significant to be ignored. As translator of Piketty's C_{21} book, Arthur

Goldhammer puts it,

> Piketty's data on inheritance flows thus strengthen the notion that the pattern of class domination tends to persist over lengthy periods—a notion that had fallen into neglect with the ascendancy of neoliberal ideology in the final decades of the twentieth century. Robert Lucas, whom Paul Krugman calls "the most influential macroeconomist of his generation," declared in 2004, for instance, that "of the tendencies that are harmful to sound economics, the most seductive, and in my opinion the most poisonous, is to focus on the question of distribution." By making it once again respectable to raise distributional questions and to question the efficacy of competition alone, Piketty earned the gratitude of historians aware from their own work that economists like Lucas were entirely too sanguine in their belief that the normal operation of the market sufficed to ensure that wealth and its concomitant power did not settle all too comfortably into the hands of a restricted and (to a degree) self-reproducing class of capitalists.[12]

Piketty's prediction about the future of ever-increasing inequality are based on his fundamental inequality, $r > g$ (where r stands for average annual return on capital, g stands for the rate of growth of economy). Piketty's estimates of r and g are based on the analysis of historical observations.

A higher value of r in comparison to g in Piketty's model causes 'a redistribution of income away from labour and towards holders of capital.' As explained by Krugman,

> A rising share of capital, in turn, directly increases inequality, because ownership of capital is always much more unequally distributed than labour income. But the effects don't stop there, because when the rate of return on capital greatly exceeds the rate of economic growth, "the past tends to devour the future": society inexorably tends towards dominance by inherited wealth.[13]

Grewal summarises Piketty's contribution very succinctly as follows:

> One of the prime virtues of C_{21} is that it returns us to these classical debates on capitalism and inequality. Of course, it is neither Smith nor Marx but rather the twentieth-century economist Simon Kuznets who seems as Piketty's main foil. Over the longer time-horizon that Piketty

> studied, the Kuznets curve is revealed as a temporary aberration: the post-war moderation of economic inequality turned out to have been the exception rather than the trend. With Kuznets dispatched, as Piketty recognizes, the study of economic inequality opens once again to the consideration of the deeper theoretical issues that concerned nineteenth-century classical political economy and the earlier discourse of eighteenth-century moral philosophy. C_{21} shows us the way back to these debates—indeed, to the necessity of reengaging them—via the recognition that the decline in inequality during the mid-twentieth century was an anomaly.[14]

From the foregoing analysis, it is quite evident that in the current phase of advanced capitalism, particularly in the 21st century, inequality has been on the rise in the period of growth as well as in the period of stagnation or recession. Stiglitz is in broad agreement with many analysts in economics and other social sciences when he argues that 'inequality is the result of political forces as much as of economic ones.'[15] The most significant remedial measure to save capitalism that emerges from Piketty's work is focused on a 'progressive global tax on capital.' In addition to a tax on capital, Piketty also argues for a progressive tax on income as well as progressive real estate tax.[16] In prevailing political conditions, all these remedies/suggestions are, however, just utopian ideas. These can have practical significance only if there is a political change in every nation such that the common people take control of the situation in their own hands.

PART III

Hunger and Food Insecurity

The enormous growth of production in the modern world has theoretically undermined the Malthusian population trap. The growth of production of food has increased the possibilities of food for all. But the real picture of the contemporary world shows that millions of people are living in acute hunger and food insecurity. Despite the enormous growth of production in the world, 2 billion people are making less than \$ 2 a day—most of them living in rural areas of developing countries. One cannot study the widespread hunger, malnutrition and poverty in isolation by divorcing it from the existing capitalist economic system.

Historically, hunger and food insecurity have been endemic to capitalist development. The recent report of Food and Agricultural Organisation (FAO) titled *The State of Food Security and Nutrition in the World* (2017) has highlighted that in 2016, the number of undernourished people in the world increased to an estimated 815 million up from 717 million in 2015, a hundred million added in one year. Of the world's hungry and undernourished people, 98 per cent live in developing countries. The question of hunger and food insecurity is not only an ethical and moral issue but also a political and economic concern because hunger and food insecurity is not persisting due to the shortage of production.

This clearly demands an explanation: why despite the world's food production continuously increasing, the incidence of hunger, food insecurity and real poverty is not decreasing at the same rate? The growth of GDP and per capital income that developing countries have experienced after the introduction of neoliberal policies is a false indicator which does not reflect the actual reality of living standard of the common masses in these countries. The increased income has only been experienced by a small fraction of population whereas the vast majority of the population has remained untouched by growth. Therefore, the distribution rather than production becomes the more important issue in the present era of global capitalism. The persistence of hunger in the contemporary world is due to the increasing inequality between and within the societies produced by the uncontrolled growth of capitalist market network. The empirical evidences presented by the FAO show that recently the food security situation has worsened in many part of Sub-Saharan Africa and South Eastern and Western Asia.

FAO has tried to relate the dire situation in these economies with the rising conflict, compounded by droughts and floods in these regions. However, the integration of these economies with the world capitalist system and violence caused by the plunder by multinational corporations is not addressed by the FAO as a cause of hunger and food insecurity. It is evident from the facts that food availability has got deteriorated in those settings where governments have introduced the neoliberal reforms under the guidelines of the IMF, World Bank and WTO. In the name of fiscal discipline there is continuous decline in subsidies in developing economies which were a means to protect the poor households against rising food prices. Since the early 1990s the volatility of food prices has become much higher that has increased uncertainties and insecurities of food and nutritional intake by the majority of population in developing countries.

The increase in food prices in recent years has increased the number of people around the globe that are undernourished. It is not the shortage in production of food that has resulted in the increase in food prices and therefore food insecurity. It is rather the withdrawal of the state and increased involvement of the private players in distributional chains. Speculation in the future market and hoarding at the local level are certainly playing a part in the increase in food prices that make food inaccessible. The increase in speculative activities in food and creation of artificial shortage by the big corporate players has resulted in increase in prices and therefore the import bill of food deficit underdeveloped and developing regions has soared. Dismantling of food stock by government agencies, reduced state intervention in price control and purchase and sale of food articles have also contributed to increase in food price volatility. The increase in food prices has put a huge burden on the net importer countries of food. Out of the total food import bill of the world, the share of Africa and Asia is 40 per cent.

The replacement of the local traders by transnational corporations that process agriculture products, manufacture various food, and sell food to the public only benefit the latter (Magdoff and Tokar, 2010). They create artificial shortage that results in price increase leading to increase in their profit margin. But the price rise causes grave hardship among the poor and is a major factor behind the increase in hunger and food insecurity.

Extent of Hunger and Food Insecurity

According to FAO, in 2016, among the major regions of the world,

Sub-Saharan Africa seemed to be in the worst situation with 22.7 per cent of undernourished people followed by the Caribbean (17.7 per cent) and Southern Asia (14.4 per cent). Among the Sub-Saharan African regions the situation is more alarming in Eastern Africa where one-third of the population is estimated to be undernourished.

FAO has also collected data in almost 150 countries on Food Insecurity Experience Scale (FIES).[17] According to FIES, nearly one in ten (9.3 per cent) of the world's population suffered from severe food insecurity. According to FIES, the absolute number of population under severe food insecurity increased from 645.1 million in 2015 to 688.5 million in 2016. Africa has highest level of food insecurity with 27.4 per cent (333.2 million people) living in severe food insecurity (almost four times higher than the other regions). Food insecurity in Sub-Saharan Africa has increased 3 percentage points from 2014 to 2016. Near about half of the world's food insecure population is living in Africa. More than 615 million out of 688.5 million population (89.32 per cent) under severe food insecurity lives in two regions of the world (Africa and Asia). The number of undernourished people in the world has increased from 775 million to 845 million from 2013 to 2016.

The data on various essential indicators of quality of life highlights that Sub-Saharan Africa is the most deprived region of the world. In 2014-16, 29.4 per cent of the total population was under severe food insecurity and 33.6 per cent of the children under the age of 5 are stunted. The prevalence of anaemia among women between the age group of 15-49 was 39.2 per cent. The situation of Asia in terms of prevalence of stunting among children and anaemia among the women is also very severe. In Asia, South Asia is the most deprived region. The situation in South Asia is the worst in the world in case of three indicators of quality of life. According to recent data of 2016, prevalence of wasting and stunting in children less than 5 years of age is highest in the South Asian region. The prevalence of anaemia among women in the age group of 15 to 49 was as high as 48.7 per cent (highest in the world).

Conflict, Food Insecurity and Nutrition

FAO argues that there is a correlation between hunger, food insecurity and conflict. A vast majority of the severely food insecure and malnourished population lives in countries affected by conflict. It is estimated that out of 815 million undernourished people, 489 million live in conflict-prone regions. Hunger and undernourishment are more significant where conflict are prolonged and compounded by weak institutional capacity and/or adverse climate related events. According to the United Nations' *Global Report on Food Crisis* (2017), the causes of food insecurity in conflict are diverse but often coupled with disruption in food production and food system, plundering of crops and livestock, loss of assets and income or population displacement which all directly or indirectly impact availability, access and utilization of food. The countries where conflict or widespread insecurity has acutely impacted food security are mainly in Africa (Burundi, Central African Republic, Congo, Nigeria, Somalia, South Sudan and Sudan), Asia and the Middle East (Afghanistan, Iraq, Syria and Yemen).

The increase in the number of conflicts and unrest in African and Asian regions is, however, closely linked to the capitalist penetration in these economies. This is not a natural outcome of the growth process and transformation of these economies. It is rather dictated by the imperialist interests of Western capitalism. Therefore, the situation of disempowerment of vulnerable groups among the developing economies, as far as access to food and other essential commodities is concerned, is closely related with the introduction of neoliberal policies.

In the name of efficiency and superiority of free market forces, the IMF, and World Bank are promoting neoliberal polices among the developing and underdeveloped countries of Asia and Africa. The fundamental objective of these policies is to integrate the pre-capitalist production and distributional system of the Third World economies with the world capitalist system. According to the policies dictated by the IMF in the form of the structural adjustment programme (SAP), the Third World countries are forced to dismantle the elaborate system of public agencies that provide the farmers access to land, credit, insurance, inputs and cooperative organisations. This approach holds that the state should stop subsidising farmers, stop being involved in the storage and transportation of food, and stop subsidising food for poor people and leave all these to the market (Magdoff, 2008). This has increased the threat of hunger and food insecurity in the Third World economies. The increased intervention of the big private foreign and domestic capital in the production of primary commodities in these economies has resulted in the dispossession of the common people from the commons.

The promotion of the corporate agriculture by the World Bank and other institutions of the developed countries is forcing most of the peasantry in Asian and African countries to give up the traditional forms of agricultural activities in favour of commercialisation. This process of imposed commercialisation and growth of free market forces in the countryside after the withdrawal of the state has seriously undermined the self-sustained food production system of family farming. The involvement of big corporations in agro-processing, agro-input and contract farming has resulted in the displacement of family farming by the corporate capital. This process has further accelerated the process of depeasantisation in the Third World economies. This process of depeasantisation was characterised by Eric Hobswbam (1994), an eminent historian, as 'the death of peasantry' that he referred to as the most dramatic and far-reaching social change of the second half of the 20th century. The widespread depeasantisation and dispossession caused by the introduction of neoliberal policies has forced the peasant farmers off the land and petty producers from their independent means of production.

In the pre-capitalist economies of the Third World, agriculture is not simply an economic activity but rather a way of life—an integral part of their culture and social system. This is the reason that the forced integration of this pre-capitalist agriculture with the world capitalist system has produced disastrous effects on the livelihood of the majority of countryside population. The increased control of the corporate capital over the agriculture production and distributional system has brought food into the commodity market like any other commodity. This transformation has increased the hunger and food insecurity for the displaced population that is not absorbed by the organised urban labour market. The data on agriculture production at the world level shows that hunger is not due to the failure of production but rather due to a lack of appropriate amount of resources to command the required amount of food. The encroachment of the resources of the peasant farmers and petty producers in the Third World countries by big corporate capital has resulted in the decline in means of livelihood and real incomes of the common masses in these countries. A small fraction of population who benefited from the neoliberal policies have experienced improvement in their economic position substantially, thereby commanding a bigger share of the available food. This has resulted in the decline in access to food on the part of less favourable sections of the population who have lost their means of livelihood in the competitive market.

So the increase in incidence of hunger and food insecurity in Africa and Southern Asia is an integral part of the process of globalisation of capitalism that has uprooted millions of people from their ties to land and natural resources. The austerity measures introduced by the African and Asian governments in the name of fiscal discipline, have resulted in the squeezing, or in majority of cases a decline, in real income of the masses. These developments have also eroded the national food self-sufficiency and food security in African and South Asian economies. The problem is further being aggravated by the continuous process of commodification of health and education services that have increased the cost of access to these services and put an additional burden on the poor. The solution to end hunger and food insecurity lies in transforming the power structures and institutional framework of the Third World economies that have become totally subordinate to the interests of the imperialists. If Third World countries really want to end hunger and poverty, the most important thing is to de-link their economies from the imperialist accumulation network and offer (economic and political) power to their own poor people.

PART IV

The present volume covers a wide range of issues from conceptual questions to empirical investigation of the major challenges posed by contemporary capitalism. The sequence of the papers nowhere reflects the importance of one paper over the other. All the papers are equally important to understand the theoretical foundations and major challenges posed by contemporary capitalism.

Anjan Chakrabarti's paper is a methodological one which presents historical materialism as a method of inquiry of economy and society. In the present scenario, it is essential to understand the concept of historical materialism and method to expose the exploitative nature of capitalism and role of the superstructure in shaping the economy and society as per the requirements of the capitalist mode of production. Surinder Kumar's paper explains the basic concepts of Marxian political economy which are important to set the foundation for detailed analysis. Prabhat Patnaik's contribution explains the Marxian critique of Classical Political Economy. This paper highlights in the Marxist framework the misery of classical political economy to understand the accumulation logic of capitalism and nature of capitalist production. The contributions by Paramjit Singh and Greg Albo explain the capitalist mode of production and the nature of its contemporary phase. Both contributions are important to understand the basic structural principles of capitalism and how it has evolved in recent decades. The next three contributions explain the questions of employment and unemployment under capitalism. Deepankar Basu's paper, along with a theoretical exposition, has empirically tested Marx's conception of the reserve army of labour. The paper by Satyaki Roy is rooted in Marxian political economy that traces the employment-unemployment phenomenon under capitalism that is an outcome of the nature of the capitalist production process. V. Upadhyay's paper examines the nature of technological progress under contemporary capitalism and its implications for labour and employment growth.

The next two papers deal with the agrarian question that has not been appropriately addressed by the Marxist political economists of the Global North in general and has not been part of the global political economy curriculum in particular. The paper by the late Samir Amin is a detailed analysis of the agrarian question under capitalism. It addresses one of the key dimensions confronting the Russian and Chinese revolutions, that of the agrarian question for the peasantry which constituted popular majorities in each of these countries at the time of their revolutions. Amin argues that the new agrarian question is the key issue to be addressed in the processes of building socialism in the 21st century. The contribution by Goran Durfeldt discusses capitalist and family farming, fetching illustrations from India and China, Sub-Saharan Africa and occasionally also South America. He has challenged the widely held view of 'big is beautiful.' He has presented sound reasons why family farming is still thriving in the age of global capitalism.

The next five contributions cover the major themes which expose historical and contemporary dimensions of the exploitative nature of capitalism. John Bellemy Foster's contribution defines monopoly capitalism as a special stage of capitalist accumulation. It traces monopoly capitalism and its various dimensions covered by the leading political economists since Hilferding. The explanation followed by the rich sources would be of immense worth to those students and researchers who want to explore various dimensions of the monopoly phase of capitalism. Paul Zarembka's contribution challenges the conception of "accumulation of capital" that is generally propagated by scholars based only on Marx's work. He argues that accumulation of capital requires an in-depth analysis. He has argued that the complete understanding of accumulation of capital requires for Marxist scholars to build upon Marx's works and understand the concept in a horizontal manner by incorporating the contribution of Rosa Luxemburg. Gerald Epstein's contribution is important in the sense that it clarifies the much debated concept of "financialisation", the term that had been developed long before the crisis of 2008 but, understandably, became even more popular since the crisis. He discusses various theoretical contributions in order to provide a comprehensive understanding of financialisation. Along with this, he argues that there are still many conundrums and open questions about "financialisation" which means it will remain a fruitful area for multi-disciplinary research and an important arena for political battles and structural reforms for the foreseeable future. The next two contributions by Paramjit Singh and V. Upadhyay explore the other important debatable issue of Marxian political economy that is imperialism. Paramjit's contribution traces imperialism historically whereas Upadhyay's contribution challenges the accepted conception of imperialism in order to understand its contemporary significance.

The last three papers focus on the life-threatening crisis of climate change. V. Upadhyay's paper provides a brief outline of various dimensions of global warming and discusses the debates around the idea of degrowth. Pritam Singh's paper is an attempt to contribute to an eco-socialist critique of the widely prevailing theoretical perspectives on capitalism, its crisis and the solutions offered to this crisis. His contribution focuses on examining Keynesianism, monetarism/neo-liberalism, traditional Marxist and the Green perspectives. He concludes by arguing that a critical synthesis of Marxian and Green perspectives best captures the complexity of the current crisis of capitalism—the global environmental crisis—and offers a creative way of dealing with this crisis. The last but no less important Erald Kolasi's paper examines the relationship between energy, economic growth and the ecological crisis under capitalism. He argues that even most political leaders and economists who support the current capitalist order have begun talking about a series of alternative narratives about the relationship between human economies and the natural world.

NOTES

1. See Rouche (2020).
2. See Hudson (2020).
3. See Peng (2020).
4. See Upadhyay (2016).
5. See Harari (2020).
6. See Chomsky (2020).
7. See Sen (2010).

8. See Degdeviren et al. (2004).
9. See Delong et al. (2017).
10. See Krugman (2017), p. 61.
11. Ibid.
12. See Goldhammer (2017), pp. 43-4.
13. See Krugman (2017), p. 65.
14. See Grewal (2017), pp. 474-5.
15. See Stiglitz (2012).
16. See Piketty (2014).
17. FIES is an experience-based metric of the severity of food insecurity, relaying on direct yes/no response to eight questions regarding access to adequate food. For details about the indicators and methodology of FIES, see report of FAO (2017), *The State of Food Security and Nutrition in the World.*

REFERENCES

Boushey, H., J.B. Delong and M. Steinbaum (eds.) (2017), *After Piketty*, Cambridge, Massachusetts: Harvard University Press.

Chomsky, N. (2020), Interview with Pressenza Athens, March 30, 2020, Pressenza.com.

Dagdeviren, H., Rolph van der Hoeven and J. Weeks (2004), Redistribution Does Matter: Growth and Redistribution for Poverty Reduction, in Anthony Shorrocks and Rolph van der Hoeven (eds.), *Growth, Inequality and Poverty—Prospects for Pro-poor Economic Development*, London: Oxford University Press.

Delong, J.B., H. Boushey and M. Steinbaum (2017), Capital in the Twenty-First Century: Three Years Later, in Boushey et al. (eds.), *After Piketty*, Cambridge, Massachusetts: Harvard University Press.

FAO (2017), *The State of Food Security and Nutrition in the World*, Rome: Food and Agriculture Organisation of United Nations.

Goldhammer, A. (2017), The Piketty Phenomenon, In Bosuhey et al. (eds.), *After Piketty*, Cambridge, Massachusetts: Harvard University Press.

Grewal, D.S. (2017), The Legal Constitution of Capitalism, in Boushey et al. (eds.), *After Piketty*, Cambridge, Massachusetts: Harvard University Press.

Harari, Y.N. (2020), The World After Coronavirus, *Financial Times,* March 20, 2020.

Hobsbawm, E. (1994), *The Age of Extreme: A Short History of the Twentieth Century (1914-1991),* London: Abacus Books.

Hudson, M. (2020), De-dollarization—Towards the End of the US Monetary Hegemony, YouTube. April 23, 2020.

Krugman, P. (2017), Why We're in a New Gilded Age, in Boushey et al. (eds.), *After Piketty,* Cambridge, Massachusetts: Harvard University Press.

Magdoff, F. (2008), The World Food Crisis: Sources and Solutions, *Monthly Review,* Vol. 6, No. 2.

Magdoff F. and B. Tokar (2010), Introduction, in Magdoff F. and B. Tokar (eds.). *Agriculture and Food in Crisis: Conflict, Resistance, and Renewal,* New York: Monthly Review Press.

Peng, Y. (2020), Coronavirus Pandemic and a Once-in-a-Century Change, Available at: https://www.readingthechinadream.com/yuan-peng-coronavirus-pandemic.html.

Piketty, T. (2014), *Capital in the Twenty-First Century,* Cambridge, Massachusetts: The Belknap Press of Harvard University Press.

Rouche, Julia La (2020), Economist Roubini Expects "Anaemic US Recovery" and a "Greater Depression" Looms, *Yahoo Finance,* June 30, 2020.

Sen, A. (2010), *The Idea of Justice,* London: Allen Lane.

Stiglitz, Joseph E. (2012), *The Price of Inequality: How Today's Divided Society Endangers Our Future,* New York: W.W. Norton and Co.

Upadhyay, V. (2016), The World at Crossroads: Understanding the Modern-Day Multipolarity, in V. Upadhyay (ed.), *Essays on Distribution, World Systems, Ecology, and Left Politics.* New Delhi: Daanish Books.

United Nations (2017), *Global Report on Food Crisis,* Rome: World Food Programme.

1

Introduction to Historical Materialism: A Theory of Society and History[1]

Anjan Chakrabarti

Taking off from Marx's insights, Marxism emerged as a broad tradition sharing the common objective of pursuing a critique of exploitative systems such as capitalism and seeking a transition towards a post-exploitative, post-capitalist society.[2] Nevertheless, it will be an error to reduce any tradition to one theory. Like all traditions, Marxism too comprises many, often clashing, theories, each operating with diverse entry points, logics, modes of analysis, techniques, claims, etc. While these pull and push Marxism in different, often contesting directions it also makes for over 150 years of lineage that is extraordinarily rich, complex and dynamic. If not anything, it represents the space for the most rigorously developed critique of capitalist system that we know of.

Expanding on some interpretation of Marx's works particularly with reference to his book *Capital: Critique of Political Economy*, diverse theories of society and of its transition in the Marxian tradition can be classified into, by no means exhaustive or conclusive, three broad approaches: (i) historical materialist approach of Orthodox/traditional Marxism of Kautsky-Plekhanov which reached its highest sophistication through the logic of functionalist explanation in the hands of G.A. Cohen who claimed to defend stage-based, deterministic Marx's theory of society and history (1978, 1986a, 1986b, 1988), (ii) historical materialist approach of broadly speaking Classical Marxism which reaches its greatest sophistication through a developed philosophy of dialectical materialism (DM) in the hands of Luxemburg-Gramsci-Althusser and subsequent thinkers expanding on them (Althusser, [1969] 2010; Althusser and Balibar 1975; Hindess and Hirst 1977; Harvey 2010)[3] and (iii) class focused approach that developed following the pioneering theoretical intervention of Resnick and Wolff based on defining class as process of surplus labour and understanding dialectical materialism by using a post-Althusserian[4] epistemology of overdetermination and contradiction (Althusser, 1969; Resnick and Wolff, 1987, 2006, 2012).[5] The first two in their own specific ways deploy a deterministic mode of explanation, i.e. reduces their respective understandings of society and its transition to ultimately some chosen essence (say, forces of production or relations of production) or law of motion (say, of capital accumulation); the third is a non-deterministic approach implying that explanation of anything—individuals, institutions, society and its transition—cannot be reduced to one or a set of pre-given elements (Chakrabarti and Cullenberg, 2003; Chakrabarti and Dhar, 2017). A training in Marxist tradition requires a knowledge of these broad approaches, the theories therein, their critique of the ruling ideas of political economy and their ideas of post-capitalism (which could be dissimilar despite sharing the common problematic) and of the debates within Marxian tradition as such.[6]

Given the above qualification, I will only focus on G.A. Cohen's rigorous presentation of historical materialism (henceforth HM). Moreover, given space constraints, I organise some of the criticisms and debates within the Marxian tradition around Cohen's theory of HM. (see Chakrabarti, 2016 for details) My focus here is to introduce a prototype model of HM ala Cohen—its concepts, modes of analysing causality, intersecting theories of society and history it delivers and the derived politics that surface. In the process, some propositions and suggestions that emerge will be so organised as to alert the reader to their controversial nature. Indeed, the optimistic view is that a detailed understanding of one theory within the Marxian tradition may serve the important purpose of clearly distilling out some debatable methodological and substantive issues/problems; they can be used by the readers to further delve into other contending theories within the Marxian tradition which take these issues/problems as their points of reference and departure.

Two crucial intersecting and reinforcing steps compose HM—one, a theory of society and secondly, a theory of history. Cohen's seminal intervention came in the form of functional explanation proposed as a deterministic causal mechanism of explaining the connection between the various components of society and of why societies rise and fall. Cohen used the explanatory device of functionalist explanation to challenge the usage of dialectics in HM as a sloppy explanation of rise and fall of societies—whether in its mechanistic version of quantity-quality transformation in other varieties of Orthodox Marxism or as 'structure in dominance' marked by overdetermination and contradiction in Althusser. On the other hand, he is silent on Resnick and Wolff's class-focused approach that challenges (i) and (ii) version of HM with its own rigorous, non-deterministic logic of overdetermination and contradiction.

Components and Definition of Society in Historical Materialism

> In the social production of their existence, men enter into definite, necessary relations that are indispensable and independent of their will, relations of production which correspond to a definite stage of development of their material productive forces. The sum total of these relations of production constitutes the economic structure of society, the real basis, on which rises a legal and political superstructure, and to which correspond definite forms of social consciousness. The mode of production of material life conditions the social, political and intellectual life-process in general. It is not the consciousness of men that determines their being, but on the contrary their social being that determines their consciousness. (Marx, 1977 [1857])

Cohen uses this quote in Karl Marx's Preface to *A Contribution to the Critique of Political Economy* to describe and defend his theory of society and its history. Society or social totality is an articulation of the components of forces of production, relations of production (the economic structure) and superstructure, where the forces of production is given a privileged status. The structure in turn determines the social consciousness. In so far as this overarching social totality is taken as the basic representation of reality, HM adopts a frame of absolute realism (its claim through knowledge of the world is taken as the world per se), implying that all essential ingredients of society—as represented in the diagram below—are present in its proposed depiction of society. And, because this theory flags what is essential in society to know, the truth about society can be unpacked by exploring the anatomy and dynamics offered by the theory. Moreover, following its self-proclaimed scientific basis, the truth of society (the character of the relation between their components, and of the entire society) and its transition (in which some societies fall and others rise) can be derived from an underlying privileged determinant/essence and law of motion respectively. Cohen is clear in what he seeks to do: defend such a theory of society and of its history.

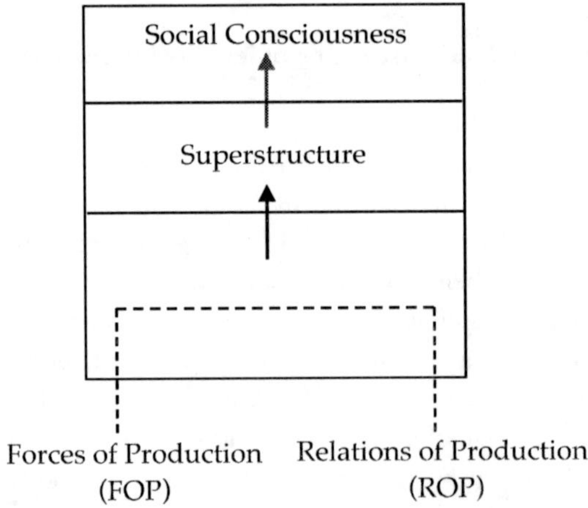

Forces of Production (FOP) consist of facilities and devices used in the process of production; it is the sum total of productive forces at the disposal of organisers of production in any society at any point in time. It includes raw materials (directly connected to nature), instruments of production, the brains, muscles, skills and knowledge of the labour force and so forth. At times, for convenience sake, the FOP is clubbed into labour power (mental and physical capacity to labour and not labour per se, two conceptually different things) and means of production (all material forces besides labour power). Like the means of production, labour power is devoid of any specific social content and is to be considered as a stock of brains and muscles (inclusive of skills and knowledge they possess) that can be deployed for production. Labour power is considered more important than the means of production; even if the means of production are destroyed, the retained knowledge to produce enables the labourers to recreate the means of production. At times, the technology (broadly here the technical ways and means of producing goods and services which clearly embodies knowledge) and its autonomous accumulation is taken as a rough index of FOP and its development.

If FOP emphasise the material condition, the relations of production (ROP) highlight (social) relations between people in the process of producing goods and services with the help of a given stock of FOP.[7] More particularly, ROP takes a specific social form, that of class relations which following Cohen is the basis/base/foundation of society. More on ROP later. In HM, the ***Primacy Thesis*** states that FOP is assumed to be exogenously given and determines the ROP and everything that appears subsequently. The primary relation in HM is thereby marked by FOP or technological determinism.

One qualification before proceeding further. Scholars interpret Marx as having used mode of production in different ways (Hindess and Hirst, 1977; Cohen, 1978 and Harvey, 2010). For one, mode of production is seen as the actual methods and techniques used in production under the given forms of specialisation and division of labour (material mode of production). Second, the mode of production captures the social properties of production process in the form of direct producer's surplus labour and mode of exploitation (social mode of production). Third, Marx would practically refer to society (for example, in his work on 'Grundrisse'), its entire technical and social configuration, as a mode of production (the mixed mode of production). Fourth, the mode of production is interpreted as the specific articulation of FOP and ROP without incorporating social superstructures and social being. We infer from Cohen that deploying mode of production as the articulation of FOP and ROP must guarantee the causal primacy of FOP over ROP in that articulation, something that Althusser and Balibar (1975) tried to argue against by highlighting the centrality of ROP. Because of its multiple mode of deployment by Marx and Marxists, Cohen tends to avoid using the term mode of production although, if any one way is rigorously developed then there is no reason why it cannot be used in an adopted theory.

Forces and Relations of Production: For Cohen, the 'economic structure/base'[8] is the set of ROP; it is not to be confused with FOP which are the facilities and devices—devoid of any social content—used in the process of production. In production, through a labour process, the material (which includes elements of natural world) and social are combined to produce use values for the purpose of consumption or to add new facilities and devices for further expansion of production. If one chooses to deploy mode of production at all then the centrality of primacy thesis—prior presence of FOP to that of ROP in a cause and effect relation—must be guaranteed in it.

One fact that all major Marxist theories agree upon is that the 'relations' in ROP must be class relations. That is, ROP must be class ROP. That is where the consensus ends. Marxist theories differ from one another in terms of what they mean by class, the unit of defining it and the contrasting logics (reductionist or non-reductionist) used to explain the relation of class and non-class elements. Regarding the 'what', class has been defined in various ways within the Marxian tradition, predominantly as economic power, property and surplus labour. Power theory of class (predicated upon power), property theory of class (predicated upon property) and surplus labour theory of class (predicated upon surplus labour) are irreducibly different class theories; debates within Marxism can henceforth be partly construed in terms of each theory's focus on the importance of a specific set of class effects and outcomes that they project (Resnick and Wolff, 2006, 118-136; Chakrabarti and Cullenberg, 2003, Chapters 2 and 3). Moreover, theories differ in terms of the 'unit of defining class i.e. whether class is to be considered a noun (homogenous group of people) or an adjective to a verb (process); classes as homogeneous groups of people and class as process, class struggle as struggle between two or more homogeneous groups or classes and class struggle as struggle over class process are very different in terms of what class effects are underscored and how their ramifications are understood. The final point concerns the logic deployed to analyse the relation between class (no matter how it is defined) and non-class aspects. Non-determinist approaches like that of the class-focused theory of Resnick and Wolff contend that class (no matter how it is defined) and non-class processes mutually constitute one another; as cause and effect of one another, their relation cannot be reduced exclusively to class effects. In contrast, deterministic HM theories, one of whose varieties we are emphasising here, tend to reduce the relation between non-class and class aspects to the adopted class effects/character.

Defining class as a homogeneous group of people predicated in terms of economic power over the FOP, Cohen (1978, 1986a, 1986b, 1988) adopts and delivers a reductionist class analysis. Specifically, different kinds of class ROP can be distinguished by the criterion of whether the direct producers have no, some or total economic power over his/her own labour power and the means of production. Following Cohen's typology:

Amount of Economic Power Over	*His Labour Power*	*The Means of Production He Uses*
Slave	None	None
Serf	Some	Some
Proletarian	All	None
Independent	All	All

How does Cohen relate the aspect of ownership/property to power? He differentiates between legality and control with respect to ownership of property. While accepting that 'ownership is a legal phenomenon' (and arises at the level of superstructure) ownership of property can also be seen in term of economic power as in effective control over the property irrespective of whether that right is legally conferred or not. Those who have economic powers over the means of production and labour power are assumed to have real or imputed (as if) ownership rights over them as well.

What about surplus labour and exploitation? While property relation is predicated on economic power as we saw, exploitation (and for that matter, surplus labour, without which exploitation cannot be located) too is reducible to power relations. A correspondence emerges: the class which more or less exercise economic power necessarily exploits the class (i.e. excludes the direct producers from the appropriation of surplus) who do not have that power.[9] By reducing exploitation to relations of power structure, Cohen displaces the focus upon exploitation per se by rendering the effects and mechanisms flowing directly from the processes of surplus labour as passive, waiting to be derived from, or reflected by, other categories (property, power, etc.).

Cohen defines 'economic structure' as the sum total of coexisting ROP. However, typically in HM, one class ROP is considered to be dominant, with the others subordinated to it. The economic structure of a society thereby comes to be designated by the dominant ROP. The explanation of what happens to that society, its function and the transition it undergoes is reducible to the extant dominant ROP and its effects to which the other ROPs are subordinated, and consequently the society gets its designated name from the identified dominant ROP.[10] For example, a feudal/capitalist society is one in which the feudal/capitalist ROP is predominant. Or, to say that the Indian economy is capitalist is to say so by the same reasoning.

Superstructure: Superstructure consists of only those political, legal and cultural aspects of society (institutions and apparatuses of state, law, education, religion, etc.) that enable the reproduction of ROP. While FOP provide the natural/material foundation of ROP, in turn ROP is the (economic) foundation on which culture and political rises. For example, law facilitates the capitalist ROP by securing for "capitalists effective power over means of production. What confers them that power on a given capitalist, say an owner of a factory? On what can he rely if others attempt to take control of the factory away from him? An important part of the answer is this: he can rely on the law of the land, which is enforced by the might of the state…The content of the legal system is explained by its function, which is to help sustain an economy of a particular kind" (Cohen, 1988, 9). However, to be careful, not everything is part of the superstructure (such as singing among friends or art per se if disconnected from a relation with ROP).

The significance, theoretical and practical, attached by Marxists to the state has been extensively discussed. Whether wholly or partially (with relative autonomy), the state is seen as an instrument of political organisation of the ruling class, especially when it comes to securing capitalist society. In many Marxian approaches it is at times offered as a collective embodiment of all other elements of superstructure. In those treatments, the objective of the state is to create, regulate and control social institutions that will reflect, justify, protect, serve and uphold the existing class relationship. Lenin's insistence on the centrality of the state in securing capitalist ROP and the counter force of vanguard party needed to institute a delinking between the two by capturing the state on behalf of the working class was a benchmark moment in the history of the 20th century. However, without subsuming the entire superstructure to the state, Cohen's approach insists on maintaining the distinct features and roles of each of the elements in the superstructure. Nevertheless, the importance of the state in capitalist society is flagged in his treatment.

Others such as, to name a few, Lukacs, Gramsci, Althusser, Frankfurt school and Jameson have highlighted the importance of cultural apparatuses pertaining to institutions of education, religion, art and entertainment, advertisements, etc. These apparatuses create a socialised system of production and dissemination of meanings, symbols, rituals, morality, etc. that help rationalise and justify the dominant ROP, say the capitalist ROP. The subjects are embodied within these apparatuses, and their consciousness, history and texture, constituted by their effects. Somewhat sidestepping Lenin's insistence on the centrality of the state, Gramsci in particular insisted that it is these social apparatuses and their effects, and not the state per se, that constitute the first and immediate firewall in defence of capitalist ROP; his insistence on the effects of these on consciousness and the production of common sense became a benchmark for future analysis. Taking off from Gramsci, Althusser sought to combine the state and social apparatuses as also the intertwined system of meanings, signs, habits, morality and rituals they help shape to explain the production of willing subjects for the reproduction of capitalist ROP; it is this cultural production that seek to produce the mentioned intertwined system as the social norm (something socially specific taken as naturally/universally true) that enable the reproduction of capitalist ROP.[11] Both Gramsci and Althusser insisted on the indispensability of counter apparatuses and the role of 'organic intellectuals' to help create a current for alternative cultural formation and subject formation in the struggle against capitalism and for a post-capitalist society.[12]

Understandably, the domain of superstructure is the site of stabilisation (of ROP) and conflict (over issues related to the dominant ROP or to transit from it). Class struggle between homogeneous social actors (derived from their structural class positions) for winning economic control over the ROP materialize at this level.

Social Consciousness and Subjects: Finally, there are forms of social consciousness capturing the mindset/disposition of the subjects in a manner that are broadly consistent with the superstructure and ultimately the economic structure of a society. Cohen invokes Marx's Preface once again where he contends, "it is not the consciousness of people that determines their being, but, on the contrary, their social being that determines their consciousness". He argues that "what Marx meant by 'social being' was a particular one or set of a person's social roles, namely, his economic role(s)." Cohen sketches the connection thus. "The foundation is an economic structure, a set of production relations, whereas the social being of a person is his position in it; and the superstructure is a set of non-economic institutions (of law, politics, religion, education, etc.) in which persons participate with a consciousness grounded in their being." (Cohen, 1988, 45-46) Superstructure being the site of stabilisation and conflict, he contends that "none of this occurs except through the agency of human beings, whose actions are inspired by their ideas, but whose ideas are more or less determined by their economic roles." (Cohen, 1988, 45-46) From the slightly differently angle of Gramsci-Althusser, the linkage of superstructure and economic structure with the production of consciousness and subject formation takes a more sophisticated route for understanding the dexterity of social systems, particularly capitalism.

Determinism/Essentialism: We use these terms interchangeably, focusing on its logic. Expressed simply, determinism/essentialism is a mode of explanation based on a structure of causality in which one aspect is explained or caused (being determined) by another aspect (determinant) which is taken as given, self-constituted totality that is intelligible, knowledgeable and rational on its own basis in need of no further explanation in that order of relationship. Structured by a strict separation of cause and effect, the determinant/cause to which the determined/effect is being reduced to is called essence; such kinds of reductionist explanation are called essentialist (Chakrabarti and Cullenberg, 2003, 25-40). HM models such as that of Cohen's have tended to embrace variants of determinist logics (choosing this or that essence of their theory) which in turn became a source of tension and debate amongst Marxists for over a century now. Among many others, one important source of friction with determinism has been that it tends to render passive or secondary other dimensions that could be equally important in explaining something; as a mode of explanation, it has been considered incomplete and misleading with possible destructive social consequences. The ensuing criticisms have given rise to a search for non-deterministic logics and modes of explanation to help produce alternative ways of constructing the knowledge of society and history (Resnick and Wolff, Chapters 1 and 2).

Coming back to our model, superstructure and forms of consciousness are included within the social totality but they do not possess primary explanatory power so far as the reproduction, crisis or development of society is concerned. According to HM, the superstructure and forms of consciousness depend on and are caused/explained by the class ROP. This is what we call class determinism.

Since class ROP comprise the economic structure which determines the superstructure and consciousness, economic determinism and class determinism coincide at that level. From another perspective, the mode of production (combination of FOP and ROP) is posited as causally prior to and determining all other aspects of society. Notwithstanding how the 'economic' is situated, its deterministic property is commonly held and known as economism or economic essentialism/determinism. Moreover, as explained earlier, the explanation of ROP by FOP can be seen as an instance of FOP or technological determinism. Finally, the structure (consisting of FOP, ROP and superstructure) determines the subject/consciousness producing in turn structural determinism. Notwithstanding on the kind of relations analysed in society implying variations in the types of determinism (class, economic, technological, structural), what is nevertheless true is that determinism as a logic uniformly inflects and fastens all such relations between the components of society into a totality. This complex social totality or whole has a centre or essence (FOP) to which every other aspects of society owe their existence, role and historical lifespan.

A final clarification on determinist logic might be helpful. It is not always the case that the element that causes would determine other elements on its own. As had been attempted in many Marxist theories, a more sophisticated argument would be to say that any element of the superstructure is determined by a combination of forces of production, relations of production and other elements of superstructures but that forces of production are not determined by any of them. However, in this case, even though the superstructure may not be solely determined by forces of production, its specific form of existence crucially hinges on the stage of development of the forces of production and this dependence takes precedence over other forms of dependence.[13] Not all elements of superstructures are consistent with the prevailing stage of development of the forces of production. Accordingly, even though many factors come together to determine the existence of any element of the superstructure, one factor—the forces of production—is accorded a privileged status of being the most important factor.

Fundamental Puzzle of Historical Materialism

Recall Marx's observation in the Preface stating: "In the social reproduction of their life, men enter into definite, necessary relations that are indispensable and independent of their will, namely relations of production which correspond to a definite stage of development of their material productive forces". Cohen turned his attention to the term correspondence. Does correspondence means that the relation between FOP and ROP is symmetrical? "If relations correspond to forces, forces must correspond to relations." In that case, the primacy thesis entailing that "the level of development of productive power explains the nature of the economic structure" get violated. According to Cohen, "correspondence is not always symmetrical...'correspond' means, roughly, 'are explained by'" (Cohen, 1978, 137). Given this asymmetry inferred in the term correspondence, one must accept that productive forces explain ROP which he argues is clearly asserted in Marx.

'Correspondence' would also mean that ROP might have influenced and through it advanced the development of the FOP. Cohen argues that Marx gives enough indication to this effect in the Preface: "No economic structure (set of production relations) ever perishes before all the productive forces for which there is room in it have developed...new higher relations of production never appear before the material conditions of their existence have matured in the womb of the old society itself" (Cohen, 1978, 140-41). This asserts that ROP have a role in developing FOP and does so till it has exhausted its ability to do so.

The term 'correspond' accordingly harbours a puzzle. On the one hand, it is claimed that FOP exist independently and is causally prior to ROP; it explains the existence of relation of production. That FOP causes ROP must hold true. On the other hand, it is also claimed that ROP influence and control the FOP. How can both be true?[14] Here, Cohen argues that this type of correspondence between the different levels of society can only be consistently explained by functional explanation. In his elaborate defence of this casual explanation from analytic philosophy for HM, Cohen dismissed other modes of explanation including the philosophy of DM as inadequate for resolving the fundamental puzzle.

Functional explanation refers to a logic of relationship in which the cause is explained in terms of the effect; e is the cause and f the effect holds true only under the circumstance: when e occurred because the situation was such that an event like e would cause an event like f. Putting the same in a different way, "something which has a certain effect is explained by the fact that it has that effect." (Cohen, 1988, 8).[15] Take the case of the relations between FOP and ROP. The numbers indicate propositions.

1. The level of development of productive power explains why certain relations and not others would advance productive power,
2. Relations which advance productive power obtain because they advance productive power,
   It follows that:
3. The level of development of productive power explains the nature of the productive relations.

Cohen designates 3 as the Primacy Thesis. Proposition 1 asserts which ROP, say of k type, would be appropriate to develop the FOP. It states the possibility that to develop the FOP which type of relations (or, economic structure) is appropriate for selection and which not. It says nothing about whether the ROP will actually obtain or not. The role of functional explanation appears here. Proposition 2 affirms that the feature that relations of type k facilitate the development of FOP explains why that type of relations obtain. This "production relations prevail because they are relations which advance the development of the productive forces" (Cohen 1988, 10). The order of relationship—FOP first and then ROP—is fixed by 1. Proposition 2 imply that, courtesy functional explanation, only the ROP appropriate for selection by FOP will obtain by virtue of its effects of developing the level of the FOP. Combining 1 and 2 gives proposition 3 which guarantees the primacy of the FOP over ROP even as ROP facilitates the development of the FOP. The fundamental puzzle is resolved.

Extending functionalist explanation into other levels of society, the economic base of ROP at any historical time select that superstructure (hence, ROP is the causal prior) which would be suitable for its functioning (which in turn would advance the development of the productive forces); the fact that a specific superstructure can protect and regulate the class relations explain why the superstructure of that kind obtains. Together, they give rise to proposition 4.

4. The economic structure explains the nature of the superstructure.

Cohen argues that (3) and (4) can only be explained by functional explanations because that is the only way to reconcile the following two theses:

5. The economic structure promotes the development of the productive forces, and

6. The superstructure stabilises the economic structure.

As Cohen avers, "(5) and (6), in conjunction with (3) and (4), do force us to treat historical materialist explanation as functional… No other treatment preserves consistency between the explanatory primacy of the productive forces over the economic structure and the massive control of the latter over the former, or between the explanatory primacy of the economic structure over the superstructure and the latter's regulation of the former" (1988, 13).

Similarly, social being and consciousness is explained by the superstructure and ultimately by the economic structure. This gives us the following.

7. Economic structure and superstructure determines the social being (subject) and embedded consciousness.

Based on the primacy of FOP and the logic of functionalist explanation that preserves the primacy, an internally coherent theory of society emerges. Cohen further supplements this axiomatic conception of society with the ***Development Thesis*** entailing an axiom of history.

8. The productive forces tend to develop throughout history.

Not only is there a primacy of FOP in the conceptualisation of society (the Primacy Thesis (3)), but it additionally enjoys a privileged status in the transition of this society (the Developmental Thesis (8)).

Transition and Development: Cohen's Defence of Karl Marx's Theory of History

That FOP tends to develop throughout history is a historical exigency derived from the rationality saying that people "are disposed to reflect on what they are doing and to discern superior ways of doing it" in the face of material scarcity which does not allow them to advance their wants. Given this rationality and material scarcity (both derived from nature, human and material), people will when the necessity arises exploit the opportunity to expand productive forces to fulfil their wants.[16] Not to do so is irrational which is ruled out. People's rationality works in another way. As a logical extension, they reject or accept ROP depending upon its capacity to improve or not improve the FOP. Again, not to do so is irrational and hence ruled out. There is, in Cohen, two further implicit axioms: that of material scarcity and that of embedded principle of rationality amongst humans. Given material scarcity, there is an assumed 'rational' human agency impetus to go on developing the FOP. Putting it in another way, naturalism (explanation being reduced to some elements of nature) in the form of material nature (FOP) and human nature (rationality) become a guiding force to rationalise why history moves in a certain direction and not others.

The backdrop of the human agential rationality to develop the FOP in the face of material scarcity is also the reason as to why class divisions appear. This is because getting control over the productive forces means that the cost of material scarcity will not be shared equally amongst people. That is, those who enjoy effective powers over means of production will have access to the products and the surplus as compared to the rest of the population who become dependent on them. It is also the case that "class struggle is...a principal means whereby the forces assert themselves over the relations." (Cohen, 1986, 233). Clearly, the existence and utility of classes and their struggles are reduced to FOP and its development. Two kinds of struggles arise: one between the mentioned two classes—ruling versus ruled—in any epoch and second between the ruling classes versus those who want to take control over the FOP. Note that in any era the ruled class (say, serf under feudalism) and the class wanting to overthrow the existing ruling class (say, capitalist class under feudalism) may not be the same. Which struggle—between lord and self or between capitalist and lord—will triumph? Referring to feudalism as an example, Cohen's answer is unambiguous. "Part of the answer is that there is a general stake in stable and thriving production, so that the class best placed to deliver it attracts allies from other strata in society. Prospective ruling classes (capitalist class, emphasis ours) are often able to raise support among the classes subjected to the ruling class (feudal lord class, emphasis ours) they would displace. Contrariwise, classes unsuited to the task of governing society (serfs; emphasis ours) tend to lack the confidence political hegemony requires, and if they do seize power, they tend not to hold it for long." (Cohen, 1986, 233) Other contenders like some of the feudal lords or merchants too will modify their operations on a capitalist basis and undergo a change in class character. Therefore, "the class which rules through a period, or emerges triumphant from epochal conflict does so because it is best suited, most able and disposed, to preside over the development of the productive forces at the given time" (Cohen, 1988, 15). Accordingly, the ROP which will procreate the economic power of the class with the above property will appear. In short, the rise and fall of classes are ultimately determined by the development of the FOP.[17]

Given this Development Thesis, the society is stable if all other aspects of society, notably class ROP, are such that they do not impede the development of the FOP in any manner. If, at any point, ROP do create barriers to the free development of the FOP, a condition of social crisis arises which can be resolved only with the advent of new ROP. Who creates the fetters of whom? Existing ROP fetter productive forces signifying that they are no longer optimal in providing scope for the latter's development. In Marxist literature, this incompatibility or non-optimality or disequilibrium between forces and ROP is at times captured by the term contradiction.[18]

It is worth mentioning that the disequilibrium is not solvable since at this stage the extant ROP has exhausted its potential to develop the FOP; in fact, with time, the state of disequilibrium can only worsen. Expressing it in another way, deepening of the contradiction signals that the time for fundamental change in ROP as per the Development Thesis has arrived.

This new ROP will be so selected by FOP that it will provide maximum scope for the productive use and development of FOP. Evidently, the drive form the presumed rationality of the people trying to overcome material scarcity will ensure that such a kind of ROP obtains. Anything else (that is, other ROP) again will be irrational and hence rejected in the course of history. This change in economic structure in turn brings about a change in the superstructure, and the latter in turn brings about a change in the forms of consciousness.

Does the stage of history follow a certain pattern that ties together the optimal/progressive change from one epoch to another? Here, Cohen draws upon a detailed correspondence between the images of history in Hegel and Marx. (1978, 1-27, 175-215) It is however the case, Cohen contends, that Marx's materialism triumphs over Hegel's idealism. Unlike Hegel, his is not just a philosophy of history but a theory of history of a materialist society containing a logically sound explanation of the inner dynamics of society and its transition. One does not need Hegel to theorise society and its history as perceived by Marx.

Superimposing functionalist explanation driven Marx's theory of history over the imagery of Hegelian triad of affirmation, negation and negation of negation, one can nevertheless conveniently picture transition as already theorised by Marx. Undifferentiated unity (primitive communism where there is no class division/conflict) is the affirmation which is negated by differentiated disunity (slave, feudal and capitalist society respectively, that is, societies divided by optimality crisis and class division/conflict) which is in turn negated (therefore, negation of negation) by differentiated unity (communism or a materially abundant society with no optimality crisis and consequently no class and class conflict). The contradiction between the forces and ROP within each complex society leads, via class struggle to a process of selection of another type of ROP conducive to the development of the FOP and subsequently new superstructure and social consciousness that arises on the basis of it. That is, contradiction in each society is resolved to give rise to a new complex society—a higher form of the society that assimilates the previous society—and subsequently develops another round of contradiction within it. This new complex totality is a higher moment in the qualitative sense that the FOP are freer to develop and hence achieve higher material prosperity as compared to the previous stage.

Clearly, this way of looking at history is teleological meaning that parts of the structure/whole, of their relationship to one another and of their transition, have an underlying purpose. This teleological conception of transition induces a historicist logic: a rational, ordered, progressive movement of society from a preordained origin to a predestined end. The rational element is the essence—here, the FOP; its development signals progress which is coterminous with a higher order of society and this progressive movement starts from a given point—primitive communism—and moves with a law like ordered motion to end where history is destined to reach, finally—communism. Steered on by the iron logic of functionalist explanation, the transitional process is guided by an underlying purpose of the development of the FOP such that, prodded by it, every turn, bend and shift in stages comes to be explained in terms of the more general journey of the society towards its destined end—communism; 'progress' is judged by the proximity of a stage to communism. That class is deemed revolutionary which drive the movement of society forward and the one named reactionary is by virtue of its intention to retain the existing one.

Can stages be skipped (say, skip stage 2 to go straight from 1 to 3)? Cohen argues against that possibility by defending the rationale of the following proposition in Marx's Preface: "No social formation ever perishes before all the productive forces for which there is room in it have developed; and new, higher ROP never appear before the material conditions of their existence have matured in the womb of the old society itself." Cohen's argument can be used to claim, as has been done by some Marxists, that the Russian, Chinese and other 'socialist' revolutions in so-called 'backward' nations were premature attempts to overthrow the still-nascent capitalist ROP and were bound to fail; this is because the capitalist ROP has not exhausted its full potential to facilitate the development of FOP.[19] Equally forceful was the contrary argument of other Marxists who defended the revolutions by stating that during the 20th century history marked by monopoly/cartel, colonialism, imperialism and wars/plunder/occupation for resources and markets the capitalist ROP in advanced countries and elsewhere have turned into a regressive force that impede rather than impel the development of FOP (the underdevelopment, centre-periphery or articulation of modes of production theories are some examples). Given that capitalist ROP have shackled the development of FOP which they were supposed to promote, the 'socialist' revolution telescoped into its logic the blocked progressive content of capitalist ROP, namely propel the development of FOP so as to unchain the forward march of history. Rather than being seen as failures, these erstwhile 'backward socialist' countries, despite taking diverse strategies often forced by circumstances, succeeded in achieving high growth through modernisation, rapid poverty reduction and unprecedented levels of social security in a short span of history. The point is that there is no absolute winner in this long dragging debate since, despite valiant efforts by both sides, there is no way to disprove one another.

We surmise that in HM if essentialism/determinism is the undisputed logic of society then historicism is the undisputed logic of transition; the two logics supplement one another. The essence (FOP) serves as the rational element, the engine, in whose terms history unfolds and the logic predicated on the telos in turn captures the inexorable ascent of society in stages.

Under communism—the end of (class) history—the FOP reach a state of development such that the ROP can no longer act as fetters to technological development; the fundamental contradiction responsible for transition disappears. This epoch signals a change from material scarcity to material abundance such that human wants are satisfied. Rather than being driven by the rationality of a perennial conflict amongst classes to control the ROP, particularly the means of production, so as to become the chief organiser, appropriator and dispenser of income and wealth derived from surplus in society, the rational organisation of society in a society of material abundance comes to be based on: 'from each according to his ability to each according to his need". As Cohen states, "Marxism sees history as a protracted process of liberation–from the scarcity imposed on humanity by nature, and from the oppression imposed by some people on others. Members of the ruling and subject classes share the cost of natural scarcity unequally, and Marxism predicts, and fights for, the disappearance of society's perennial class division." (1988, vii).

On the route to the establishment of communism, property is socialised; the source to draw economic power for one group as against another is taken away. Resultantly, the basis of class ROP disappears and so does class struggle. To sum up: like the category of surplus and property, the basis for the existence of classes and consequently class struggle disappears from human history. Finally, with the establishment of a classless society, the reason for the existence of the state too is no longer there. Its superstructure role as facilitator of class ROP becomes redundant and unwanted. Under communism, we have statelessness accompanying classlessness. In its place, different kinds of institutions aimed at reproducing a new society appear.

This depicted blueprint of communist society must be followed by a warning. Marx himself expressed scepticism about an ideal in terms of which a blueprint for a communist society can be established. An expression of this deep scepticism is present in *A Critique of Germany Ideology*, "Communism is for us not a state of affairs which is to be established, an ideal to which reality [will] have to adjust itself. We call communism the real movement which abolishes the present state of things. The conditions of this movement result from the premises now in existence." By this account, the make-up of the final station of history presented by HM is not so certain, uniform and frictionless. How do we think of a post-capitalist society then?

Perhaps it is not so out of order to pay more attention to what some have and many more presently are trying to imagine and produce through their actions from within this world: a pluriverse world (a world where many worlds are possible) of a variety of post-capitalist societies in the spirit expressed by Marx (Gibson-Graham, 2006, Klein and Morrero, 2019).

Role of Class Struggle

Class struggle is secondary in the sense that it arises on the basis of the 'fundamental explanation of the course of history and the structure of society'. This is not to say that class struggle is unimportant but to accept that it appears at the level of "main events of that course (of history) and the surface relief of society" and not the "fundamental explanation of the course of history and the structure of society" (Cohen, 1988, 14). Let us explore this point somewhat further.

As an existing ROP fetter the development of the FOP, class conflict intensifies. Since classes (defined in terms of property or power) embody diverging groups' location vis a vis the creation and appropriation of surplus, the conflict expresses itself in the inability of the ruling class to extract its desired surplus from within the existing ROP. It also means that the fulfilment of wants of the mass of people becomes increasingly difficult to attain. The scenario is made murkier by the entry of a new class force that is attempting to usurp the economic power from the hands of the old ruling class. As we exemplified earlier, the sharpening of the conflict between lord and serf during the crisis of feudalism saw the rise of the nascent capitalist class intent on usurping power. The conflict erupts into and disrupts the reproduction of the extant superstructure as well making its institutionalised socio-political order (say, the feudal political system, the central role of church in education, etc.) difficult to sustain. Under the growing challenges, the ruling order is no longer seen as capable of securing the existing class ROP; it is resolved through a change in economic power that takes the form of a new revolutionary class ultimately defeating the existing ruling class. Therefore, the bourgeoisie appeared as revolutionary class under feudalism to defeat the ruling class of lords putting in place a new class ROP that will provide ample scope for the arrested FOP to develop freely once again and thus allow the new ruling capitalist class to achieve a desirable level of surplus extraction. As the previous revolutionary capitalist class becomes the new ruling class, its ROP secures the rise of a new revolutionary class, the working class; conflict between the two classes emerges. Thus, as FOP changes, so does the class relationships of production, so does the new elements of superstructure conducive to the new class ROP leading to newer forms of class struggle and conflict in the new society born out of the womb of the old and so history moves on till its final station.

Dual Definitions of Class and Class Formation: Politics of Transition

The rest of the discussion is on the presented theory of class in HM which brings into the forefront a bagful of issues and problems, some of which are covered now. There are clearly two definitions of class in HM. The first pertains to a given group of people structurally positioned within the ROP. Because this definition of class encapsulates the ROP or economic structure, this is often referred to as an economic definition of class. Nevertheless, this presence of class does not have any mechanism of explaining why and how such a class will act. Sans class as social actor there cannot be any class struggle and consequently the transition of society cannot materialise. Therefore for change in the structurally given ROP to

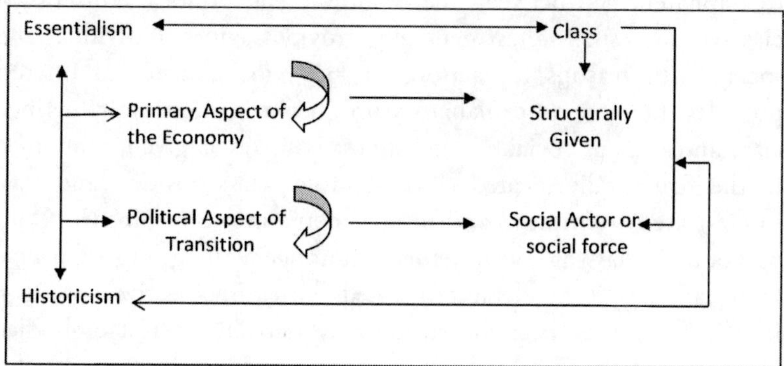

transpire to remove the fetters on the development of FOP, class must also be a designated social actor capable of decision-action. There is then another definition of class—a political definition—that refers to class as a homogeneous group of conscious people who can act.

One of the enduring puzzles that has since emerged in Marxism is how to reconcile the economic definition (i.e. the structural definition) of class with the political definition (i.e. the subjective definition) of class, that is, make consistent the two claims or rather make the singular claim: those who occupy a structurally given class position will also be ones who will form themselves according to their position as a social actors in order to struggle for or against progressive social change. While Cohen assumes embodied rationality to achieve material prosperity in class subjects which provides it with a reason for collective action for progressive change in history this assumption is hardly a resolution to the class problem of reconciling the two levels. Because of the importance of class politics in Marxism, let us explore this issue of class dichotomy somewhat more with the help of new concepts.

Class positions are those structurally defined (economic) positions that individuals occupy in ROP. Roughly, a group embodying a specific class position in ROP constitute class in itself. Class formation refers to the transformation of class in itself to class for itself, where class for itself is the social consciousness demanded of a class to congeal into a social actor. The missing element in this apparent gap between the economic and political concepts of class is 'interest'. Interest generally provides actors, individual and social, with reasons for action. In HM, the concept of interest provides therefore an explanatory link between structurally defined class and class as social actor. Interest is taken as given, embodied in the structurally located class positions; class position and class interest are coterminous and in fact merge into one another. Once so granted, class as social actor (a homogeneous group of people who can act) is by default instilled with an objectively defined intelligibility reflecting the structurally derived interest embodied in class positions. For example, defining working class in capitalist

ROP is also laying down the working class interest that provides it with the collective will for directing its specific course of action along that line. Classes now become actors for class interests—class-for-itself. In the historical plane, class actors with preformed interest struggle with one another—clash of classes is a clash of class interest—to fulfil their assigned goal and role in society and history.

The basic contour comprising the problem of class formation in HM is then this linkage:

Structurally Given Class Position → Pre-Given Interest → Class as Social Actors → Class Struggle.

From a different but related angle, the presence of working class consciousness and actual consciousness of individual members of working class signals a dichotomy that present a further complication. Ideally, working class consciousness would automatically translate into the consciousness of individuals holding that class position. This is the concept of 'imputed consciousness' i.e. consciousness reflecting the true (working class) interest that in turn is structurally given. Since the working class is derived from a structural disposition, the imputed consciousness reflects the intelligibility flowing from the working class interest. Imputed consciousness is thus said to have an objective basis. The problem is that while interest is said to have an objective or structural basis it may not be necessarily recognised by those whose interests they are presumed to be. The actual consciousness may be in discord with the desirable true interest personified in imputed consciousness. This difference is false consciousness whose extent for any individual is a function of the difference between true and false interest. The individuals holding working class positions and hence belonging to the working class may not recognise the "truth" of their class interest and consequently of what their social and historical role ought to be.[20] Class identity as social actor with a collective will cannot be formed i.e. the class formation problem from class in itself to class for itself cannot be resolved in the presence of false consciousness.

Marxist practitioners working with some variant of HM model with dual class dichotomy—starting from Lenin, Luxemburg, Gramsci and Lukacs to many in contemporary times—have long recognised the problem of class formation for working class politics associated with this schism between true and false interest, between imputed and actual consciousness. In flagging false consciousness as a political problem, they however do not question the assumption of pre-given true interest. Taking interest as objectively and structurally given and hence as true, they then proceeded to analyse the apparent problem of reconciling imputed consciousness with actual consciousness. Putting it somewhat simply the individual is not yet a political subject and false consciousness a measure of this lack. In order to transcend false consciousness which the working class (members) on their own are definitionally incapable (otherwise you will not have this dual problem in the first place), it was argued that one needs an external force for precisely this purpose. The conception of a vanguard party of the working class—a party of 'revolutionaries'—emerged whose purpose is to educate the members about their true interest and historical role, and help to forge the class identity with a collective will to initiate class struggle against capitalism for its overthrow. In the erstwhile socialist countries, vanguard parties embodied the very basis of so-called working class domination.[21] Forging class interests and class identity for the purpose of revolution through the medium of re-education, trade union activism, social movements such as general strike, insurgency, vote politics, etc. become the said goal of the vanguard party. The following diagram presents our arguments schematically.

Careful theoretical and political introspection pointed to the two other controversial consequences of class determinism: one, by reducing the relevant object of social struggle to that of changing the structurally defined class relations pre-assigned as the most essential structural component of society and two, by reducing the relevant subject of social struggle to a unified, uniform and closed class subject, both at the individual and social level. Consequently, the individual and social subject as also the object of social struggle which the subject addresses are presumed as subsumed by class. Taken together, the class saturated social space fails to explain why both the relevant object and subject of social struggle should be considered as reducible to class per se when it can be neither theoretically nor empirically defended; for one, it begs the question of how can its claim of a class saturated space be taken as what that space actually is. The fallout of class determinism has long been acknowledged as a problem within Marxism.

SOCIETY

Consciousness

Superstructure

Relations of Production

Forces of Production

(Class Struggle)

Agency → **Class-for-itself**

False Consciousness

Party

Structural Location → **Class-in-itself**

Among other things, it has led to a renewed effort to rethink the issue of subject/consciousness, class identity and struggle.[22] Rather than emphasise upon false consciousness or the dual existence of true/false interest/consciousness, other approaches have tried to understand the subject—his disposition, consciousness, practice, etc.—as a combined effects of cultural, political, natural and economic aspects of society. Subjects need to be theorised as a constitutive product of these aspects including the kind of superstructures and economic structures within which the subject is embodied. Social struggles too are likewise rethought as transpiring in a contested plane. When the subject formation and social struggle is in such a mired space, the role of the ruling order to impregnate the subject's psyche and common sense with the ruling ideas (which is produced and disseminated at the level of superstructures) that does not challenge the dominant class ROP becomes crucial. Having learnt from and absorbed the historical lesson of the threat of the working class movement to capitalists' social position as a class which is by no means omniscient or omnipotent, the ruling order (much in the same way as Gramsci and Althusser argued) in trying to shield the capitalism system may reorganise and recast, as the need arises, the superstructure elements to secure the system (through aspects of education, media, politics, law, religion, race, ethnicity, ownership pattern, etc.). The uncited, unacknowledged intent of this ever changing imperial architecture of shaping subjects is to produce and transform subjects into ones who themselves, of their own free will, reject any rejection of the capitalist system. This phenomenon of accumulation of men to accompany accumulation of capital as Foucault referred to in *The History of Sexuality* has been the subject of much analysis in Marxism, from Gramsci (who foregrounded the importance of cultural apparatuses in shaping social beings) to Althusser (who theorised the ideological state apparatuses by combining state and culture). Others, following Gramsci, Althusser, Jameson, Resnick and Wolff have proceeded to argue for a thorough transformation of both the understandings of structure and subject and of their relation. They argue that defeating the festering class determinism in Marxism can only be achieved by recasting the definitions of class and epistemology. These tendencies and the theories they produce inject into the contested Marxian tradition a different trajectory and history of Marxism as also of its politics.

Conclusion

As stated in the introduction, my expansion of Cohen's work to present a prototype deterministic model was to unpack carefully some of the basic positions and modes of analysis of HM. Variants of this prototype HM model, more or less similar to it, have flourished in Marxism and we have also recorded some line of extensions, deviations and debates. Another embodied purpose had been to prepare the readers to self-identify the channel through which they can start to make sense of how and why deterministic

HM models become a fertile ground for launching fundamental challenges to its logics, descriptions, histories and actions from within the tradition of Marxism. The history of Marxism, including in many of its developed forms, have witnessed the rise of new theories in the course of this challenge—flourishing with different sets of logics, focuses, strategies, analysis and positions. Moreover, responses to newer socio-economic development have in turn led to production of new concepts and tools that are consistent with whatever kind of Marxist theory is produced. Marxism is neither a singular nor a dogmatic field, not to say static. Rather, it is a sophisticated, changing, rich space of contesting and often clashing theories which not only challenge the mainstream discourses but also one another. In the process, it produces a deeper understanding of what this tradition seeks to broadly highlight and pursue.

These internal clashes within Marxism transpired over multiple aspects. We will end by mentioning a few, by no means exhaustive, debates and disputes that have and continue to inflect this tradition: over the concept of dialectics, over deterministic versus non-deterministic epistemologies, between varieties of determinism (structuralism versus theoretical humanism), between teleological versus non-teleological understanding of history, over class definitions whether to predicate it upon power, property or surplus labour and whether the unit of class should be a group of people or process, over whether the dual structure of class should be retained or not, over whether false consciousness as an explanation of consciousness should be abandoned, over understandings of what constitute consciousness, subject and identity, over whether the associated concept of vanguard party is flawed, over the meaning and content of politics, over that of power whether it should be accounted for in terms of the categories of HM that we have described or whether we need a distinct theory of power in the form of hegemony, whether the erstwhile 'socialist' countries were/are exploitative or not and hence deserving to be critically engaged with, over how to account for colonial and post-colonial societies, histories and experiences along with the often-mentioned problems of orientalism, ethnocentrism and modernism, etc. For each question and many others not mentioned, different debates and disputes have contributed to bolster existing and new theories adding to the overall rich complexity of Marxism. The question of the relation of Marxism to politics has accordingly been undergoing serious rethinking and transformation (Gibson-Graham, 2006; Wolff, 2012; Chakrabarti and Dhar, 2019; Dhar and Chakrabarti, 2019; Klein and Morrero, 2019; Chakrabarti, Dhar and Kayatekin, 2020), raising new discussions not only regarding what the objective and scope of transformation should be but also on what the means of doing politics ought to be.

NOTES

1. This is a shortened albeit reworked version of "Historical Materialism: A Critical Assessment" in *Contemporary Readings in Marxism: A Critical Introduction* (ed. Ravi Kumar). Aakar Books: Delhi, 2016. I thank Ravi Kumar for his permission to use some parts of the chapter in the book.
2. It tells us that, as Étinnie Balibar had noted, Marx and Marxism are not the same. Just as in the instance of Marxism, socialism and communism too are not the same nor can be readily reduced or collapsed to one another; even what is meant by socialism is not singular (see Wolff, 2019 for an introduction to their differences and complex relations).
3. See Olsen (2009) for a good review.
4. Louis Althusser's battle with determinisms of both Hegelian structuralism and theoretical humanism in Marxist theory is well-known and much dissected. At the same time, his conception of overdetermination was criticised for holding onto a structural residue of economic in the last instance in the determination of society. By giving up on any such residue of determinism (economic or otherwise), Resnick and Wolff develops overdetermination and contradiction as a wholesale non-deterministic epistemology. The 'post' in 'post-Althusserian' thus signifies a theoretical movement after Althusser but in relation to him.
5. Sharp debates have transpired in India too, something that is well documented in the Indian modes of production debate and that over passive revolution of capital in the context of India's economic transition (Chakrabarti and Cullenberg, 2003, Chapters 2-5).

6. Absorbing lessons from all the three broad approaches, thinkers and practitioners from the erstwhile colonial countries have combined what they find relevant in them with critical indigenous literature and experience to highlight the importance of outside (say, world of the third) in the constitution of (global) capitalism (Cesaire, 2010, Chaudhury, Dhar and Chakrabarti, 2000, Dhar and Chakrabarti, 2019, Chakraborty, Chakrabarti, Dasgupta and Sen, 2019). We can call theories emphasising this constitutive connection as world of the third Marxism. In this paper, we do not pursue this brand of Marxian theoretical field.
7. Alternatively, how FOP and ROP combines captures a critical dimension of human-nature relation that is central to the reproduction of both human life and natural life; this has given rise to a rich eco-socialist literature in recent times (Saito, 2018).
8. Economic base is not to be confused with the essence of society (to which we will come later).
9. See Resnick and Wolff (2006) and Chakrabarti and Cullenberg (2003) for why this correspondence would not be true in a non-reductionist class theory.
10. One of the richest formulations and debates on the issue of transition and subordination of one ROP by another in the early 20th century and the role of the nation-state in it has come from Japan (Walker, 2016).
11. This is not to say that Althusser, undisputedly influenced by Gramsci, did not differ from him; for one, he did not accept the idea of hegemony that Gramsci proposed.
12. Organic intellectual is not the same as vanguardism (to be discussed later).
13. See Althusser (1969), for instance.
14. Interestingly, this puzzle is also acknowledged at the level of mode of production and superstructure by Althusser (1969, 1975) who tries to resolve the primacy of the former and the important role of the latter through concepts such as 'determination in the last instance' of the economic, 'effectivity', 'relative autonomy' and 'reciprocal action.' His detailing of the mode of production can be found in Althusser (2014).
15. An example given by Cohen might be helpful for a preliminary understanding of functional explanation. 'Birds have hollow bones because hollow bones facilitate flight.' The functional explanation is:

That birds having hollow bones facilitate flight is explained by the fact that it has the effect of facilitating flight.

16. This emphasis on human rationality in the face of scarcity bears an uncanny affinity with the liberal tradition, particularly in the neoclassical economics.
17. Cohen's reduction of class ROP and class struggle to FOP was criticised by many scholars of HM. They insisted on the primacy of class struggle to resolve which ROP will appear as central in the Marxian theory of history (for example, Brenner, 1986).
18. It must be said though that Cohen does not have much use for the category of contradiction. In him, the aspect of (sub)optimality is a good enough way of depicting the social (in)stability. I still use it here, without compromising on Cohen's rendition, to make the readers aware of the manner of usage of contradiction in the historical sense in deterministic Marxian theory.
19. Cohen argues that the changes in ROP, when they come, would be revolutionary although it is not clear why his version of orthodox Marxian would not be consistent with the revisionist approach in Marxism. From the late 1890s onwards, Eduard Bernstein, especially in *Evolutionary Socialism and The History and Theory of Socialism* forwarded his revisionist Marxist approach, directing another path of socialism, a peaceful road, which has had a lasting influence in many parts of the world (Laclau and Mouffe, 1985). Following Bernstein, the politics of socialism, influenced by Marx or otherwise, became split into two roads: the revolutionary and the reformist path. Following Bernstein, (i) socialism does not follow from the collapse of capitalism (rejects inevitability), (ii) history is not an objective process but interaction between objective and subjective (will) factors and (iii) socialism is achieved through party programmes that requires an ethical and not entirely scientific decision. This requires the autonomy of ethical subject. The ethical subject is a (transcendental) subject. How is it possible then to have a unification of economic and political? Here, Bernstein forwards his evolutionary thesis entailing that the ethical subject is also transcendental subject guided by, and adapting to the laws of evolution. Thus, revisionism collapses into gradualism, and a peaceful parliamentary path towards socialism within the purview of the nation-state follows. For a critique of Bernstein's position, see Rosa Luxemburg's *Reform or Revolution*.
20. Misrecognition is not the same as non-recognition, a difference we do

not discuss any further except to say that the latter becomes important in the literature on hegemony.

21. The vanguard party was assumed to uphold the pure interest of the working class. As a result the interests of the working class and the vanguard party became synonymous. Since the totality of the subject directly translates the objective interest of the working class, the interest of an individual holding a working class position should coincide with that of the working class as a whole and the vanguard party. The subject is represented by a working class that, in turn, is represented by the vanguard party. Any dissent or revolt against the vanguard party is considered a revolt against the working class and its true interests. I leave it for the reader to count the effects and consequences of this correspondence relation.
22. Lenin maintained historical subjects as personification of classes that entails the presence of pure class identity. Luxemburg in "Mass Strike, The Political Party and the Trade Unions" argued that one cannot take, fix, a priori the meaning of the strike or party as moments in the socialist transition; instead it is in the process of revolution—through overdetermination of many struggles—that the unity of the working class is achieved. Once the meaning of social events has been unfixed, we get a unity—involving spontaneity—that cannot be reduced to any necessity attributed to social and individual actions derived from their structural position. Class identity cannot be taken as given. However, Luxemburg still maintains that this composed unity, achieved through overdetermination of many struggles, at the political sphere is a class unity even though why it should be referred to as so is not clear. This essentialism of class is also present in Gramsci. Sharply distinguishing between the economic and political sphere, he uses the conception of hegemonic articulation of non-class and class relations in the formation of class subjects and politics. Yet, he continues to maintain the reduction of this hegemony to the class core in the economy (Laclau and Mouffe, 1985, Chapters 1 and 2). As we understand, while both Luxemburg and Gramsci correctly identify the problem and take the first basic step to break out of it (the same is true for Althusser later on), the framework of historical materialism within which they operate holds them back from resolving the matter decisively. While the economy in the last instance haunted their framework it is nevertheless true that the extraordinary phase of political thought has in turn led to a fertile territory over which theories, questions and debates continue to appear till today.

REFERENCE

Althusser, L. (1969 [1965]), *For Marx,* trans. Ben Brewster, Allen Lane: The Penguin Press.

Althusser, L. and E. Balibar (1975), *Reading Capital,* London: Verso Books, Indian edition (2013), Delhi: Aakar Books.

Althusser, L. (2014), *On the Reproduction of Capitalism: Ideology and Ideological State Apparatuses.* London: Verso.

Brenner, R. (1986), The Social Basis of Economic Development, In J.E. Roemer (ed.), *Analytical Marxism,* Cambridge: Cambridge University Press.

Césaire, A. (2010 [2000]), *Discourse on Colonialism,* Translated by Joan Pinkham, Delhi: Aakar Books.

Chakrabarti, A. and S. Cullenberg (2003), *Transition and Development in India,* London and New York: Routledge.

Chakrabarti, A and A. Dhar (2017), Transition, In Brennan D., D. Kristjanson-Gural, D.C. Mulder, and E. Olsen (eds.), *Routledge Handbook of Marxian Economics,* New York and London: Routledge.

Chakrabarti, A. and A. Dhar (2019), Non-Violent Socialism: Marx and Gandhi in Dialogue in Chakraborty A., A. Chakrabarti, B. Dasgupta and S. Sen (eds.), *'Capital' in the East: Reflections on Marx,* Singapore: Springer Nature.

Chakrabarti, A., A. Dhar and S. Kayatekin (2020), *Marx, Marxism and the Spiritual,* New York and London: Routledge.

Chakraborty A., A. Chakrabarti, B. Dasgupta and S. Sen (eds.), (2019), *'Capital' in the East: Reflections on Marx,* Singapore: Springer Nature.

Chaudhury, A., D. Das and A. Chakrabarty (2000), *Margin of Margin: Profile of an Unrepentant Postcolonial Collaborator,* Kolkata: Anushtup.

Cohen, G.A. (1978), *Karl Marx's Theory of History: A Defence,* Oxford: Oxford University Press.

Cohen, G.A. (1986a), Forces of Production and ROP, In J.E. Roemer (ed.), *Analytical Marxism,* Cambridge: Cambridge University Press.

Cohen, G.A. (1986b), Marxism and Functional Explanation, In J.E. Roemer (ed.), *Analytical Marxism,* Cambridge: Cambridge University Press.

Cohen, G.A. (1988), *History, Labour and Freedom,* Oxford: Oxford University Press

Dhar, A., and A. Chakrabarti (2019), Praxis in World of the Third Contexts: Beyond Third Worldism and Development Studies, In E.

Klein and C.E. Morrero (eds.), *Postdevelopment in Practice: Alternatives, Economies, Ontologies*, Oxon and New York: Routledge.

Gibson-Graham, J.K. (2006), *A Postcapitalist Politics*, Minneapolis: University of Minnesota Press.

Harvey, D. (2010), *A Companion to Marx's Capital*, London: Verso Books.

Hindess, B. and P. Hirst (1977), *Mode of Production and Social Formation: An Auto Critique of Pre-Capitalist Modes of Production*, London: Macmillan.

Klein, E. and C.E. Morrero (eds.), (2019), *Postdevelopment in Practice: Alternatives, Economies, Ontologies.* Oxon and New York: Routledge.

Laclau, E. and C. Moufee (1985), *Hegemony and Socialist Strategy*, London: Verso Books.

Marx, K. (1977), *A Contribution to the Critique of Political Economy*, Moscow: Progress Publishers.

Olsen, E.K. (2009), Social Ontology and the Origins of Mode of Production Theory, *Rethinking Marxism*, Vol. 21, No. 2, pp. 177–95.

Resnick, S.A. and R.D. Wolff (1987) *Knowledge and Class*, Chicago: University of Chicago Press.

Resnick, S.A. and R.D. Wolff (2006), *New Departures in Marxian Theory.* London and New York: Routledge.

Resnick, S.A. and R.D. Wolff (2012), *Contending Economic Theories: Neoclassical, Keynesian and Marxian*, Cambridge: MIT Press.

Saito, K. (2018), *Karl Marx's Ecosocialism: Capitalism, Nature, and the Unfinished Critique of Political Economy*, New York: Monthly Review Press.

Walker, G. (2016), *The Sublime Perversion of Capital: Marxist Theory and the Politics of History in Modern Japan*, Durham & London: Duke University Press.

Wolff, R.D. (2012), *Democracy at Work: A Cure for Capitalism*, Chicago: Haymarket Books.

Wolff, R.D. (2019), *Understanding Socialism*, New York: Democracy at Work.

2

Essential Concepts in Marxian Political Economy

Surinder Kumar

We recognise a phenomenon in our minds through its attributes, which are generalised in the form of 'concepts'. Concepts facilitate reflection of the world in our minds. Concept is abstraction from reality and it is just a logical construct. It is through concepts that we comprehend the reality. For example, shirt, school, commodity, capitalist, landlord, and labourer are different concepts. A concept should be defined as precisely as possible to avoid any confusion and gap in our communications. Most of the misunderstandings emerge because we may use a concept for communication through spoken words or writing, which may not be precisely defined and may mean different things to different people. Therefore, the first task in any scientific communication or discussion is to clearly and precisely define the 'Concepts' in terms of which we enter into dialogue with others and communicate our ideas or views.

Most people find it difficult to comprehend Marx because they are not familiar with the Marxian concepts. Marxian Political Economy uses some terms/concepts, which were formed by British classical economists, French political thinkers and German philosophers and were further evolved, refined and precisely defined by Karl Marx over time. We need to comprehend Marxian concepts as precisely as possible so that there is no confusion in our comprehension of the Marxian theoretical formulations.

1. Marxian Political Economy

Psychology deals with individual human behaviour. However,

society is more than a collection of individuals. Social behaviour has its own dynamics. Individuals enter into certain definite and somewhat enduring relations among themselves. The social sciences comprise all those branches of knowledge, which aim at studying and understanding these social relations and their changes over time. Political Economy/Economics is a social science. Subject matter of economics deals with production and distribution of goods and services, which people need and want. Unfortunately, the way economics has evolved over time, the social character of economics as a discipline has got concealed under the high-sounding technical economics, especially in the neoclassical economic theory. The Classical Political Economy approach to the study of economic problems is associated with Adam Smith, Ricardo and others. Karl Marx developed it further and put it on a scientific basis. It has had an enduring impact on the development of social sciences in the world.

There was a long debate over which economics has been reduced from the study of social relations to technical relations of production with labour as one of the explanatory variables, especially since Alfred Marshal (see Lionel Robbins and others). Many motives have been attributed to this shift in the paradigm and economic thinking. Some scholars have observed that Classical Political Economy formulated social relations in terms of class relations and class interests, and contradictions were exposed which were not suited to the ruling classes. Therefore, the shift from class conflict to class harmony as in formulations of the neoclassical economics were encouraged and promoted by the ruling elite. In the neoclassical paradigm, all factors of production join harmoniously and contribute to production in the production process and it is assumed that they are rewarded according to their contribution/ marginal productivity. Thus, there was no conflict and every economic decision may be left to the market forces, which leads to the most efficient allocation of resources and distribution of income. The fact that different people own these factors of production and rewards are distribution according to ownership, which is a social process, is concealed in mainstream economics.

The depression of the 1930s sent alarm signals and the neo-classical economic theory was called into question. Keynesian economics emerged out of that economic crisis. However, since the 1950s, the ruling classes again restored legitimacy of market forces and neo-classical economic thinking. However, the economic and financial crisis of 2008 has again forced economists to have a close look at the mainstream macroeconomics (Wolff and Resnick, 2012). The political economy approach and Marxian approach to economic analysis, which have an interdisciplinary framework of analysis of socio-economic phenomena, are again gaining popularity in social sciences. Therefore, the need of the hour is to reappraise the Marxian Political Economy and its method of analysis and explore its explanatory power of the socio-economic phenomena.

2. Marx's Method

The methodology evolved by Marx is perhaps his greatest contribution, along with his study of capitalism. Marx's method of analysis was the abstract-deductive method. Concrete cannot be understood without first being analysed into the abstract relationships, which make it up. However, our 'a priori' construct must be validated by empirical reality. Further, Marx adopted what modern theorists call the method of 'successive approximation' which consists in moving from more abstract to more concrete in a step by step fashion removing simplifying assumptions at successive stages of the investigation so that theory may take into account and explain an ever-wider range of actual phenomena.

Marx's objective of study was to discover the 'economic laws of motion of capitalist society'. Marx came to an early realisation that human progress was rooted in the material conditions of life and anatomy of the civil society is to be sought in political economy. Marxian formulation of these laws is radically different from that of non-Marxian schools of thought (it embodies a different epistemology of human knowledge). Marx retained the elements of Hegel's thought, which emphasised dynamics of a process and development through the conflict of opposed or contradictory forces (dialectical process). He traced decisive historical conflicts to roots of mode of production in economic relations, which underlie and express themselves in the form of class conflict. These are the essential elements, which must be isolated and analysed through the method of abstraction.

Classical economists, especially Ricardo, identified class conflicts in the 'distribution of the produce of the earth'; but this conflict was between industrial capitalists and landlords. But for Marx, in capitalist society, primary economic relation are between capitalists and workers. The relation between wage labour and capital determines the entire character of the mode of production. This relationship should be at the centre of investigation.

As a method, Marx's method involves two fairly distinct steps: (i) all social relations except those between capital and labour must be assumed away, to be reintroduced, one at a time, only at a later stage of the analysis, and (ii)capital-labour relations which arise in the sphere of industrial production as the most significant relationship in the capitalist system. Capitalists and workers alike are reduced to certain standard types, from which all characteristics irrelevant to the relation under examination are removed. They are the personification of economic categories; represent certain class relations and class interests. Nature of capital-labour relations is an exchange relation in the production process and the capitalist buys labour power from the worker and the worker gets wages from the capitalist with which he acquires the necessities of life.

(Marx's *Capital* Volume 1 remains on a high level of abstraction. It may be taken as provisional as it undergoes extensive modifications on the lower level of abstraction in Volumes 2 and 3.)

3. The Historical Character of Marx's Thought

Marx's method is historical. For Marx, social reality is a historically dynamic process; a process that, in principle, knows no finality and no stopping places. Marx premised that social systems, like individuals, go through life cycles and pass from the scene (is changed/transformed) when relations of production among people change. The process of social change is not purely mechanical. It is dialectical. It is rather a product of human action, but action is definitely limited by the kind of society in which it has its roots. Society is both changing and, within limits, can be changed. To a Marxist, the specific historical forms are transitory in character.

4. Basic Premise of Karl Marx

The essence of Marx's understanding of society and its dynamics is laid down in his work, *A Contribution to The Critique of Political Economy (1859),* which was published eight years before publication of the first volume of *Das Kapital* (1867).

In the social production, which men carry on, they enter into definite relations that are independent of their will; these relations of production correspond to a definite stage of development of their material powers of production. The sum total of these relations of production constitutes the economic structure of society—the real foundation on which rise legal and political superstructures and on which correspond definite forms of social consciousness. The mode of production of material life determines the general character of the social, political, spiritual processes of life. It is not the consciousness of men that determines their existence, but, on the contrary, their social existence determines their consciousness. At a certain stage of their development, the material forces of production in society come in conflict with the existing relations of production, or—what is but a legal expression for the same thing—as the property relations within which they had been at work before. From forms of development of the forces of production these relations turn into their fetters. Then comes the period of social revolution. With the change of the economic foundation the entire superstructure is rapidly transformed (Sweezy, 2016).

5. Labour and Theory of Value

Theory of Value in Economics is a theory which was formulated to explain why a 'good' has a value. What is the source of value? If the producers exchange these goods, how is their exchange value determined? If production and exchange of goods is generalised, how are their prices determined in the market?

In every society, from the most primitive to the most advanced, it is essential that labour is applied to produce goods, and that goods are distributed among the members of society. What changes in the course of history is the way in which these productive and distributive activities are organised and carried out. Adam Smith successfully assured the people that historically the economic fate of people was in their own hands and was not predetermined by the fate of natural resource endowments or control over gold and silver deposits as argued by the Mercantilists. The essence of Smith's labour theory of value was that human activity was the source of prosperity and wealth rather than God-given fertility of land or natural resource endowment or hoards of treasure.

Goods produced for exchange with other producers are called commodities. A commodity is anything that is produced for exchange rather than for the own use of the producer. The study of commodities is therefore the study of the economic relations of exchange. For exchange, we need to develop a common measure of value of various commodities. Preferably it should be quantitative, and invariant (constant over time and space) like kilogram or litre. Historically, the search for a common measure/denominator to be used as a measure of value of different commodities has been a great challenge. In barter exchange, people used to exchange goods on the basis of some subjective notion of value of different commodities. As the exchange process became more generalised, producers started measuring value of commodities in terms of some scarce but divisible commodity like silver and gold. The moot question was, what is the source of value of various commodities? As production of different goods needs different inputs, the only common element/denominator among various goods was that they were all produced by the labour of the producers. Classical economists took labour used as the common measure of value of various commodities.

The labour theory of value has played a pivotal role in the development of Political Economy as a science. Some scholars have argued that the labour theory of value parallels the philosophical and theoretical innovations of Galileo and Newton in the physical sciences as the founding idea of a science (Foley, 2000). The labour theory of value started taking shape during the second half of the 17th century with increasing production and exchange of commodities. Sir William Petty (1623-87) 'came remarkably close to the idea that the exchange value of a commodity is determined by the quantity of labour needed to produce it' (Meek 1973, 35). The labour theory of value became the cornerstone of the classical political economy in the 18th century.

Adam Smith, David Ricardo and Karl Marx each used the labour theory of value in their own way and for their own purpose. Each emphasised the facet of theory most relevant to their own vision. For Adam Smith, labour embedded in production of a good was the measure of its value and labour commanded as a measure of its price. Ricardo's main focus was on the use of the labour theory of value to develop a logically consistent macroeconomic framework for the analysis of the distribution of value of the produce between wages, profit, and rent.

Marx believed in Historical Materialism, the idea central to his thinking was that the ideas and societies organise themselves into classes based on control of surplus production. He further argued that the pattern of political and social power and their associated cultural manifestations in religion, literature, and art, rested on the appropriation of the share of output by a small ruling class in excess of the basic reproduction requirements (subsistence wage). The key to understanding basic evolution and change in human societies lay in uncovering the exact mechanisms through which ruling classes secure the control over surplus produce and the "contradictions" or instabilities producing change (class struggle), that these mechanisms implied (Foley 2000). Marx developed his labour theory of value to explain how value of a commodity is determined as well as how surplus value emerges in a capitalist economy and employed it in his theory of exploitation.

6. Marxian Labour Theory of Value

Marx following the classical economists propounded his labour theory of value. He begins his analysis with simple commodity production. Simple Commodity Production is production of goods in a society in which each producer owns his means of production and satisfies his material needs by exchange with other similarly situated producers. He stated that in this simplified world, a producer uses his labour and with the help of instruments of labour (tools, equipment etc.), acts on the object of labour (land/ raw materials) to produce goods, which have a use value as well as exchange value. Labour theory of value states that exchange value of two commodities is in proportion to the labour consumed in the process of production of those commodities.

The device developed as a measure of 'labour' was the 'time' taken to produce that commodity. Now the time taken to produce a good may differ from one producer to the other, depending on their level of skills. The tools as well as technology embedded in them also help to reduce time consumed in the production of a good. Under these conditions search for an invariant measure of value remained elusive. All the issues, which emerged in the use of labour as a measure of value, are dealt with in the Labour Theory of Value.

For Marx, commodity production is not a natural phenomenon (something which is governed by laws of nature), it is a socio-economic phenomenon and it becomes a valid subject of socio-historical investigation. Therefore, along with quantitative relations arising in commodity production, he directed his attention to the character of social relations (qualitative relations) which underlie the commodity production. The great originality of Marx's value theory lies in his analytical distinction and recognition of two elements or aspects of the value problem: (i) the quantitative value problem, and (ii) the qualitative value problem, and in his attempt to deal with them simultaneously within a single conceptual framework. It has been noted that to deal with these two aspects simultaneously has been the major source of confusion and difficulty in understanding Marx's formulation of Labour Theory of Value. Following Paul Sweezy (2016), we will deal with qualitative and quantitative aspects of value theory separately.

A. The Qualitative Value Problem

The general dictionary meaning of term 'Value' is 'worth'

'importance' or 'usefulness' of something. In political economy we talk of two types of value: Use Value and Exchange Value.

(i) *Use Value*: We produce goods and services as they satisfy various human needs. These goods have a need/want satisfying power or have a utility. An object of human consumption always possesses a 'use value'. Use value is an expression of a certain relation between the consumer and the object consumed by him. Therefore, it is not a social relation.

However, Marx stated that political economy is a social science of the relations among people in the process of production and distribution of goods and services. It follows that 'use value' as such lies outside the sphere of investigation of political economy, as it does not directly embody a social relation (a relation among producers or people). But it does not mean that use value plays no role in Marxian Economics. Use value is a prerequisite to consumption, and is in no sense excluded by Marx from the causal chain of economic phenomena.

Marxian formulation is in sharp contrast to the practice of all non-Marxian schools (in particular, the neo-classical value/price theory), which regards the economic system as a series of, interdependent but conceptually discrete relationships between men and economic goods. Therefore, use value or utility takes a central position among various categories of neoclassical economics.

(ii) *Exchange Value*: As stated before, commodities possess exchange value as well as use value. Exchange is a regular method of realising the purpose of social production (exchange makes available goods produced by different producers to each other). Exchange value appears to be a quantitative relation between things/commodities themselves. The quantitative relation between things, which we call exchange value, is in reality only outward form of the social relation between the commodity owners, or (as in case of simple commodity production) between the producers themselves. The exchange relation as such is an expression of the fact that individual producers, each working even in isolation, are in fact working for each other. Thus, the exchange of commodities is an exchange of products of the labour of individual producers. Thus, production and exchange of commodities is a social process.

As stated before, a commodity is produced as it has a use value. An individual commodity also has a 'value', because human labour was consumed in its production. If it were a free good provided abundantly by nature, it would not have exchange value. Value of a commodity is assumed to be equal to the amount of labour consumed in its production. Thus, a commodity has a 'use value' and a 'value'. Marx has stated that labour is the source and substance of 'value of a commodity'. Exchange value comes into existence when goods are exchanged or sold in the market. Thus, exchange value is a derived concept. Exchange value is an independent method of displaying the value contained in the commodity.

(iii) *Labour and Value*: Human labour (physical and mental capabilities of producer) is used on raw materials (natural resources) to produce goods, which have use value. For example, a coat has a use value. It is produced by labour: raw cotton into thread and thread into cloth and cloth into a coat. This labour is concrete labour (also called useful labour) of the producer. Thus, nature co-operates actively and passively in the process of production of use values. As William Petty puts it, 'labour is the father and the earth its mother' in the creation of use values.

Concrete labour of every producer has his own, individual specific, attributes and as such cannot be compared with concrete labour of another producer. If we assume that value of a commodity is determined by labour embodied into its production, we need to evolve a common measure of labour. Marx evolved another concept of labour called 'abstract labour' used in the production of a commodity. He defined abstract labour as labour of an average producer used in the process of production employing tools embedded with average level of technology.

The requirement that all economic categories must represent social relations led Marx directly to labour as 'value' that lies hidden behind the exchange value. Commodities are the bearer and expression of social relation as they are products of labour. If we abstract from the use value of a commodity, it exists simply as a value (we have stated that a commodity has 'use value' as well as 'value'. If we ignore 'use value' for the time being in our analysis, we are left with 'value' of a commodity). Productive activity, which creates 'value', is the expenditure of human labour power. Value of a commodity represents human labour in the abstract, the expenditure of human labour in general.

Qualitative relation of 'Value' to 'Labour' can be summarised as follows:

> Marx makes a sharp analytical distinction between two aspects of human labour used in the process of production of goods or commodities: Concrete labour and Abstract labour. Concrete labour is the labour of a producer used in the production of a good. This labour is specific to each individual. Marx states that this concrete labour creates 'use value' of a good. Concrete labour of one producer cannot be compared with concrete labour of another producer as concrete labour includes specific attributes of labour of each individual producer. As labour is consumed in the production of a commodity, it has a 'value'. We need to measure this value when we want to exchange this commodity with another produced by some other person. For development a comparable measure of value, Marx evolved the concept of 'abstract labour'. Abstract labour expresses the social relation in which labour is exchanged among people under the condition of commodity production. This formulation provided foundation to the quantitative labour theory of value.

On the one hand, all labour is, speaking physiologically, an expenditure of human labour power, and in its character of comparable form 'abstract human labour', it creates and forms the values of commodities. On the other hand, all labour is the expenditure of human labour power in a special form (production of every commodity required different type of labour/skill) and with a definite aim, and in this, it is character of concrete useful labour; it produces use values. Concrete labour and abstract labour are not two different forms of labour. They are merely two aspects of the same labour. People must engage in various forms of concrete labour in production of various use values for the satisfaction of various needs. Concrete labour expresses the relationship between man and nature/raw materials. On the other hand abstract labour provides a unified measure to compare the labour expended on the production of various commodities. Therefore, abstract labour expresses the social relation in which labour is exchanged among people under the condition of commodity production.

(iv) *Abstract Labour*: Abstract labour (which is represented in the value of commodities) is a concept, which has an important place in Marx's thinking. Abstract labour is abstract in the sense that 'all special characteristics which differentiate one kind of labour from another are ignored.' Abstract labour is equivalent to 'labour in general'; it is what is common to all productive human activity. Labour is the substance of the value of everything.

To sum up, reduction of all labour to abstract labour enables us to see clearly, behind the special forms labour may assume at any given time, an aggregate social labour force which is capable of transference from one use to another in accordance with social need, and on the magnitude and development of which society's wealth-producing capacity in the last resort depends. Marx defined abstract labour as labour of an average producer using common/average tools/technology, used in the process of production.

(v) *The Relation of the Quantitative to the Qualitative Aspects in Value Theory:* Abstract labour is the substance of value. A commodity absorbs a part of society's total available labour force. Production of Commodities uses available labour force (i.e. they are all materialized abstract labour) and it is this characteristic of commodities (which presumes use value and manifests itself in exchange value) that makes of 'commodities' the starting point and central category of the political economy of the modern period. Main tasks of quantitative–value theory are determined by the qualitative analysis.

From a formal point of view, it appears that quantitative-value theory is concerned solely with discovering the laws, which regulate the relative proportions in which commodities exchange for each other. But for Marx, exchange value is merely the 'phenomenal form' behind which hides value itself. Critics of Marx have concentrated on quantitative aspects of value and the exchange ratios to the neglect of the character of the social relations, which lie hidden beneath the surface.

Suppose there are two persons (producers), A & B in the economy, person A produces q_a amount of commodity X using L_a amount of his labour. Similarly, person B produces q_b amount of commodity Y using L_b amount of his labour. Now these two persons A&B exchange commodities X & Y produced by them. Question is what principles determine the rate at which commodity X will be exchanged for commodity Y? Quantitative theory of value studies how much quantity of commodity X will be exchanged for commodity Y? As we know these commodities X & Y are produced by A & B using their labour L_a & L_b, when two producers exchange X& Y, this exchange not only imply exchange of goods X & Y, it also implies exchange of labour L_a & L_b of the two producers. Thus, when these producers produce X& Y and exchange these goods, they are in fact, working for each other and therefore, it implies a social relationship. Study of this social relationship, Marx characterised as qualitative value problem.

Marx argued that bourgeois economics studies only quantitative relations and not qualitative relations that underlie exchange relations of commodities. As these relations are social relations, they are the proper subject matter of political economy/economics as a social science. These social relations, which underlie commodity exchange relations, take what Marx call Fetish character in bourgeois economics.

B. Quantitative Labour Theory of Value

Now we propose to examine the initial and most simplified formulation of the quantitative value theory and the conditions under which it may need to the reformulated. In a commodity producing society, exchange value of commodities is a quantitative aspect of the value theory. Given market demand, market exchange rate determines the allocation of productive activity in an economy.

As stated before, we need a stable measure of value of a commodity. Labour was used as a 'measure of value', as labour was the common denominator (factor) in the production of all commodities. How to determine the exchange value of one commodity with another with another commodity was the next issue to be sorted out. As a first approximation, Marx assumes quantities of commodities exchange in the same ratio in which labour time is consumed in the process of production of these commodities. To determine exchange value, labour time used to produce these commodities has to be quantified and standardised. 'Labour unit' was defined as the number of hours of labour used in the process of production of a commodity. As discussed before, concrete labour of all the labourers is different and cannot be compared; Marx evolved a concept of 'Abstract Labour'. To standardise unit of (abstract) labour, the 'average number of hours' used by an 'average producer' under the existing (normal) conditions of production, skill of workers and technology was defined to be the labour consumed/embedded in a commodity. The average labour time consumed in the production of one unit of a commodity is also called socially necessary labour required to produce one unit of that commodity. For Example: If 'N' workers use 100 hours to produce 50 units of a commodity 'X' with normal technology and production conditions, then we say that two units of labour is required (socially necessary) to produce one unit of that commodity.

Labourer who is more skilled than a simple labourer must have a corresponding greater power of producing value. Skilled labour counts only as simple labour intensified (a multiplied simple labour). Skilled labour may be more proficient because of two reasons: (i) superior natural ability, and (ii) superior training. If a person has a natural superior ability, that person will be more efficient in most of the labour activities. To make a comparison, both the producers may be put in same line of production and quantitative relation (ratio) in value creation of two persons can be determined. If difference in skill is because of training, then it can be assumed that a superior worker expends in production not only his own labour but indirectly a part of the labour of his teachers who are responsible for his superior productivity. In practice, difference in skills is likely to be the result of a combination of difference in ability and difference in training. Thus, there is a theoretical feasibility of reducing skilled labour to simple labour. As a first approximation, it can be stated that commodities exchange with one another in proportion to the quantity of socially necessary labour embedded in each of the commodity. This proposition may be modified in further analysis of quantitative theory of value.

(Karl Marx (1992) in Chapter 1 of Volume I of *Capital* used this simple formulation of Labour Theory of Value. This proposition is reasonable for the purpose of initial analysis of commodity exchange. It has been further extended for complex analysis.)

Let us inquire under what conditions exchange ratios may or may not correspond exactly to labour-time ratios.

The Role of Competition

Let us assume an ancient society of hunters in which they did not have accumulation of capital as well as ownership of land. For hunting they use their labour only. How to determine the exchange rate of objects of hunting by the hunters? In such a society, quantity of labour required to prey the object (animal) was the only plausible common denominator for determining the exchange rate. If a hunter takes X hours to hunt an animal A and 2X hours to hunt the animal B, i.e. time taken for production of B is twice of production of A, then the plausible exchange rate between A & B will be 2:1, i.e. 2 units of A= 1 unit of B.

Adam Smith's deer-beaver example, which was used by Ricardo, provides the convenient starting point (an early economy of hunters with simple tools): Deer and Beaver will exchange in proportion to the quantity of time required to kill each. It is the competition among hunters, which will determine the exchange ratio and finally the equilibrium exchange ratio among values of different commodities.

Given this kind of competition in the society of simple commodity production, supply and demand will be in equilibrium only when the price of every commodity is proportional to the labour time required to produce it. Thus, competitive supply-and-demand theory of price determination is consistent with the labour theory of value. Supply and demand are in fact, summary expression of competitive forces at work in the market—a mechanism for eliminating deviations between market prices and values. Supply represents competition among suppliers and demand represents competition among consumers to acquire that commodity. At the moment when supply and demand equilibrate each other, and therefore cease to act, the market price of a commodity coincides with its real value (embedded labour).

Thus, in a perfectly competitive market, market prices are consistent with the labour theory of value.

The Role of Demand

Marx is often accused of having ignored the role of demand in the sense of consumer's needs and desires, in determining quantitative–value relations. Paul Sweezy has argued that Marx did not ignore the significance of demand in quantitative value theory as is clear from his analysis of the problem in Vol. III of *Capital* wherein he grappled with the problem of transformation of values into market prices repeatedly.

Marx was primarily interested in investigating the process of social change and discovering the economic laws of motion of the capitalist society. The relative price determination was given a subordinate position in his analysis. For Marx, distribution of income was more powerful determinant of market demand than subjective valuation of consumers. Therefore, he extended his analysis in the direction of the theory of Surplus Value, which is the basis of more advanced form of commodity production in the capitalist society. Even Schumpeter's theory of trade cycles and Keynes' macroeconomic analysis, are dominated by distribution of income rather than the subjective value problem.

(iii) *Values and Price of Production:* Price as Marx uses the term in Vol. I of *Capital* is merely the money expression of value. In Vol. III, however, there is the quite different concept of 'price of production'. Prices of production are modifications of value. However, the differences in prices of production and values are attributable to certain features of capitalism such as monopoly, etc. The introduction of the monopoly element into the economy interferes with the operation of the law of value as regulator of the quantitative relations of production and exchange. The monopolist's control over supply enables him to take advantage of demand conditions. In this case, therefore, demand acquires a special significance, and both price and quantity produced (hence also allocation of labour) are different from what they would be in a regime of competition.

Quantitative-value relations are disturbed by monopoly. However, qualitative–value relations are not disturbed. In other words, the existence of monopoly does not in itself alter the basic social relations of commodity production i.e. the organisation of production through private exchange of the individual products of labour. Under monopoly conditions, we can continue to measure and compare commodities and aggregates of commodities in terms of labour-time units in spite of the fact that the precise quantitative relations implied in the law of value no longer hold. (Further extensions in labour of theory require advanced treatment, which is not discussed here. For that, students may refer to the specialised literature.)

7. The Fetish Character of Commodities

Commodity fetishism is a very powerful doctrine formulated by Marx in his critique of the classical political economy. Commodity fetishism highlights the social character of commodity production and exchange in the capitalist system. As various persons are involved in the process of production and exchange, these relationships are social relations of production and exchange. These relations may or may not be exploitative. An exploitative relation is one in which each individual is not rewarded according to his contribution to the production of that commodity. Bourgeois economics in its theories tries to conceal the true social character of production and exchange relations as they are exploitative and it is objectively and morally difficult to justify them.

Marx observed that commodity fetishism is the perception of the social relationship in the process of production and exchange of commodities not as relationship among people, but as economic relationship between the money and commodities exchanged/traded in the market. In preceding classical political economy, it was assumed that commodities have 'intrinsic value' of their own.

Exchange value between two commodities was in proportion to their intrinsic values. Thus, it was only an economic phenomenon and its human contents were underplayed. Marx argued that it was only a perception and not the reality. It is an illusion as it conceals their true social character. Commodities are produced by the expenditure of labour of their producers. When the commodities are exchanged or sold to others in the marker, it is, in fact, an exchange of labour embedded in one commodity with labour embedded in the other commodity. Therefore, Marx argued that market exchange should be visualised as a social process and not just as a pure economic process in which exchange of one commodity for the other takes place. Thus appearance, the form (economic relationship) takes precedence over the substance (social relationship) in the commodity exchange market process.

Thus, in commodities and commodity production, the way classical political economy visualizes them, there is a gap between 'form' and 'substance'. In commodities, if we see only the exchange relationship (form) and not their true social relationship (substance), Marx calls it 'Commodity Fetishism'. Form is not unimportant, as reality is perceived in terms of the form but we must not lose sight of the substance, which underlies the form. If we see beneath the forms, we discover the substance of social relations in the social organisation of production and exchange. Marx argued that in economic analysis, the social character of production and exchange process should be preserved. Political Economy/Economics should continue to remain truly a social science.

In the pre-capitalist production of commodities or simple commodity production, relations of production have direct personal character; reification of social relations was not possible as producers themselves enter into exchange market. But, in generalised commodity production, i.e. capitalist commodity production, phenomenon of reification of social relations acquires decisive importance. In capitalist exchange relations, individual producers deal with fellow producers only through 'the market', where prices and amounts sold are the substantive realities and human beings appear to be merely their actors/instruments. 'These quantities (prices and quantities sold) vary continuously, independently of the will, foresight, and action of the producers.' In such a situation, the real character of the relations among producers themselves is both obscured and distorted from the view.

Once the world of commodities has achieved its independence and subjected the producers to its sway, as under capitalist production, the producers come to look upon commodities in much the same way as they regard that other external world to which they must learn to adjust themselves. The existing social order becomes in the apt expression of Lukcas, a 'second nature' (acquired habit or tendency in one's character that is so deeply ingrained as it appears automatic as instinctive or genetic which is first nature). The consequences for such a structure of thought are both extensive and profound. If we start believing that men are born unequal, which is a social process, then we will not see exploitation as a social phenomenon.

Historically, application of the ideas and method of natural science to society is one of the most striking features of the capitalist period. This changed the attitude towards society, which was the reflex of the flowering of commodity production. In the field of political economy, the results of transition are most clearly observable in the 18th century economic doctrines of the physiocrats (use of laws of nature) in France and classical school in England (invisible hand, wisdom of laissez-faire as an economic policy). All attest to a profound belief in the impersonal and automatic character of the economic order i.e. economic laws like laws of nature are independent of society. This bias against conscious social action in economic affairs, which grew in the 18th century and remained a very prominent feature of capitalist ideology until emergence of monopoly and imperialism and the 1930s Depression which exposed its weaknesses. Keynes exposed the myth of natural economy and rejected the automatic optimality of the free market economy. He argued that government/society needs to intervene to ensure that economy behaves in a sustained fashion without trade cycles.

Marx's theory of fetishism has brilliantly illuminated the specific roots in the characteristics of commodity production, as well as its connection with associated doctrine of natural law and social automatism. Marx showed that commodity production and exchange process involved exploitation of workers by the capitalist and was not a natural process and it was governed by social laws and not automatic natural laws. Classical economists stated that equilibrium of the economy will be automatically at full employment, Marx proved them wrong.

Reification of social relations has exercised a profound influence on traditional economic thinking in at least two further important aspects. In the first place, the categories of the capitalist economy—rent, wages, profit, interest, etc., which were being treated as though they were the inevitable categories of economic life have been questioned. These categories conceal their social character. Secondly, it is the appearance that the commodity-producing form constitutes the most effective veil over the true class character of the capitalist society. Class relations are concealed as if all commodity owners are standing on the equal footing, i.e., there is no master-servant relations in the process of production and its distribution and all human beings are equal. There is no dispossession of the labour power.

The doctrine of fetishism has implications, which far transcend the conventional limits of economics and economic thinking. Doctrine of Commodity Fetishism is the first essential step in the Marxian analysis of capitalism. He who has not understood this has understood little of Marx's critical method. Marx stated that 'reification' is at the heart of commodity fetishism in general and economics in particular.

REFERENCES

Foley, D.K. (2000), Recent Developments in the Theory of Value, *Review of Radical Political Economy*, Vol. 21, No. 1.

Marx, K. (1859), *A Contribution to the Critique of Political Economy*, Moscow: Progress Publishers.

Marx, K. (1992 [1867]), *Capital: A Critique of Political Economy*, Vol. I, London: Penguin Books.

Meek, Ronald L. (1973), *Studies in the Labour Theory of Value*, New York:

Monthly Review Press, Indian edition (2017), Delhi: Aakar Books.

Sweezy, Paul M. (2016 [1942]), *The Theory of Capitalist Development*, Delhi: Aakar Books.

Wolff, Richard D. and Stephan A. Resnick (2012), *Contending Economic Theories: Neoclassical, Keynesian, and Marxian*, Cambridge, Massachusetts: The MIT Press.

3

Notes on Marx's Critique of Classical Political Economy[1]

Prabhat Patnaik

Marx summed up the essence of Classical Political Economy as the belief that "there has been history but there is no longer any". He explained: "There has been history since there were the institutions of feudalism, and in these institutions of feudalism we find quite different relations of production from those of bourgeois society, which the economists try to pass off as natural and as such, eternal." In other words, the movement of history ends with the coming into being of bourgeois society whose relations is "in conformity with the laws of nature." We find here a remarkable parallel with Hegelian philosophy which saw the movement of history as culminating in the Prussian State.

Marx's basic task regarding bourgeois economics therefore was to "historicise" it, to go beyond it so that the present is seen not as the end of history but as a part of history itself. But "historicising" bourgeois economics did not consist simply in adding on a "preferred" or "anticipated" *denouement* in the shape of a socialist transformation to the development of bourgeois society. It necessitated a theoretical revolution in the matter of studying bourgeois society itself. Bourgeois society had to be studied from a supra-bourgeois theoretical perspective, with the same objectivity with which pre-bourgeois societies are studied, i.e. from the vantage point of an observer who comprehends the "historical process as a whole" and is capable, conceptually, of transcending bourgeois society itself. If bourgeois society is to be studied objectively, on a par with other pre-bourgeois societies, then the question to ask is: how is the process of appropriation of surplus, which is so transparent in pre-bourgeois societies, effected in a bourgeois society where there is formal equality, voluntary exchange among "free" commodity owners, and equivalent exchange under free competition? The answer clearly cannot be found in the sphere of circulation, which precisely is the sphere where exchange is carried out among commodity owners on an equal footing. The answer must lie beneath the sphere of circulation, in the sphere of production itself. Surplus, Marx argued, takes the form of "surplus value" in a bourgeois society, which arises in the sphere of production itself. This surplus value is already present in the higher value of the commodity capital with which the capitalist emerges from the sphere of production, compared to what he had thrown into it; it is realised, i.e. converted into money form, in the sphere of circulation, through the sale of the commodity which the production process yields.

Marx's calling this process of surplus appropriation "exploitation" has misled many into thinking of Marxism as being based on some Lockean "natural rights" doctrine. Marx's theory is often believed to have postulated that workers are "cheated" out of their "just share". Such an interpretation however is incorrect. Marx's approach was historical not moral. He held Proudhon's dictum "property is theft" to be absurd, since the term "property" referred merely to the prevalent social rules governing the appropriation of the fruits of production. There could never be social production without such rules, i.e. without "property". The transcendence of capitalism meant not the abolition of property as Proudhon thought, but the substitution of socialist property for capitalist property. Likewise the proposition that society needed capital but could do without capitalists, so that the latter constituted a bunch of parasites appropriating a part of the product that "justly" belonged to the workers, is not a Marxian proposition; it belongs to the theoretical corpus of Ricardian socialists like Hodgskin. For Marx the concept of "surplus value" is not based on any postulation of a "norm" or of a notion of "fair share" relative to which the workers get less. It is a part of a historical datum.

Since the secret of capitalist society was that surplus value emerged in the sphere of production (a proposition of immense importance as we shall see), any scientific analysis of this society must focus on the sphere of production, if it is not to fall into the trap of believing that the formal equality of the sphere of circulation was substantially true, i.e. if it is not to degenerate into apologetics (of taking bourgeois society's claim about itself as the truth). It follows that "historicising" Classical Political Economy necessarily meant penetrating behind the veil of circulation, into the sphere of production. But Marx at the same time drew a sharp distinction between "classical political economy" and "vulgar economy", the latter exclusively caught up in the sphere of circulation, taking the appearances of the sphere of circulation as the reality of capitalism, a trait which the former did not share. In other words classical political economy is "classical" precisely because it does analyse the sphere of production. Indeed Marx called Ricardo the "economist of production *par excellence*". But then if the analysis of production did not begin with Marx, if classical political economy had already developed such an analysis, how can we argue that it was Marx who ushered in the "historicisation" project with the analysis of production at its core? In what sense can it be said that the pre-Marxian analysis of production did not amount to a proper analysis of production?

Marx himself has provided a succinct answer to this question. Classical political economy did not distinguish clearly between the spheres of production and of circulation. It telescoped the two instead of keeping them conceptually separate and examining their mutual relationship. In other words instead of an integrated and structured analysis of the totality in which both spheres figured with their specificities and inter-relationships, classical political economy flattened out this structured relationship by putting the two on the same level, and hence producing an eclectic mixture that obscured the significance of some of its own insights. More generally, its failure consisted in not distinguishing between "essence" and "form". In other words even while going beyond "appearances" (in which it was much superior to "vulgar economy") to "reality" it did not see the two as a linked totality; and hence it could not even properly pursue its journey beyond "appearances".

There are three obvious ways that this failure manifested itself: first, classical political economy could not see surplus value as a single homogeneous category. Surplus value as such is never visible; what is visible are the different forms in which it manifests itself, viz. profit, rent, and interest. It took each of these manifestations as separate and investigated the determination of each, but did not see them as forms in which surplus value appears, and hence did not see the category called surplus value. Secondly, "price" is what prevails in the market, in the sphere of circulation. Underlying these "prices" however are "values" which are not visible and which arise from the fact that any commodity embodies a certain amount of homogeneous social labour. Commodities do not exchange at their values because if they did then the rates production would be different, because of which prices represent a "modification" of values. Instead of seeing the totality of this inter relationship, classical political economy in the person of Ricardo (who represented its highest development) talked eclectically of "two determinants" of prices: the total labour embodied in a commodity and its time-distribution in the production of that commodity. In the process therefore it obscured the origins of value and surplus value, including whatever insights it had itself developed. Thirdly, this mixing up of levels meant that it could not locate the origin of surplus value in the sphere of production. In fact it did not pursue the question of the origin of surplus value, which prevented its seeing capitalism in the same historical light in which it had seen pre-bourgeois societies.

If surplus value emerges in the sphere of production, then it follows that capitalism must be characterised by a duality: on the one hand like all modes of production it must be characterised by "production in general" at the core of which is the man-nature dialectic but in which, since men act socially, the general needs of social production must be getting met. On the other hand however there must be the specific capitalist stamp on the production process, which must be highly *sui generis* because of the very opaqueness of the mode of production. This duality which characterises capitalism in a way that it does not characterise any other mode of production imprints itself on every category of capitalism: "products" are also "commodities", the "labour process" is also "the value-creating process", "surplus" is also "surplus value", "means of production and subsistence" are also "capital", "use value" is also "exchange value", "concrete labour" is also "abstract labour", and so on. Putting it differently, all specifically capitalist categories, such as "commodities", "capital", "value" and "surplus value", etc. have a relational dimension to them. As Marx put it for the category "capital": "In themselves money and commodities are no more capital than are the means of production and subsistence. They want transforming into capital. But this transformation itself can only take place under certain circumstances that centre in this, viz. that two very different kinds of commodity possessors must come face to face and into contact; on the one hand the owners of money, means of production, means of subsistence, who are eager to increase the sum of values they possess, by buying other people's labour-power; on the other hand free labourers, the sellers of their own labour-power, and therefore the sellers of labour. Free labourers in the double sense that neither they themselves form part and parcel of the means of production, as in the case of slaves, bondsmen, etc., nor do the means of production belong to them, as in the case of peasant proprietors; they are, therefore, free from, unencumbered by, any means of production of their own." The essence of "historicising" political economy therefore consists in recognising the relational (and hence historically specific) nature of capitalist categories.

The contrast with the approach of the Ricardian socialists (and indeed of all socialists who base their argument on a moral-ethical critique of capitalism) could not be sharper. Hodgskin had said: society needed capital but not capitalists; Marx argued: there can be no capital without capitalists, since capital is a relation between the capitalists and the workers. On this basis, Marx not only provided a precise definition of capitalism, "a system of generalised commodity production where labour power itself has become a commodity", but explored the precise historical circumstances under which capitalism came into being, i.e. "the two very different kinds of commodity-possessors" were originally formed (the process of the so-called "primitive accumulation of capital" which was based on a concept of Adam Smith but acquired a precision because of Marx's relational approach). He unearthed the antagonistic character of capitalism (the fact that surplus value accrued to a particular class behind the facade of equality in the marketplace), and hence its necessarily transient presence in history. Above all, however, Marx drew attention to the spontaneous character of capitalism, and the profound implications of that spontaneous character.

The idea of the bourgeois society being a "self-acting economic order" (with the implicit inference that it did not interference from kings and priests) was first advanced by the French Physiocrats and was taken over by English Classical Political Economy. The latter conceptualised this economic order differently: the myriads of decisions taken by individuals, each motivated by self-interest, produces not chaos but an order, and, what is more, a benevolent order, which is governed by objective laws independent of human will and consciousness and capable of being scientifically discovered. The view that the aggregation of self-interest-based individual actions yields something unintended by the individual participants, had once again a clear parallel in Hegelian philosophy: "The whole is not the sum of the parts." And implicit in this view was a recognition also of the spontaneous character of capitalism, its "self-acting" property.

While Marx took over this basic perception of capitalism as a spontaneous, law-governed system, his break from Classical Political Economy made him comprehend the system not as benevolent, but as anarchic, crisis-prone, and subject to a unique trajectory of development. Any system of commodity production necessarily produces differentiation among producers. This is true of capitalism as well. "One capitalist kills many". Typically that "one capitalist" is the one controlling large capital. Large capital in other words drives out small capitals because of which every capital wishes to become large through accumulation. Marx, in other words, visualised a Darwinian struggle among capitalists which makes accumulation an externally-imposed coercive drive. To accumulate one must garner as much surplus value as possible, and to do so, in a world where surplus value originates in the sphere of production, each capitalist constantly strives to revolutionise his production process through innovations. Notwithstanding this striving however some capitalists continuously go under, leaving fewer and fewer, and larger and larger, blocs of capital in each branch, what Marx called "centralisation of capital". Accumulation, continuous increase in the scale of production, and centralisation are the three chief moments in the accumulation process, which result on the one hand in enormous increases in the productive forces, and on the other in a progressive polarisation of society between a few large capitalists and large masses of concentrated workers forced to develop a spirit of collective action. The journey of capitalism, from its beginnings in "primitive accumulation" of capital is a continuous concentration of the control over mean of production in fewer and fewer hands; its counterpart is a continuous increase in the socialisation of labour which reaches both its climax and its transcendence in socialism. This journey (though not obviously the achievement of the climax) is a spontaneous one.

There are, it follows, two very different kinds of "laws" discussed by Marx. On the one hand there are the "laws" referring to the relational aspects of capitalism, such as centralisation of capital, progressive socialisation of labour etc. These, even though their operation may be temporarily checked, prevented, or shifted (in terms of the universe where they apply), are inexorable. On the other hand there are other "laws" mentioned by Marx, such as the "law of the falling tendency of the rate of profit" which are quantitative. Their purpose is to highlight the contradictions of the system, its possible points of vulnerability to crises, and the manner in which it might attempt to overcome such vulnerability. They do not inexorably manifest themselves; their purpose is to lay bare the constraints within which the system operates. Marx, it is interesting, does not have a theory of crisis; he does not have a theory of growth; he does not have a theory of how the system would quantitatively evolve. Here he sees various possibilities which apparently mutually contradict one another if we attribute to him one theory. But he is not looking for one theory of this kind. His concern is not with the quantitative trajectory of capitalism, but with its qualitative trajectory, with changes in its relational aspects. When he is discussing these, there are no apparent contradictions whatsoever. Having two different kinds of "laws" is thus in conformity with Marx's overall approach.

While capitalism creates the condition for its own transcendence, the precise manner of that transcendence requires revolutionary political intervention in a particular conjuncture (when revolution "comes on the agenda"). The first question that arises in this context is: when does the revolutionary stage arrive? Marx does not give a concrete answer to this question (though Lenin was to do so later). From Marx's remark that "No social order is ever destroyed before all the productive forces for which it is sufficient have been developed", it might appear as if material circumstances alone determine whether a revolutionary transformation has appeared on the agenda; but this is not true. Marx also remarked: "Of all the instruments of production, the greatest productive power is the revolutionary class itself. The organisation of revolutionary elements as a class supposes the existence of all the productive forces which could be engendered in the bosom of the old society." This suggests that the working class' organising itself into a revolutionary force, a process intimately linked to the development of its consciousness, is the true index of the revolution coming on the agenda, a much more open-ended formulation.

The second question that arises is: how does the working class acquire revolutionary consciousness? Again, Marx does not discuss this issue concretely (which Lenin was to do later). But Marx too drew a distinction between "trade union consciousness" and "revolutionary class consciousness". Lenin's idea that the latter had to be introduced "from outside" figures already in the *Manifesto.* In addition there is the suggestion in *The Poverty of Philosophy* that the working class, in the course of its own economic struggles, also tends spontaneously to develop a political consciousness, in so far as it is increasingly confronted by state power that comes to the aid of the capitalists even in the course of economic struggles.

The third question that arises is: why should capitalism be, according to Marx, the last antagonistic mode of production? If arrival of capitalism, represented a flawed perspective, then why should Marxism, which saw the end of capitalism as the end of antagonism, not be accused of the same error? Putting it differently, what is so specific about capitalism that its end, unlike the end of earlier modes of production, signals the end of antagonism? Marx's answer to this was as follows: capitalism is the first antagonistic mode of production where the most directly oppressed class is simultaneously the most revolutionary class. This fact, which has to do with the spontaneous nature of capitalism, discussed earlier, creates a unique situation in human history.

Lenin, as already mentioned, gave concrete answers to many of these very questions, and did so via his theory of imperialism. Revolution comes on the agenda in the era of imperialism which is punctuated by wars that give the working class in each country one and only one choice: either to kill fellow workers across trenches or to turn the gun against capitalism in one's own country. Imperialism moreover presupposes the completion of the partitioning of the globe among a handful of imperialist powers; hence all these wars entail the use of the colonial and oppressed people as "cannon-fodder" even as they are trained as fighters. They too are given only one choice: either kill fellow-oppressed people across trenches, or train the guns on the colonial masters. Not only does the era of imperialism then signify the beginning of social revolution, but it generates and brings together two different, independent and inter-linked revolutionary streams: a workers' revolution in the metropolis and an anti-colonial struggle in the periphery. (The recognition of these two streams is already there in Marx and Engels though they thought for most of their lives that a European revolution was on the immediate agenda).

How, it may be asked, do we critique Marx's critique of Classical Political Economy today? Marx's critique is incomplete in one crucial respect, which, though it might not have appeared important at the time (when all attention was in any case focused on a European revolution), cannot be ignored today. And this is his treatment of the capitalist system as a "closed system". Though he is acutely aware of the fact that capitalism rests on a particular pattern of international economic relationships, his main opus discusses capitalism entirely as if it consists of capitalists and workers and no other *dramatis personae.*

It may be thought that his basic concept of a mode of production is responsible for this incompleteness, since the concept directs attention to the question of appropriation of surplus from direct producers within a certain closed universe: masters and slaves, feudal lords and serfs, capitalists and labourers constitute the exclusive binary relations within particular modes of production. There is no reason however why we should not recognise capitalism as a very different kind of mode of production. It is universal from its very inception in the sense that it acquires control over a variety of labour processes apart from the one directly and visibly under its supervision. From its very inception it is not a "closed system", with trade being only a secondary phenomenon, or a phenomenon concerned only with the exchange of use-values but not the acquisition of surplus value, i.e. a phenomenon that occurs to promote the mutual advantage of the trading parties but does not constitute an instrument of exploitation. This is what Ricardo postulated. Marx, notwithstanding his recognition of the limitations of such an approach in his writings on the colonial question, never broke away from it in his theory. Lenin, to be sure, did, but in his case imperialism is a feature of late capitalism. It is not just that capitalism ceases to be a "closed system" in its old age; it was never a "closed system" to start with.

To say this does not mean that the specific form in which the labour process is carried on is of secondary importance, as the world system theorists would have us believe. It does matter a great deal through what mediations capitalism controls a particular labour process; and it opens up complex patterns of class struggle in a world that is under the overall hegemony of capitalism. World revolution would have to proceed through these complex patterns. A recognition of this fact via a critique of Marx's critique constitutes not a negation of Marx, but precisely the way of carrying forward his theoretical agenda. Marx, in Althusser's words, opened up a continent; it is important for us to map it out properly instead of remaining satisfied with his initial sketches.

NOTES

Reprinted with permission from the editor of *Social Scientist* and Author. The earlier version was published in *Social Scientist,* Vol. 30, Nos. 3-4, March-April 2002.

4

Capitalist Mode of Production: A Basic Interpretation[1]

Paramjit Singh

Introduction

The financial crisis of 2008, followed by recession in the world economy, has put a question mark on the stability and working of capitalist economic system. The debate among the pro-people intellectuals has once again intensified to expose the real character of capitalism. There is no better work than Marx's *Capital* to meet this objective. Marx's *Capital* is a comprehensive critique of classical political economy that is primarily concerned with the working of the capitalist mode of production. The best method to understand capitalism is to examine what differentiate it from pre-capitalist societies. Like the pre-capitalist modes (slavery and feudalism), capitalism is also a class society. The fundamental difference between capitalism and pre-capitalist societies is that the method of exploitation in pre-capitalist societies rested upon the direct domination by the owner of the means of production and the method of exploitation was quite visible. For example, slaves were the property of their master and the master exploited the slaves directly. The relations of production in a slave society were based on the master's ownership of the means of production (the land, instruments of labour, labourers- the slaves). Slaves were not considered more than just an instrument of production. As Marx (1970) argued "the slave did not sell his labour power to the master, any more than ox its service to the peasant. The slave, together with his labour power, has been sold once and for all to his owner."

On the other hand, in the capitalist economic system the method of exploitation is flexible as well as complex. Under capitalist production relations, wage labourers are formally free and they can sell their labour power to any capitalist, such freedom was absent under slavery and feudalism. Another fundamental difference is that pre-capitalist societies were 'consumption dominant societies'. The exploitation of the dominated class served primarily the consumption of the dominant class. Contrary to this, the capitalist society is a 'production dominant society'. Under the capitalist relation, the aim of production is to increase the capacity to produce in order to generate an ever greater surplus. A large proportion of the produce is used for sale in the market in order to enhance the production base for the future. Contrary to pre-capitalist societies, the comfortable life and luxurious consumption for the capitalist is merely a by product of the production process, but not a principal goal. Earnings under capitalism not only serve the consumption, but also the continuous 'valorisation of capital', that is, the restless movement of more-and-more accumulation (Heinrich, 2012). As Marx and Engels (2002) said about the uniqueness of capitalist mode of production, "the bourgeoisie cannot exist without constantly revolutionizing the instruments of production, and thereby the relations of production, and with them the whole relations of society ... Constant revolutionising of production, uninterrupted disturbance of all social conditions, everlasting uncertainty and agitation distinguish the bourgeois epoch from all earlier ones."

The historical analysis of capitalism shows that there are various ways to realise the surplus. In the case of the internal bearing of capital, money is lent at interest. This interest thus constitutes surplus. In the case of merchant capital, the purchase of product cheaply in one place and sold dearly in another place generates surplus. In the case of industrial capital, the production process is organised on capitalist lines in which the selling price of final produce is greater than the input and process cost. The base of production under capitalism is not 'need oriented', in which exchange and money play subordinate roles, but rather 'profit oriented', in which exchange and money play primary roles. Capital is a driving force of capitalist mode of production, always seeking out the best possibilities for profit and leaving the less profitable options for the time being. The domination of various forms of production and exchange in the valorisation process (bank capital, merchant capital, industrial capital, finance capital, etc.) presents this dichotomy.

In the light of these facts, the present chapter is an attempt to develop an understanding of the capitalist mode of production. The first part of the chapter defines major categories which Marx has developed (or hired from classical political economy and modified) to analyse the production, distribution and exchange under capitalism. The second part explains the simple and capitalist commodity production. The third part examines the capitalist production process and means used by the capitalists to extract the surplus value. The concluding part explains the factors that lead to the capitalist crisis and possibilities of the alternative mode of production.

Capitalist Mode of Production: Object and Categories of Analysis

In order to unfold the working of the capitalist economic structure and its real essence, Marx put emphasis on analysis of its various forms- commodity-form, value-form, money-form, etc. In order to study these economic forms, he realised the importance of the 'power of abstraction' in his analysis. Marx was concerned neither with the history of capitalism nor with a specific historical phase of capitalism, but rather with the concrete foundations of capitalist system which remain the same regardless of all historical variations. He was concerned with the foundational elements of capitalism, universal categories to understand the working of capitalism as an economic structure. The Marxian political economy approach is different from bourgeois political economy because it analyses capitalism and its working from the workers' perspective. Unlike bourgeois political economy, it does not view the capitalist order as absolute and ultimate form of social production. As Marx (1992) wrote in the postface of second edition of *Capital* Vol. I, "in bourgeois political economy the impartial investigation was absent or under the existing circumstance was not permitted. They view the capitalist order as the absolute and ultimate form of social production, instead of as a historical transient stage of development." However, Marx viewed capitalism (like other pre-capitalist socio-economic formation) as being in a fluid state, in motion.

In order to understand the working of capitalism Marx has applied the Hegelian dialectics not in a same manner as it was given by Hegel but in just the opposite manner. Regarding the method of analysis used by him, he himself wrote in the pre and postface of the French edition that the method of analysis which he had employed had not previously been applied to economic subject. In the first part of *Capital* Vol. I, Marx has discussed the main categories of classical political economy and developed some new categories in order to explore and expose the real foundations and logic of capitalist economic system. The first category that Marx deals with in *Capital* Vol. I is the 'commodity'. Regarding the importance of commodity in capitalist economic systems, Marx wrote, 'the wealth of the society in which the capitalist mode of production prevails appears "as immense collection of commodities"; the individual commodity appears as its elementary form. Our investigation therefore begins with the analysis of the commodity.'

From here, Marx starts unfolding the commodity. He starts generalising it by explaining that its importance for human beings may be as a consumable commodity or may be as a raw material. Therefore, the common thing that he abstracts from the commodity is its 'usefulness', i.e. use value. According to Marx (1992), the use value of something is nothing other than its usefulness. "It is conditioned by the physical properties of the commodity, and has no existence apart from the latter. It is therefore the physical body of the commodity itself, for instance iron, corn, a diamond, which is the use value of useful thing. ...use values are only realised in use or in consumption."

However, in society, which is the subject matter of Marx's Capital (capitalism), things are not only produced for their use value, rather they are produced for the purpose of exchange. Therefore, according to Marx, exchange value is a necessary precondition for an object to be a commodity. Exchange value in addition to use value is not a 'natural' property of things, but rather a 'social' one. The natural form can be distinguished from the social form of a commodity. For instance, the natural form of the chair is simply its material composition, whereas its social form means that the chair is a commodity, something that constitutes value and qualifies the conditions of exchange for something else, therefore possess exchange value. As Marx pointed out, exchange value appears first of all as the quantitative relation, the proportion, in which use value of one kind exchange for the use value of another kind. This relation changes constantly with time and place. Commodities have a dual character, i.e. as an object of utility and a bearer of value. Use value (utility) is a qualitative form of value. It is a 'transhistorical category' applicable within all modes of production. Use value does not present a social relationship, rather it presents a direct relationship (for example, the relationship between the consumer and the object of consumption). The subject matter of political economy of capitalism is commodities which possess exchange value rather the commodities which merely contain use value. Hence, one important feature of capitalist mode of production is production of those commodities which are subject to exchange value.

The other category that constitutes as an important component of capitalist mode of production is 'value'. What constitutes value? Long before Marx, this question was addressed by Adam Smith and David Ricardo: they considered the quantity of labour necessary to produce something constitutes its value. In other words, labour embodied in commodity constitutes its value. However, Marx, in his analysis of value, took the analysis further and specified the quantity of labour that produces the value as 'social necessary labour time'. The social necessary labour time refers to the as 'labour time required to produce any use value under the conditions of production normal for a given society and with the average degree of skill and intensity of labour prevalent in that society.

Contrary to classical and neoclassical economists who begin their analysis with isolated individuals, Marx's aim was to uncover the specific social structure through his analysis. For that purpose,

Marx presented individual exchange relations as an undivided part of the social totality. The objective character of value is social—it can only appear in relations between commodities. At this point, Marx unfolds another category, i.e. 'labour power'. As commodity has two-fold character- use value and exchange value— commodity producing labour must also have a twofold character—concrete labour (producer of specific use value) and abstract labour (producer of exchange value). The concrete labour constitutes the aspect of labour activity that is a condition of human existence which is independent of all forms of society: "It is an eternal natural necessity which mediates the metabolism between man and nature and therefore between human life itself (Marx, 1992)." Qualitatively different concrete labour produces qualitative different use value.[2] On the other hand, abstract labour constitutes an expenditure of human labour power, human labour pure and simple, the expenditure of human labour in general. In other words, abstract character of labour unfolds in the process of exchange at immense scale, the private concrete labour of various types is reduced to equal human labour, i.e. the amount of labour contained in the commodity regardless of its specific character. Marx argued that concrete labour and abstract labour are not different activities rather they are the same activity considered in different aspects. More specifically, Marx (1992) summarised it as "on the one hand, all labour is an expenditure of human labour power, in the psychological sense, and it is this quality of being equal, or abstract, human labour that it forms the value of commodities. On the other hand, all labour is an expenditure of human labour power in a particular form and with a definite aim, and it is this quality of being concrete useful labour that it produces use value." Marx argued, "A product of labour, considered in isolation, is not value, nor is it a commodity. It only becomes value in its unity with another product of labour. The substance of value and thus value objectively, is something only obtained by things when they are set into relation to one another in exchange (Heinrich, 2012)."

Marx continued his analysis of value by analysing 'value-form' with the examination of the simple, isolated or accidental form of value. This is the expression of a commodity's value in another. The simplistic value-form can be expressed as follows:

20 yards of linen = 1 coat

In the above representation, the value of the linen is expressed and the coat serves as a means of expressing the value of linen. In this way, the value of the linen is expressed as 'relative value' and the coat serves as 'equivalent' for the value of linen and vice versa.

From here we can obtain the expanded form of value:

20 yards of linen are worth 1 coat

20 yards of linen are worth 10 lbs of tea

20 yards of linen are worth 40 lbs of coffee, etc.

In the above presentation, the value of linen stands in relation to entire world of commodities. From this equivalent form we can obtain the 'general-form of value' or general equivalent:

1 coat
10 Ibs. of tea
40 Ibs. of coffee
1 quarter of corn
— = Worth 20 yards of linen

In the above scheme, 20 yards of linen serves as general equivalent, an expression of value for all other commodities. According to Marx (1992), "A commodity only acquires a general expression of its value if, at the same time, all other commodities express their value in the same equivalent."

From this general equivalent-form, Marx reaches 'money-form of value'. The money-form of value is ultimately distinguished from the general-form of value merely by the fact that the equivalent-form has coalesced 'by social customs' with the specific natural-form of particular commodity (historically this has been gold, and to a lesser extent silver). As Marx (1992) wrote, "as soon as gold had won a monopoly of this position in expression of value of world of commodities, it became the money commodity and only then, when it had already become the money commodity, ... the general-form of value came to be transformed into money-form." This commodity becomes the money commodity.

20 yards of linen
1 coat
10 lbs. of tea — = Worth 2 ounces of gold
40 lbs of coffee
1 quarter of corn

The important point that one should note is that in the above discussion of value, Marx reached the most modern form of value, i.e. the money-form, through conceptual development of relationships without discussing the historical facts and figures of its evolution. In a commodity dominated economy, the money-form appears because the commodity owner does not wish to exchange his commodity for any arbitrary commodity, but rather for definite, particular commodities. The overall scheme of the main categories discussed by Marx in Part-I of *Capital* Vol. I unfolds as follows:

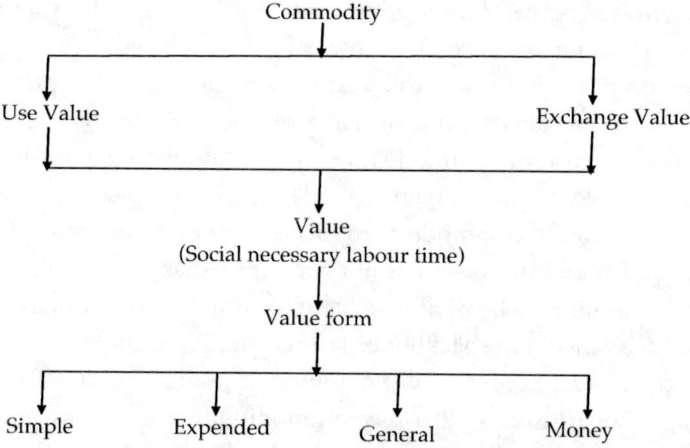

In the above discussion, Marx's aim was to develop the labour theory of value solely on conceptual grounds within which the peculiarities of specifically capitalist production could be studied. Capitalist production as a way of organising human labour socially through exchange is a special form of commodity production, and it depends on the emergence of the money-form of value. Money is necessary to express the value of commodities, to comprehensively relate commodities to one another as value. So money which came into being to facilitate exchange among the different producers of use value becomes a driving force of production and exchange transactions under capitalism. The importance of money increases more when it presents itself as a real source of surplus value and real vehicle of production and exchange.

Simple and Capitalist Commodity Production

In a pre-capitalist system of economic transactions, simple circulation dominates and money played only a role of medium of exchange. It can be expressed through the following scheme:

C—M—C′

In this presentation, a simple commodity producer produces commodities C with a particular use value, and he takes this use value to the market for money M and uses that money M to buy a different bundle of commodities C′ with a different use value. The aim of the whole process is the consumption of different commodity that the producer cannot produce of his own. In this form of transactions, money plays a subordinate role and commodities play the primary role. In this type of economy, the labour power of an individual does not take the form of commodity, i.e. the ability of the labour is not bought or sold at the marketplace. Hence in a simple commodity production (SCP), commodity product does not take the generalised form because labour power has not been treated as a commodity. In a society dominated by SCP no systematic process of 'accumulation' takes place which is the backbone of the capitalist production process. The crucial feature of capitalist commodity production (CCP) that distinguishes it from SCP is the commoditisation of labour power, i.e. the purchase and sale of ability to produce. The other feature of the capitalist mode of production is that money (M) becomes generalised and independent representative of value.

M—C—M

The above M—C—M process contains the same elements, M—C and C—M as the sequence C—M—C, only the order differs. Now, money is the starting point and end point of the process. A capitalist producer/investor only enters into the circulation process with his money M if he holds the expectation that the amount of money at the end of circuit will be greater than the amount of money at the beginning of the circuit. This is what Marx calls the 'general formula for capital'.

M—C—M′

The capitalist begins with money M and converts M into commodity C with an objective to get more M. The objective of the circuit, unlike the circuit of SCP, is exchange value. In this scheme M′>M the aim of the process is quantitative increase of original amount of money. The sum of value that is produced in this process is the 'capital'. The linking of the various processes with the purpose of increasing the initial sum is what Marx calls 'surplus value'. According to Marx, in capitalist production process the only aim of the movement of capital is to increase the sum of the value that is initially advanced. Unlike the SCP process (where production and exchange takes place for the satisfaction of one's own needs), the aim of the capitalist production process and circulation is surplus value and not necessarily the satisfaction of own needs.

The next question is where surplus value comes from. According to Marx, the owner of money M (initiator of production) must find a commodity on the market whose use value processes the quality of a source of value. In other words, the use value of this commodity creates value more than the value of this commodity itself. Marx called this special commodity 'labour power'.[3]

There are two necessary conditions to use labour power as a commodity to realise surplus value in the production process:

(1) There must be people who are legally free and voluntarily ready to sell their labour power; and
(2) They must not own any of their own means of production.

Thus capitalist mode of production presents a specific social relationship: on the one hand, there must exist a class of property owners or owners of means of production, and on the other hand, there must be a class of property less, but legally free workers. Marx writes, 'the value of labour power is determined as in case of every other commodity, by labour time necessary for the production and consequently also the reproduction, of this special article.' In a capital dominant society, the value of labour power is determined by the value of the means of subsistence necessary for the maintenance of its owners (Heinrich, 2012).

The capitalist ensures the value of labour power to be equal to the cost of its reproduction. This is fundamentally necessary for the capitalist to generate more and more surplus. The difference between the value of labour power, which Marx refers to as equal to the necessary labour time (the labour time required to reproduce the value of the labour power) and the total value is the surplus value. In this way, the newly created value can be firmly divided into two parts—the value of labour power and surplus value. In this whole process, the workers (real producers) receive a lesser value from the capitalist than the value they produced. Marx calls this extra value 'exploitation'.

The second volume of Marx's *Capital* deals with the process of circulation of capital.[4] M—C—M′ is an abstract depiction of the circuit of capital. The real circuit of capital can be written as follows:

```
       MP
      /
M—C—P—C′—M′
     \
      L
```

In the real circuit of capital, capital assumes three successive forms:

(1) Money capital, M, which capitalists convert into a commodities C, has a special material content, i.e. the capitalist buys means of production (constant capital) and labour power (variable capital). The combination of means of production and labour power in the capitalist production process is known as productive capital P.

(2) The result of the capitalist production process is a new quantity of commodities. This quantity of commodities is commodity capital C′.

(3) The selling of commodities C′ in the market for M′ money capital, but M′ > M

M′ is the money capital increased in value by the amount of surplus value. We can clarify above relation as follows:

$M = C$
$C' > C$ therefore $C' > M$
$C' = M'$ therefore $M' > M$

The time spent by capital in the production process is the 'time of production'. The time spend by capital in the circulation process, whether in the form of money capital seeking commodity sellers or as commodity capital seeking buyers, is capital's 'turnover time'. Capital that passes through the above three forms (money capital, productive capital and commodity capital) is characterised by Marx as industrial capital. In this sense, capital investment in services also belongs to the category of industrial capital. The main difference consists in the fact that the finished product is not a 'material object' acting as independent commodity capital (Heinrich, 2012). In Marxian scheme this can be written as follows:

```
        MP
       /
M—C—P—M′
    \
     L
```

In the above process C′ is missing because a service is consumed simultaneously with its production. Hence pure merchant capital such as trading capital, commercial capital etc., and interest bearing capital which includes banking and insurance services do not belong to the category of industrial capital. These activities appropriate a share of surplus value, but the production of surplus value does not belong to their capital function (Heinrich, 2012). Thus, the economy ruled by the capitalist commodity production, capital enters into various levels of circuits in order to realise the surplus value.

Capitalist Production Process and Surplus Extraction

The main objective of the capitalist production process is to extract the surplus. Within the capitalist process of production, the labour process exhibits two distinctive characteristics: first, it proceeds under the control of the capitalist, and second the product of the labour process is the property of the capitalist. As we explained in the previous section, the general formula for capital is M—C—M′

as the valorisation process. Valorisation is only possible because a particular commodity (i.e. labour power) is purchased and consumed in a production process of a new commodity. However, in order to consume labour commodity, the means of production (machinery, raw material and related equipment) are necessary condition. In the capitalist production process, the capitalist advances capital both to buy the non-labour means of production which Marx calls constant capital c and labour power which he refers as variable capital v. The value of produce can be explained as under:

$$c + v + s$$

c, the Constant capital, can be further subdivided into two parts: fixed capital, such as machinery, instruments of labour, buildings, labouring animals, etc., and circulating capital, such as materials of production, raw and auxiliary materials, semi-finished products, etc. v, the variable capital, is the value of social labour-power employed in production. In other words, it is equal to the sum of the wage paid to the workers whose labour power is hired in production process. s, surplus value, is the value produced by the labour over and above the value of their wages and appropriated by the capitalist.

The capacity of capitalist production to produce surplus value determines what Marx calls the 'rate of surplus value s/v' or in other words 'rate of exploitation.' The capitalist's measure of valorisation is the 'rate of profit':

$$s/(c + v)$$

With s/v as a measure of rate of surplus value there arise two basic possibilities for increasing the valorisation of capital, which Marx refers to as the production of 'absolute surplus value' and the production of 'relative surplus value'. One way to increase the surplus value is lengthening the workday, e.g. from 8 to 10 or 12 hours. However, the length of working day has absolute limits. Marx calls this way of increasing surplus value the absolute surplus value. The production of absolute surplus value refers the early phase of development of capitalism. It constitutes the phase when the techniques of production are relatively unchanged. The other way to increase the surplus value is to decrease the necessary labour time. Marx calls this way of enlarging of surplus value the relative surplus value. The relative surplus value can be intensified by either lowering the real wages or increasing the productivity of labour, leading to a reduction of necessary labour time.

There are three visible ways for capitalist to increase the relative surplus value:

(1) Cooperation among workers in the production process.
(2) Division of labour or specialisation of production activities in order to enhance the efficiency; and
(3) Speeding up labour or mechanisation of production process.

The first two ways to increase the surplus value have natural limits. The third way that is the mechanisation of production process produces the fear of technological unemployment that was also realised by Ricardo (2006) prior to Marx and Keynes (1933) after him.[5] The change in technical composition of capital, as Marx (1992) argued, results in the growth in mass of the means of production, as compared with the mass of labour power. It changes the value composition of capital by increase of constant constituent of capital at the expense of its variable constituent. This process what is prevalent at different scale in different industries and countries inevitably produces reserve army of labour hourly and daily. In other words, owing to the introduction of machines in the production process, demand for labour power declines, that results in involuntary unemployment. The mass of workers who are willing to sell their labour power at prevailing wages but are not able find any work are referred by Marx as the 'reserve army of labour'.

The labour displacing technology is an important feature of an economy ruled by capital. In a capital-dominant society, in order to valorise its produce, an individual producer interacts with other producers in the market. The circuits of individual capitals intervene and presuppose one another. The reproduction of an individual capital does not take place in isolation. The total reproduction of individual capital is part of the reproduction of total social capital. The total social capital can be reproduced under the condition that a certain amount of means of production is required by individual capitals as a whole, and so as many means of subsistence have to be produced as are consumed by capitalists and workers. For Marx, the reproduction of capital is fundamentally the reproduction of the class relations of capitalist production. If the reproduction process in various segments of the economy is repeated in the same manner (with the same capital labour composition), Marx calls this process 'simple reproduction'. Simple reproduction refers to a capitalist system which preserves indefinitely the same size and same proportion among its various parts. Every year, capitalist replace all capital worn out or used up and spend all their surplus value on consumption and workers must spend all their wages on consumption (Sweezy, 1942).

In order to differentiate the simple and expanded reproduction (ER), Marx, in *Capital* Vol. 2 has divided the economy into two broad sectors: Department-I, which produces the means of production and Department-II, which produces means of consumption. Simple reproduction (SR) of two Departments can be presented as follows:

Department- I (Producer goods) = $c_1 + v_1 + s_1$

Department-II (Consumption goods) = $c_2 + v_2 + s_2$

SR means the output of producer goods must be equal to the constant capital of both the sectors, i.e.

$$c_1 + c_2 = c_1 + v_1 + s_1$$

In the same manner, the output of consumption goods sector must be equal to consumption of capitalist and workers

$$v_1 + s_1 + v_2 + s_2 = c_2 + v_2 + s_2$$

Simplification of the two equations gives the famous equation of Marx showing balance between two departments in SR

$$c_2 = v_1 + s_1$$

It states that the value of the constant capital used up in consumption goods sector is equal to the value of commodities consumed in by workers and capitalist engaged in production of means of production (Sweezy, 1942).

However, if the reinvestment of surplus value was merely to expand capital's existing operations (for example building new factories to expand the production) both constant and variable capital would grow in the same proportions. If wages were to remain constant, the total labour power purchased would grow at the same rate. This situation Marx calls 'expanded reproduction'. SR does not reflect the picture of mature capitalist society. In other words, SR is equivalent to Say's law of market in which production process is driven by the use value. However, the real aim of the capitalist is not the use value but to expand his capital. It is achieved by converting a proportion (often major proportion) of his surplus value into additional capital that enables him to earn more and more surplus value. If the capitalist uses the surplus value to buy additional means of production, capital accumulation takes place. If the capitalist does not consume the entire surplus value, then purchase of means of production for the next period exceeds current use.

$$c_1 + c_2 < c_1 + v_1 + s_1$$

$$c_2 < v_1 + s_1$$

This inequality presents the expended scale of reproduction (Fine and Saad-Filho, 2014). ER represents the real aim of the capitalist that is to expand the value in the form of accumulation of capital.

The third volume of *Capital* synthesises the process of production and circulation, with an objective of discovering the concrete form which grows out of the process of capital's movement. In other words, the third volume of *Capital* presents clarification of everyday mystification of surplus value and profits. In capital-dominant production relations, money is not only a medium of exchange but becomes 'potential capital'. As Marx pointed out, 'in this capacity of potential capital, as a means to the production of profit, it becomes a commodity, but a commodity of a special kind or what comes to the same thing, capital becomes commodity' (Heinrich, 2012). As money becomes a unique commodity, the price paid for this unique commodity is 'interest'. Interest is the reward for money because it yields profits. It can be expressed with the following scheme:

M—M—C—M′—M″

Money as interest-bearing capital is advanced twice: one by its owner to the industrial capitalist, then by the industrial capitalist to finance profit yielding commodity production. The first return goes to the industrial capitalist (M″) and then from the industrial capitalist to the lender (M′). The return to the industrial capitalist contains a profit, and the return to the lender contains interest, which is paid from the industrial profit (Heinrich, 2012). Marx refers to the capitalist who owns interest-bearing capital as the 'money capitalist', whereas the person who borrows funds from them is the 'functioning capitalist'.

What is peculiar to interest-bearing capital is not interest—this is merely a particular expression of valorisation as expressed in the equation M—M′: money appears to multiply all by itself. The money capitalist owns the abstract position in a capitalist economy, but it is considered the primary force of surplus realisation. The functional capitalist, who owns a concrete position in the working of the capitalist economy, is largely ignored by bourgeois economics. The theories of stabilisation and accumulation in the present phase of capitalism largely address the abstract part in order to accelerate the surplus extraction. Marx therefore referred to interest-bearing capital or speculative capital as the 'most superficial and fatishised form' (Marx, 1959).

The institutions that mediate the movement of interest-bearing capital are banks and capital markets. The credit system—granting of loans, trade in stocks and bonds—lives on expectations and insecurity. The speculative nature of finance capital leads to 'bubbles' (excessive share prices) and the subsequent crash (a sudden fall in prices). The financial crisis of 2008 is an important example of crisis produced by the speculative nature of financial capital.

Capitalist Crisis and Society Beyond Capitalism

Marx had not given a systematic theory of crisis of capitalism. In the third volume of *Capital*, Marx speaks of the barriers to the capitalist mode of production, but not in the sense of its temporal end. In *Capital* Vol. I, Marx highlighted the logical contradiction of capital that can lead to capitalism's collapse but in his analysis of capitalism in three volumes of *Capital* he does not address the question of collapse or crisis in particular. According to Marxian tradition, capitalism is subject to two types of crises: general crisis and partial crisis. General crisis refers to the widespread collapse of economic and political relations of production and reproduction under capitalism. Partial crisis or business cycles is a regular feature of economic activities under capitalism. The tendency of rate of profit to fall is a form of general crisis that is caused by the internal factors (inherent to capitalist development).

The fall in surplus value produces the forces that could lead to the general crisis of capitalism. The first contradiction of capitalism that produces the general crisis can be explained as follows.

Rate of surplus value = s/v

This rate expresses the 'degree of exploitation' of labour by capital. The rate of profit is related to the total capital advanced in commodity production.

Rate of profit = s/(c + v)

The measure of valorisation for capitalist is not the rate of surplus value (s/v) but the rate of profit (s/(c + v)). Marx showed that the average rate of profit (s/(c + v)) falls owing to the increase in productivity at the general level of capitalist production. This argument of Marx of the tendency of the rate of profits to fall is based on the rise in value of organic composition of capital c/v along with condition that s/v remains constant. The fall in rate of profit in Marxian explanation is caused by the increase in constant proportion of capital in production process that results in increase in 'organic composition of capital'. It can be illustrated as follows.

Following equation expresses the total output for a capitalist economy.

$$c + v + s$$

Organic composition of capital is expressed as

$$q = c/(c + v)$$

If at initial level c= 200, v = 50, s = 50, then total value of output is 300. As per these numeric values, the rate of profit is

$$p' = s/(c + v)$$

$$p' = 50/\ 250 = 20\%$$

Here organic composition of capital is:

$$q = 200/250 = 80\%$$

The increase in proportion of constant capital relative to variable capital causes the increase in organic composition of capital, therefore a fall in the rate of profit. It can be explained as under.

With the introduction of more machines in production process by keeping the proportion of variable capital and surplus capital as before, we reach the following results:

$$c = 400, v = 50, s = 50$$

$$p' = 50/ 400 = 11\%$$

$$q = 400/ 450 = 88.89\%$$

The other form of general crisis of capitalism is under-consumption or demand gap. Due to the mechanisation of the production process two tendencies emerge under capitalism. Firstly it makes workers redundant and weakens the bargaining power of the active labour. Second, it enhances the productivity of labour without corresponding increase in real wages. Since workers get less wages, their consumption is never sufficient to buy back their produce (Sheikh, 1991). On the other hand, capitalists consume only a proportion of total profits and bulk of their profits remains unconsumed that results in unsold produce in the economy. The excess credit creation to fill the demand gap to avoid the general capitalist crisis is not a permanent solution. It rather deepens the roots of those forces that ensure the general structural crisis to be more severe in future. The forces that lead to the general capitalist crisis are internal and inherent to capitalism which exposes the exploitative nature of the capitalist mode of production (such as production structure and production relations).

In order to unfold the real character of capital, Marx outlines the various fetish forms and mystifications in the three volumes of *Capital.* In the forty-eighth chapter of *Capital* Vol. III, Marx discussed the 'trinity formula'. Marx presented this trinity formula as 'capital–profit (profit of enterprises plus interest), land–ground rent, labour–wages'. According to him, this comprises all the secrets of the social production process under capitalism. Marx (1959) points out that "capital is not a thing, but rather a definite social production relation, belonging to a definite historical formation of society, which is manifested in things and lends this thing a special social character. Capital is not the sum of the material and produced means of production. Capital is rather the means of production transformed into capital, which in themselves are no more capital than gold or silver in itself is money." So capital, for Marx is a social relation and Marx's project was to study specific social relations, i.e. of bourgeois society and the main determinant factors which move the wheels of this society. People in bourgeois society live in an enchanted world, in which a personification of things occurs. In bourgeois society, the subject of social progress is not people but commodity, money and capital. All members of bourgeois society are subordinate to fetishism of social relations which revolves around capital. The fetish social relations of bourgeois society takes root as an objective form of thought that structures the perception of all the members of society.

In order to bring humanity out of crisis produced by the capital driven fetish social relations, the critique of the capitalist mode of production is a necessary condition. In the three volumes of *Capital*, one could be disappointed that Marx did not write even a short chapter on communist society.

There are two widespread conceptions regarding what constitutes communism in Marx's sense. One conception emerged from the early writings of Marx, the ideal explanation of communist society based on ethical reason. According to this explanation, in communist society people should not exploit and oppose their fellows; they should not seek to gain material advantage over them, but rather show solidarity and helpfulness. In the *Economic and Philosophical Manuscripts*, Marx said that communism as such is not the aim of human development rather the aim of communism is to bring human welfare center to production and social relations. It is to create a form of production and an organisation of society in which man can overcome alienation from his product, from his work, from his fellow man, from himself and from nature, in which he can return to himself and grasp the world with his own power, thus becoming one with the world. Socialism for Marx is society beyond alienation, as he wrote in the third volume of *Capital*, that 'socialised man, the associate producers, regulate their interchange with nature rationally, bring it under their common control, instead of being ruled by it as by some blind power;

they accomplish their task with least expenditure of energy and under conditions most adequate to their human nature and most worthy of it.' This is quite a humanistic and positive conception, which Marx referred to as the aim of communist society.

The other conception which we have witnessed is communism as the nationalisation of the means of production and centrally planned economy. The Soviet Union's attempt in the 20th century is regarded as in accordance of this conception of communism. The collapse of the Soviet Union is falsely propagated as a proof for the failure of Marx's idea of communism. However, that was one attempt (but not the last attempt) towards socialism and can be called as Soviet style socialism. In *The Communist Manifesto* of Marx and Engels and Engels's *Anti-Duhring,* one can clearly find that the nationalisation of production is a first step and never the last to build a communist society.

Marx's project of communism was concerned with the comprehensive emancipation of human beings from the social nexus and fetish social order that takes on a life of its own and imposes itself upon individuals as an anonymous compulsion. Not only should the capital relations as a specific characteristic of exploitation that generates bad and insecure working and living conditions for the majority of population be overcome, but the fetishism that attaches to the products of labour as soon as they are produced as commodities should also be abolished. Social emancipation, the liberation from self-produced and therefore gratuitous constraints, is only possible when the social relations that generate the various forms of fetishism have disappeared. The members of such a society would have to regulate their social life, organise production in individual workplace, coordinate between workplaces, harmonius interactions as producers and consumers, have harmony with nature, find ways of dealing with minority positions, different forms of discrimination and inequality. The communist project which Marx and Engels have visualised is an outcome of their concrete understanding of working of capitalism. It is the responsibility of pro-people intellectuals to explore the real foundation of capitalism and its exploitative character and work towards and alternative social order.

NOTES

1. This paper is a revised and updated version of article published in 2017 in *Critique: Journal of Socialist Theory*, Vol. 43, No. 3, pp. 409-26, titled 'Understanding Marx's Capital'.
2. The specific character of particular type of labour can be defined as, for example, carpentry produces a chair; linen weaving produces a linen sheet. Concrete labour is the basis on which we differentiate products of different labour.
3. The term labour power refers to the ability of human beings to perform labour. So labour is application of labour power.
4. This volume is further subdivided into three parts: The Metamorphoses of Capital and Their Circuits; The Turnover of Capital; and The Reproduction and Circulation of the Aggregate Social Capital.
5. It was first highlighted by Ricardo (2006 [1817]) with an argument that due to the introduction of machinery in production process, no doubt, the one fund, i.e. net income, from which the capitalist class derives their revenue in the form of profits, may increase, but other funds, i.e. gross income from which the labour class is employed, may diminish. Capital formation or investment in the forms of introduction of new machinery will reduce the funds to employ labour. Ricardo's fundamental proposition was that capitalists do not employ the new machinery from their shares of profits, i.e. net income but from the gross part of revenue. The introduction of machinery in the production process has two effects- one, it reduces the availability of funds for the employment of labour and second, it also reduces the requirement of labour for given production unit. Thus, it has a positive effect of saving labour for the capitalist class along with a negative effect on working masses in the form of redundancy of labour from production process. No doubt, the technological revolution during in 19th and beginning of 20th century had resulted in sustained increase in the material standard of living but fears of adverse employment consequences of technological advancement had also been aggravated in the 20th century. This fear was also raised by Keynes during the era of the Great Depression with a prediction that in the near future we may be able to perform all the operations of agriculture, mining, and manufacturing with a quarter of the human effort. But the rapid change will bring a new disease, namely, technological unemployment (Keynes, 1963 [1933]).

REFERENCES

Fine, B. and A. Saad-Filho (2014), *Marx's Capital*, New Delhi: Viva Books.

Foley, D.K. (1986), *Understanding Capital: Marx's Economic Theory*, Cambridge, MA: Harvard University Press.

Heinrich, M. (2012), *An Introduction to the Three Volumes of Karl Marx's Capital*, New York: Monthly Review Press, Indian edition (2013), Delhi: Aakar Books.

Keynes, J.M. (1963 [1933]), Economic Possibilities for Our Grand-children, In *Essays in Persuasion*, pp. 358-76, London: W.W. Norton & Co.

Marx, K. (1970), Wage, Labour and Capital, In *Selected Works*, Vol. I, Moscow: Progress Publishers.

Marx, K. (1992), *Capital: A Critique of Political Economy*, Vol. I, London: Penguin Books.

Marx, K. (1956), *Capital: A Critique of Political Economy*, Vol. II, Moscow: Progress Publishers.

Marx, K. (1959), *Capital: A Critique of Political Economy*, Vol. III, Moscow: Progress Publishers.

Marx, K. (1961), The Economic and Philosophical Manuscripts, in E. Fromm (eds.), *Marx's Concept of Man*, London: Continuum Publications.

Marx, K. and F. Engels (2002), *The Communist Manifesto*, London: Penguin Books.

Ricardo, D. (2006 [1817]), *On Principles of Political Economy and Taxation*, Third Edition, Canada: Ontario: Reprinted by Batoche Books.

Sheikh, A. (1991), Economic Crisis, pp. 160-64, In T. Bottomore et al. (eds.), *A Dictionary of Marxist Thought*, London: Blackwell Publishers Ltd.

Sweezy, P.M. (1942), *Theory of Capitalist Development*, New York: Monthly Review Press, Indian edition (2016), Delhi: Aakar Books.

5

Contemporary Capitalism

Greg Albo

The study of capitalism has entailed both the interrogation of the capitalist mode of production as an abstract-formal object and investigation of the diverse historical forms that capitalism has taken across time and place. From this duality, a distinction in Marxist theory has often been drawn between the examination of the capitalist mode of production as such—the 'pure' theory of capitalism with its distinct 'laws of motion'; and specific historical periods of capitalist development—monopoly capitalism, post-war capitalism, neoliberal capitalism as examples; and particular spatially circumscribed cases—East Asian capitalism, German capitalism, or capitalism in New York City. The notion 'contemporary capitalism' has been invoked in Marxist debates as a general term to speak to the historical phasing and evolution of capitalism.

The term contemporary capitalism has, however, no particular bounded conceptual foundation. It is a notion often intertwined with the more sharply delimited theoretical debate within Marxism about the 'periodisation' of capitalism. Periodisation can, in general terms, be defined as "the effects of the development of the forces and relations of production on the form of social relations within a mode [of production] ... such a periodisation will reveal itself in the methods of appropriating and controlling surplus value. These methods will assume increasingly socialised forms as the socialisation of production proceeds" (Fine and Harris, 1979, 109). The notion of contemporary capitalism has often then been appealed to in suggesting that a new phase of capitalism has succeeded the historical features and class struggles of earlier ones.

Historical debates about contemporary capitalism have typically, then, been about transformations in 'patterns of social reproduction' characteristic of different periods of capitalism that require theoretical clarification, and the identification of emerging features, sectors, regions or countries seen as typifying the most 'advanced' features of capitalism.

In terms of the patterns of social reproduction aspect, it is often claimed that contemporary capitalism has fundamentally altered the economic dynamics of accumulation and the form of the capitalist state. All zones of capitalist society are being compelled to adjust to new organisational and competitive imperatives and, as will be seen, this leads to its being characterised abstractly in a number of ways. For example, the shift from mass production technologies to micro-electronic ones has often been interpreted as a transition from Fordism to post-Fordism; and changing forms of macroeconomic intervention as a shift from a Keynesian state to a neoliberal one. In identifying particular ascendant features of capital accumulation are taken to be the essence of contemporary capitalism. These features might be, for example, the organisation of the labour process or the internationalization of capital, or the organisational features of a particular state with respect to the forms of coordination and regulation of financial and industrial capital. Debates about contemporary capitalism with Marxian political economy have, therefore, attempted to explain current developments in light of the 'general laws' of the capitalist mode of production; identify new patterns and features of the production, appropriation and distribution of value; and indicate other qualities of social relations and class struggles that appear to be more conjunctural and spatially-bounded. This is what Mandel has referred to as a "synthesis of economic history and economic theory" (Mandel, 1968, 17).

This two-sidedness to the debates about contemporary capitalism reflects the Marxist methodological commitment to the position that capitalism is, in all times and places, a social system driven by the encompassing accumulative imperatives of a world market; yet capitalism is always differentiated by temporally and spatially specific processes accumulation and statification and particular class relations necessary for the production of value. Marx made the point that capitalism imposes "one specific kind of production which predominates over the rest, whose relations thus assign rank and influence to the others. It is a general illumination which bathes all the other colours and modifies their particularity" (Marx, 1973, 106-07). And in the *Communist Manifesto*, Marx and Engels contend that capitalism spreads through imitation and emulation—the bourgeoisie fashioning a "world after its own image" (Marx and Engels, 1998, 40). The appeal to developments in 'contemporary capitalism' make the point that the remaking of capitalism never stops, and competitive imperatives ensure that new developments spread across the world market, although always in a process of uneven development and thus varying in their social form according to specific institutional contexts, places, and class struggles.

In this approach, it is important to distinguish Marxian political economy from other theoretical frameworks. In neoclassical economics, universal categories of economics and politics means that debate about 'contemporary capitalism' is simply and always about whether the essential human essence to 'truck, barter and exchange' is unfolding as it should with the expansion and intensification of market relations, or if this essence is being thwarted by market intervention (Friedman, 1953). There exists no methodological precept or theoretical tools in neoclassical economics to distinguish different historical epochs, let alone phases of capitalism, except on such a singular market continuum that identifies social, political and technological factors that allows the market to spread. In contrast, institutional political economy conceives of all historical economies as embedded in more general socio-economic logics, such as forms of rationality, with capitalism dominated by, but not reduced to, profit maximisation (Lazonick, 2008; Castells, 2000). In turn, each phase of capitalism is marked by a dominant organisational and technical paradigm determined by its particular forms of organisation. The policy challenge is to ensure that the institutions of corporate governance and the administrative form of the state match the socio-technical logics of production. This evolution, for institutional political economy, can be understood by certain universal categories although always with temporal and spatial variations formed as ideal-types.

The essential difference in theorising contemporary capitalism, and the underlying concern to periodise phases of capitalist development, is located in Marx's fundamental methodological point of departure and his critique of bourgeois political economy in its failure to ask: "Why this content has assumed that particular form, that is to say, why labour is expressed in value, and why the measurement of labour by its duration is expressed in the magnitude of the value of the product" (Marx, 1976, 174).

Capitalist Development

Development in capitalist societies takes the general form of accumulated money-capital being continually reinvested in expanding means of production and the purchase of labour power for the purpose of increasing the amount of value accumulated as money. The unending search for profits leads to specific tendencies of development, or 'laws of motion' of capitalism. This accumulation implies a continual transformation of the commodities, social relations and class struggles; and thus in the 'social forms' which mediate the tendencies of the capitalist mode of production in concrete history. A number of these tendencies have figured, repeatedly, in debates about contemporary capitalism.

First, Marxian political economy identifies the labour process as the location for the extraction of surplus value from workers, the organisation of production, the changing form of the subsumption of workers, the contestation over work-time and the development of the forces of production. The history of capitalism is defined by transformations internal to the labour process in terms of skills, technology, work organisation and conflict over work control (Braverman, 1974). Thus the development of the modern factory system or the implementation of Taylorist work organisation and Fordist assembly-line production have often been hailed as the central features defining contemporary capitalism and its dominant mode of capital accumulation. The changes in the labour process from the adoption of new computer technologies in workplaces, for example, is often seen having several new features: the intensification of Taylorism to match the rhythms of new technologies for production and service workers and a multi-skilling for a range of technicians and production support workers; a recomposition of the form in which the conception of work is undertaken by designers and developers and the execution of the work by production workers; a relative decline of individualised piece-work and increase in team-work; and a shift from dedicated machinery to flexible manufacturing systems.

Second, the consumption of labour power in the labour process is premised on the commodity labour power being available for sale. There is a range of factors—skilling, unions, household relations, education—that are necessary to transform workers into a properly constituted supply of labour power available for exploitation. These institutions form the wage-relation that underpins the reproduction of workers. Further, the accumulation of capital tends to increase the technical and social divisions of labour as the machines being deployed increase in sophistication and new sectors develop. The demand for labour power is, therefore, continually shifting. A fundamental contradiction exists between a changing labour demand and the need for a stable supply of labour power that is dependent on the extra-market institutions that produce workers. This contradiction can only be worked out historically in specific places as it is explicitly embedded in class struggles and class formation. It is common to identify the most contemporary of capitalism not with the labour process, but with the conflicts, social compromises and institutions which determine the historical form of the wage-relation (Gordon, Edwards and Reich, 1982).

Third, the imperatives of competition lead to the concentration and centralisation of capital into ever more complex and larger firms. This entails larger units of capital in terms of the economies of scale forming individual plants, but also more differentiated units of capital and labour processes under the control of any given ownership group. This raises a number of deep-seated problems of control: the process controls over increasingly complex labour processes; the operational controls over spatially dispersed labour processes, particularly of the commodity chains of multinational corporations; the strategic controls necessary to coordinate market strategies across horizontally differentiated units of capital; and the accounting and administrative controls to enforce competitive imperatives on the individual units of capital internal to the firm (Hymer, 1979). As well, the forms that legal ownership of firms takes between different shareholder groupings, and the ways that top managers exercise their power to make decisions to invest and fund the expansion of the firm, also take on particular features. The different forms of organisational controls has sparked heated debate about contemporary capitalism as being characterised by highly institutionalised distributional relations associated with large bureaucratic firms, or more flexible distributional bargains and 'networked' firms.

Fourth, capital accumulation always occurs within the context of a world market, and individual capitals confront competitive imperatives to internationalise their production. The tendency to the internationalisation of capital drives further innovations in communications and transportation in the process building a new foundation for the world market. The internationalisation of commodity, productive and financial capital takes on varied features and relations in different phases of capitalism. The form internationalisation takes in different phases also transforms the class alliances of the power bloc between the internal and imperialist fractions of capital in national social formations. This, in turn, carries implications for the specification of the autonomy and sovereignty of the state, the allocation of state functions to international agencies, and the coordination of the political-economic relations between the hierarchy of states in the world market (Panitch and Leys, 2004). The periodisation of the forms of the nation-state and international competition figures prominently in all debates about contemporary capitalism.

Fifth, extra-market institutions and political mediation are always necessary to secure the socio-political conditions that underpin accumulation. States provide both these capacities and the requisite political coercion and legitimation. The tendency towards the increasing socialisation of production within capitalism is also entails stratification, that is, the increasing role of the state in ensuring the reproduction of capital through infrastructure, support for education and research and development and economic coordination. The social forms of state economic intervention, the technical organisation of state apparatuses and the relations between branches of the state vary considerably. For example, during the post-war phase of capitalism the wage-relation was often directly inserted into the state via incomes policies and corporatist institutions such that the nominal reference wage was formed via political mediations as opposed to market mechanisms. But more recently, state policies helped recompose the reserve army of labour and market disciplines were reasserted in wage formation. The self-expansion logic of capital remains, but the social form of the state and its political mediations become indispensible in locating the most contemporary features of capitalism.

Contesting Contemporary Capitalism

While Ernest Mandel (1975, 23) claimed that there was "no satisfactory history as a function of the inner laws of capital … and still less a satisfactory explanation of the new stage in the history of capitalism", there have been many signal contributions to the understanding of modern capitalism. The classic text which began to raise the question of emergent features of capitalism shifting the form of capitalist development was Rudolf Hilferding's *Finance Capital* (1981), itself a response to Eduard Bernstein's revisionist argument that the socialisation of capitalism meant that the law of value no longer held and capitalism was simply evolving into socialism. Hilferding presented his book as a diagnosis of the most recent developments in capitalism from the vantage of Marx's laws. But he extended the theoretical analysis to take into account transformations in money, credit and banking to offer a unique interpretation of modern capitalism as 'finance capital', a fusion of industrial and bank capital into monopolies which were transforming competition and extending it into the international arena. This sparked additional responses from Luxemburg, Bauer, Grossman, Lenin and Bukharin about the features of 'monopoly capitalism' and new tendencies towards economic crisis, nationalisation and imperialism. But they all held in common with Hilferding, while arguing within a value-theoretical approach, that a new stage of capitalism had been arrived at, driven by the increasing socialisation of production and the monopolistic concentration industry.

The Great Depression and the long boom of 'post-war capitalism' suggested to many that the fundamental dynamics of accumulation had changed as the concentration of economic power altered competition and thus the specific way that the law of value operated. The key statement setting the framework for much modern debate, and certainly for US interpretations of postwar capitalism, came from Paul Sweezy's *Theory of Capitalist Development* (1942). After surveying classical Marxism, Sweezy argued that monopoly pricing power fundamentally altered the pattern of accumulation by forming a tendency for the surplus produced by capitalists to rise, the consumption of workers to be constrained, with military spending, marketing and other factors deployed to counteract permanent stagnation. This interpretation reflected a commonly asked question in radical political economy circles with the emergence of the so-called Keynesian welfare state: 'Has capitalism changed?' (Strachey, 1957; Tsuru, 1961).Theorists for the communist parties in particular took the suspension of competition by monopolisation even further and argued that contemporary capitalism had now taken the form of 'state monopoly capitalism'. This concept inferred a particular 'fusion' between the state and the monopolies which, at one and the same time, represented the stabilisation of capitalist economies and the possibility of coexistence of two rival systems, and yet the inexorable decay of capitalism as it inevitably gave way to socialism. But other theorists of state monopoly capitalism rejected the notion that the fundamental accumulation dynamics of capitalism had changed, but insisted that the socialisation of production had altered the form, magnitude and substance of state intervention into the economy.

Although explicitly rejecting the position that capitalism had fundamentally changed its dynamic, Ernest Mandel (1968; 1975) identified a new stage of capitalism, which he variously referred to as 'neo-capitalism' or 'late capitalism'. Mandel insisted that the basic laws of motion still regulated capital accumulation, but what had changed in 'neo-capitalism' was the character of the science and technology deployed, market relations and class struggles that mediate these abstract tendencies in concrete history and that allow for long-term tendencies in the rate of profit and long waves of economic growth. For Mandel, the uniqueness of 'late capitalism' lay in the third technological revolution driving up profit rates, increased military spending, permanent inflation, the increased role of the state and the spread of planning across all organisations. This was a list of features of contemporary capitalism remarkably similar to Sweezy's and holding in common the view that capitalism was moving into an epoch of decline, in opposition to the thesis that the contradictions of capitalism had been superseded by state management.

The economic crisis of world capitalism across the 1970s gave special urgency to reexamining the laws of motion of capitalism in light of current developments. A slew of new interpretations of contemporary capitalism resulted with a relative focus on 'intermediate concepts' needed to penetrate the various stages of capitalism and their transition (Aglietta, 1979). The French regulation school, for example, argued that abstract laws of motion were modified into particular modes of regulation and regimes of accumulation. Thus post-war assembly-line production dominated by semi-skilled workers was governed by the monopolistic regulation of Fordism, while the new flexible production systems have been regulated by a mix of markets and associational governance institutions of post-Fordism. In parallel, the 'social structures of accumulation' approach of American Marxists interpreted contemporary capitalism in terms of a 'capital-labour accord' institutionalised in economic and state structures, while Japanese Marxists developed the 'Unoist' approach to interpret the transition to a new stage of capitalism (Kotz, McDonough and Reich, 1994; Itoh, 1990). Distinctively, Nicos Poulantzas located contemporary capitalism in the changing form of the state. He linked the new forms of integrated production to transformations in the relations of production and capitalist ownership structures to new alliances in the power bloc and functions in the state. In opposition to prevailing views, Poulantzas claimed that American hegemony has "become stronger ... what is taking place at present, far from signalling as attempt by American capital to 're-establish' its hegemony, is rather an offensive on its part to even undermine the place of a secondary imperialism" (1974, 86, 88).

The most recent assessments of contemporary capitalism have continued many of these theses, particularly about the new forms of the production and the restructuring of the state and classes. But new concerns about the social form of neoliberal globalisation have also arisen. One such debate has been in how to characterise neoliberalism itself. For instance, Robert Brenner (2006) assesses neoliberal policies as the economic and political response of the capitalist classes' inability to restore profits through creative destruction over the 'long downturn' from the 1970s as firms try to preserve existing investments and government policies block exit, while others have sought to clarify the forms of neoliberalism as a specific phase of capitalism (Saad-Filho and Johnston, 2005). Another has been centred on financialisation, with Gerard Dumenil and Dominique Levy (2004) seeing the emergence of a new form of financial capital that also explains both neoliberalism and globalisation. Others, following the earlier theses of Sweezy on monopoly capitalism have contended that financialisation represents a further mechanism to cope with capitalist stagnation. Finally, an overarching debate has been how to characterise the contemporary features and competitive form of the internationalisation of capital. David Harvey (2003), for example, has defined the new imperialism as a search for a 'spatial fix' to an economic crisis in core countries via 'accumulation by dispossession' in peripheral countries. Still others have registered the new imperialism as, on the one hand, a register of US economic decline as surplus capital accumulates in East Asia and, on the other, as a measure of US hegemony as it imposes neoliberal globalisation on the world market and reinvigorates its capitalist classes in the process (Arrighi, 1994; Panitch and Gindin, 2004). This includes examining how the neoliberal state, for instance, constructs markets politically by depoliticising economic management (a so-called 'rules-based approach' that aims at targeting inflation and increasing and the international competitiveness of the national economy). In doing so, primacy within the state apparatuses and policies is given to the central bank and monetary and financial policies in order to mediate conflicts between different fractions of capital and to subordinate labour to the imperatives of competition intensified by financial markets.

The changing dynamic and form of capitalism has given rise to numerous attempts to identify and theorise its contemporary features. Mainstream accounts put emphasis on empirical shifts of a 'new economy' without any theoretical content that places these developments within the structures of capitalism. In contrast, institutional political economy has tended to analyse contemporary capitalism within a new set of concepts—post-Fordism or informational capitalism—as an entirely unique development (Hollingsworth and Boyer, 1997). It has been characteristic of Marxian political economy, however, to anchor its theorisation of new developments within the abstract concepts—value, exploitation, class, concentration and centralisation of capital, state power—necessary to understand capitalist society in general. This allows a focus on underlying determinations, specification of their current forms and theorisation of its concrete and complex processes. Following Marx's methodological mandate, this is the study of the form taken by the laws of motion of capitalism in their contemporary phase.

REFERENCES

Aglietta, M. (1979), *A Theory of Capitalist Regulation*, London: New Left Books.

Arrighi, G. (1994), *The Long Twentieth Century*, London: Verso Books.

Braverman, H. (1974), *Labor and Monopoly Capital*, New York: Monthly Review Press.

Brenner, R. (2006), *The Economics of Global Turbulence*, London: Verso Books.

Castells, M. (2000), *The Rise of the Network Society*, Oxford: Blackwell.

Duménil, G. and D. Levy (2004), *Capital Resurgent: Roots of the Neoliberal Revolution*, Cambridge: Harvard University Press.

Fine, B. and L. Harris (1979), *Rereading Capital,* New York: Columbia University Press.

Friedman, M. (1953), *Essays in Positive Economics,* Chicago: University of Chicago Press.

Gordon, D., R. Edwards and M. Reich (1982), *Segmented Work, Divided Workers,* Cambridge: Cambridge University Press.

Harvey, D. (2003), *The New Imperialism*, Oxford: Oxford University Press.

Hilferding, R. (1981), *Finance Capital: A Study in the Latest Phase of Capitalist Development*, London: Routledge.

Hollingsworth, R. and R. Boyer (eds.), (1997), *Contemporary Capitalism: The Embeddedness of Institutions,* Cambridge: Cambridge University Press.

Hymer, S. (1979), *The Multinational Corporation: A Radical Approach*, Cambridge: Cambridge University Press.

Itoh, M. (1990), *The World Economic Crisis and Japanese Capitalism*, London: Macmillan.

Kotz, D., T. McDonough and M. Reich (eds.), (1994), *Social Structures of Accumulation*, Cambridge: Cambridge University Press.

Lazonick, W. (2008), Contemporary Capitalism, In *The New Palgrave Dictionary of Economics,* London: Palgrave Macmillan.

Mandel, E. (1968), *Marxist Economic Theory,* London: Merlin Press.

Mandel, E. (1975), *Late Capitalism*, London: Verso Books.

Marx, K. (1973), *Grundrisse*, Harmondsworth: Penguin Books.

Marx, K. (1976), *Capital: A Critique of Political Economy*, Vol. 1, London: Penguin Books.

Marx, K. and F. Engels (1998), *The Communist Manifesto*, London: Verso Books.

Panitch, L. and C. Leys (eds.), (2004), *The New Imperial Challenge*, London: Merlin Press.

Panitch, L. and S. Gindin (2004), Global Capitalism and American Empire, In Leo Panitch and Colin Leys (eds.), *The New Imperial Challenge*, London: Merlin Press.

Poulantzas, N. (1974), *Classes in Contemporary Capitalism*, London: New Left Books.

Saad-Filho, A. and D. Johnston (eds.) (2005), *Neoliberalism: A Critical Reader*, London: Pluto Press.

Strachey, J. (1957), *Contemporary Capitalism*, London: Victor Gollancz.

Sweezy, P.M. (1942), *The Theory of Capitalist Development*, New York: Monthly Review Press.

Tsuru, S. (ed.), (1961), *Has Capitalism Changed? An International Symposium on the Nature of Contemporary Capitalism*, Tokyo: Iwanami Shoten.

6

Reserve Army of Labour

Deepankar Basu

Introduction

In any capitalist economy, the total labour force can be divided into two parts—the active army of labour and the reserve army of labour. The former consists of those that are currently employed in capitalist enterprises; the latter, which Marx calls the 'relative surplus population', consists of those that are not currently employed in capitalist enterprises but are potentially available for employment, if the need arises.

This dual division of the labour force into the active and reserve armies of labour is a characteristic feature of capitalism. Other than in exceptional situations, e.g. during and immediately after the Second World War in the US and Europe, a significantly-sized reserve army of labour is a permanent fixture of capitalist economies. In fact, the reserve army is produced by the logic of capitalist production.

"But in fact it is capitalist accumulation itself that constantly produces, and produces indeed in direct relation to its own energy and extent, a relatively redundant working population, i.e. a population which is superfluous to capital's average requirements for its own valorisation, and is therefore a superfluous population" (Marx, 1992, 782).

The implication of the continued existence of the reserve army of labour in capitalist economies is striking: these economies typically do not employ all of its potential labour force. A portion of the available labour force is almost always left unemployed, or is marked by different degrees of attachment to the labour force, as we will see in detail below. Workers who are unemployed and underemployed not only bear the direct loss of forgone income, but also a much larger non-monetary loss of subjective well-being. At the individual level the loss of subjective well-being increases with the duration of unemployment (Ochsen and Welsch, 2011). At the societal level, the indirect, non-monetary loss is several fold larger than the direct, monetary loss (Helliwell and Huang, 2014).

No matter how it is distributed between its monetary and non-monetary components, unemployment imposes a large cost on individual workers and on society as a whole. Why can capitalist economies not eliminate unemployment? Why must some people always remain unemployed, or underemployed, or partially employed, even when there is a large individual and social cost of unemployment? In this chapter we will offer answers to these questions from a Marxist perspective and illustrate the argument with some evidence from the United States.

The Theoretical Question

The value of a commodity produced under capitalist conditions is the sum of three components: constant capital (value of means of production used up in the production process), variable capital (value of labour power) and surplus value (value appropriated by the capitalist firm). Capitalist firms are much less interested in the specific commodity they produce and sell than in the surplus value they appropriate. The central dynamic of capitalist economies arises from the behaviour of capitalist firms as they try to generate, realise and reinvest surplus value.

Surplus value comes from unpaid labour time of workers. It is the difference between the value added by the use of labour power and the value of labour power. The former is what the worker adds to means of production in each hour of work; the latter is what the capitalist pays to purchase each hour of labour power (the ability to do useful work). If the difference between the two narrows, surplus value falls. Without adequate magnitudes of surplus value, capitalism would be under threat. And this brings us to an interesting question.

Reinvestment of surplus value is largely driven by the structural imperatives of the perpetual competitive struggle between capitalist firms. Without reinvesting surplus value and enlarging their capital values, capitalist firms risk falling behind their competitors in the race to generate and appropriate ever more surplus value. At the aggregate level, the reinvestment of surplus value generates new demand for means of production and labour power.

Elements of the means of production are largely produced by capitalist firms. Hence, their aggregate investment decisions generate demand for the output of capitalists who specialise in the production of means of production. The mismatch of demand and supply of means of production are dealt with by the market mechanism, by the fluctuations in the pace of production.

It is a wholly different story with labour power. Labour power is the ability to do useful work. This ability inheres in the body of the worker. Labour power is not produced in any capitalist firms. Labour power is produced and reproduced daily with the living worker. At the aggregate level, the total supply of labour power comes from the generational replenishment of the working class. Thus, there is no market mechanism to deal with the mismatch of demand for and supply of labour power.

If the demand for labour power increases with reinvestment of surplus value, the price of labour power might increase to a point where surplus value begins to fall. If this process continues for extended periods of time, the whole capitalist system might be under threat. After all, the central dynamic of capitalism will grind to a halt if the aggregate surplus value falls to zero. What mechanism—and this has to be a non-market mechanism—is available to the capitalist system to avert this possibility? What mechanism keeps the value of labour power from rising too much? What ensures the stability of the value of labour power that is necessary to keep generating adequate amounts of surplus value?

The Ricardian Answer

Borrowing from the writings of Thomas Malthus, the prominent classical economist, David Ricardo, offered one answer to the above question. For Ricardo, a theory of population offers an explanation of why this does not come to pass. When capital accumulation picks up and the demand for labour power rises, the result is an increase in real wage rates. Rising incomes lead to increasing prosperity of the working class, which, in turn, increases the fertility rate. As the population rises, it gradually increases the supply of labour power. This increase in the supply eventually overtakes the rising demand for labour power. The excess supply of labour power then pulls down the real wage rate (Sweezy, 1942).

Marx never accepted the validity of this theory of population, and he certainly did not use it for answering the above question. With the benefit of hindsight we can see that the Malthusian population theory is grossly inadequate in addressing the above question. Over long periods of time, increasing prosperity has been accompanied by falling, and not rising, fertility rates. This is exactly the opposite of the Malthusian claim. Resting on empirically dubious claims, the Malthusian-Ricardian explanation just does not cut ice.

The Marxian Answer

In Volume I of *Capital*, Marx offered a powerful alternative answer to the above question by developing the concept of the reserve army of labour (Marx, 1992). Marx's answer to the above question was this: the key mechanism that keeps the value of labour power within necessary bounds, i.e. necessary for the generation of surplus value, is the fluctuation in the size of the reserve army of labour.

"The industrial reserve army, during the periods of stagnation and average prosperity, weighs down the active army of workers; during the periods of over-production and feverish activity, it puts a curb on their pretensions. The relative surplus population is therefore the background against which the law of the demand and supply of labour does its work. It confines the field of action of this law to the limits absolutely convenient to capital's drive to exploit and dominate the workers." (Marx, 1992, 792).

Before we understand the reasons for the fluctuation in the size of the reserve army of labour, let us look carefully at its construction and its components. Figure 1 presents a schematic representation of the labour market of a typical capitalist economy. The representation of the labour market involves both stocks and flows.

Figure 1. A Schematic Representation of the Active and Reserve Armies of Labour in a Typical Capitalist Economy.

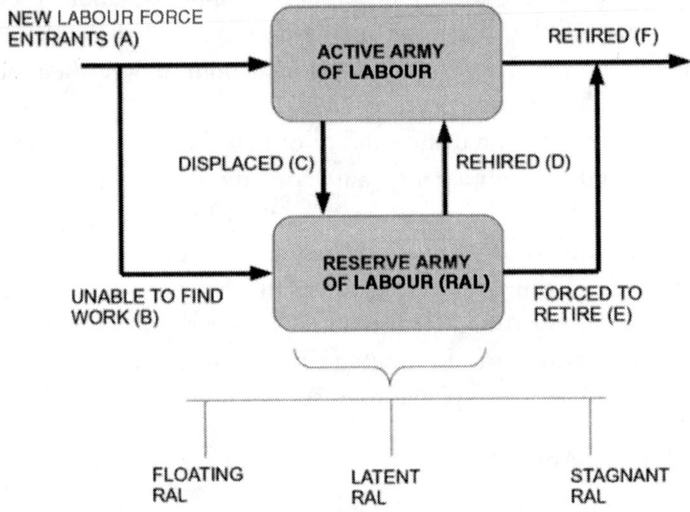

Source: Adapted from Basu (2013).

The total labour force, a stock, is divided into two parts: the active army of labour (workers employed in capitalist enterprises) and the reserve army of labour (workers not employed in capitalist enterprises but potentially available for employment). In Figure 1, the two rectangular boxes represent these two components of the labour force.

The two stock quantities are linked to the larger economy and to each other through various types of flows. Starting at the left end of Figure 1, we see the flow of new workers entering the labour force. This flow gets divided into two parts. The first part, labelled (A), represents the workers who find employment; of the new entrants to the labour force, they join the active army of labour. The second part, labelled (B), represents new workers who cannot find a job and are forced to join the reserve army of labour—at the very beginning of their working life.

The active and reserve armies of labour are connected to each other through two flows: some currently employed workers lose their job and move from the active to the the reserve army—this is represented by flow (C); there is also movement in the other direction, when some workers who are currently not employed find employment in a capitalist enterprise—this is represented by the flow (D).

At the right end is the flow of labour power out of the labour market. Some of the workers who are currently in the reserve army fall out of the labour force—represented by flow (E); and some workers who are currently employed retire and leave the labour force—represented by the flow (F).

Fluctuations in the Reserve Army of Labour

Fluctuations in the size of the reserve army of labour come from the flows represented in Figure 1 as (C) and (D). What are the causes of these flows? The flow labelled (C) represents workers losing their employment. This flow increases the size of the reserve army and is caused by three sets of factors.

The first, and most important, is labour saving technical change. When there is a sustained increase in the demand for labour power, it leads to an increase in the price of labour power. Since wage costs are an important and significant component of the total cost of production, capitalist firms have an incentive to reduce wage costs—in the context of rising prices of labour power. The search for methods to reduce wage costs often leads to the search for and adoption of new techniques of production that reduce the use of labour power relative to the means of production. The new technique of production, thus, saves on labour—the costly input—and replaces it with the relatively less costly input—means of production. Such 'labour saving technical change' leads to job loss for some currently employed workers. Hence, these workers move from the active to the reserve army of labour.

The second source of fluctuation is the regular cyclical movement of aggregate economic activity, what contemporary economists call business cycles. The cyclical fluctuations of aggregate activity is caused by fluctuations in various components of aggregate demand. Investment expenditure by capitalist firms can fluctuate due to movements in animal spirits; consumption expenditure by worker and capitalist households can fluctuate because of changes in consumer sentiments; government expenditure can fluctuate for fiscal policy reasons; and net exports can bounce around because of fluctuations in foreign economies. During the upswing phase of business cycles, jobs are created on a net basis. More workers move from the reserve to the active army than the other way round. During the downswing phase of business cycles, the opposite movement, i.e. from the active to the reserve army, dominates.

The third source of fluctuation in the size of the reserve army of labour can be relocation of production across geographical regions. The relocation can be within or across national boundaries. The location that loses economic activity, the flow from the active to the reserve army of labour is likely to be large; locations that manage to attract new economic activity, the opposite flow is likely to be bigger. In either case, geographical relocation of production, which has become especially important since the last few decades of the 20th century, will lead to a fluctuation in the size of the reserve army of labour.

Components of the Reserve Army of Labour

In Volume I of *Capital*, Marx distinguished between three components of the reserve army of labour (Marx, 1992). The three components—floating, latent and stagnant—of the reserve army of labour are indicated at the bottom of Figure 1. Considering the three components separately allows us to think carefully about the short and long run forces governing the formation and reproduction of the reserve army of labour.

The floating reserve army of labour is its part that fluctuates most with the fluctuation of economic activity and capital accumulation. It is composed of workers who have lost jobs due to labour saving technical change, recessions or geographical relocation of production. When the pace of economic activity picks up, some, or most, of these workers will be rehired. Hence, they will move back into the active army of labour—once the recession is over. Thus, the floating reserve army of labour is the part whose formation is governed by short run economic forces.

The latent component of the reserve army of labour directs our attention to longer run forces responsible for its formation. It is the part of the reserve army of labour that is gradually formed, over many decades, with the evolution and expansion of capitalism. The two important sub-components of the latent reserve army of labour are household labour, and labour involved in peasant farming and other forms of non-capitalist production.

Historically, the bulk of household labour, i.e. work involved in raising children, caring for the elderly and sick, carrying out daily activities of household labour like cooking, washing, and cleaning, have been done by women. Because of this unequal division of household labour between men and women, the latter have historically been largely confined within the household. This does not contradict the fact, highlighted by recent historical research, that women's labour was crucial during the Industrial Revolution (Burnette, 2008). While individual branches of production relied heavily on women's labour, there was an overall decline in the labour force participation of women in the 18th and 19th centuries in England (Table 1, last column, Horrell and Humphries, 1995). The declining labour force participation of women was driven largely by changes in demand arising from structural and institutional changes of an industrialising, capitalist economy. Thus, it seems fair to assert that women's labour gradually became a potential source of the reserve army that was latent. Even though the capitalist system was not using it, it could draw on this labour as and when needed.

This movement of women's labour from the household and into the labour force was seen most forcefully in Europe and the United States in the decades after the end of the Second World War. For instance, using data for the US from the Federal Reserve of St. Louis, we see that only 33 per cent of women were in the labour force in 1948. For the next five decades, the labour force participation rates of women increased secularly. In 2000, about 60 per cent of women were in the labour force. The pattern of steady increase in the labour force participation rates of women in the US has been halted since the early 2000s—perhaps indicating exhaustion of an important component of the latent reserve army of labour.

The second sub-component of the latent reserve army of labour consists of workers involved in non-capitalist production. The largest section of such workers have been involved in peasant and artisanal petty production. In Western Europe, the process of 'primary accumulation of capital' led to their destitution and dispossession over a 300-year period. Peasant producers losing access to land and petty non-agricultural producers ruined by competition from big business swelled the ranks of the working class that supported capitalist development. As the pace of capitalist production increased and industrialisation proceeded, the second sub-component of the latent reserve army was drawn into the domain of capitalist production.

In much of what is today known as the developing world, the 'primary accumulation of capital' is incomplete. A large segment of the working population in these countries work in what the development economist W.A. Lewis called the 'traditional sector' (Lewis, 1954). Distinguished from the 'modern sector', which is characterised by capitalist relations of production and the use of reproducible capital, the 'traditional sector' is the domain of non-capitalist relations, and labour intensive techniques, of production—small-scale family farming in agriculture and petty non-agricultural commodity production. These workers form a large latent reserve army that is potentially available to capital, not only domestic capital in these countries, but also global capital (Foster, McChesney and Jonna, 2011).

The third, and final, component of the reserve army is the stagnant component. This is composed of workers who live on the margins of society, who have fallen out of the labour force due to illness, loss of skills, or psychological reasons. There is neither a stable short run nor a steady long run logic to its formation. The formation of the stagnant component of the reserve army seems to be related to the institutional setting of capitalism, to the existence, or its lack, of a strong social safety net and a social environment that can help workers come back to the labour force if they fall out of it.

Reserve Army of Labour in the United States

Drawing on, and extending, Basu (2013), I will now present empirical estimates of the reserve army of labour in the postwar US economy. The main source of the data that has been used to construct these estimates is the Current Population Survey (CPS) conducted every month by the US Bureau of Labour Statistics.

The Data

The starting point for estimating the reserve army of labour (RAL) is the civilian non-institutional population (CIV). CIV is an estimate of every person 16 years and above who is neither in an institution (prison or mental health institution) nor on active duty in the US Armed Forces. Based on detailed interviews, conducted on a sample of roughly 60,000 households every month, the CPS assigns every person in CIV to either of three pools:

The pool of employed workers (EMP): these are the persons who reported doing any wage or salary work (either full-time or part-time) at the time of the interview; or, they reported as having done self employed work; or, they reported that they had a job but were not at work currently due to vacation, illness, etc.; or, they reported that they were doing unpaid family work;

The pool of unemployed workers (UNEMP): These are the people who reported that they did not have a job currently and had actively looked for a job in the previous 4 weeks (with reference to the time of the interview).

The pool of those who are not in the labour force (NLF): These are the persons who fall neither into the category of employed workers (EMP), nor can be counted as being unemployed (UNEMP).

While it is obvious that all the unemployed workers would be part of any measure of the RAL, the question as to which part of the NLF should be included in the RAL requires some more analysis. Based on answers to questions in the CPS, the NLF can be divided into two broad groups: (a) those who reported that they want a job, and (b) those who reported that they do not want a job. The second category was by far the largest component of NLF, and was primarily composed of: (i) those who were attending educational institutions, and (ii) those who had retired. Among those who wanted a job, the CPS allows us to distinguish two important groups: (i) those workers who searched for jobs some time in the past 12 months (but did not do so during the past 4 weeks), and (ii) those workers who did not search for jobs anytime in the past 12 months.

Of those who had actively searched for work some time during the past 12 months, the workers who report as being currently available for work are referred to as the 'marginally attached workers'. An important subset of the marginally attached workers are those who have stopped looking for jobs because of discouragement, with the reason for discouragement varying across respondents. Some believe that no work is available for them, or that they lack the necessary schooling or training; some believe that their employer thinks them either too young or too old; some are discouraged because of other types of discrimination in the labour market. Together, they are all referred to as the 'discouraged workers'.

These finer distinctions among workers who are all grouped together under the category of NLF will be useful in constructing various measures of the RAL. But before we do so, we must also look at another, often overlooked, category of workers: those undergoing incarceration. According to the International Centre for Prison Studies, the US has, by far, the largest prison population in the world as a share of the total population. This forms a small but significant part of the potential reserve army of labour because this population is potentially available to capital; by removing them from the labour market, pressure on wages is reduced. Hence, one must include some measure of the population in prisons and jails to get a more accurate measure of the RAL. The Bureau of Justice Statistics (BJS) has made available annual data on the 'correctional population' for the period 1980-2016. Though there are some issues of comparability of the data over years, it gives us a usable number for the population in prisons and jails.

Four Measures of the Reserve Army

Using data on the variables discussed above, we can construct four, increasingly comprehensive, measures of the reserve army of labour in the US economy over the postwar period. The first measure, RAL1, is the total number of unemployed workers, i.e. RAL1 = unemployed workers. This is the official measure of 'unemployed' workers, and for us, it is the most conservative estimate of the reserve army of labour.

The second measure, RAL2, adds the marginally attached and part-time workers to the unemployed workers, i.e. RAL2 = unemployed workers + part-time workers + marginally attached workers. This is more comprehensive than RAL1 because it includes (a) workers who are not counted as unemployed because they did not actively look for work anytime in the 4 weeks preceding the CPS but did so over the previous 12 months, and (b) part-time workers, who are counted as part of the employed pool (EMP) but whose primary and secondary jobs are both part-time. These part-time workers wish to switch to a full-time job but are unable to do so because of economic reasons.

The third measure, RAL3, adds all workers who are not in the labour force but wanted a job to the total number of unemployed and part-time workers, i.e. RAL3 = unemployed workers + part-time workers + workers not in the labour force but wanting a job. This measure is more comprehensive than RAL2 because it includes workers outside the labour force who are not even part of the 'marginally attached worker' category.

The fourth and most comprehensive measure, RAL4, is the sum of people in prison and jail and RAL3, i.e. RAL4 = RAL3 + persons in prison and jail. Data on the number of persons in prison and jail is available at an annual frequency from 1980 to 2016. Hence, the RAL4 series starts in 1980 and runs up to 2016. Note that even this measure, the most comprehensive so far, provides only a lower bound for the 'true' reserve army of labour. This is because the latent reserve army is almost certainly not properly estimated in RAL4. In a sense, the latent reserve army can only be estimated post facto, i.e. after the latent labour force has actually joined the labour force. Hence, almost always, this portion of the reserve army will be underestimated.

Estimates of the RAL

In Table 1 and in Figure 2 and 3, I present estimates of the four measures of the reserve army of labour in the postwar US economy. From the numbers in Table 1 and from the trends visible in Figure 2 and 3, we see that the reserve army of labour in the US economy has steadily increased in size over the decades. If we use a comprehensive measure like RAL3, the average size of the reserve army of labour increased from 4.9 million in the 1950s to 13.9 million in the 1980s, and further to 17.7 million in the 2010s. As a proportion of the labour force, the reserve army of labour (measured by RAL3) increased from 7.68 per cent in the 1950s to 12.21 per cent in the 1980s. From the highs attained in the 1980s, RAL3 declined in the next two decades, before rising to 11.35 per cent of the labour force in the 2010s.

Table 1: Magnitude of the Reserve Army of Labour (Decadal Averages)

	Actual Number (in thousands)				*Proportion of Labour Force (%)*			
	RAL1	RAL2	RAL3	RAL4	RAL1	RAL2	RAL3	RAL4
1950s	2946.79	3637.18	4945.79		4.58	5.65	7.68	
1960s	3514.42	4337.78	5898.47		4.78	5.90	8.02	
1970s	5822.47	7186.57	9772.22		6.22	7.67	10.44	
1980s	8303.12	10248.40	13935.66	14680.69	7.27	8.98	12.21	12.85
1990s	7568.72	9413.88	13212.10	14733.08	5.76	7.17	10.05	11.20
2000s	8269.63	10075.59	13416.91	15569.49	5.54	6.75	9.00	10.45
2010s	11158.38	13680.83	17651.61	19872.42	7.18	8.81	11.35	12.78

Notes. RAL1 = unemployed workers; RAL2 = RAL1 + part-time workers + marginally attached workers; RAL3 = RAL1 + part-time workers + workers not in the labour force but wanting a job; RAL4 = RAL3 + prison and jail population. Source: Author's calculation from data available on the website of the US Bureau of Labour Statistics.

Figure 2. Four Measures of the Reserve Army of Labour in the US Economy, 1948-2016

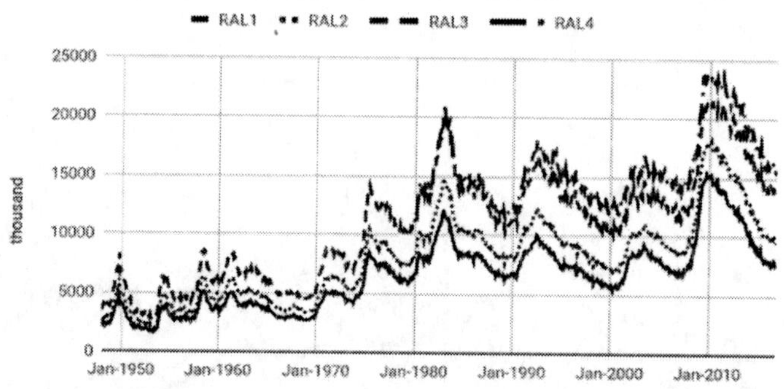

Note: For Definitions See the Note to Table 1.

The rising magnitude of the reserve army of labour is also visible in Figures 2 and 3. Starting from the left end of the graph, as we move right, we see the magnitude of the reserve army of labour steadily go up. This upward movement is true for all the four measures of the reserve army of labour. The rising movement attains its peak in the early 1980s, and then fluctuates around that value for the next three decades. All the four measures begin another pronounced rise from the end of the 2000s, and have now crossed the earlier peaks reached in the 1980s (especially in terms of magnitudes, but not yet in terms of the proportions of the labour force).

The fact that the size of the reserve army of labour was highest in the early 1980s and in the late 2000s is not surprising. These are periods of structural crises of capitalism (Basu, 2019). The late 1970s and early 1980s was a period of crisis of the regulated form of post-war capitalism. In response to the crisis, capitalism changed its institutional structure into a neoliberal form. The late 2000s marks the crisis of neoliberal capitalism. During periods of structural crisis, the circuit of capital is interrupted, which leads to production being curtailed drastically. The result is an increase in the reserve army of labour.

Figure 3. Four Measures of the Reserve Army of Labour, as Percentage of the Labour Force, in the US Economy, 1948-2016

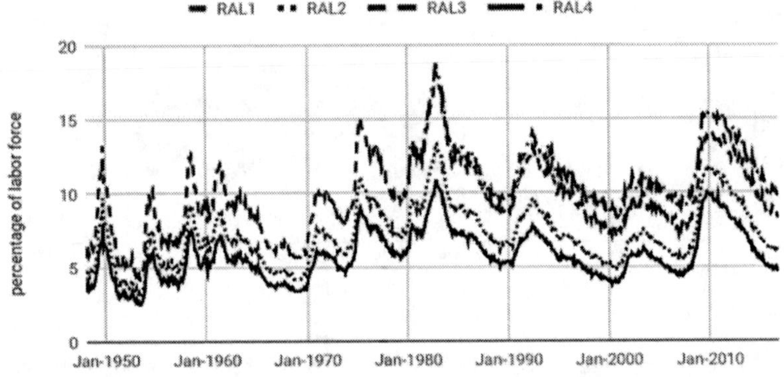

Note: For Definitions See the Note to Table 1.

Apart from periods of structural crises, we can also see in Figures 2 and 3, the pronounced fluctuation of the reserve army of labour at business cycle frequency. The reserve army of labour falls with the upswing phase of the typical business cycle; it rises with the downswing phase of the business cycle.

Conclusion

A characteristic feature of capitalist economies is the existence of a part of the labour force as unemployed or precariously attached to the labour force. The history of capitalism shows that, other than in exceptional periods, e.g. immediately after the Second World War, capitalist economies are unable to provide adequate employment, in terms of quality and quantity, to all those in the labour force. Mainstream economics tries to explain the existence of what it terms 'structural', i.e. long run, unemployment by taking recourse to various types of 'frictions'; Keynesian economics sees in inadequate aggregate demand the reason for short run unemployment. The Marxist tradition offers an alternative explanation that encompases both short run and long run factors.

Marxist analysis highlights the division of the labour force in any capitalist economy into two parts, the active army of labour (those employed) and the reserve army of labour (those unemployed and those attached to the labour force in various degrees but wishing to be employed). The existence of the reserve army of labour is a structural necessity of capitalism because this is the key mechanism through which the system keeps the price of labour power within bounds necessary for the generation and accumulation of surplus value. While the reserve army of labour fluctuates with the pace of capital accumulation, it can never disappear—without undermining the whole capitalist structure of production and authority.

The continual existence and reproduction of the reserve army of labour is a severe indictment of capitalism. Unemployment or precarious attachment to the labour force imposes enormous costs on individual workers and on the whole of society (Helliwell and Huang, 2014). The fact that even the most advanced capitalist economies are unable to permanently solve the problem of unemployment should be part of the arsenal of post-capitalist imaginaries. After all, socialist economies, with all their problems, had completely eliminated the problem of unemployment. For instance, there was virtually no unemployment at the aggregate level in the USSR after the 1930s (Kotz and Weir, 1997).

Of course, the problem of the reserve army of labour is of an altogether different magnitude in the periphery of the global capitalist system. The vast majority of these countries, in what is now referred to as the developing world, have not even managed to absorb large fractions of their labour force into the orbit of capitalist production. The overwhelming majority of working people are 'employed' in various ways in the 'informal sector'. From a Marxist perspective, a significant part of the informal sector represents the latent reserve army of labour. For instance, small-scale peasant production and petty commodity production outside agriculture, both important components of the informal sector, represent a large pool of labour engaged in commodity (or non-commodity) production under non-capitalist relations of production. It can be drawn on if capital accumulation picks up.

But various types of structural constraints, both internal and external to these economies, prevent capital from even absorbing this vast pool into stable, well-paying capitalist employment. This means that, in the periphery of the global capitalist system, conditions of existence of the vast majority of working people continue to be marked by low productivity and low income work, lack of social security, absence of job security, and most often lack of bargaining power or rights. The key problem of economic development in the periphery. i.e. generation of adequate employment for the vast majority of the working people, remains unaddressed several decades after the pioneers of development economics like W. A. Lewis, M. Kalecki and N. Kaldor identified them in the 1950s. Whether it can at all be addressed within the confines of capitalist economies is an open question.

REFERENCES

Basu, D. (2013), The Reserve Army of Labour in the Post-War US Economy, *Science & Society*, Vol. 77, No. 2, pp. 179-201.

Basu, D. (2019), Reproduction and Crisis in Capitalist Economies, In M. Vidal, T. Smith, T. Rotta and P. Prew (eds.), *The Oxford Handbook of Karl Marx,* Oxford, UK: Oxford University Press.

Burnette, J. (2008), Women Workers in the British Industrial Revolution. EH. Net Encyclopedia, URL:http://eh.net/encyclopedia/women-workers-in-the-british industrial-revolution/

Foster, J.B., R. McChesney and R.J. Jonna (2011), The Global Reserve Army of Labour and the New Imperialism, *Monthly Review*, Vol. 63, No. 6, November. URL: https://monthlyreview.org/2011/11/01/the-global-reserve-army-of-labour-and-the-newimperialism/

Helliwell, J.F. and H. Huang (2014), New Measures of the Cost of Unemployment: Evidence from the Subjective Well-Being of 3.3 Million Americans. Working Paper 16829, Cambridge, MA: National Bureau of Economic Research.

Horrell, S. and J. Humphries (1995), Women's Labour Force Participation and the Transition to the Male-Breadwinner Family, 1790-1865, *The Economic History Review, New Series*, Vol. 48, No. 1, pp. 89-117.

Kotz, D. and F. Weir (1997), *Revolution from Above: The Demise of the Soviet System,* New York, NY: Routledge.

Lewis, W.A. (1954), Economic Development with Unlimited Supplies of

Labour, *The Manchester School*, Vol. 22, No. 2, pp. 139-91.

Marx, K. (1992 [1867]), *Capital: A Critique of Political Economy*, Volume I, Translated from the third German edition by Ben Fowkes. New York, NY: Penguin Publishers.

Ochsen, C., and H. Welsch (2011), The Social Cost of Unemployment: Accounting for Unemployment Duration, *Applied Economics*, Vol. 43, No. 27, pp. 3999-4005.

Sweezy, P.M. (1942), *The Theory of Capitalist Development: Principles of Marxian Political Economy*, New York: Monthly Review Press.

7

Political Economy of Employment-Unemployment in Capitalism

Satyaki Roy

The employment of labour force has never been the main concern of capitalism despite the fact that labour used to be the only source of value creation. Classical economists as well as Keynes and Marx held the view that labour is the source of creative activity that adds value to existing inputs. But a society which is primarily driven by realisation of exchange value recognises work only when it creates commodities. Capitalism is a world of commodities where producers produce goods not for their own use but to sell their produce in exchange of money that assumes the form of universal exchange value. Labour is exchanged in the form of labour power or the capacity to produce some goods or services for sale and that is the only mode of work recognisable in the world of commodities. Any work which is an expenditure of mind and energy but primarily creates use value for the producer is not being counted as productive value addition in capitalism. Capitalism therefore is not only a system of producing and exchanging commodities but also is typical of making labour power a commodity. Employment is the engagement of labour power as commodity purchased by a typical employer. In this process of selling labour power or the capacity to work for a defined time or output based contract, the act of labour is controlled by the employer and hence the autonomy of labour as a creative human being seizes to exist. The worker is alienated not only from the means of production which are owned by the capitalist but also from the labour process which is controlled by the command structure of production deployed by the capitalist and finally from the fruits of labour which are produced goods and services owned by the employer. Work as a result loses its joy of creative engagement with the nature and society, it rather becomes tyrannical to the worker and a field of contestation between employer and employee that determines the outcomes of class process. In this article we therefore try to locate the problem of employment and unemployment through the Marxian lens of class process which involves production, appropriation and distribution of surplus value.

In the advent of capitalism unemployment had never been a concern to be reckoned with. Instead considerable force and coercion was applied to make people work in newly emerging industries. Working for others in order to earn a living was preceded by a social arrangement in which people could produce their bare necessities on their own and if some surplus was being produced it was exchanged within the community on the principles of reciprocal relations. In that sense unemployment preceded employment and working as wage labour was preceded by non-wage labour. In a particular historical context labour power becomes a commodity and that could be reproduced only in a society where exchange values emerged to be the dominant form of societal engagement. In today's world we come across a situation where the use of direct human labour in the process of capitalist accumulation is on the decline. Capitalism does not require to employ the huge number of unused labour at its disposal anymore to sustain the system with a threshold rate of profit. Growth or value addition can happen with far less use of labour compared to earlier phases of capitalist development due to improved technology. At the same time if labour happens to be the only source of value and if the current system is not in a position to use human capacities, the question of rising unemployment is no longer of a temporary nature neither is it a concern to the individual who happens to be unemployed, rather the problem is systemic and creates structural limits to the progress of human civilisation.

Capitalism: Employment-Unemployment

Marx begins his magnum opus *Capital* with the discussion on commodity as that is the primary unit of capitalist social construction. Goods and services are produced for sale and exchange value of the produce predominates and defines its use. A good has to be useful to others not to the producer, only then it can assume exchange value. But goods and services produced for the use of the producer is outside the ambit of capital relations. Similarly, a human being who is employed by someone else assumes exchange value and paid wages while if someone works or produces for his or her own satisfaction would not be considered as employed and rightly so because the person would not be able to earn a living in capitalism. Employment therefore refers to a state where a person's work is worth for the society and someone is prepared to buy that work in exchange of money. But what actually motivates someone to work for others to earn a living? The simple answer is when the person has no other alternative means to survive. In a self-sustained community there are relations of reciprocity where people are dependent on each other where there may be division of labour but the motivation for production was primarily of community use. So peasants and artisans, craftsmen and priests all had their defined roles which were asymmetric but no one was employed by others. The social hierarchy was visible where the status of men and women were defined by their position in the occupational structure. To make people work for others, one should be ripped off from his or her own way of living, from the community in which the individual exists and, most importantly, the means of production which s/he owns. Then only can one be forced to work for others so as to make both ends meet. Therefore, this particular category of people who sell their capacity to work to others or need employment to survive is a historical construct defined by Marx as primitive accumulation of capital (Marx, 1958). The act was a forcible separation of direct producers from their means of production which created the original accumulation of capital. But this process of creating labour power to be used in capitalist enterprises can be sustained only when the dominance of exchange value, the commodity-money economy is well established. Against work, workers would be paid wages by which they can buy their necessities for subsistence which these workers may not be producing on their own. A world of exchange value is a pre-condition for the sustenance of capital-wage labour relationship. The means of production which is forcefully separated from the direct producer becomes capital in the hands of the capitalist which no longer is used to produce goods or services for immediate consumption but as a means of creating surplus value. But the separation of the direct producer from the means of production and the transformation of alienated labour into wage workers is not something automatic and immediate. Between these two processes there was wide gap both in terms of time and space and involved force and cultural imposition to create the norm of the 'worker'. The origin of employment therefore is associated with a new social organisation where creating commodities is the dominant form of production. Labour is forced to sell his or her labour power or capacity to work and in that sense for the first time in human history labour power becomes a commodity and the process of production and consumption are separated and has to be mediated by market. What is even more important that the process of distribution of returns to various factors of production as wages, profits, rents or interest get intrinsically linked to the realisation or sale of the goods and services produced.

The creation of a commodity economy and that of labour power as commodity involves a process of exchange and hence comparability between diverse products, services and skills of different human beings. It therefore demands a common measuring rod which can compare goods of different use values and can also evaluate diverse forms of labour that are deployed in producing different goods and services. It involves a process of homogenisation of labour, where all diverse types of labour are reduced to a simple quantitative measure in terms of labour hours. This is 'abstract labour' which is separated from its concrete forms and can be expressed in terms of labour time. But Marx's notion of abstract labour is not a conceptual category but very much concrete as realised in day-to-day market activities, where goods, services and human labour can be expressed and exchanged in terms of quantities of money. Basically the value of the goods and services or the labour power or any form of commodity is determined by the socially necessary labour time required to produce that particular commodity. It is important to note that it is not the actual amount of labour congealed in a particular commodity that determines its value rather the amount that is considered to be socially necessary. And the determination of what is 'socially necessary' is subject to the average technology predominant at that particular point of time and also on what society gives sanction to through the interaction in the market. Therefore, if someone uses more labour time to produce a commodity than what is socially sanctioned with a given level of technology, the value of that product would not be determined by the actual use of labour hours rather on the basis of labour hours that are considered to be socially necessary to produce that particular commodity.

The value of labour power as a commodity is also determined in the same way, that is, it is derived by the socially necessary labour time required to produce the goods and services required to reproduce the mental and physical energy or capacity of the worker as well as to maintain the future stream of supply of labour power. Simply put, it is derived from the values of goods and services which is required to keep the worker and his or her future generations healthy and able bodied to serve capital. But what is required for the worker and the family is not objectively determined by any nutrition standard or measure of well-being but simply on the basis of struggle by which the working class can make the society accept some entitlements as necessary. As the surplus value accumulated by the capitalist is the total value created by the worker net of the value of labour power paid as wages, the capitalists as a class always tend to push down or lower the wages in order to create more surplus value. The 'necessary labour time' in a working day represents the value of labour power that is paid in monetary terms as wages. What is also important that capitalism recognises only labour power that is employed and 'necessary labour time' only refers to the employed workforce that are engaged in creating surplus value. People who are not employed by the capitalist class, such as unemployed, self-employed or those engaged in household work are not to be considered as productive and would not be considered while measuring what is 'necessary' for them to survive or reproduce.

The calculus of 'socially necessary labour time' also has a macro implication reflected through a mismatch of demand and supply. The value of goods and services produced has to be realised through the act of sale, meaning those should be purchased or demanded by others in exchange for money. If goods supplied are not being demanded in the market, then the labour time spent to produce unsold goods and services do not get realised as values. In some sense society signals that the excess amount of labour spent in producing those commodities does not have a social sanction and hence indicates a need of revision of the allocation of social labour. In capitalism, since the system of production and consumption are not coordinated, fluctuations and mismatch of demand and supply is not something exceptional. Rather the norm causes persistent turbulence in the allocation of social labour. Apart from the conflict between the capitalist class as a whole and the working class, the other important dimension that critically influences the dynamics of the system is the competition between capitals. As discussed earlier that the 'socially necessary labour time' is measured in reference to the average ongoing technology at a particular point in time. If an individual capitalist introduces a new technology and can reduce per unit expenditure of labour, while if the average technology remains the same in a particular industry, the value of the product remains the same and the particular individual capitalist who has deployed a new technology can earn a premium over and above the average rate of profit. This creates an inbuilt instinct of innovation in the capitalist system where capitals compete with each other and the technology once introduced by one individual capital becomes the average technology of the industry over time. Once the new technology becomes the social average, socially necessary labour time as a measure of value also changes and the premium that once the innovator was enjoying ceases to exist. But introduction and growth of new technology if moves faster than the growth of labour force and since these two growth rates are determined by factors that are independent and separated, it is always possible that the emerging production process would involve less and less direct labour. In other words, the competitive instinct of capitalists to innovate and the natural growth of labour force may diverge from each other giving rise to a structural problem of unemployment.

On the other hand, accumulation in capitalism is driven by increasing growth of investment often stimulated by growth of potential markets that kindles the expectation of higher profits. Capital is essentially a self-augmenting process and can continue as capital when it expands its value. This creates the unending drive to internalise non-capitalist space into its own ambit. But the same process also brings a huge labour force as well as natural resources which were earlier beyond the access of capital. Whether this labour force would be employed or not or if employed in what differential terms depends on diverse historical and conjectural factors. But what seems to be certain in this erratic process that a huge number of labour force is at the behest of capital and plays a significant function in the dynamics of capitalism. Marx calls it relative overpopulation constituting the industrial reserve army of labour. Expanding capital with increasing scale of operation recruits more labour in the process of production but with increasing use of machines and new technology in the same process also 'sets free' existing labour. Marx contradicts with Malthus that it is not the absolute number of population that sets limits to production but more importantly it is the relative overpopulation caused by the 'inclusion-exclusion' of the labour force that is crucial for the accumulation process of capitalism. To quote Marx, "The production of a relative surplus population, or the setting free of labourers, goes on therefore yet more rapidly than the technical revolution of the process of production that accompanies, and is accelerated by, the advance of accumulation; and more rapidly than the corresponding diminution of the variable part of capital as compared with the constant. If the means of production, as they increase in extent and effective power, become to a less extent means of employment of labourers, this state of things is again modified by the fact that in proportion as the productiveness of labour increases, capital increases its supply of labour more quickly than its demand for labourers" (Marx, 1958, 635-36). He further suggests that this creation of relative over population is the crux of demand-supply in the capitalist labour market. It on the one hand makes a part of the active labour force forcefully redundant while the same process allows the capitalist to extract more labour from the existing workers. This relative overpopulation helps capitalism to contain wages in periods of expansion when there is more demand for labour and can get rid of the burden of excess labour during downturn.

Marx (1958, 642-44) discussed three distinct layers of the reserve army which are as follows. The first refers to those who are in the cities and towns, temporarily thrown out of the active industrial labour force and can be called again when industrial activity rises. The second layer is a continuous flow of labour set free from the country side due to increased capital relations and mechanisation of agriculture and people released want to make their future in the towns in industrial activity. They do not get immediately absorbed in industrial activity and have to wait for long or may not be able to make it at all. The third layer consists of those who are low waged and heavily exploited in sweatshops, the lowest segment of the domestic industry. The lowest segment also consists of paupers, vagabonds, criminals, prostitutes, orphans and destitute who work as a dead weight to the industrial reserve army. The industrial reserve army however is not created by any grand design but it has structural relations with the functioning of capitalism. It is crucial for the accumulation process of capitalism to continue as the relative oversupply of labour helps capitalism to contain the wages.

In the discussion so far capital-labour relation is largely seen as wage labour, that is human beings are selling their creative capacity involving mind and body for the production of goods and services owned by someone else and receives wages or salary against their work. The worker who is selling his labour power can be a factory worker, an engineer or a doctor or a professor employed by a capitalist enterprise. Depending on the goods and services or inputs required to create and reproduce these various forms of labour, the value of their labour power will be determined. At a level of analytical abstraction, a particular skill can be conceived as a complex combination of simpler tasks performed at one go. Hence conceptually the value of a unit of skilled labour can be conceived as a product of several units of simple labour and can be measured accordingly. But one should not have the false impression that capitalism is only about wage labour and cannot live with other forms of non-capitalist relations. In fact, the contrary is true. Capitalism as a pure system existed only in the level of conceptual abstraction and it has mingled with various forms of non-capital relations and labour forms given the concrete conditions of space and time. Capitalism always existed with petty-producers, subcontracted devalued labour, labour by chattel, slave labour, lumpen and various other forms of proletariat and unemployed.

Globalisation and Employment

Global integration of markets of goods and services and free flow of capital has been the hallmark of globalization. We had similar phases of global integration but the current phase of globalisation is the most interpenetrative of all the phases. Liberalising the flow of capital and technology as well as reducing trade barriers have virtually erased the difference between foreign and domestic market. The larger implication of this fact is that even if the flow of labour has been restricted across borders by stringent immigration laws, movement of capital and flow of goods and services have made labour implicitly accessible to global capital. In other words, huge relative surplus population of the developing world is being accessed by global capital while the wage differences between countries continue to exist. According to the IMF the 'export weighted global workforce' or the effective global workforce quadrupled in size between 1980 to 2003 (IMF, 2007, 162). The massive labour force, particularly located in China, India, Indonesia, Thailand and ex-Soviet countries, are easily accessed by global capital either through foreign direct investment or through arms-length transactions in way of production networks. The general assumption was that globalisation would facilitate specialisation on the basis of factor intensities and developing countries with huge labour force would be the destination of labour-intensive jobs and hence create employment. In spite of the fact that there had been relocation of production towards the developing world, it did not increase gainful employment in the net. In fact, import intensities of exports in global trade have increased over the years and hence the difference between gross exports and domestic value added in exports has increased over time. This simply implies that exporting of jobs has not been limited to western countries alone rather jobs gravitate to low wage segments of the world giving rise to a 'race to the bottom'. What is more important that in this process, the bargaining power of workers vis-à-vis capital has declined across the world. Labour lost their share in advanced countries as well as in developing countries. Therefore, even if developing countries were competing with each other to grab a larger part of jobs that are relocated from the North, it came with a declining share of value added which is also reflected in declining terms of trade between exports and imports of developing countries. The crucial fact is relocation was driven by the opportunity to take advantage of global labour arbitrage where huge wage differences for similar kind of work became the prime source of rising profit.

In the advanced countries unemployment was largely caused by the introduction of new technology where repetitive jobs were increasingly being replaced by machines. As finance became cheaper with the free flow of capital, the relative cost of investment in machines also declined. In sectors where elasticity of substitution is high, employers preferred to replace workers and in sectors where elasticities were low they sought for places where the labour cost is relatively low. As a result of which jobs were destroyed in the advanced countries which is primarily 'technology unemployment' and that reduced the bargaining power of existing workers as well. This has caused a decline in labour's share in the advanced countries. Labour's share declined for 19 advanced countries who account for 78 per cent of the aggregate GDP of advanced economies and for 32 developing countries accounting for 70 per cent of total GDP of developing economies. The median labour share for OECD countries declined from 66.1 per cent in the early 1990s to 61.7 per cent in the late 2000s (IMF, 2017, 127). In the developing world because of this relocation not many new jobs were created as expected. This is because the sectors which attracted new foreign investments are labour-intensive according to Western standards but not so according to developing country standards. As a result, relocation in fact increased the average capital intensity of industries in the developing world.

Moreover, the process of globalisation facilitated concentration of capital through cross border mergers and acquisitions on the one hand and fragmentation on the other. MNCs and TNCs control the production networks in which developing country production facilities are inserted as a result of which local monopolies are destroyed and local capital lost control over the production structure and became junior partners in actualising the imperatives of global capital. Because of the global integration, technology choices are hardly available for local industries. The tastes and preferences of Western markets create hegemonies as a result of which technologies available in the global shelf are largely incorporated in domestic production structures to sustain competition. In this process, local capital prefer to face competition only on the basis of pushing down wages in order to reduce production costs. This gives rise to a labour process which increasingly relies on casualisation and informalisation of labour. In the case of India during the period March 2014 to July 2015, there had been an addition of 0.32 million in organised manufacturing. Notable is the fact that out of this total new employment created in the organised manufacturing, 85 per cent has been contracted workers. In the case of unorganised manufacturing, the only segment that recorded growth in employment is the Own Account Manufacturing Enterprises (OAMEs) which are basically one person enterprises meaning self-employed who do not hire any labour and mostly employ unpaid family labour. According to the NSSO survey on Unincorporated Non-Agricultural Enterprises (excluding construction), total employment in unregistered manufacturing increased from 34.8 million in November 2010 to 36.04 million in 2015-16, an increase of 1.24 million in five years

(NSSO, 2017). The rise has been higher in OAMEs to the tune of 1.84 million, while employment declined in establishments that are relatively larger in size within the unregistered segment that employ one to ten hired workers, which have employed 0.67 million less workers during the same period. Increased informalisation and casualisation was facilitated by rising subcontracting in the domestic production process which not only reduces the wage costs but also transfers a part of wage cost to capitalist profits. Although it is not true that pushing down wages is the only way to remain competitive in the global market. Competition works rather on the basis of unit labour cost which is a combined effect of labour productivity and wages. If the productivity of the worker rises faster than the growth of wages, unit labour costs tend to decline. In case of India the return to labour has been squeezed in the organised sector even though their productivity increased much faster. In fact, such a trend of relying more on informal contracts reduces the average productivity over time. In case of India, productivity of labour in the informal sector is on an average one-seventh of those working in the formal sector. Thus as informal work contracts increase, a downward trend in productivity may also set in.

One of the distinctive features of the employment-unemployment scenario in today's world is the rising proportion of self-employed within the workforce. In case of India, it remained consistently more than half the workforce independent of growth fluctuations (Roy, 2011). The general perception has been that during high growth periods, the demand for labour increases and proportion of wage employment rises within the workforce. On the other hand slackening of growth reduces demand for labour and proportion of self-employment rises as many existing workers lose their jobs and opt for self-employment as a survival strategy. But during the recent period the weakening of growth-employment linkage has also disrupted the relation between growth and self-employment. In other words, the high share of self-employment has become a structural feature of contemporary capitalism and not only confined to developing countries anymore. This raises a conceptual problem as well which is the following. If capitalism accumulates on the basis of surplus value and that is extracted from wage labour who sells labour power as a commodity then how do we appreciate this high share of self-employed even in situations of high growth? Self-employment is also portrayed as a rise in entrepreneurship where the producer has control over the means of production and the process of production. In spite of the fact that even the self-employed person apparently carries a sense of autonomy but in countries such as India, most of the self-employed face greater uncertainty and vulnerability than the wage employed. For the wage worker, at least in the medium term payment of wages cannot depend on the realisation of value or sale of produced goods or services. It is part of a contract where the worker is supposed to get wages against work for stipulated labour hours. In case of self-employed this is not the case. The return of the self-employed can only be realised once the value of produced goods and services are realised. Furthermore, self-employment as a non-capital relation does not invoke exchange based on equivalence of value as it is in the realm of capital relations. But non-capital can realise its return only through exchanges in the market. And the return to self-employed articulated through the market is completely arbitrary and asymmetric vis-a-vis capital relations.

The rise of self-employment and the informal sector at large has sometimes been seen as a process of de-capitalisation or a reunion of the labour to the means of production. Kalyan Sanyal's conceptualisation of post-colonial capitalism rests on the division between accumulation economy and the need economy (Sanyal, 2007). The accumulation economy is that part of the economy which contributes to the production, appropriation and distribution of surplus value. The other part of the vast majority which constitutes the informal economy has no contribution to the process of capitalist accumulation. They are the need economy who survives on the basis of transfer of surplus from the accumulation economy. Such a characterisation actually undermines the crucial role of this vast unprotected labour in the process of capitalist accumulation. There are various dimensions of value capture on which the current neoliberal regime relies upon. Marx's discussion on surplus value primarily focuses on exploitation that assumes workers are paid wages equivalent to the value of labour power. Marx's intention was to show that even if exchanges take place on the basis of equivalence of value and if worker is paid the full value of labour power then also exploitation takes place because the value created by the expenditure of labour is much higher than the value of labour power. Labour receives wages on the basis of what s/he sells rather than what is being produced by the labour. But in the real world there is no pure capitalism existing where wages are at least paid as equivalent to the value of labour power. Rather in most of the cases labour are paid wages that are below the value of labour power. In other words more the fragmentation of production takes place through subcontracting and outsourcing, undervaluing labour has become the norm of competition. A vast majority of the informal labour are engaged in productive activity in subhuman conditions that feed into super profits of multinationals as well as that of domestic capital. This regime of expropriation is intrinsic to the current process of accumulation and rising self-employment and tiny enterprises reflect capitalism's incapacity to employ people on conditions that it had to concede during the 'Golden Age'.

Unemployment has also been caused by various dimensions of dispossession. It is important to note that the current phase of dispossession is markedly different from Marx's narration of primitive accumulation of capital. In Marx's narrative, primitive accumulation was characterised as a combination of three distinct processes which may be separated by time and space. The first process is of alienating direct producer from their means of production; secondly, the appropriated means of production is turned into capital and thirdly, dispossessed people are forcibly turned into commodity, labour power. It is also not the case that people displaced during the Industrial Revolution in the West were absorbed entirely by emerging factories. Rather capitalism found the solution by moving people from metropolitan areas to new white settlements. In the current scenario people who were displaced and dispossessed either because of 'developmental projects' or because of facilitating corporate mining or 'land acquisition' are hardly being absorbed as wage labourers (Roy, 2020). Instead the huge mass of dispossessed people lose their livelihood and essentially earn their living either by offering low waged work in the informal segment or as beggars, rag pickers, hawkers, vegetable vendors, rickshaw pullers, drug peddlers and prostitutes in urban areas which constitute the dark underbelly of modern capitalism. This is the 'wretched of the earth' which survives by negotiating with capitalism mostly by accepting undervaluation of their labour or are simply excluded from the realm of capital relations.

New Technology and Unemployment

The spurt of new technological innovation has been a major impetus of growth, new investment, new productive activities, demand and employment that saved capitalism from sinking into perpetual stagnation. In fact technological innovation and state intervention are the two most important social forces that triggers necessary bouts of investments required to maintain the minimum profit rate for capitalism to sustain. The processes that influence innovation are largely being determined by the competition between capitals as introducing new technology creates possibilities of profit over and above the general rate of profit so long as the new technology is not being diffused as the average technology of the industry. The growth of labour force is mostly determined by natural factors and there is no reason in capitalism as a system driven by uncoordinated profit motives that the growth of innovation and that of labour force would converge. Instead the growth of innovation is likely to be faster than the growth of labour force and as in capitalism the prime motive of innovation is to transfer and internalise idiosyncratic human skills into standardised machines; technological progress essentially means less use of 'living' labour. However new technologies although reduce the use of labour in the existing production process but it may create new jobs that are employed to produce new machines and their components or allied services. Only if the diffusion of technology is widely spread and fast enough, then productivity may increase at all levels giving rise to a real income effect and hence higher demand for goods and services. In such a scenario employment can increase in the net even if a particular technology may be labour displacing.

In fact technologies are meant to reduce human effort and human civilisation is simply a progress featured by discoveries of simple tools to complex machines that allow people to produce similar things with much less effort. The important question however is why such innovations bring in considerable anxiety and pain to a vast section of employed mass who see the threat of job loss. Reducing human effort to produce the necessaries of life should provide enough disposable time to people who can use that time into more creative activities. But responses on the contrary had been rise in working time of existing employees together with large number of people facing the threat of unemployment.

Introduction of new technology such as Artificial Intelligence, Internet of Things and Robotics are posing new challenge to the existing labour force. AI internalises processes that involve formal reasoning and can replace human beings easily in repetitive jobs. Machines can easily translate and create regular texts as newspaper articles, can write legal petitions, make predictions on stock market trading, can replace humans in a whole range of customer service and business processes. We are entering the age of driverless cars, assessing repayment capacity in banks can be done by a machine and human resource management would be efficiently done by a machine. Robots are used in the shop floors for material handling, assembling of parts and so on. A drastic fall in computing cost, digital storage and cloud computing allow firms to reduce their fixed costs and real time management of resources. All these developments are likely to make a large number of existing human activities redundant in the coming decades.

In the earlier Industrial Revolutions, particularly in the 19th and 20th centuries rise in productivity growth in agriculture led to a release of an enormous number of unskilled workers who were to be employed in industrial activities. One of the important features of early technological revolutions was that they could employ huge number of unskilled workers because most of the technologies were labour-intensive in nature. Apart from that, capitalism could find new areas of investment and employment in new found lands as well could generate huge profits by extracting wealth from colonies. The current technological revolution is markedly different from the earlier ones as new innovations and machines are primarily a response to the huge supply of educated workforce that grew over time both in advanced and developing countries. As a result of which low skilled repetitive jobs which would be lost in the process would not be absorbed anymore. According to a World Bank estimate that 35 per cent of workers in the United Kingdom and 47 per cent of those in the USA are at the risk of being displaced in the next 20 years. Such estimates on developing countries done by the World Bank suggest that 69 per cent in India, 72 per cent in Thailand, 77 per cent in China and 85 per cent in Ethiopia would be facing technology-led displacement (ILO, 2015, 143). It is also argued that as the use of robots increases and their costs decline, relocation of labour-intensive jobs to developing countries in search of low wages would no longer remain relevant.

Moreover studies suggest that the productivity growth triggered by new technology has not been very significant to the level the growth was impacted earlier by inventions of electricity and so on (David, 1990). But in future this may not be the case as the diffusion of technology takes time to emerge as a paradigmatic shift in the production process. What is even more significant is the fact that the diffusion of new technology in earlier phases of capitalism was largely driven by the market. The current phase of technological change depends on knowledge and knowledge being a non-rival input, the market mechanism is not the appropriate mode to trigger competition and diffusion of technology. In fact many information and knowledge in today's world is accessible through internet free of cost. And unlike all other inputs the stock of knowledge does not deplete through its uses rather increases through interaction and exchange. In such a context internalising natural processes in new machines that increases productivity is a result of social knowledge to which assigning private property rights become detrimental to the progress of knowledge itself. For instance, by the use of robots the productivity of the supervisor in a shop floor increases manifold but that cannot be appreciated as the result of rise in individual efficiency or productivity of the particular supervisor. Rather it is the outcome of social wisdom that evolved through various layers of interaction. In other words, production is immensely socialised while capital wants to establish property rights on this knowledge which essentially restricts the flow of knowledge.

The other problem with the introduction of new technology as discussed is the possibility of rising unemployment which finally leads to chronic demand shortage. One of the distinctive features of capitalism is that it only recognises labour power as commodity and the only means of distribution of output is wage or salary against employment. In other words, work which is not hired as a commodity is beyond the radar of capitalism and hence there is no rationale to share income or benefits for work which is not being hired. Therefore the burgeoning army of unemployed should not have any income according to capitalist logic. But capitalism has to reconcile to the fact that such a large share of population cannot be deported to new found land anymore and also cannot be left without income because that becomes politically unsustainable beyond a point. Therefore, there has to be a transfer of surplus for those excluded in the form of credits, income transfer or even an overarching scheme of universal basic income. In fact the increasing debates and discussion on UBI basically reflect the fact that capitalism is no longer able to employ the available labour force and since it can only recognise labour power as a commodity, it is not able to find a mechanism to reconcile the burgeoning gap between production and consumption.

Conclusion

The current phase of capitalism is characterised by high concentration of ownership together with increased fragmentation of the work process. On the one hand there are waves of mergers and acquisitions through which MNCs and TNCs give rise to the global edifice of capital control, on the other hand it unleashes labour processes that stretches from large factories to tiny homework integrated at the global scale. The inclusion/exclusion dynamics of capitalism is articulated through layers of exploitation, expropriation and exclusion. Every bit of the human life process gets subordinated to the imperatives of global capital. From formal wage contract to various layers of subcontracting and outsourcing capital internalises the large chunk of non-capital relations and self-employment into its own ambit. Moreover there seems to be an explosion of the working day which defined the boundaries of working time and disposable labour time and actually the realm of production and reproduction collapses into one. Capital establishes control over the life process of human beings, colonises every bit of human engagement and destroys existing norms of contract. Bare survival and reproduction of life demands more working hours and gradual erosion of protective institutions erases the differences between formal and informal workers. Wage employment, self-employment, bonded labour, slave labour and various other precarious forms of labour with the most modern forms of platform labour collude into one whole of the 'social labour'. This objectivity extends capital-labour conflict beyond the realm of factory and invokes a society wide class struggle.

It is also important to note that measures of returns to labour based on individual productivity is increasingly becoming meaningless. Human civilisation has entered into a phase of technological progress where individual capabilities are increasingly embedded into social capabilities. Direct human labour has a limited role in managing the functioning of social knowledge embodied in machines. Production would require less and less direct human effort with the use of new technology. The labour time saved in this process should enable human beings to engage in more creative work rather than being bogged down into producing bare necessities. But the current system does not allow such development because it is based on private property and tries to appropriate the gains of technology in terms of profit accumulation. Technological development is not the problem in itself rather the real evil is capitalism which restricts the fruits of technology in terms of private appropriation. With the use of machines people should get more free time, to think, to create and enjoy labour at their will. But since in capitalism machines, labour process and fruits of labour are appropriated by a handful of capitalists, instead of free time new technology creates unemployment on the one hand and hyper-work on the other.

The production of knowledge demands a space for cumulative learning. And knowledge being non-rival in nature grows with continuous interaction and dissemination. Capitalism on the contrary reproduces a structure and facilitates property rights on knowledge. If we are really heading towards more use of knowledge inputs, a supportive environment of learning needs to be created. Instead of repetitive and routine work, existing labour force should get ample time to accumulate new knowledge, to think and apply them in solving new challenges and a collabourative milieu needs to be created that is far beyond the drudgery of wage labour. Employment-unemployment is a social construct which emerged in a particular juncture of history when human labour is being turned into commodity labour power in capitalism. Such a structure no longer seems to be appropriate regarding the progress of human knowledge. New technology demands a new collabourative environment that breaks the division of employment and unemployment, reinstates labour as the most creative, free and joyful act of human species and distributes the gains of social knowledge according to the needs of social progress.

REFERENCES

David, P.A. (1990), The Dynamo and the Computer: A Historical Perspective on the Modern Productivity Paradox, *American Economic Review Papers and Proceedings*, pp. 355-61.

ILO (2015), *World Employment Social Outlook 2015: The Changing Nature of Jobs*, Geneva: International Labour Organisation.

IMF (2007), *World Economic Outlook, April 2007: Spillovers and Cycles in the Global Economy*, Washington, DC: International Monetary Fund.

IMF (2017), *World Economic Outlook, April 2017: Gaining Momentum?* Washington, DC: International Monetary Fund.

Marx, K. (1958), *Capital: A Critique of Political Economy*, Vol. I, Moscow: Foreign Languages Publishing House.

NSSO (2017), Key Indicators of Unincorporated Non-Agricultural

Enterprise (excluding construction) of the 73rd Round (2015-16) KI (73/234).

Roy, Satyaki (2011), High Non-wage Employment in India: Revisiting the Paradox in Capitalist Development, *Indian Journal of Labour Economics*, Vol. 54, No. 2, pp. 251-67.

Roy, Satyaki (2020), *Contours of Value Capture: India's Neoliberal Path of Industrial Development*, UK: Cambridge University Press.

Sanyal, K. (2007), *Rethinking Capitalist Development: Primitive Accumulation, Governmentality and Post-Colonial Capitalism*, London, New York, Delhi: Routledge.

8

Can Capitalism Survive the High Degree of Automation? A Comparison with Thomas Piketty's Argument[1]

V. Upadhyay

There is a growing recent debate in the West whether we are witnessing the phenomenon of technological unemployment caused by increasing automation in all spheres of economic activity, unemployment that is distinct from cyclical unemployment, or structural unemployment caused by trade and globalisation, or even that existing in the form of the reserve army. Mainstream economists reject outright this possibility. They point out that this argument is not a new one.[2] It has been made many times earlier during the two-century long history of industrial growth and that it especially springs up during the recessionary phases. When the economy recovers from downturn, it is argued, employment also grows with output and productivity.

If we look at the historical experience, this assertion generally holds. There have been many recessionary episodes during this long period in the industrially advanced countries of Europe and North America, but these economies eventually recovered and resumed the growth process. This is even true of the Great Depression during the early 1930s. Here, however, one has to acknowledge the fact that the Second World War played a decisive role in the process of economic revival.

The main argument in support of the proposition of the 'impossibility of technological unemployment' runs as follows: Labour-saving technological change reduces demand for labour.

However, at the same time, by reducing costs and prices of products, it 'frequently leads to increases in output demand; greater output demand results in increased production, which requires more labour, offsetting the employment effects of reduction in labour requirements per unit of output stemming from technological change.'[3]

According to this view, 'automation and other forms of technological progress, in aggregate, create more jobs than they destroy.[4, 5]

This view, however, has been challenged by Jared Bernstein, Erik Brynjolfsson, Andrew Mcafee and others[6], who, through their research, reveal decoupling of productivity and employment. As Brynjolfsson and Mcafee (2014) point out,

> While these two key economic statistics tracked each other for most of the post-war period, they became decoupled in the late 1990s. Productivity continued its upward path while employment sagged. Today, the employment-population ratio is lower than any other time in at least the last twenty years, and the real income of the median worker is lower today than in the 1990s. Meanwhile, like productivity, GDP, corporate investment and after-tax profits are also at record highs (Brynjolfsson and Mcafee, 2014, 78).

As Summers (2014) puts it,

> It is not always true that innovation creates more employment. There is nothing in the logic of the market or human experience to suggest that it must necessarily be so that there will be jobs for all at acceptable wages, no matter how technology evolves.

Summers points out that, 'In 1965, in the US, one in 20 men between the ages of 25 and 54 were not working, now it is one in six.'

Over the past century, agriculture has shed most of the jobs it used to provide. Now very few people are employed in agriculture, for example, between 1-2 per cent of the labour force in the industrialised countries. With mechanisation, agricultural productivity rose spectacularly, reducing the demand for agricultural workers. What has happened in agriculture is now happening in manufacturing and services sectors. Like in agriculture earlier, output per worker in these sectors is increasing rapidly. It means that with the application of technology, far more output is being produced with far fewer workers.[7] In China, which is the global manufacturing workshop, manufacturing employment is only 15 per cent of the workforce. Between 1995 and 2002, China has suffered heavy loss in manufacturing jobs, about 16 million according to some estimates. South Korea, which has experienced one of the fastest rates of industrial growth during the later part of the 20th century, had 28 per cent share of manufacturing jobs in the total workforce in 1989, which since then, has declined to by 10 percentage points.[8] In all major industrialised countries manufacturing sector is not creating any new jobs. The situation in services sector is no different. Workers displaced by mechanisation in agriculture could move to manufacturing or services. But when all sectors in the economy are losing jobs, where can people find jobs?

The effects of new technologies are now not limited to loss of low-skill jobs only. Its effects have now reached the middle-level segment. The new information and communication technologies, by automating many routine tasks, are in fact eliminating clerical and professional employment opportunities.

According to Autor and Dorn (2013), a process of "polarisation" of the workforce has been taking place in most industrialised countries for the last several decades. This process is leading to "hollowing out" of the middle class: jobs that fall in the middle part of the job hierarchy, jobs that provided middle-class pay, are now increasingly being handled by computers.[9] At the same time, higher paying jobs that require sophisticated skills needed for the development of new technologies are not under threat.

The rapid acceleration of technological progress is also contributing to increasing income inequalities in the industrialised countries. Large scale displacement of workers by automation is an obvious causal factor. This is creating a large pool of people who are being rendered jobless as well as without any source of purchasing power. This will increase the gap between the rich and the poor, which has already become unsustainable, both economically as well as socially. There is, however, another factor that is also at work here. As mentioned above, the higher-paying jobs are not affected that much by the automation process. Not only that, digital technologies are creating a world which favours "superstars". These are the people who actually occupy central positions in the technology development arena and they are paid "super salaries", salaries in millions or even billions of dollars. This is the world where the winners take all; and the losers get zero. The role of this phenomenon in increasing income inequalities cannot be underestimated.

As pointed out by Marx in the middle of the 19th century, the capitalist system knows no limits to the accumulation of capital. It is within reason to imagine that the process of automation could acquire such an accelerating pace that, in the coming decades, production activities would mostly be performed by robots. In an experiment that 'reflects the reality that there is no 'iron law' that technological progress must always be accompanied by broad job creation', Brynjolfsson and Mcafee (2014) write,

> Imagine that tomorrow a company introduced androids that could do absolutely everything a human worker could do, including building more androids. There's an endless supply of these robots, and they're extremely cheap to buy and virtually free to run over time. They work all day, every day, without breaking down.

Clearly, the economic implications of such an advance would be profound. First of all, productivity and output would skyrocket. The androids would operate the farms and factories. Food and food production will become much cheaper to produce. In a competitive market, in fact, their prices would fall close to cost of their raw materials. Around the world, we'd see an amazing increase in the volume, variety and affordability of offerings. The androids, in short, would bring great bounty.

They would also bring severe dislocations to the labour force. Every economically rational employer would prefer androids, since compared to the status quo they provide equal capability at lower cost. So they would very quickly replace most, if not all, human workers. Entrepreneurs would continue to develop novel products, create new markets, and found companies, but they'd staff these companies with androids instead of people (Brynjolfsson and Mcafee, 2014, 84).

The historical experience of capitalism also reveals a tendency of concentration of productive capital in ever fewer hands. In an extreme case scenario, the ownership of all robots may be vested in the hands of a few people. In such a situation, Brynjolfsson and Mcafee (2014) predict that: 'The owners of the androids and other capital assets or natural resources would capture all the value in the economy, and do all the consuming.'[10] There is, however, a logical fallacy in this proposition. In such an extreme situation, most people are unemployed and thus have no income. There is thus no labour income in the economy other than superstars' incomes. As the ownership of robots is highly concentrated, capital income accrues to only a handful of people. Then the question who will do the consuming acquires special importance. In a completely robotised economy, production of commodities will necessarily be on a large scale. But as general masses have no income or purchasing power, they are not part of the demand for the produced items. Is it then possible that a few multi-billionaire owners of robots will be able to generate sufficient demand for the mass produced items even if they have the purchasing power to do so? To put it differently, will a robot owner with hundreds of billion dollars of capital income purchase a fifty thousand cars? The answer is a clear no. He or she might only purchase a few dozen highly expensive cars. But these cars are not a product of a robotised system: the high value of cars is solely due to branding.

This raises a serious question about the survivability of capitalism, a system that works for profit motive. In a highly automated system of mass production with highly concentrated ownership of productive capital, profit realisation becomes impossible as demand for items produced on a mass scale does not exist.

In the foregoing analysis, we have focused on income inequalities generated in the production system. But there are huge income and wealth inequalities whose sources lie beyond the production system.

Income and wealth inequalities are not only influenced by economic forces but also by changes in political power relations.[11] Workings of markets, of assets (physical or financial) or of natural resources, produce enormous inequalities. At the same time distribution of income and wealth is impacted, crucially, by the balance of class power and changes therein as it determines government policies and laws related to taxation, finance, inheritance, gifts, etc., which have a tremendous bearing on the final amounts received by individuals in the forms of incomes from capital and labour, or wealth transfers. Thomas Piketty's recently published magnum opus *Capital in the Twenty-First Century* deals with these issues in such great details and so thoroughly as not seen for a long time.

Piketty's basic proposition is that: 'When the rate of return on capital exceeds the rate of growth of output and income, as it did in the 19th century, and seems quite likely to do again in the 21st century, capitalism automatically generates arbitrary and unsustainable inequalities....'[12]

In order to understand Piketty's argument, it is necessary to understand his use of the term 'capital'. He uses the terms 'capital' and 'wealth' interchangeably, as if they were perfectly synonymous. According to his definition, national wealth or national capital is:

> (T)he total market value of everything owned by the residents and government of a given country at a given point in time, provided that it can be traded on some market. It consists of the sum of total non-financial assets (land, dwellings, commercial inventory, other buildings, machinery, infrastructure, patents and other directly owned professional assets) and financial assets (bank accounts, mutual funds, bonds, stocks, financial investments of all kinds, insurance policies, pension funds, etc), less the total amount of financial liabilities (debt) (Piketty, 2014, 48).

His definition of capital thus is much wider than the commonly used definition of capital, productive capital to be precise: industrial plants, official buildings, machinery, infrastructure, etc.

His fundamental inequality, r>g (where r stands for average annual return on capital, and g stands for the rate of growth of the economy), is not a law in the sense of being derived from any theoretical framework or abstract model. It is basically an empirical observation, spanning a very long period of more than two hundred years.

Piketty estimates the average annual rates of return on capital in the advanced industrial countries in the late 20th and early 21st centuries to be around 4-5 per cent and takes this level as the level likely to prevail in the future as well. His prediction for the long term per capita growth in the wealthy countries is of 1.2 per cent (which he calls the median scenario). This is slightly higher than the prediction of growth made by Gordon (2012) for the advanced countries including the United States.

According to Piketty's estimates, the capital-income ratio in Britain and France in 2010 is roughly 5-6 and is about 4 in the United States. Based on the trend analysis of the data pertaining to recent decades in the rich countries, he predicts that the capital-income ratio is likely to rise in the future.

On the basis of the estimates of r, g and the capital-income ratio and the current trends, Piketty predicts 'a durable increase in capital's share of national income' in the twenty-first century, implying a secular fall in labour's share of national income.[13]

One major criticism of Piketty's approach is that he does not explain 'where the rate of return comes from.' David Harvey points out that the valuation of capital and calculation of rate of return are difficult technical problems that have no agreed upon technical solutions. According to Harvey, one major weakness of Piketty's framework is that it does not provide any theoretical explanation for high rate of return on capital. Harvey's own explanation for the phenomenon is:

> If the rate of return on capital that is being used is high then this is because a part of capital is withdrawn from circulation and in effect goes on strike. Restricting the supply of capital to new investment (a phenomenon we are now witnessing) ensures a high rate of return on that capital which is in circulation. This creation of such artificial scarcity is not only what the oil companies do to ensure their high rate of return: it is what all capital does when given the chance. This

> is what underpins the tendency for the rate of return on capital (no matter how it is defined and measured) to always exceed the rate of growth of income.

Harvey's criticism here, however, is not valid for two reasons. One, Harvey's focus is largely on productive capital whereas by capital Piketty means wealth. Secondly, Harvey shows high rate of return on 'used' capital, whereas Piketty talks about average rate of return on total capital, used as well as unused.

As mentioned earlier, Piketty's estimates of r, g and capital-income ratio and the predictions about their future tendencies are based on the analysis of historical observations. There is thus not much consideration given to production and its linkages to distribution, technology, productivity and employment and unemployment. The question of technological unemployment, therefore, does not arise in his framework. He, in fact, does not appear to be overly worried about the prospect of unemployment caused by automation as is clear from his following remarks:

> We are free to imagine an ideal society in which all other tasks are totally automated and each individual has as much freedom as possible to pursue the goods of education, culture and health for the benefit of herself and others. Everyone would be by turns teacher or student, writer or reader, actor or spectator, doctor or patient (Piketty, 2014, 308).

Piketty's main concern is about rising inequalities caused primarily by rising share of capital income of total income. 'The distribution of capital ownership (and of income from capital) is always more concentrated than the distribution of income from labour….the bottom 50 per cent of the wealth distribution owns nothing at all, or almost nothing (less than 10 per cent and generally less than 5 per cent of total wealth, or one-tenth as much as the wealthiest 10 per cent).'[14] According to Oxfam, the richest 85 people on the planet owned as much wealth as the poorest half of humanity. In Piketty's view, 'the growth of a true patrimonial (or propertied) middle class was the structural transformation of the distribution of wealth in the developed countries in the 20th century.'[15] If the present inequality trends continue in the future along with worsening concentration of wealth, the picture of the world that emerges is indeed very frightening. To quote Piketty:

> Will the world in 2050 or 2100 be owned by traders, top managers, and the superrich , or will it belong to the oil producing countries or the Bank of China? Or perhaps it will be owned by the tax havens in which many of these actors will have sought refuge. It would be absurd not to raise the question of who will own what and simply to assume from the outset that growth is naturally "balanced" in the long run (Piketty, 2014, 15-16).

It is interesting to compare the scenarios regarding the level of inequalities in the future generated by the two clearly different frameworks: One, that focuses on increasing automation of the production process combined with high concentration of the ownership of productive capital, and the other, that argues that the rate of return on capital (wealth) is likely to remain higher than the growth rate of income in future, leading to high concentration of the ownership of capital (wealth). The similarity in the projected outcomes is quite striking. Both viewpoints see inequalities taking extreme forms in the coming decades to the extent that the vast majority of people are left with no income or purchasing power. As discussed above, this raised the question about the survivability of capitalism in the long run. There are, however, important differences between the two approaches and these have implications with respect to the remedies suggested to save capitalism from demise.

Piketty's massive book's main focus turns out to be on the capital (wealth) inequalities. The most significant remedial measure to save capitalism that emerges from his work is therefore naturally focused on "a progressive global tax on capital." To quote Piketty:

> Can we imagine a 21st century in which capitalism will be transcended in a more peaceful and lasting way, or must we simply await the next crisis or the next war (this time truly global)? On the basis of the history, I have brought to light here, can we imagine political institutions that might regulate today's patrimonial capitalism just as well as efficiently?..........the ideal policy for avoiding an endless

> inegalitarian spiral and regaining control over the dynamics of progressive accumulation would be a progressive global tax on capital (Piketty, 2014, 471).

In addition to a tax on capital, Piketty also argues for a progressive tax on income as well as progressive real estate tax. These three progressive taxes, in his view, could play 'distinct and complementary roles.'

As we have discussed above, Piketty's work lacks a serious analysis of the production system. In that sense, no serious consideration is given to the possibility of mass unemployment caused by technological progress. Generally speaking, his system allows for the possibility of near-full employment continuing prevailing in the future. If that is the case, raising minimum wages could be an effective way of lowering the rate of return on capital. As Galbraith (2014) observes:

> If the heart of the problem is a rate of return on private assets that is too high, the better solution is to lower the rate of return. How? Raise minimum wages! That lowers the rate of return on capital that relies on low-wage labour.

In the framework that focuses on technological unemployment, mass unemployment is the reality. Here, the minimum wages solution would not work. If people are not working, how would they be paid wages? The most appropriate solution in such a situation would be 'sharing of work': the work week could be reduced to 15 or even 10 hours.[16] It could be argued that social control of productive capital could prevent all capital income from going to only a few people. But here we are talking about more than transcending capitalism 'in a more peaceful and lasting way.' This is, in fact, a case for building a socialist society.

In the prevailing political conditions, all these remedies/ suggestions are non-starter; they are just utopian ideas. These can have practical significance only if there is a political change in every nation such that the common people take control of things in their own hands and there is cooperation between nations regarding control over cross-border movements of capital.

NOTES

1. This paper was published in Upadhyay, V. (2016), (ed.), *Essays on Distribution, World Systems, Ecology, and Left Politics.* New Delhi: Daanish Books.
2. During the second decade of the 19th century, a group of textile workers in England, led by Ned Ludd, attempted to destroy automated looms as they feared that these machines would destroy their jobs. If technological unemployment is becoming a reality now, then it can be said that 'the Luddite moment' has arrived, even if two hundred years late.
3. Brynjolfsson and Mcafee, 2014, p. 81.
4. Ibid.
5. This viewpoint is very succinctly expressed by the CEO of a major Indian IT company in the following words: 'I want to make a big mention of automation. Artificial intelligence as a domain is not very well understood. It is often associated with precipitating...the irrelevance of humanity. Having studied at Stanford and other places at the feet of the pioneers of this domain, I see the world fundamentally differently. Technology has always been about the amplification of the human being. About augmenting them with new capabilities, not about making them irrelevant.' (Infosys CEO, Vishal Sikka, quoted in *The Economic Times*, October 17, 2014).
6. In his 1949 article "Why Socialism?" Albert Einstein commented, "Technological progress frequently results in more unemployment rather than in an easing of the burden of work for all."
7. In the early 1980s, W. Leontif warned that 'the role of humans as the most important factor of production is bound to diminish in the same way that the role of horses on agricultural production was first diminished and then eliminated by the introduction of tractors.' (W. Leontif quoted in Brynjolfsson and Mcafee, 2014) However the US economy's performance in the area of growth and employment during the last two decades of the 20th century made people ignore such fears.
8. Robots, automation and 3D printing pose a threat to human involvement at the workplace not only in the industrialised countries but also in the emerging economies. In India, for example, for about two decades, the IT services industry has been a major job provider to the college-educated. But now the big firms are planning to deploy automation in a big way, especially in the areas such as software testing

and maintenance of infrastructure. This is certain to impact job opportunities, especially at the middle level: the case of "hollowing" of the middle class (see *The Economic Times*, September 30, 2014).

9. See Brynjolfsson and Mcafee, 2012.
10. Brynjolfsson and Mcafee, 2014, p. 84.
11. Stigtitz (2014) writes: 'What we have been observing—wage stagnation and rising inequality, even as wealth increases—does not reflect the working of a normal market economy, but of what I call "ersatz capitalism." The problem may not be with how markets should or do work, but with our political system, which has failed to ensure that markets are competitive, and has designed rules that sustain distorted markets in which corporations and the rich can (and unfortunately do) exploit everyone else.'
12. Piketty, 2014, p. 1.
13. Economic Report of the President, Transmitted to the Congress, March 2013, shows: 'The labour share in the United States was remarkably stable in the post-war period until the early 2000s. Since then, it has dropped 5 percentage points.' (p. 60).
14. Piketty, 2014, p. 244.
15. Ibid., p. 260.
16. The suggestion of 'sharing of work' also emerges from the Degrowth perspective that stresses that, in order to avoid the irreversible damage to our ecology that threatens life on earth, economic growth in industrialised countries would need to be checked. The problems of poverty and unemployment that arise due to lack of economic growth could be tackled through distributional measures involving not only sharing of income and wealth, but also work. As Onaran (2010) puts it, full employment can only be achieved through shorter working times.

REFERENCES

Autor, David H. and D. Dorn (2013), The Growth of Low-Skilled Service Jobs and Polarisation of the US Labour Market, *The American Economic Review*, Vol. 103, No. 5.

Brynjolfsson, E. and A. Mcafee (2012), *Race Against the Machine*, Cambridge: The MIT Centre for Digital Business.

Brynjolfsson, E. and A. Mcafee (2014), *The Second Machine Age*, New York: WW Norton and Company.

Economic Report of the President Transmitted to the Congress (2013), United States Government Printing Office.

Galbraith, James K., Thomas Piketty's *Capital in the Twenty-First Century*, Alertnet (https://www.alertnet.com).

Gordon, R. (2012), Is US Economic Growth Over? Faltering Innovation Confronts the Six Headwinds, *NBER Working Paper*, No. 18315, August.

Harvey, D. (2014), Afterthoughts on Piketty's *Capital*, Website: https://davidharvey.org/2014/05/afterthoughts-pikettys-capital/

Onaran, O. (2010), The Crisis of Capitalism in Europe, West and East, *Analytical Monthly Review*, Vol. 8, No. 7.

Piketty, T. (2014), *Capital in the Twenty-First Century*, Cambridge, Massachusetts: The Belknap Press of Harvard University Press.

Stiglitz, Joseph E. (2014), Democracy in the Twenty-First Century, Project Syndicate (https://www.project-syndicate.org/)

Summers, L. (2014), Robots are Already Taking Your Jobs, Interview Published in *Financial Times*, August 11.

9

The Agrarian Question a Century After 1917: Capitalism in Agriculture and Agricultures in Capitalism[1]

Samir Amin

Introduction

Authored in commemoration of 1917, this article addresses one of the key dimensions confronting the Russian and Chinese revolutions, that of the agrarian question for the peasantry which constituted popular majorities in each of these countries at the time of their revolutions. These two great revolutions were confronted by three other major challenges. The first challenge originated in the fact that these revolutions with socialist goals had triumphed in 'single countries'—albeit the size of continents; two countries, moreover, situated in the peripheries of the global system of capitalism. An important issue concerned the question of how to progress towards a perspective with a universal reach, under conditions of permanent hostility and violence characterising the intrinsically imperialist processes of capitalist globalisation.

The second challenge concerned the question of democracy. How to construct practices capable of promoting the democratisation of society? How to create institutions for a new participative democracy, which would guarantee a role for all workers in the decision-making processes at all levels of economic and social governance? How was this to be achieved without sacrificing personal rights, but, instead, integrating individual emancipation, through the deployment of personal liberty and creativity, as a key dynamic in the development of society?

The third challenge concerns the ecological dimension which 21st-century socialism must boldly address as a fundamental point of departure in shaping a vision of a socialist future and the concrete policies required to achieve it. Establishing a harmonious relationship between society and nature demands a radical break with the dominant logics of capitalism predicated on the essential destruction of the material basis of society and the reproduction of life on the planet.

My book entitled *October 1917 Revolution, A Century Later* (Amin, 2017) proposes a comprehensive analysis of these challenges, organised around the central theme of Soviet isolation imposed by imperialist globalisation. This work places the focus on the particular challenge posed by the peasant question. I emphasise the examination of this issue primarily because contemporary and largely urban social movements generally ignore it, thereby constraining the formulation of a coherent strategy for socialism in the 21st century. In this respect, this work is situated alongside publications inspired by the works of Sam Moyo, whose authors recognise the importance of the new agrarian question.

The first issue presented here concerns the manner through which historical capitalism has 'settled' the (agrarian) question, in favour of minorities comprising the populations of the developed capitalist economies of the centre (about 15 per cent of the total world population). Is the reproduction of this model of 'development' feasible or achievable for the populations of contemporary Asia, Africa and South America? My response to this question is negative, and as a result, the contemporary world is confronted with a challenge which, I argue, can only be solved by a bold vision of socialism.

The second issue concerns the strategy of stages which I propose as a longer-term process of constructing a socialist alternative for the populations of these three continents. As it must, the new agrarian question is the key issue to be addressed in the processes of building socialism in the 21st century.

Historical capitalism provided its own types of solutions to the agrarian problem in Europe and the USA. Theorists and ideologists of capitalism all imagined that this same solution would result from the transfer and application of organisational models derived from large-scale industry to agriculture. History has proved them wrong. The solution has actually operated in a very different manner; notably, through the emergence of new strata of the bourgeoisie, made up of 'agriculturalists' (who are no longer peasants). Today, the capture of agriculture by large-scale corporate capital in the financial monopolies places the future of family farming in jeopardy while new strategies deployed by the agro-industrial complex aim to substitute family farms with agri-business.

Soviet socialism inherited the dominant conception of the 19th century, transmitted by Kautsky and inspired by the model of Soviet collectivisation. In my book cited above, I articulate the reasons why I consider this as the fundamental mistake underlying the rupture of the worker-peasant alliance—which had itself assured the success of the October Revolution. By avoiding this mistake, Maoism, on the other hand, opened up to a different path for the resolution of the peasant question founded on the principle of equal access to land for all rural people. This continues to be relevant for the future of the populations of Asia, Africa and South America. The distinction I make between capitalist agriculture and agriculture under capitalism constitutes, in my humble opinion, a new contribution which historical Marxism and, *a fortiori*, bourgeois theories, have ignored (Kautsky, [1899] 1988).

In the North: An Efficient Family Agriculture Perfectly Integrated into Dominant Capitalism

Modern family agriculture, dominant in Western Europe and in the USA, has clearly shown its superiority when compared to other forms of agricultural production. Annual production per worker (the equivalent of 1000–2000 tons of cereal) has no equal, and it has enabled a minimum proportion of the active population (about 5 per cent) to supply the whole country abundantly and even produce exportable surpluses. Modern family agriculture has also shown an exceptional capacity for absorbing innovations and much flexibility in adapting to demand.

This agriculture does not share the specific characteristic of capitalism, its main mode of labour organisation. In the factory, the number of workers enables an advanced division of labour, which is at the origin of the leap in productivity. In the agricultural family business, labour supply is reduced to one or two individuals (the farming couple), some- times helped by one, two, or three associates or permanent labourers, but also, in certain cases, a larger number of seasonal workers (particularly for the harvesting of fruit and vegetables). Generally speaking, there is not a definitively fixed division of labour, the tasks being polyvalent and variable. In this sense, family agriculture is not capitalist.

However, this modern family agriculture constituted an inseparable part of the capitalist economy into which it is totally integrated. In this family agricultural business, its self-consumption no longer counts. It depends entirely for its economic legitimacy on its production for the market. Thus, the logic that commands the production options is no longer the same as that of the agricultural peasants of yesterday (analysed by Chayanov, 1966), or of today in Third World countries.

The efficiency of the agricultural family business is due to its modern equipment. They possess 90 per cent of the tractors and other agricultural equipment in use in the world. These machines are 'bought' (often on credit) by the farmers and are therefore their 'property'. In the logic of capitalism, the farmer is both a worker and a capitalist and the income earned should correspond to the sum of the wages for the work and the profit from the ownership of the capital being used. But it is not so. The net income of farmers is comparable to the average wage earned in industry in the same country. The state intervention and regulation policies in Europe and in the USA, where this form of agriculture dominates, have as their declared objective the aim of ensuring (through subsidies) the equality of 'peasant' and 'worker' incomes. The profits from the capital used by farmers are therefore collected by segments of industrial and financial capital further up the food chain.

In the family agriculture of Europe and the USA, the component of the land rent, itself meant to constitute, in conventional economics, the remuneration of the productivity of the land, does not figure in the remuneration of the farmer/owner, or the owner (when not the farmer). The French model of 'anaesthetising the owner' is very telling: in law, the rights of the farmer are given priority over those of the owner. In the USA, where 'respect for property' always has the absolute priority, the same result is obtained by forcing, de facto, almost all the family businesses to be owners of the land that they farm. The rent of ownership thus disappears from the remuneration of the farmers.

The efficiency of this family agriculture is also due to the fact that it farms (as owner or not) enough good land: neither too small nor pointlessly large. The surface farmed corresponds, for each stage of the development of mechanized equipment, to what a farmer alone (or a small family unit) can work. It has gradually expanded, as Marcel Mazoyer has extremely well demonstrated (by the facts) and illustrated (as an efficiency requirement) (Mazoyer and Roudard, 1997).

Control over agricultural production also operates down the food chain by modern commerce, particularly the supermarkets. In actual fact, the agricultural family unit, efficient as it is (and it is), is only a sub-contractor, caught in the pincers between upstream agribusiness (which imposes selected seeds today, Genetically Modified Organisms (GMOs) tomorrow), industry (which supplies the equipment and chemical products), finance (which provides the necessary credits), and downstream in the commercialisation of the supermarkets. The status of the farmer is more like that of the artisan (individual producer) who used to work in the 'putting out' system (the weaver dominated by the merchant that supplied the thread and sold the material produced).

It is true that this is not the only form of agriculture in the modern capitalist world. There are also large agribusiness enterprises, some- times big owners who employ many waged labourers (when these estates are not leased out to tenant family farmers). This was generally the case with land in the colonies and still is the case in South Africa (this form of *latifundia* having been abolished by the agrarian reform of Zimbabwe). There are various forms in Latin America, sometimes not very 'modernised' and sometimes very 'modernised' (i.e., mechanised), as in the Southern Cone. But family agriculture remains dominant in Europe and the USA.

'Really existing socialism' carried out various experiences in 'industrial' forms of agricultural production. The 'Marxism' underlying this option was that of Karl Kautsky who, at the end of the nineteenth century, had 'predicted', not the modernisation of the agricultural family business (its equipment and its specialisation), but its disappearance altogether in favour of large production units, like factories, believed to benefit from the advantages of a thoroughgoing internal division of labour. This prediction did not materialise in Europe and the USA. But the myth that it transmitted was believed in the Soviet Union, in Eastern Europe (with some nuances), in China, in Vietnam (in the modalities specific to that country) and, at one time, in Cuba. Independently of the other reasons that led to the failure of these experiences (bureaucratic management, bad macroeconomic planning, reduction of responsibilities due to lack of democracy, etc.), there were also errors of judgement about the advantages of the division of labour and specialisation, extrapolated—without justification—from certain forms of industry and applied to other fields of production and social activity.

While if the reasons for this failure are now recognized, this cannot be said for the forms of capitalist agriculture in the regions of Latin America and Southern Africa mentioned above. And yet, the failure is also obvious, despite the profitability and the competitiveness of these modernized forms of *latifundia*. For this, profitability is obtained through horrific ecological wastage (irreversible destruction of productive potential and of arable land), as well as social exploitation (miserable wages).

In the South: Poor Peasant Cultivators as Part of a Dominated Peripheral Capitalism

Peasant cultivators in the South constitute almost half of humanity— three billion human beings. The types of agriculture vary, from those that have benefited from the green revolution (fertilisers, pesticides and selected seeds)—although they are not very mechanized, their production has risen to between 100 and

500 quintals per labourer—to those which are the same as before this revolution whose production is only around 10 quintals per labourer. The gap between the average production of a farmer in the North and that of peasant agriculture, which was from 10 to 1 before 1940 is now from 100 to 1. In other words, the rate of progress in agricultural productivity has largely outstripped that of other activities, bringing about a lowering of the real price from 5 to 1. This peasant agriculture in the countries of the South is also well and truly integrated into local and world capitalism. However, closer study reveals immediately both the convergences and differences in the two types of 'family' economy.

There are huge differences, which are visible and undeniable: the importance of subsistence food in the peasant economies, the only way of survival for those rural populations; the low efficiency of this agriculture, not equipped with tractors or other materials and often highly parcellised; the poverty of the rural world (three-quarters of the victims of under-nutrition are rural); the growing incapacity of these systems to ensure food supplies for their towns; the sheer immensity of the problems, as the peasant economy affects nearly half of humanity.

In spite of these differences, peasant agriculture is already integrated into the dominant global capitalist system. To the extent of its contribution to the market, it depends on purchased inputs (at least chemical products and selected seeds) and is the victim of the oligopolies that control the marketing of these products. For the regions having 'benefited' from the 'Green Revolution' (half of the peasantry of the South) upstream and downstream, the siphoning off of profits on the products by dominant capital are very great. But they are also, in relative terms, for the other half of the peasantry of the South, taking into account the weakness of their production.

Is the Modernisation of the Agriculture of the South by Capitalism Possible and Desirable?

Let us use the hypothesis of a strategy for the development of agriculture that tries to reproduce systematically in the South the course of modern family agriculture in the North. One could easily imagine that some 50 million more modern farms, if given access to the large areas of land which would be necessary (taking it from the peasant economy and, of course, choosing the best soils) and access to the capital markets enabling them to equip themselves, they could produce the essential of what the creditworthy urban consumers still currently obtain from peasant agriculture. But what would happen to the billions of non-competitive peasant producers? They would be inexorably eliminated in a short period of time, a few decades. What would happen to these billions of human beings, most of them already the poorest of the poor, but who feed themselves, for better and/or for worse—and for a third of them, for worse? Within a time horizon of 50 years, no industrial development, more or less competitive, even in a far-fetched hypothesis of a continual annual growth of 7 per cent for three-quarters of humanity, could absorb even a third of this labour reserve. Capitalism, by its nature, cannot resolve the peasant question: the only prospects it can offer are a planet full of slums and billions of 'too many' human beings.

We have therefore reached the point where, to open up a new field for the expansion of capital ('the modernisation of agricultural production'), it is necessary to destroy—in human terms—entire societies. Fifty million new efficient producers (200 million human beings with their families), on the one hand, and three billion of excluded people, on the other. The creative aspect of the operation would be only a drop of water in the ocean of destruction that it requires. I thus conclude that capitalism has entered its phase of declining senility: the logic of the system is no longer able to ensure the simple survival of humanity. Capitalism is becoming barbaric and leads directly to genocide. It is more than ever necessary to replace it by other development logics which are more rational.

So, what is to be done?

It is necessary to accept the maintenance of peasant agriculture for all the foreseeable future of the twenty-first century. Not for reasons of romantic nostalgia for the past, but quite simply because the solution of the problem is to overtake the logics that drive capitalism and to participate in the long, secular transition to world socialism. It is, therefore, necessary to work out regulation policies for the relationships between the 'market' and peasant agriculture. At the national and regional levels, these regulations, specific and adapted to local conditions, must protect national production, thus ensuring the indispensable food sovereignty of nations—in other words, delinking the internal prices from those of the so-called world market—as they must do. A gradual increase in the productivity of peasant agriculture, which will doubtless be slow but continuous, would make it possible to control the exodus of the rural populations to the towns. At the level of what is called the world market, the desirable regulation can probably be done through interregional agreements that meet the requirements of a development that integrates people rather than excludes them.

There is No Alternative to Food Sovereignty

At the world level, food consumption is assured, through competition for 85 per cent of it, by local production. Nevertheless, this production corresponds to very different levels of satisfaction of food needs: excellent for North American and West and Central Europe, acceptable in China, mediocre for the rest of Asia and Latin America, disastrous for Africa. One can also see a strong correlation between the quality and the levels of industrialisation of the various regions: countries and regions that are more industrialised are able to feed their populations well from their own agricultural produce.

The USA and Europe have understood the importance of food sovereignty very well and have successfully implemented it by systematic economic policies. But, apparently, what is good for them is not so for the others. The World Bank, the OECD and the European Union try to impose an alternative, which is 'food security'. According to them, Third World countries do not need food sovereignty and should rely on international trade to cover the deficit in their food requirements, however large. This may seem easy for those countries which are large exporters of natural resources (oil, uranium, etc.). For the others, the 'advice' of the Western powers is to specialise their agriculture, as much as possible, in the production of agricultural commodities for export (cotton, tropical drinks and oils, agrofuels in the future). The defenders of 'food security' (for others, not for themselves) do not consider the fact that this specialisation, which has been practiced since colonialism, has not made it possible to improve the miserable food rations of the peoples concerned, especially the peasants. Nor is the above-mentioned correlation taken into account.

Thus, the advice to peasants who have not yet entered the industrial era (as in Africa) is not to engage in 'insane' industrialisation projects. These are the very terms used by Sylvie Brunel, who goes so far as attributing the failure of agricultural development in Africa to this 'insane' option of their governments! It is precisely those countries that have taken this option (Korea, Taiwan, China) that have become 'emerging countries', as well as able to feed their population better (or less badly). And it is precisely those who have not done so (Africa) that are sunk into chronic malnutrition and famine. This would not appear to embarrass the defenders of the so-called principle of 'food security' (more accurately, 'food insecurity'). There is little doubt that, underneath this obstinacy against Africa committing itself to paths inspired by the success of Asia, lies more than a touch of contempt (if not racism) towards the peoples concerned. It is regrettable that such nonsense is to be found in many of Western circles and organisations with good intentions—NGOs and even research centres.

Bruno Parmentier (2007) has clearly demonstrated the total failure of the 'food security' option. Governments who thought they could cover the need of their poor urban populations through their exports (oil, among others) have found themselves trapped by the food deficit that is growing at an alarming rate as a result of these policies. For the other countries—particulary in Africa—the situation is even more disastrous.

On top of this, the economic crisis initiated by the financial collapse of 2008 is already aggravating the situation—and will continue to do so. It is sadly amusing to note how, at the very moment when the crisis underway illustrates the failure of the so-called food security policies, the partners of the OECD (such as the EU institutions) cling to them. It is not that the governments of the Triad (the USA, Europe and Japan) do not 'understand' the problem.

This would be to deny them the intelligence that they certainly possess. So can one dismiss the hypothesis that 'food insecurity' is a consciously adopted objective? Has the 'food weapon' not already been implemented? Thus, there is an extra reason for insisting that without food sovereignty, no political sovereignty is possible.

But while there is no alternative to food sovereignty, its efficient implementation does, in fact, require the commitment to the construction of a diversified economy and, hence, industrialisation.

Land Tenure Reform is at the Heart of the Choices Concerning the Future of Peasant Societies

The main issue of the debate on the future of peasant agricultures concerns the question of the rules governing the access to land. The necessary reforms of land tenure systems in Africa and Asia must be made with the perspective of a development that benefits the whole of society, in particular the working and popular classes, including, of course, the peasants. It must be oriented towards reducing inequalities and radically eliminating 'poverty'. This development paradigm involves a combination of a mixed macroeconomy (associating private enterprise and public planning) based on the double democratisation of the management of the market and of the state and its interventions, and the option for a development of an agricultural system based on peasant family cultivation.

Implementing this set of fundamental principles—the special ways and means of each country and phase of development having to be worked out—constitutes, in itself, the construction of the 'alternative' in its national dimensions. This must, of course, be accompanied by evolutions that can support it, both at the required regional levels and at the world level, through the construction of an alternative globalisation, negotiated and no longer imposed unilaterally by dominant transnational capital, the collective imperialism of the Triad and the hegemony of the USA.

The regulations governing access to the use of agricultural land must be conceived in a perspective that 'integrates and does not exclude', that is to say, which enables cultivators as a whole to have access to the land, a prior condition for the reproduction of a 'peasant society'. This fundamental right is certainly not enough. It has also to be accompanied by policies that help the peasant family units to produce in conditions that help maintain the growth of national production (guaranteeing, in turn, the food sovereignty of the country) and a parallel improvement in the real income of the peasants involved as a whole. A collection of macro- economic proposals and forms for appropriate policy in managing them has to be implemented, and negotiations concerning the organisation of international trade must be subordinated to them.

Access to land must be regulated by the status of its ownership. The terminology used in this field is often imprecise, because of a lack of conceptualisation. In English, the words 'land tenure' and 'land system' are often used interchangeably.

First of all, it is necessary to distinguish two families of land tenure systems: those that are based on the private ownership of land and those that are not.

Land Tenure Systems Based on the Private Ownership of Land

In this case, the owner disposes of, to use the terms of Roman law, the *usus* (right to develop), the *fructus* (ownership of the products of this exploitation) and the *abusus* (the right to transfer ownership). This right is 'absolute' in that the owner can cultivate his/her own land, rent it out, or even keep it out of cultivation. Ownership can be given or sold, it is part of a collection of assets deriving from the rights of inheritance.

This right is no doubt often less absolute than it appears. In all cases, usage is subordinated to laws governing the public order (prohibiting its illegal use for growing drug-producing crops, for example) and increasing numbers of regulations concerned with preserving the environment. In certain countries that have made an agrarian reform, there is a fixed ceiling to the size of the property of an individual or a family. The rights of tenant farmers (length and guarantee of lease, the amount of land rent) limit the rights of the owners in different degrees, to the point of giving the tenant farmer the greater benefit of protection by the state and its agricultural policies (as is the case for France). The freedom to choose crops is not always the rule. In Egypt, the state agricultural services have always imposed the size of the plots of land allocated to the different crops in accordance with their irrigation requirements.

This land tenure system is modern in the sense that it is the result of the constitution of 'really existing' capitalism, starting from Western Europe (first in England) and from the colonies of European extraction in America. It was set up through the destruction of the 'customary' systems of regulating access to the land in Europe itself. The statutes of feudal Europe were founded on the superimposing of rights on the same land: those of the peasant concerned and other members of the village community (serfs or freedmen), those of the feudal lord and those of the king. The assault on these rights took the form of the Enclosures in England, imitated in various ways in all the European countries during the 19th century. Marx very soon denounced this radical transformation that excluded most of the peasants from access to the use of land—and who were destined to become emigrant proletarians in the town, or remain where they were as agricultural labourers (or sharecroppers)—and he classified these measures as primitive accumulation, dispossessing the producers of the land and the use of the means of production.

Using the terms of Roman law to describe the statute of modern bourgeois ownership imply that it dates from time immemorial, that is, the ownership of the land in the Roman Empire, and more precisely the slave-labour land ownership. In actual fact, these particular forms of ownership, having disappeared in feudal Europe, make it impossible to talk of the 'continuity' of a 'Western' concept of ownership (itself associated with individualism and the values that it represents) that has never existed.

The rhetoric of the capitalist discourse—the 'liberal' ideology—has not only produced this myth of 'Western continuity'. It has produced another myth that is still more dangerous: that of an 'absolute and superior rationality' of the management of an economy based on the private and exclusive ownership of the means of production, which include agricultural land. Conventional economics does, in fact, claim that the 'market', that is, the alienability of the ownership of capital and land, ensures the optimal usage (the most efficient) of these 'factors of production'. According to this logic, therefore, land must be turned into 'a commodity like the others', which can be alienated at the price of 'the market' to guarantee that the best use is made of it for the owner concerned and for the whole society. This is only a miserable piece of tautology, but it is what the whole discourse on which the bourgeois economy is based. This same rhetoric thinks it can legitimise the principle of ownership of the land by the fact that it alone gives the cultivator who invests to improve the yields per hectare and the productivity of his work (and of those that he employs, if this is the case) the guarantee that he will not suddenly be dispossessed of the fruits of his labour and savings.

This is not true at all, for other forms of regulations on the right of land use can produce the same results. Finally, this dominant discourse extends the conclusions that it believes to draw from the construction of Western modernity, to propose them as the only 'rules' necessary for the progress of all other peoples. Giving over the land everywhere to private ownership in the current sense of the term, such as that practised in the centres of capitalism, is to apply to the whole world the policy of the Enclosures—in other words, dispossessing the peasants. This is not a new process: it was initiated and continued during the centuries preceding the world expansion of capitalism, particularly in the colonial systems. Today, the World Trade Organisation (WTO) actually proposes to accelerate the movement, whereas the destructions that this capitalist option involves are increasingly foreseeable and calculable. For this reason, the resistance of the peasants and the peoples involved can make it possible to build a real alternative, one that is genuinely human-oriented.

Land Tenure Systems Not Based on the Private Ownership of Land

This definition, being negative, cannot apply to a homogeneous group. For, in all human societies, access to the land is regulated. But this is done either through 'customary communities', 'modern local authorities', or the state. Or, more precisely, and more often, by a collection of institutions and practices that concern individuals, local authorities and the state.

The 'customary' management (expressed in terms of customary law or so-called customary law) has almost always excluded private ownership (in the modern sense) and has always guaranteed access to the land to all the families (rather than individuals) concerned—that is, those who constitute a distinct 'village community' and identify themselves as such. But it hardly gave 'equal' access to the land. First, it usually excluded 'foreigners' (very often what remained of the conquered people) and 'slaves' (of various status); it also unequally distributed land according to membership of clans, lineage and castes, or status ('chiefs', 'freed-men', etc.). So it is inappropriate to indiscriminately praise these customary rights as is done by numerous ideologues of anti-imperialist nationalism. Progress will certainly require them to be questioned.

Customary management has almost never been that of 'independent villages', which were in fact nearly always integrated into some sort of state, stable or shifting, solid or precarious, but seldom absent. The usage rights of communities and of the families that composed them have always been limited by those of the state that received tribute (which is the reason why I described the vast array of pre-modern production modes as 'tributary').

These complex kinds of 'customary' management, which differ from one country and epoch to another, now only exist, at best, in extremely degraded forms, having suffered from the attack by the dominating logic of globalised capitalism for at least two centuries (in Asia and Africa) and sometimes five centuries (in Latin America). The example of India is probably the most striking in this regard. Before British colonisation, access to land was administered by the 'village communities' or, more exactly, their governing castes, excluding the inferior castes—the Dalits—who were treated as a kind of collective slave class, similar to the helots of Sparta. These communities, in turn, were controlled and exploited by the imperial Mughal State and its vassals (rajas and other kings), who levied the taxes. The British raised the status of the zamindars (whose responsibility it was to actually collect the taxes) to becoming 'owners', so that they constituted a kind of allied large land-owning class, regardless of tradition. On the other hand, they maintained the 'tradition' when it suited them, for example excluding the Dalits from access to land. Independent India did not challenge this heavy colonial inheritance, which is the cause of the unbelievable destitution of most of the peasantry and, thus, of its urban population (Amin, 2006, Chapter 4).

The solution to these problems and the building up of a viable peasant economy of the majority thus requires an agrarian reform, in the strict sense of the term. The European colonisation in South East Asia and that of the USA in the Philippines have had similar consequences. The regimes of the 'enlightened' despots of the East (the Ottoman Empire, the Egypt of Mohamed Ali, the Shahs of Iran) also mostly supported private ownership in the modern sense of the term for the benefit of a new class (incorrectly described as 'feudal' by the main currents of historical Marxism), required from the senior agents of their power systems.

As a result, the private ownership of land is now applicable to most agricultural land—particularly the most fertile ones—in all Asia, except for China, Vietnam and the former Soviet republics of Central Asia. There remain only the vestiges of para-customary systems, particularly in the poorest areas and those less attractive to prevailing capitalist agriculture. This structure is highly differentiated, juxtaposing large landowners (rural capitalists in my terminology), rich peasants, middle peasants and poor peasants without land. There is no peasant organisation or movement that transcends these acute class conflicts.

In Arab Africa, in South Africa, Zimbabwe and Kenya (but not in Egypt), the colonial authorities had granted their colonisers 'modern' private property, generally of a *latifundia* type. This inheritance has certainly been eliminated in Algeria, but there the peasantry had practically disappeared and been proletarianised or reduced to vagrancy by the extension of the colonial properties, while in Morocco and Tunisia the local bourgeoisie took over (which also partially happened in Kenya). In Zimbabwe, the revolution underway has challenged the colonial heritage on behalf partly of new owners who are more urban than rural and partly of the 'communities of poor peasants'. South Africa, for the time being, has not taken part in this movement. The strips of degenerated para-customary systems which remain in the 'poor' regions of Morocco and Berber Algeria, as in the Bantustans of South Africa, are suffering from the threat of private appropriation, encouraged by elements inside and outside the concerned communities.

In all these situations, the peasant struggles (and sometimes the organisations that support them) should be identified more precisely: do they constitute movements and represent claims by 'rich peasants' that are in conflict with some state policies (and the influence of the dominant world system on them)? Or are they poor and landless peasants? Could they both form an alliance against the dominant (so-called 'neoliberal') system? On what conditions? To what extent? Can the claims—whether they are expressed or not—of the poor, landless peasants be 'forgotten'?

In intertropical Africa, the apparent persistence of these 'customary' systems is certainly more visible. Because, here, the colonisation model took off in a different direction known as the économie *de traite*: the meaning of this concept, which has no English translation, is that the management of access to land was left to the so-called 'customary' authorities, nevertheless controlled by the colonial state (though genuine traditional chiefs or false ones fabricated by the administration). The objective of this control was to force the peasants to produce, beyond their cotton, coffee, cacao. The maintenance of a land tenure system that did not recognise private property was convenient for the colonisers, as land rent did not have to be taken into account in calculating the price of the products. This resulted in the degradation of the soils, destroyed by expanding crops, sometimes definitively (as, e.g. the desertification of Senegal where groundnuts had been cultivated). Here, once again, capitalism demonstrates that the 'short-term rationality' inherent in its dominant logic is largely responsible for ecological disaster. The juxtaposition of subsistence food crops and exports crops also made it possible to pay the work of the peasants at levels close to zero. For these reasons, to talk about the 'customary land tenure system' is grossly misleading: it is a new regime that conserves only the appearance of 'tradition', often its least interesting aspects.

China and Vietnam provide a unique example of a system for managing access to the land which is based neither on private ownership, nor on 'custom', but on a new revolutionary right, unknown elsewhere, which is that of all the peasants (described as the inhabitants of a village) having equal access to land—and I stress the 'equal'. This is the most beautiful acquisition of the Chinese and Vietnamese revolutions.

In China, and still more in Vietnam, which had a deeper colonisation experience, the 'old' land tenure systems (those I have described as 'tributary') were already fairly eroded by dominant capitalism. The old governing classes of the imperial power system had taken over agricultural land as owners, or almost as private property, while capitalist development encouraged the creation of new classes of rich peasants. Mao Zedong is the first—followed by Chinese and Vietnamese communists—to have prescribed an agrarian revolution strategy based on the mobilisation of most of the poor peasants, without land or other assets. The victory of this revolution made it possible to abolish the private ownership of land right from the beginning—which was replaced by that of the state—as well as the organisation of new forms of equal access to land for all peasants. True, this procedure has passed through several successive stages, including the Soviet-inspired model based on production cooperatives. The limits of their achievements led both countries to return to the idea of family peasant units. Are they viable? Can they produce a continual improvement in production without freeing up too much rural labour? On what conditions? What kinds of support are required from the state? What forms of political management can meet this challenge?

Ideally, the model involves the double affirmation of the rights of the state (the only owner) and of the usufructuaries (the peasant family). The state guarantees the equal division of the village lands among all the families and it prohibits all other usage other than family cultivation— for example, the renting of land. It guarantees that the result of investments made by the usufructuaries is given back to them immediately through their right of ownership of all the produce of their land, which are marketed freely, although the state guarantees purchase at a minimum price. On the longer term, the children who remain on the land can inherit from the usufructuaries (those who definitively leave the place lose their right to the land, which reverts to the lands for future redistribution). This is the case, of course, for fertile land, but also for the small, even dwarf-sized plots, so that the system is only viable if there is vertical investment (the green revolution without much mechanisation), which proves as effective in increasing production through rural activities as horizontal investment (extension of the holdings, supported by intensified mechanisation).

Has this 'ideal' model ever been implemented? It was surely close to it, for example, during the period of Deng Xiaoping in China. Nevertheless, even if it has created a greater degree of equality within a village, it has never been able to avoid the inequalities between one community and another, which are created by the difference in the quality of the soils, the density of population, or the proximity to urban markets. No other system of redistribution (even through the structures of cooperatives and state marketing monopolies during the 'Soviet' stage) has managed to resolve this challenge.

What is certainly more serious is that the system itself is subject to internal and external pressures that undermine its aims and social impact. Access to credit and favourable conditions for the supply of inputs are the object of bargaining and interventions of all kinds, legal and illegal: 'equal' access to the land is not the same as 'equal' access to the best conditions for production. The increasing popularity of the 'market' ideology promotes this erosion: the system tolerates tenant farming (if not re-legitimising it) and the hiring of wage labour. The discourse of the right-encouraged from the outside—repeats that it is necessary to give the peasants 'ownership' of the land and open up 'the market in agricultural land'. It is very clear that those supporting this are the rich peasants (if not agribusiness), who want to increase their holdings.

The management of this system of access to land for the peasants is ensured up till now by the state and the Party together. It may well be that this is because of the village councils that have been genuinely re-elected, and it has been necessary because there is no other way to mobilise the opinion of the majority and reduce the intrigues of the minorities of profiteers who would eventually benefit from a more marked capitalist development. The 'dictatorship of the Party' has shown that this has been largely solved through careerism and opportunism, if not corruption. The social struggles underway in the Chinese and Vietnamese countryside make their voices heard in these countries, just as they do elsewhere in the world. But they remain very much on the 'defensive', that is, attached to defending the heritage of the revolution: the equal right of everyone to land. Defence is necessary, because this heritage is more threatened than would appear, in spite of repeated affirmations by the two governments that 'the ownership of land by the state will "never" be abolished for the benefit of private ownership'. But now this defence requires recognition of the right to do it through the organisation of those concerned, the peasants.

Not Only One Formula for Peasant Alternatives

'Agrarian reform' should be understood as the redistribution of private ownership when it is considered to be unequally distributed. It is a land tenure system that is based on the principle of ownership. This reform becomes necessary both to satisfy the demand (perfectly legitimate) from poor and landless peasants and to reduce the political and social power of the large landowners. But where it is implemented, in Asia and Africa after the liberation of old forms of imperialist and colonial domination, it has been carried out by hegemonic non- revolutionary social blocs who were not governed by the dominated and poor majority classes. The exceptions were in China and Vietnam where, also for this reason, there had not been an 'agrarian reform' in the strict sense of the term but, as I have said, private ownership of land was suppressed, the principle of state ownership was affirmed, and the 'equal' access to the use of land by all the peasants was put into operation. Elsewhere, real reforms only dispossessed the large landowners for the profit, ultimately, of the middle and even rich (long-term) peasants, ignoring the interests of the poor and those without land. That was the case in Egypt and in other Arab countries. The reform underway in Zimbabwe risks ending up in the same way. In other situations, reform is always on the agenda of what should be done: in India, in South East Asia, in South Africa and in Kenya.

The progress created by agrarian reform, even where it exists as an immediate and essential requirement, is nevertheless ambiguous for its more long-term implications. For it reinforces attachment to 'small property', which becomes an obstacle to the questioning of a land tenure system based on private ownership. Russia's history illustrates this drama. The developments that followed the abolition of serfdom, in 1861, were accelerated by the revolution of 1905, because Stolypin's policies had already produced a 'claim for ownership' that was (finally) fulfilled in the radical agrarian reform after the 1917 Revolution. And, as we know, the new small owners did not enthusiastically renounce their rights for the benefit of the unfortunate cooperatives, which were dreamt up at the time, in the 1930s.

'Another path' to development, based on the peasant family economy of the generalised small owners, would have been possible. But it was not attempted. And what about the regions (other than China and Vietnam) where, in fact, the land tenure system had not (yet) been based on private property? This was, of course, the case of intertropical Africa.

Here we find the old debate. Towards the end of the 19th century, Marx, in his correspondence with the Russian Narodniks (Vera Zasulich, among others), dared to say that the absence of private ownership could constitute an advantage for the socialist revolution, enabling a leap forward towards a regime for managing the access to land other than the one governed by private ownership. But he did not specify what forms this new regime should take, the adjective 'collective', correct as it was, being insufficient. Twenty years later, Lenin believed this possibility no longer existed, eliminated by the penetration of capitalism and the spirit of private ownership that accompanied it. Was this a correct assessment? I cannot say, as I do not know enough about Russia. However, Lenin was hardly able to give decisive importance to this question, having accepted the viewpoint of Kautsky in *The Agrarian Question.*

Kautsky made generalisations about the extent of the model in modern European capitalism and believed that the peasantry was destined to 'disappear' because of the capitalist expansion itself. In other words, that capitalism would be able to 'resolve the agrarian question'. While this was true (for 80 per cent) of the other capitalist countries (the Triad: 20 per cent of the world population), it is not the case for the 'rest of the world' (80 per cent of the population). History has shown that not only has capitalism not solved this question for the 80 per cent of the world population, but that, as it pursues its expansion, it cannot resolve it, other than by genocide—what a marvellous solution! It was necessary to await Mao Zedong and the Communist Parties of China and Vietnam to give an adequate response to this challenge.

The question came up again in the 1960s, when Africa attained its independence. The national liberation movements of the continents, the states and the State-Parties which it had produced received, in different degrees, the support of the peasant majorities of their people. Their natural tendency to populism was to imagine a 'specific ("African") path to socialism'. This could be described as very moderately radical in its relationships both with dominant capitalism and with the local classes associated with its expansion. Nevertheless, it posed the question of reconstruction of peasant society in a humanist and universalist spirit. This spirit was often very critical of 'traditions' that the foreign masters had, in fact, been trying to mobilise for their own profit.

All the African countries—or almost all—adopted the same principle, formulated in the 'eminent ownership right of the state' over all the land. I am not among those who consider this declaration to have been 'a mistake', nor that it was motivated by extreme 'statistim'. To grasp the extent of the challenge it is necessary to study the way in which the current system controls the peasantry and how it is integrated into the world capitalist system. This control is ensured by a complex system that calls upon 'custom', private (capitalist) ownership, and the state, all at the same time.

'Custom', as we have just seen, has degenerated and only serves as decoration in the discourses of dictators appealing to what is known as 'authenticity', the fig leaf to cover their appetite for pillage and betrayal to imperialism. The tendency for private appropriation to expand has not met with any serious obstacle, apart from some resistance by the victims. In certain regions, which are more suitable for profitable cultivation (irrigated areas, market gardens), land is bought, sold and rented without any formal ownership titles.

The eminent state ownership of land, which I defend as a principle, is itself promoting private appropriation. The state can thus 'give' the land necessary for installing a tourist area, a local or foreign agro-business enterprise, or a state farm. The title deeds required for access to the areas to be developed are the object of a distribution process that is rarely transparent. In all cases, the peasant families that occupied the areas and are forced to clear off are the victims of these practices that amount to abuse of power. But to 'abolish' eminent state ownership of land to transfer it to the occupiers is not, in fact, feasible (all the village territories would have to be registered!), and if it were attempted it would enable the rural and urban notables to make off with the best bits of land.

The right response to the challenges of a land tenure system that is not based on private ownership (at least not dominated by it) should be to reform the state and its active involvement in setting up a management system of access to land that is modernised, efficient (economically), and democratic (to avoid, or at least to reduce inequalities). Above all, the solution is not to 'return to custom', which is, anyway, impossible and which would only serve to increase the inequalities and open up the way to unbridled capitalism.

However, it cannot be said that the African states have never tried to take the path recommended here. In Mali, the Sudanese Union, just after independence in September 1961, started on what was very inaccurately called 'collectivisation'. In fact, the cooperatives that were established were not production cooperatives, which remained the exclusive responsibility of the family farmers. They constituted a form of modernised collective power, replacing the so-called 'custom' which the colonial power used to support. The party that took over this new modern power was also clearly aware of the challenge and aimed at eliminating the customary forms of power—which were judged to be 'reactionary', if not 'feudal'. It is true that this new peasant power, formally democratic (the leaders were elected), was only as democratic as the state and the party. However, it did exercise 'modern' responsibilities, seeing that access to land was carried out 'correctly', that is, without 'discrimination'. It managed the credits, the distribution of the inputs (which were partially supplied by state trading) and the marketing of produce (also partially delivered for state commerce). Nepotism and extortion were certainly not eliminated in these procedures. But the only response to these abuses was the gradual democratisation of the state, not its 'withdrawal', which was later imposed by liberalism, through an extremely violent military dictatorship, for the benefit of the traders (the *dioulas*).

Other experiences, like those in the liberated areas of Guinea Bissau, inspired by the theories advanced by Amilcar Cabral, in Burkina Faso during the Sankara era, have also openly confronted these challenges and sometimes produced unquestionable advances. There are now efforts to obliterate them from people's minds. In Senegal, the establishment of elected rural authorities constitutes a response that I unhesitatingly defend in principle. Democracy is a practice whose apprenticeship never ends, no less in Europe than in Africa.

What the dominant discourse at the moment means by 'reform of the land tenure system' is the exact opposite of what is required for the building of an authentic alternative based on a prosperous peasant economy. What this discourse means by land reform—conveyed by the propaganda instruments of collective imperialism, the World Bank, many development institutions, but also a number of NGOs that are richly endowed—is the acceleration of the privatisation of land, and nothing more. The aim is clear: to create the conditions that would enable some 'modern' islands of agribusiness (foreign and local) to take over the land they require to expand. But the supplementary produce that these 'islands' could supply (for export or for local 'effective demand') could never meet the needs for building a prosperous society for all, which would involve the development of the peasant family economy as a whole.

Need to Define Role of the State in Land Reform

I do not exclude complex and mixed formulas, which can be specific for each country. Private ownership of the land can be accepted—at least where it is established and considered legitimate. Its distribution can— or must—be reviewed where this is the case, by agrarian reforms (for Sub-Saharan Africa, South Africa, Zimbabwe and Kenya). I do not even necessarily exclude the opening up of space—under control—of the setting up of agribusiness. But what the essential question lies elsewhere: how to modernise peasant family production and democratise its integration into the national economy and globalisation. I have no readymade solutions to propose in these fields. I shall just mention some of the great problems that this reform raises.

The question of democracy is the indisputable issue to be tackled in responding to this challenge. It is a complex and difficult issue that cannot be reduced to the insipid discourse of good governance and electoral multipartyism. It has, of course, a genuine cultural aspect: democracy wants to abolish the 'customs' that are hostile to it—prejudices about social hierarchies and, above all, the treatment of women. It includes juridical and institutional aspects: the construction of systems of administrative, commercial and personal rights that are consistent with the aims of social construction and the setting up of adequate institutions (elected, for the most part). But, above all, the progression of democracy will depend on the social power of its defenders. The organisation of peasant movements is, in this sense, absolutely irreplaceable. It is only to the extent that the peasantry can express itself that the advances towards what is called 'participatory democracy'—in contrast to reducing it to the problem of 'representative democracy'—can clear the path (Amin, 2005).

The relationship between men and women is no less important in the democracy challenge. Those who speak of 'family cultivation' (peasant) evidently refer to the family, which till now and almost everywhere has structures that impose the submission of women and the over-exploitation of their labour. The democratic transformation will not take place if there are no organised movements of the women concerned.

Attention should be given to the question of migrations. 'Customary' rights generally exclude 'foreigners'—that is, all those who do not belong to the clans, lineages, and families of which the original village community is constituted—from right to the land, or their access is conditioned. The migrations caused by colonial and postcolonial development have sometimes taken on dimensions that upset the ethnic 'homogeneity' of the regions concerned. The emigrants who come from outside the country (like the Burkinabe in Cote d'Ivoire), or those who are formally citizens of the same country but of 'ethnic' origin that is foreign to the regions where they settle (like the Hausa in the Plateau state of Nigeria), have faced questioning of their rights to the land which they have cultivated by narrow-minded and chauvinistic political movements, which also benefit from foreign support. One of the most unavoidable conditions for real democratic advance is to dismiss ideological and political 'communitarianisms' and firmly denounce the paracultural discourse that underlies them.

All these analyses and proposals which were the object of past developments only concern the status of ownership and the rules of access to land. These questions are, indeed, a major issue in the debates about the future of agricultural and food production of peasant societies and of the individuals who constitute them. But they do not cover all dimensions of the challenge. Access to land cannot be a potential transformer of the society if the peasants who benefit are unable to get access to the indispensable means of production on favourable conditions (credit, seeds, inputs, access to the markets). National policies, like the international negotiations that aim to define the framework in which the prices and incomes are determined, are another dimension of the peasant question.

We refer the reader to the writings of Jacques Berthelot (2001) on these questions. He is the best and most critical analyst of the projects to integrate agricultural and food production into the 'world' markets. We shall just mention two of the conclusions and most important proposals that we have reached.

First, it is not possible to accept that agricultural and food production, as well as land, be treated as ordinary 'goods', and thus allow them to be integrated into the project of globalised liberalisation promoted by the dominant powers and transnationalized capital.

The WTO agenda must just be rejected, purely and simply. Opinion in Asia and Africa must be convinced of this, and particularly of the need for food sovereignty, beginning with the peasant organisations, but also all the other social and political forces that defend the interests of the popular classes and those of the nation. All those who have not renounced a project for development that is worthy of the name must realise that the negotiations underway in the framework of the WTO agenda will only be catastrophic for the peoples of Asia and Africa. Capitalism has reached the stage where the pursuit of profit requires 'enclosure' policies at the world level, like the enclosures that took place in England in the first stage of its (modern) development. Now, however, the destruction of the 'peasant reserves' of cheap labour at the world level will result in nothing less than the genocide of half of humanity.

Second, it is impossible to accept the behaviour of the main imperialist powers, the USA and Europe, that are associated with the assaults against the people of the South within the WTO. These powers, that try to unilaterally impose the 'liberalism' proposals on the countries of the South, have freed themselves from the same restrictions by ways that can only be described as systematic trickery.

The Farm Bill of the USA and the agricultural policies of the European Union violate the very principles which the WTO intends to impose on other states. The 'partnership' projects proposed by the European Union, following the Cotonou Convention, as from 2008, are nothing less than 'criminal' to use the strong, but appropriate, expression of Jacques Berthelot. These powers can and must be accused in the very courts of the WTO set up for this purpose. A group of countries from the South can do this—and they must.

The alternative consists of national policies to construct/reconstruct national funds for stabilisation and support for production, completed by the establishment of common international funds for basic products, enabling an effective alternative reorganisation of the international markets of agricultural products. Jean-Pierre Boris has elaborated such proposals in detail.

The peasants of Asia and Africa organised themselves during the stage prior to the liberation struggles of their peoples. They found their place in the strong historical blocs which made it possible to win victory over the imperialism of the time. These blocs were sometimes revolutionary (China and Vietnam), and they then had their main rural bases in the majority classes of middle peasants and poor, landless peasants. Or, elsewhere, they were led by the national bourgeoisie or sectors who aspired to become so, among the rich and middle peasants, thus isolating the large landowners in some places and the 'customary' chieftaincies in the pay of the colonisers.

That page of history having been turned, the challenge of the new collective imperialism of the Triad will only be got rid of if historical blocs are constituted in Asia and Africa. But this cannot be a remake of the preceding blocs. The challenge faced by the so-called alternative world movement and its constitutive components of social forums is to identify, in the new conditions, the nature of these blocs, their strategies and immediate and long-term objectives. This is a far more serious challenge than is realised by many of the movements committed to the struggles.

A Complex and Multidimensional Challenge

Is the capitalist modernisation path as 'effective' as the conventional economists claim? Let us imagine that, in this way, we can double production (from an index of 100 to one of 200), but that this is obtained by the elimination of 80 per cent of the surplus rural population (the index of the number of active cultivators falling from 100 to 20). The apparent gain, measured by the growth of production per active producer is considerable: it is multiplied by 10. But, if it is seen in terms of the rural population as a whole, it is only multiplied by two. Therefore, it is necessary to distribute freely all this growth in production in order simply to keep alive the peasants who have been eliminated and cannot find alternative work in the towns. This was what Marx wrote concerning the pauperisation associated with the accumulation of capital.

The challenge, which is to base development on renewing peasant societies, has many dimensions. I will just call attention here to the conditions for constructing the necessary and possible political alliances that will enable progress to be made towards solutions (in the interests of the worker peasants, of course) to all the problems that are posed: access to the land and to the means to develop it properly; reasonable wages for peasant work; improvement of wages parallel to the productivity of this work; and appropriate regulation of the markets at the national, regional and world levels.

New peasant organisations exist in Asia and Africa that are visibly activating the struggles underway. Often, when political systems make it impossible for them to constitute formal organisations, the social struggles in the rural world take the form of 'movements' with no apparent direction. These actions and programmes, where they exist, should be analysed more carefully. Which peasant social forces do they represent and whose interests are they defending? The majority mass of the peasants? Or the minorities which aspire to participating in the expansion of dominant globalised capitalism? We should mistrust quick answers to these questions that are complex and difficult. We should be careful not to 'condemn' a number of organisations and movements on the pretext that they are not mobilising the peasant majorities on radical programmes. This would be to ignore the need to formulate broad alliances and strategies by stages. But we should also be careful not to support the discourse of the 'naïve alternative world people' who often set the tone in the forums and fuel the illusion that the world is on the right path only because of the existence of the social movements. This is a discourse that belongs more to the many NGOs—with good intentions, perhaps—than to the peasant and worker organisations.

I myself am not so naïve as to think that all the interests that these alliances represent can naturally converge. In all peasant societies, there are the rich and the poor, who are often without land. The conditions of access to land result from different historical experiences which, in some cases, have rooted aspirations to ownership in people's minds, while in others, it is to protect the access to land of the greatest number. The relationships of the peasantries to state power are also the result of different political paths, particularly as concerns the national liberation movements of Asia and Africa: populisms, peasant democracies, state anti-peasant autocracies show the diversity of peoples' heritages. The way in which international markets are run favour some, penalise others. These divergences of interest are sometimes echoed in many of the peasant movements and often in the divergences of the political strategies adopted.

NOTE

1. Originally published in *Agrarian South: Journal of Political Economy*, Vol. 6, No. 2, Copyright 2017 © Centre for Agrarian Research and Education for South (CARES), New Delhi. All rights reserved. The paper is reproduced with the permission of the copyright holders and the publishers, Sage Publications India Pvt. Ltd., New Delhi.

REFERENCES

Amin, S. (2005), *Les Luttes Paysannes et Ouvières Face Aux Défis du Xxe Siècle,* Paris: Les Indes Savantes.

———. (2006), *Beyond US Hegemony,* New York: Zed Books.

———. (2017), *October 1917 Revolution, A Century Later*, Nairobi: Darja Press.

Berthelot, J. (2001), *L'agriculture, Talon d'Achille de l'OMC,* Paris: L'Harmattan.

Chayanov, A.V. (1966), *On The Theory of Non-Capitalist Economic Systems*, In D. Thorner, B. Kerblay and R.E.F. Smithy (eds.), *The Theory of Peasant Economy,* pp. 1–28, Homewood, IL: Irwin.

Kautsky, K. (1988 [1899]), *The Agrarian Question*, Winchester, MA: Zwan Publications.

Mazoyer, M. and L. Roudard (1997), *Histoire des Agricultures du Monde,* Paris: Seuil.

Parmentier, B. (2007), *Nourrir l'humanité,* Paris: La Découverte.

10

'Big is Not Always Beautiful': Family Farms and Capitalism

Goran Djurfeldt

According to the counting by the FAO, there were 600 million farms globally in 2009 (FAO, 2014). An overwhelming majority of all these farms, or 570 out of 600 million (95 per cent) were family farms. The remaining 5 per cent were under diverse forms of ownership and management: governments, cooperative and institutional like for example religious institutions. Very few were owned by private corporations.

One of the great paradoxes in social science is why there is so little theoretical interest in the livelihoods of family farmers in contrast to the loosely defined category of smallholders. Family farmers continue to be a more than marginal part of the global population and responsible for much of world food production.

There is much more tumult about capitalist farming, although, in terms of numbers, it remains a minor part of world agriculture. Deininger and Byerlee in 2012 tried to estimate the number of capitalist farms worldwide, but found only one good example of such a farm: Black Earth AB, that bought or rented large tracts of land in the black earth areas of Ukraine, cultivating them with so-called precision agriculture, in which tractors and combine harvesters are steered by Global Positioning Systems (GPS) and in which fertilisation regimes are worked out by means of satellite imagery (Deininger and Byerlee, 2012).

Furthermore, and looking at the US, the authors cited found only two agri-business companies listed on the Nasdaq. They were

Farmland Partners, which used to be a cooperative union, figuring in Forbes' list of the biggest companies in the world. Founded in 1929, it was privatised in 2003 to 2006 and continues to be active, but not in farming as such. The same is true of the Nasdaq-listed Gladstone Land Corporation which is a real estate investment trust.

Returning to the Black Earth AB, it is, or rather was a public limited corporation, listed on the Stockholm Stock Exchange. The corporation fulfilled a rigorous definition of an ideal type capitalist farm, dependent for its long-term survival on generating profit on the capital invested, including the land. But it did not survive, went bust and was delisted in Stockholm in 2017.

What a paradox! After more than 200 years of global capitalist development inside and outside agriculture, observers at or close to the World Bank, like the authors cited, found only one capitalist farm in the whole world—and that firm did not survive for more than a decade. Given that we have been fed with prognoses of the imminent take-over of world agriculture by capitalism, at least since Lenin's *The Development of Capitalism in Russia* (Lenin, 1960 [1899]), this paradox calls for an explanation.

I define a capitalist farm as an agricultural production unit in which all factors of production (land, labour, capital and management) are procured on the market. Moreover, a capitalist farm is: (i) worked by labourers hired for wages (rather than recruited by non-market means); (ii) managed by professional managers (rather by family members); (iii) owned by a corporation investing capital into the farm, including the land, whether owned or leased. Black Earth AB fulfilled these three criteria, but it did not succeed in giving its owners the required return on capital. Obviously, it is not easy for a farm to satisfy these criteria. Why?

In the following I will discuss capitalist and family farming (to be defined below), drawing on examples from all over, fetching illustrations from India and China, Sub-Saharan Africa and occasionally also South America. In the process we will learn why it is not true that 'big is beautiful', especially not when talking about capitalist farms. There are sound reasons why family farming is still thriving, many having to do with what I call Chayanov's principle, after the great Russian economist, A.V. Chayanov.

Land

The first reason for the paucity of capitalist farms is the common but erroneous inference that capitalist farms are identical to large landed estates. Such units are seldom constrained to making a profit on the (imputed) value of the land, either because the land is not mortgaged at market value and therefore not liable to pay interest, or because the owners, whether corporate or individual, may have acquired the land cheaply or free of cost, like inheritance.

Large landed estates often have an interesting history, worth digging into. Take the Indian case: Simply put, what still remains of large landed estates after land reforms and other developments since Independence, either have a colonial background, for example tea plantations, or a feudal one, like the zamindari and other types of estates created by the Mughals, by the East India Company, or other pre-colonial rulers.[1] Such estates were often referred to as 'tax farms', because they were created by rulers to facilitate tax collection from the tillers of the land, by 'farming it out' to people with the means, that is the arms and the men needed to collect taxes on the part of the ruler. In the process, taxable land was converted, more or less formally, into private property. Thus, large estates were not created because they were superior in terms of productivity, or because of economies of scale.

In fact, outside the plantation sector, economies of scale seldom obtain in agriculture, which is one reason why capitalist farms, unlike large estates are rare and a main reason why the Leninist expectation of the form that capitalism would take in agriculture was off the mark, both in Europe and in the US.

Labour

Another presumption underlying the expectation that capitalist farms would prevail in agriculture is that such farms rely on hired labour, whose wages are formed in a process of free negotiation between the labourer and the employer. Labour hiring is usually regarded as the capitalist relation of production. Marx himself spent much space in the first chapters of the first volume of *Capital* to show what goes on behind the backs of the 'free' agents in labour hiring. Our point is that hired labourers in agriculture are seldom 'free' to negotiate their wages; on the contrary they are constrained by gender, race, citizenship and other institutional factors to negotiate wages which are not equivalent to the ones obtained by labourers who are not discriminated against by non-market factors.

Instead of being 'free', agricultural labour markets tend to be segmented along the lines mentioned. Three examples will illustrate, one from the US, one from India and from today's Scandinavia. A classic study from the 1980s (Thomas, 1985) of salad farms in California, USA, showed that farm workers were recruited from highly segmented niches in the labour market, with illegal immigrants at the lower rungs doing the most tedious jobs at the lowest wages. Green Card holders occupied a higher and somewhat better niche, as overseers, quality controllers, etc. Wages at competitive rates were only paid to US citizens, typically as managers, security staff and the like.

Or take the Indian case: the majority of those working as hired labour in Indian agriculture either are so-called Scheduled or Backward Castes. Moreover, many of them are women. When we studied agrarian labour relations in what was then Tiruchy District in Tamil Nadu (Athreya, Djurfeldt, and Lindberg, 1990), we found that in the 'wet', canal-irrigated villages, both male and female labourers were organised in caste-based gangs, under male or female *mistries* who negotiated piece rates in highly competitive markets. Outside these 'wet'villages however, wages did not fluctuate much and were set by village and season by the elders with women usually getting half of that paid to men. The high percentage of Scheduled Castes (SC) in these villages contributed both to the low wage levels and to the high rates of poverty in the SC colonies.

Taking finally the example of Sweden and the Scandinavian countries, before Sweden's entry to the EU in 1995, hired labour had more or less disappeared in the family farm sector and farmers were working round the clock and the year to manage with only their own machinery and family labour (Djurfeldt and Waldenström, 1996). They managed thanks to mechanisation and to swapping of services with neighbours. This resembled what Bailey once dubbed the one-man mechanised farm (Bailey, 1973). We have to remember though that farmers who were married had wives who tended to work off-farm, and whose incomes were often a hidden subsidy to the farm.

Since the expansion of the EU and the entry of the ex-communist countries, the tendency has been reversed and currently goes towards low wage, ethnically segmented labour markets all over Western Europe, especially in horticulture and vegetables, while one-man mechanised farms persist in grain and other arable cropping. Labour unions are absent in these markets and unionised labour tends to be found working mainly in golf courses, urban parks and other non-farming sectors.

As industrialisation proceeds and the service sectors grow in middle income countries like India, competition for labour is likely to lead to further emancipation of agricultural labour from gender, caste and other discrimination. As I will argue, this will boost the resilience of the family farm sector.

Management

In Andalusia in Spain, as well as in latifundist areas in South America and also currently in India, there are farm management firms, taking on large landholdings on the part of their owner families, proffering professional management of the farms, using up to date methods, much machinery and recruiting specialised workers and small 'armies' of casual labour. Another variety of this is firms owning combine harvesters, negotiating directly with farm owners and moving along a harvest frontier, like South to North on the Gangetic plain, or in the Yangtse River valley in China.

These arrangements presuppose everyday management by owner families, or by salaried managers in the case of larger estates; they do not in any way threaten the family ownership characteristic of all the mentioned cases. Corporate ownership of machinery, yes, but corporate land ownership, in no way!

The Dismantling of Landed Estates in Europe

According to our definition, a capitalist farm tills land procured on the market, that is, land rented rather than owned. This was true of the English case on which Marx built his analysis; he presumed that it was the first case of its kind, but it was unique and, as we will see, it turned out to be short-lived.

Starting a telescoped historiography in the 16th century, the majority of the rural population in the UK lacked property and were compelled to seek their subsistence in the commons, till the early 17th century when the Enclosure Acts privatised many commons and deprived the peasantry also of this source of sustenance. From the 18th century onwards the poverty of the rural population drove the poor and property-less to seek work as agricultural labourers, industrial workers, domestic servants or, alternatively to seek poverty relief (Polanyi, 2001 [1944]).

Besides the property-less and the landlords, the most important group, although small in terms of numbers, was the estate tenants. The landowners generally did not cultivate their land themselves, but leased it out. Property-owning peasants, in England called yeoman farmers became a small minority in the countryside. Britain had a distribution of land reminding us of some Latin American countries before the land reforms of the 1960s.

The British agrarian structure before 1870 lay quite close to the ideal typical capitalist farming described earlier: It had a small group of aristocratic landowners, renting out their land to capitalist tenants and with a mass of agricultural labourers slogging in fields and stables. The system fulfilled one of the definitional requirements of capitalist agriculture, viz. capitalisation of the land. The nobility lived from their rents, and their tenants had to run an enterprise, which could finance not only the wages and the inputs of capital, but also the capitalised value of the land, in the form of rent. It is a historical irony that this system was at its high 150 years ago and that since then it decayed.

The agrarian crisis from the 1870s onwards and what we today describe as the first period of hyper-globalisation brought about the downfall of the British system of capitalist tenants. Falling food prices are a deadly threat to landlordism, since they decrease the rental value of land. Landlord incomes tumble; the nobility cannot maintain their castles, their extravagant style of living or pay their servants. This was the destiny that befell many British landowners.

The agrarian crisis can be seen as a delayed effect of the Corn Laws, adopted in the 1840s by the British Parliament in opposition to the landlords (Perry, 1972, 14). The Corn Laws opened Britain to imports of farm products, but their impact was delayed by about 30 years, due to high transport costs that curbed international trade in bulky products like cereals. Freight prices came down after 1870 and allowed American and Argentinian cereals to compete with European ones, which set the bells tolling for British landlordism:

> The dismantling of the landed estates—the aristocratic diaspora from the land—although usually dated from the period immediately following the First World War… began much earlier. Nevertheless a deluge of land sales began in 1919, on a scale unprecedented since the dissolution of monasteries in the sixteenth century. Within three years, it has been estimated, one-quarter of the land surface of the United Kingdom changed hands. (Newby, Bell, Rose and Saunders, 1978, 36-37), cited in (Djurfeldt and Sircar, 2017).

The agrarian crisis thus brought a land reform, not by the state, but by the market. British estates were divided and taken over by smaller landowners. They were often ex-tenants, but land was also sold in smaller portions to family farmers (Harrison, 1975). Although Britain still has a higher concentration of landownership than Western Europe, its structure is similar to that found in the rest of Europe (Gasson, 1987).

The British case is a good illustration, of the role of agricultural labourers in the structural transformation. As prices of output fell, wages increased in real terms: This forced landlords to divest in land and made it possible for family farms to invest in it. The development in the rest of Europe was parallel (Dovring, 1965 [1955]).

Farm Size and Productivity

One might think that this story would have brought an end to the ever-ongoing debate on economies of scale in agriculture; but it has a tendency to periodically upsurge. It thrives on the myth about 'big is beautiful': This myth says that if we organise production on scientific, factory-like principles, it certainly will be superior to the small and scattered plots tilled by 'peasants' or smallholders working on 'unscientific' principles, as handed down by tradition. This myth informed political decision-making all over. It was the rationale for the collectivisation of small-scale agriculture in the Soviet Union in the 20s and 30s; in China after the land reforms carried through in the late 40s and early 50s, and it was a guiding principle for forming People's Communes in the late 50s. The same myth informed political decision-making in Ethiopia during the military regime in the 1970s; and the villagisation policy in Tanzania about a decade earlier. We will not continue the enumeration of what turned out to be grandiose failures, but also point to the numerous cases where the myth of 'big is beautiful' has been the rationale for reneging on promises of small-scale land reform, instead keeping large landed properties intact and handing them out to cronies, like in Zimbabwe to mention just one example. Thus, innovations have been adapted to farming systems in which family farming has been prominent, which in principle means all over, not only in Japan, but all over Asia, in Europe and the US (a classic source is Hayami and Ruttan, 1971). Low-yield small holder systems can be found in Asia, prominently in India, in large parts of Central and South America and in Africa south of the Sahara. In few if any of these cases, low-yield smallholder or family farms systems exclusively depend on farming, but on non-farm income in various forms, including remittances, both international and domestic (see below on pluriactivity).

Chayanov's Principle[3]

A.V. Chayanov (1888-1937) was a Russian economist, statistician and sociologist belonging to the so-called *zemstvo* school who worked for the decentralised local governments set up as part of the 1861 reforms under Tsar Alexander II in Russia. Chayanov was shot 20 years after the Revolution, as part of the Stalinist purges. Rehabilitated in 1987 during *glasnost,* Chayanov was introduced to an English-reading audience by scholars like Basile Kerblay, Daniel Thorner and Teodor Shanin. The English translation of his book on *The Theory of Peasant Economy* (Chayanov, 1986 [1966]) had a great influence on peasant studies as these developed in the West from the late 1960s and onwards.

What I call Chayanov's principle was formulated by Chayanov in various ways, from Marxist to marginalist inspired. As I see it, the principle works on the contrast between capitalist farming, as earlier defined, and family farming:

(i) Although from time to time making a financial surplus, unlike capitalist farming, family farming requires no such surplus to reproduce, at least short-to mid-term.

(ii) Family farming depends on family labour that does not require payment of wages according to market rates

Within the Marxist tradition since Marx himself,[4] family farms have been seen as a class facing extinction. For Lenin, the peasantry was doomed to disappear and split into two parts, a minority that would develop into an agrarian capitalist class, and a majority that would lose their land and be forced either to join the ranks of the agricultural proletariat, or its counterparts in the cities (Lenin, 1960 [1899]; Djurfeldt, 1981). Underpinning this vision is a presumption of superior productivity within capitalist agriculture: When compared to family farms, capitalist agriculture, or factories in the field would be like industry compared to crafts.

The difficulties for craft production to compete with industrial organisation are evidence of the superiority of what Marx called the capitalist mode of production (1977 [1887]). Like Adam Smith before him (Smith, 1904 [1776]), he argued that this superiority stemmed, not only from mechanisation, but also from the advanced division of labour within the factory, with labourers specialising in different parts of the production process rather than producing the whole product, as the artisan would. This type of specialisation of labour holds only to a limited extent on really existing large estates. Such farms depend on masses of workers to perform repetitive tasks that are not easy to mechanise, like picking of strawberries, grapes or tomatoes.

Capitalist farms have difficulties in competing with family farms, precisely because they are not factories in the field, as this discussion clearly illustrates. Historically, as well as currently, large estates access few technologies, which are not also available to family farms. Both in Europe and the US, there are small differences in technology between the two sectors. The main difference between them lies in the armies of labour, often from segmented or unfree labour markets, absorbed by farms dependent on such labour. This is in contrast to a much greater dependence of family farms on own labour.

While theoretically it is plausible that their mode of organisation gives a competitive edge to farms dependent on hired labour, historically as well as currently, this is seldom the case. By contrast, given the access to the same technologies the 'staffing' of farms under family management provides their competitive advantage. Hired (non-family) labour is less motivated to work, and more prone to foot dragging than family labour (Scott, 1985; Chayanov, 1986 [1966]; Eswaran, Kotwal, Ramaswami and Wadhwa, 2009). Family members, on the other hand, work for themselves or for their families, including for their children and future generations. This is a potent motivating force. During farm crises family labour is often prepared to work for minimal or no remuneration, which is the fundamental reason for the resilience of family farms. This is in contrast to farms dependent on hired labour, for which the wage bill is largely inelastic.

There is an ongoing debate within agricultural and development economics on economies of scale within farming (for overviews see, Eastwood, Lipton and Newell, 2010; Chand, Prasanna, Lakshmi and Singh, 2011). With few exceptions, scale in many studies is proxied by area, either of farm or of area under specific crops. There are evident problems with this operationalisation, however. Area is not a homogeneous variable. Whether we speak of farm or plot size, the productivity differences between different farms or plots are vast and depend not only on soil fertility, but also on irrigation, drainage and other factors. Models regressing productivity on farm or plot size, as a result, get large residuals, not easy to minimise and not prone to be normally distributed, as is required of a good-fit model. In our view, this is the fundamental reason why many studies on farm size have yielded little in terms of generalisable results. Thus, we would argue that farm (or even plot) size is not the relevant operationalisation, while farm type is. We know of only one study, which has used this insight, a World Bank study of the profitability of a selection of crops, comparing family farms and large estates in Sub-Saharan Africa (World Bank, 2009). The study concluded that in most crops, family farmers are competitive with the estate sector.

Eastwood and Lipton argue that the competitive advantage of family farms over capitalist ones will gradually disappear and Deininger and Byerlee would seem to agree (Eastwood et al., 2010), (Deininger and Byerlee, 2012). The authors cited mention precision agriculture and geo-sensing, which at the prices then prevailing required large farm areas to motivate the investment. But the authors seem to neglect Moore's law, which implies that technology that currently is large-scale is likely soon to be available to smaller-scale farmers. Be that as it may be, our sketchy overview seems to indicate that we are far from the point of time when capitalist farms will replace family farms because of their superior productivity.

This argument can be put in economic terms by referring to Coase's theory of the firm (Coase, 1937) and the concept of transaction costs (Williamson, 1979). Coase's article became a classic because he pointed out that neoclassical economics could not explain the emergence or existence of the firm. This is where Williamson and his terminological innovation enter: the firm is a way of minimising transaction costs by internalising them into an organisational unit. One can argue along the same lines about family farming, and family business in general. By internalising labour costs into the farm (or firm), one reduces transaction costs. Using family instead of hired labour, lowers transactions costs because the need for supervision is nearly eliminated and shrinkage or foot dragging avoided. This is not necessarily a disadvantage to family workers and thus does not necessarily imply self- exploitation, as has sometimes been alleged. On the contrary, by increasing the quality of the labour input, the remuneration of family labourers may be higher than it would have been for the hired labour it replaced.

The remuneration of family labour is crucial. While hired labour is paid a sum of money, family labour is remunerated with a bundle of utilities, food, shelter, affection and love, not easy to evaluate in economic terms. The economic parts of the remuneration can be regarded as the correspondence of a wage, or what Eastwood, Lipton and Newell call a reservation utility (Eastwood et al., 2010). Thus, one can say that as long as the reservation utility of family labour is higher than prevailing agricultural wages, one can expect a tendency for hired labour to be replaced by family labour (Schmitt, 1991). An upward pressure on wages, for example due to competition with the industrial and service sectors, would have similar effects. But family labour is not bound to the farm; it can be pluriactive.

Pluriactivity

Family farmers are not always specialised in arable farming, horticulture and animal husbandry, but more often combine these activities with others, outside the farm and often outside agriculture. We refer to this as 'pluriactivity', which is a mongrel of a word: with the prefix 'pluri' from Greek and 'activity' from Latin. Pluriactivity refers to a family or household, often spanning more than a generation; and reliant upon the activities of their members. Thus the term refers to the reproduction of the whole. Had it not been for pluriactivity then, the resilience of family farming would have been much less.

It lies near at hand to think of pluriactive families these days, when individual members of rural and agrarian families are migrating all over, nationally and internationally, looking for income opportunities and for money to send to their families back home. Internationally, remittances sent home by migrants supersede both foreign investments and aid received by the migrants' countries of origin, or at least they did so till the current crisis (Ratha, 2016). Think of the giant movements of internal migrants in huge countries like India and China. When India imposed the Covid-19 lockdown in the summer of 2020, millions of migrants were caught between the cogs of the bureaucratic machine. Many of them walked over enormous distances from Mumbai, Chennai and Bengaluru, scorched by the sun, caned by the police. Daily news made the point that these people fell between categories and into multiple traps. When they reached their villages, authorities did not welcome them: with empty pockets and potential bearers of a killer virus, they were often forced to stay outside village borders, receiving food from their families whom they were prevented from meeting at home.

The Aftermath of 2008-09 Scramble for Land

After the financial crisis in 2008 and the following increases in food prices, investors on Wall Street, hedge fund managers and risk capitalists in general, re-valued prospects of investments in land; and a boom followed. Taking a quick stock of the situation a decade later, some of the main points made above get reinforced: Decision-makers all over are still taken in by the 'big is beautiful' and expect quick returns to large-scale investment in land. Deals often fail for various reasons, a common one being that large is not as superiour as imagined.

During the boom, giant contracts were signed between investors, bureaucrats and politicians in a set of semi-failed states: In Madagascar in 2009 a long-term lease of 1 million hectares was granted to the South Korean Daewoo company. The deal involved the sitting president, over the heads of the present occupants of the land. Scandal was created in both countries, which led to the fall of the President and the liquidation of the deal. Another example is Congo, former Zaire, where a similar deal covered more than one million hectares leased to foreign interests; the apparent presumption being that the land was vacant; nobody in Kinshasa nor in Western capitals seemed to bother about its present users, agriculturalists, herders and hunters. This murky deal never materialised. In Tanzania local interests ganged up with an Emirate sheik and hunter and transferred an entire nature reserve, to be converted to hunting grounds, completely nonchalant of the people inhabiting the park, an ethnic minority described as untouched by 'civilisation'. NGOs and local protests succeeded to kill the deal.

These cases are misleading if they are taken as representative, because the deals are apparently abandoned while most similar deals still survive at least on paper if nothing more. The following case recently reported in *The Economist* may be more representative:

> The plan was to transform farming in southern Ethiopia. Twelve years ago Fri-El, an Italian conglomerate, signed a lease with the state government for 30,000 hectares of farmland in South Omo to make palm oil. But the palms needed more water than the copper-coloured Omo river could supply and production was so disappointing that in 2011 its lease was cut by a third in size. Even a switch to cotton production did not help. Many bolls are left unpicked owing to labour shortages. A ginnery lies idle for want of electricity.

The Economist offered an explanation as follows:

> In Ethiopia, where the government offered tax breaks, low rents and vast tracts of allegedly empty farmland, more was leased than almost anywhere else. One study calculated that around 1m hectares were allocated between 2005 and 2012; others suggested two or even three times that. The idea was that poor, remote places like South Omo, near Ethiopia's south-western border, would become paragons of development. Mechanised cotton estates would feed Ethiopia's burgeoning textile factories. Nomads would ditch their cattle for jobs as labourers on commercial farms. (*Economist,* Why big farms flopped in Ethiopia, April 8, 2020)

The general and global situation seem to be well captured in Land Matrix Database.[5] When accessed for this paper, the database covered 1822 land deals globally, entered since 2000 and over 200 hectares in size; of these only 8 per cent were concluded and another 7 per cent were failed. The highest number of deals (585 deals), or 30 per cent of cases were from the Africa region with a huge majority from Sub-Sahara. Africa had the highest percentage of failures followed by Eastern Europe and Asia with much fewer failures reported from Latin America.

That so many land deals failed and that so few were concluded especially in Sub-Saharan Africa would seem to illustrate the general point that political decision-makers are easily taken in by the myth of 'big is beautiful'. Even if this is true, it may be milder but not eliminate the threat that land grabbing undoubtedly is.

Supermarketisation and Vertical Integration

Many perceive the spread of supermarkets in middle- and low-income countries as the new threat to the world's family farms. The basic argument is that the giant supermarket chains, WalMart, Carrefour and the others prefer to deal with a few big suppliers rather than a whole lot of small-scale producers. As supermarkets invest in building procurement chains for fresh fruit and vegetables, with the quality demands of discerning middle-class consumers in view, supermarkets tend to prefer large estates for production and delivery. Thus supermarkets deprive family famers of many of their markets. So goes the argument.

While supermarket chains are undoubtedly becoming an immense part of all food retailing and procurement, we believe that its consequences for family farming worldwide may not be as apocalyptic as could be feared. Even in markets controlled by huge corporations, family farms enjoy advantages that serve them well.

In his mostly unspoken criticism of Lenin and the Bolsheviks, Chayanov proffered an alternative scenario to Lenin's horizontal concentration, which he styled vertical integration. Chayanov studied how urban-based merchants contracted with family farmers to produce cotton and other cash crops and offered credit to facilitate farmers' investments. He also studied the European cooperative movement during travels in Europe and wrote about his vision for the future of family farming (Chayanov, 1977):

> If to this we add in the most developed capitalist countries, such as those in in North America, widely developed mortgage credit, the financing of farm circulating capital, and the dominating part played by capital invested in transport, elevator, irrigation, and other undertakings, then we have before us the new ways in which capitalism penetrates agriculture. These ways convert the farmers into a labor force working with other people's means of production. They convert agriculture, despite the evident scattered and independent nature of the small commodity producers, into an economic system concentrated

> in a series of larger undertakings and, through them, entering the sphere controlled by the most advanced forms of finance capitalism." (Chayanov, 1986 [1966], 262)

It is important to stress the enormous speed with which the process has enveloped the developing world, including the poorest parts of Sub-Saharan Africa. It is worth noting however that, with its restrictions on foreign direct investment in retailing, India has hitherto been less drawn into the process than many other countries (see for example, Reardon, Timmer, Barrett and Berdegué, 2003). Reardon et al. summarise studies on sub-contracting to farmers as follows:

> Companies in general tend to source from larger farmers and eschew smaller farmers in scale-dualistic contexts. However, there are various exceptions to this pattern, where companies source from small farmers even when large farmers operate in the same sector… Companies source from small farmers in contexts where small farmers dominate the agrarian structure… When companies source from small farmers, they tend to source from the subset with the requisite non-land assets (such as irrigation, farmers' associations, farm equipment, and access to paved roads). However, where companies need or want to source from small farmers but the farmers lack needed credit, inputs, or extension, companies sometimes use "resource-provision contracts" to address those constraints.... [Studies] tend to show positive effects on small farmers of inclusion in modern channels, including on incomes and assets of farmers, and positive externalities to the local labor markets. (Reardon, Barrett, Berdegué and Swinnen, 2009)

We can only conclude from the above that alarm bells must be prematurely ringing to announce the pending demise of the world's family farmers. Apocalyptic messages are too rash. In the longer run, neither supermarketisation, nor precision farming need be as deleterious to family farming as is often imagined.

Conclusions

In sum, big is not always beautiful, especially not when talking about capitalist farms. There are sound reasons why family farming is still numerically predominant in world agriculture. Many of these has to do with what I call Chayanov's principle. Thus I contend that together with small-scale mechanisation, family labour accounts for the resilience of family farming. Chayanov was right in believing about a hundred years ago that family farming will continue to predominate in world agriculture. His principle will hold for some time still.

The ongoing pandemic threatens to halt if not reverse the continued transition of poor countries in Asia, Latin America and Africa from low to middle income levels. If the process resumes, it implies that real wages for agricultural labour will rise in countries like India, due both to competition with industry and services and continued emancipation of labour from discrimination by gender, caste, race and citizenship. Will the post-pandemic future create new space for family labour as well as for mechanisation? Will output markets imply more vertical integration, creating niches for farmers specialising in horticulture and fruit and deliveries to supermarkets (whether cooperative or private)? If so, we might expect further atrophy for many large landed estates and for capitalist farming because large is not beautiful.

NOTES

1. The classical source is (Habib, 1963). *The Agrarian System of Mughal India, 1556-1707,* Asia Publishing House, Bombay. On company rule, see Dalrymple, W. (2019). *The Anarchy: The Relentless Rise of the East India Company,* Bloomsbury Publishing.
2. Other examples in Europe, Latin America or Africa are given in (Djurfeldt and Sircar, 2017, chapter 1).
3. The following draws heavily on (Djurfeldt and Sircar, 2017).
4. Shanin argues that the late Marx revised the evolutionism in his earlier views and, among other things, he realised that the development in Russia, with the peasant communes, was pointing in another direction than the English case. This view is largely supported by Stedman Jones in his Marx biography (Shanin, 1984); (Stedman Jones, 2016).
5. The Land Matrix is an independent global land monitoring initiative of large-scale land acquisitions in low- and middle-income countries across the world (See Land Matrix, 2020).

REFERENCES

Athreya, V.B., G. Djurfeldt and S. Lindberg, (1990), *Barriers Broken: Production Relations and Agrarian Change in Tamil Nadu*, New Delhi: Sage Publications.

Bailey, W.R. (1973), *The One-Man Farm* (ERS 519), Washington, DC: US Department of Agriculture.

Chand, R., Lakshmi Prasanna and A. Singh (2011), Farm Size and Productivity: Understanding the Strengths of Smallholders and Improving Their Livelihoods, *Economic and Political Weekly*, Vol. 46, Nos. 26/27, pp. 5-11.

Chayanov, A.V. (1977), The Journey of My Brother Aleksei to the Land of Peasant Utopia, In R.E.F. Smith (ed.), *The Russian Peasant 1920 & 1984*, pp. 63-108, London: Frank Cass.

Chayanov, A.V. (1986 [1966]), *A.V. Chayanov and the Theory of Peasant Economy*, Madison, Wisconsin: The University of Wisconsin Press.

Coase, R.H. (1937), The Nature of the Firm, *Economica*, Vol. 4, No. 16, pp. 386-405.

Deininger, K. and D. Byerlee (2012), The Rise of Large Farms in Land Abundant Countries: Do They Have a Future?, *World Development*, Vol. 40, No. 4, pp. 701-14.

Djurfeldt, G. (1981), What Happened to the Agrarian Bourgoisie and the Rural Proletariat Under Monopoly Capitalism?, *Acta Sociologica*, Vol. 24, No. 3, pp. 167-91.

Djurfeldt, G. and S. Sircar (2017), *Structural Transformation and Agrarian Change in India*, New York and London: Routledge.

Djurfeldt, G. and C. Waldenström (1996), Towards a Theoretically Grounded Typology of Farms—A Swedish Case, *Acta Sociologica*, Vol. 39, No. 2, pp. 187-210.

Dovring, F. (1965 [1955]), *Land and Labor in Europe in the Twentieth Century: A Comparative Survey of Recent Agrarian History, (Third Revised Edition of Land and Labour in Europe, 1900-1950)*, The Hague: Martinus Nijhoff.

Eastwood, R., M. Lipton and A. Newell (2010), Farm Size, In P.L. Pingali and R.E. Evenson (eds.), *Handbook of Agricultural Economics*, North Holland: Elsevier.

Eswaran, M., A. Kotwal, B. Ramaswami and W. Wadhwa (2009), Sectoral Labour Flows and Agricultural Wages in India, 1983-2004: Has

Growth Trickled Down?, *Economic and Political Weekly*, Vol. 44, No. 2, pp. 46-55.

FAO (2014), *The State of Food and Agriculture: Innovation in Family Farming*, Rome: Food and Agricultural Organisation of the United Nations.

Gasson, R. (1987), Family Farming in Britain, In B. Galeski and E. Wilkening (eds.), *Family Farming in Europe and America*, pp. 5-37, Boulder, Col.: Westview Press.

Habib, I. (1963), *The Agrarian System of Mughal India, 1556-1707*, Bombay: Asia Publishing House.

Harrison, A. (1975), *Farmers and Farm Businesses in England*, Miscellaneous Study No. 62, Reading: Reading University, Department of Agricultural Economics and Management.

Hayami, Y. and V.W. Ruttan, (1971), *Agricultural Development: An International Perspective*, Baltimore: Johns Hopkins University Press.

Land Matrix (2020), Online Public Database on Land Deals, https://landmatrix.org.

Lenin, V.I. (1960 [1899]), *The Development of Capitalism in Russia*, Moscow: Foreign Languages Publishing House.

Marx, K. (1977 [1887]), *Capital: A Critique of Political Economy* (Vol. I), London: Lawrence & Wishart.

Newby, H., C. Bell, C. Rose and P. Saunders (1978), *Property, Paternalism and Power*, London: Hutchinson.

Perry, P.J. (1972), *British Agriculture, 1875-1914*, London: Methuen.

Polanyi, K. (2001 [1944]), *The Great Transformation: The Political and Economic Origins of Our Time*, Boston: Beacon Press.

Ratha, D. (2016), *Migration and Remittances Factbook 2016*, The World Bank.

Reardon, T., C.B. Barrett, J.A. Berdegué and J.F.M. Swinnen (2009), Agrifood Industry Transformation and Small Farmers in Developing Countries, *World Development*, Vol. 37, No. 11, pp. 1717-27.

Reardon, T., C.P. Timmer, C. Barrett and J. Berdegué (2003), The Rise of Supermarkets in Africa, Asia, and Latin America, *American Journal of Agricultural Economics*, Vol. 85, No. 5, pp. 1140-46.

Schmitt, G. (1991), Why is the Agriculture of Advanced Western Economies Still Organized by Family Farms: Will This Continue to

Be So in the Future?, *European Review of Agricultural Economics,* Vol. 18, pp. 443-58.

Scott, J.C. (1985), *Weapons of the Weak: Everyday Forms of Peasant Resistance,* London and New York: Yale University Press.

Shanin, T. (ed.) (1984), *Late Marx and the Russian Road: Marx and 'The Peripheries of Capitalism': A Case Presented by Teodor Shanin*, London: Routledge and Kegan Paul.

Smith, A. (1904 [1776]), *An Inquiry into the Nature and Causes of the Wealth of Nations,* Retrieved from http://www.econlib.org/library/Smith/smWN.html.

Stedman Jones, G.A. (2016), *Karl Marx: Greatness and Illusions,* Cambridge: Harvard University Press.

Thomas, R.J. (1985), *Citizenship, Gender, and Work: Social Organization of Industrial Agriculture,* Berkeley: University of California Press.

Williamson, O.E. (1979), Transaction-Cost Economics: The Governance of Contractual Relations, *Journal of Law and Economics,* Vol. 22, No. 2, pp. 233-61.

World Bank (2009), *Awakening Africa's Sleeping Giant: Prospects for Commercial Agriculture in the Guinea Savannah Zone and Beyond,* Washington, DC: The World Bank.

11

What is Monopoly Capital?[1]

John Bellamy Foster

"Monopoly capital" is the term often used in Marxian political economy and by some non-Marxist analysts to designate the new form of capital, embodied in the modern giant corporation, that, beginning in the last quarter of the 19th century, displaced the small family firm as the dominant economic unit of the system, marking the end of the freely competitive stage of capitalism and the beginning of monopoly capitalism.

Marx's *Capital*, the first volume of which was published in 1867, was designed to uncover the laws of motion of the 19th century era of free competition, and was based in part on the assumption that production was carried out by numerous individual capitals (or firms) (Marx, 1976). Each of these capitals accounted for a negligible portion of society's total value added, and thus had little control over their own price and output levels, which were dictated by impersonal market forces. Yet, unlike the other classical economists, Marx recognised that such an environment of atomistic competition was a transitory historical phenomenon. "The battle of competition," he wrote, "is fought by the cheapening of commodities. The cheapness of commodities depends, *ceteris paribus*, on the productiveness of labour, and this again on the scale of production. Therefore, the larger capitals beat the smaller.... [C]ompetition rages in direct portion to the number and in inverse proportion to the magnitude of the rival capitals." Hence, capital accumulation presupposed both a growth in the size of individual capitals (concentration, or accumulation proper) and the fusion together of many capitals into "a huge mass in a single hand" (centralisation). Moreover, the credit system, which begins as a "humble assistant of accumulation," soon "becomes a new and terrible weapon in the battle of competition, and is finally transformed into an enormous social mechanism for the centralisation of capitals (Marx, 1976).

As Engels observed decades later, the rise of the joint stock company or modern corporation heralded the fact that: "the old boasted freedom of competition has reached the end of its tether and must itself announce its obvious, scandalous bankruptcy" (Marx, 1981).

Thus, there can be no doubt that Marx and particularly Engels recognised that a historical turning point had been reached. Nevertheless, they saw the demise of free competition as marking not a new stage of capitalism, but as a harbinger of socialism to come. It was not till some years later, in the work of subsequent theorists, that studies of monopoly capitalism as a distinct phase in the evolution of the system arose.

The first major theorist of monopoly capitalism was Thorstein Veblen, a rebel economist of the North American left, deeply influenced by Marx, but not himself a Marxist. In *The Theory of Business Enterprise* (1904) and *Absentee Ownership and Business Enterprise in Modern Times* (1923), Veblen emphasised such characteristic themes of monopoly capital theory as the rise of corporate finance; the tendency for monopolistic profit margins to widen at the expense of less powerful firms and workers; the systematic promotion of excess capacity; and the interpenetration of sales and manufactures (Veblen, 1904; Veblen, 1923). However, Veblen's more powerful insights were largely ignored by his followers within institutionalist economics in the United States. Consequently, it was only in the Marxist tradition—where Veblen's work was not known—that a continuing stream of work on monopoly capitalism emerged.

Here the landmark study was *Finance Capital* (1910) by the Austrian Marxist Rudolf Hilferding, which attempted to integrate into the core of Marx's theory such increasingly important phenomena as the developing market for industrial securities, the growing role of banks in the concentration and centralisation of capital, and the system-wide consequences of expanding monopolisation. Aside from the emphasis that he placed on bank capital in this whole development, Hilferding's analysis is chiefly remembered for a conclusion reached in Chapter 15: "The ultimate outcome of this process [of monopolisation] would be the formation of a general cartel. The whole of capitalist reproduction would then be consciously regulated by a single body which would determine the volume of production in all branches of industry (Hilferding, 1981)."

In historical retrospect, it is clear that this picture was overdrawn. Powerful counter- tendencies such as the breakup of old firms and the founding of new ones made concentration and centralisation a more uneven process than Hilferding expected. Moreover, Hilferding's concern with this abstract notion of a "general cartel" kept him from developing a concrete theory that would explain the modifications in accumulation associated with a monopolistically competitive market, dominated by a handful of giant, "corespective" firms (Schumpeter, 1942).

Hilferding's analysis had pointed to the growth of capital export and of transnational rivalry between mammoth corporate trusts. Out of this arose Lenin's *Imperialism, the Highest Stage of Capitalism*, written in 1916, and his observation that, "If it were necessary to give the briefest possible definition of imperialism we should have to say that imperialism is the monopoly stage of capitalism (Lenin, 1939)." However, while basing his theory on the predominance of monopoly, neither Lenin nor any of his early followers in the 1920s and 30s—with the exception of E.A. Preobrazhensky, whose work, *The Decline of Capitalism* (1931) was suppressed in the USSR—examined the implications of this for the underlying theory of accumulation (Preobrazhensky, 1985). Further progress in the formation of a theory of monopoly capitalism had to await the integration of the analysis of concentration and centralisation, with the understanding of economic crisis that had evolved out of the famous debate over Marx's reproduction schemes. As with mainstream theory—which in the 1930s had produced a theory of imperfect competition in the work of Joan Robinson and Edward

Chamberlain, followed by a theory of crisis in John Maynard Keynes's *General Theory* that was still based on the assumption of free competition—these two strands of a complete theory of accumulation under modern capitalism were cut off from each other (Robinson, 1933; Chamberlain, 1933). The first to unite them was the Polish Marxist economist Michał Kalecki—often credited with having discovered in the early 1930s all the essentials of Keynes's *General Theory* before Keynes himself. In such later works as *Essays in the Theory of Economic Fluctuations* and *Theory of Economic Dynamics*, Kalecki fused the class-based analysis of realisation crisis derived from Marx and Rosa Luxemburg, with what he called a rising "degree of monopoly" (related to Marx's surplus value concept), developing a unified theory of accumulation under monopoly capitalism Kalecki, 1939; Kalecki, 1954). As Kalecki (1990) wrote: "Monopoly appears to be deeply rooted in the nature of the capitalist system: free competition, as an assumption, may be useful in the first stage of certain investigations, but as a description of the normal stage of capitalist economy it is merely a myth." This argument was carried forward by Josef Steindl, a young Austrian economist who was one of Kalecki's colleagues at the Oxford Institute of Statistics during the Second World War. Steindl's *Maturity and Stagnation in American Capitalism*, first published in 1952, explored the causes of the Great Depression of the 1930s, contending that growing monopolisation raised profit margins (or the rate of surplus value) in core industries (Steindl, 1976).

This led to excess capacity as large firms protected their higher margins in the face of weaknesses in demand by reducing capacity utilisation rather than prices. Excess capacity dampened the rate of growth of investment. Hence, stagnation, or slow growth and widening unemployment and underemployment and idle capacity, represented the general economic trend.

Monopoly Capital by Paul Baran and Paul Sweezy, published in 1966, originated with the dissatisfaction of these thinkers with their earlier major contributions in Sweezy's *The Theory of Capitalist Development* (1942) and Baran's *The Political Economy of Growth* (1957) (Sweezy, 1942; Baran, 1957; Baran and Sweezy, 1966).

Sweezy was a former professor of economics at Harvard and editor of *Monthly Review*, and Baran was a professor of economics at Stanford. *Monopoly Capital* took the Kalecki-Steindl framework as its initial point of departure, seeking to draw out the wider societal implications. In this view, Marx's law of the tendency of the rate of profit to fall, associated with the stage of free competition, had been replaced, in the monopoly capitalist stage, by a law of the tendency of the surplus to rise. The economic surplus was defined as the difference between total social output and the socially necessary labour costs of producing it. The surplus concept was employed as a complementary category to the classical concept of surplus value, facilitating the exploration of contradictions specific to monopoly capitalism such as the growing role of waste in production, which were not easily addressed using the surplus value category.

The argument of *Monopoly Capital* focused on the critical problem of surplus absorption as the chief contradiction at this stage of accumulation. Surplus could be absorbed in one of three ways: (1) it could be consumed, (2) it could be invested, or (3) it could be wasted. Capitalist consumption accounted for a decreasing share of demand as income grew, while investment took the form of new productive capacity, which served to inhibit new net investment. Although there was always the possibility that altogether new "epoch-making innovations"—resembling the steam engine, the railroad, and the automobile in their overall scale and effect—could emerge, allowing the system to break free from the stagnation tendency, such massive, capital-absorbing innovations were by definition few and far between. Hence, the system of private accumulation, if left to itself, exhibited a powerful tendency towards stagnation. If periods of rapid growth nonetheless occurred—Baran and Sweezy were writing at the high point of the post-Second World War expansion—this was due to such countervailing factors to stagnation as the sales effort, military spending, and financial expansion (the last addressed at the end of their chapter on the sales effort). All such countervailing factors were, however, of a self- limiting character and could be expected to lead to bigger contradictions in the future.

A more comprehensive theory of monopoly capital, Baran and

Sweezy noted, would have to consider the labour process, which had occupied such a central place in Marx's analysis—something that they did not attempt in what they called their "essay-sketch." Here Harry Braverman stepped in with his path-breaking *Labour and Monopoly Capital* (1974), making it clear that the degradation of work brought on by the division of labour, as Marx had described it in *Capital*, was in many ways heightened under monopoly capitalism, with the rise of scientific management (Braverman, 1974). Other works in this general tradition in the 1960s and 70s included Harry Magdoff's *The Age of Imperialism*, James O'Connor's *The Fiscal Crisis of the State*, and Stephen Hymer's *The Multinational Corporation.* The Union for Radical Political Economists, organised in 1968, brought out its first economic crisis reader in 1975, entitled *Radical Perspectives on the Economic Crisis of Monopoly Capital* (Magdoff, 1969; O'Connor, 1973; Hymer; 1979, URPE, 1975).

The concept of monopoly capital also had an enormous influence in the global south. Che Guevara, who met both Sweezy and Magdoff, and who identified closely with Baran's argument on monopoly capital and economic surplus in The Political Economy of Growth, declared in 1965: "Ever since monopoly capital took over the world, it has kept the greater part of humanity in poverty, dividing all of the profits among the group of most powerful countries (Guevera, 1965)."

Although the notion of the monopoly stage of capitalism played a key role in the work of most Marxian economists till the 1970s—e.g. Maurice Dobb in *Studies in the Development of Capitalism* (1947), Ernest Mandel in *Marxist Economic Theory* (1962), and Samir Amin in *Accumulation on a World Scale* (1970)—by the late 1970s the notion of monopoly capital had begun to wane (Dobb, 1947; Mandel, 1968; Amin, 1974). During what became known as the "back to Marx" movement, or the growth of fundamentalist Marxian political economy, it became increasingly common to assume the ascendancy of free competition throughout the history of capitalism, and to reject the notion of historical stages of capitalist development altogether. Along with this came the abandonment (or at least the downplaying) of notions of concentration and centralisation of production and monopoly profits. Economist John Weeks wrote in his *Capital and Exploitation* in 1981 that "the monopolies that stalk the pages of the writings of Baran and Sweezy have no existence beyond the work of those authors (Weeks, 1981)." Numerous critics of monopoly capital theory claimed that the internationalisation of capital—by breaking down US hegemony and making the advanced capitalist countries as a whole more vulnerable to foreign trade and capital movements—had demolished the structure of monopolistic accumulation.[2]

In contrast, a number of radical and Marxian theorists—including Keith Cowling in *Monopoly Capitalism* (1982) and John Bellamy Foster in *The Theory of Monopoly Capitalism* (1986) and (with Robert W. McChesney) *The Endless Crisis* (2012)—argued with increasing force that the reality was one of continuing concentration and centralisation of capital on a world scale, or the internationalisation of monopoly capital, with fewer and fewer firms controlling larger parts of both national and international economies (Cowling, 1982; Foster, 1986; Foster and McChesney, 2012). This was coupled with the institution of a system of "divide and rule" in relation to global labour. In an influential empirical study (carried out with the help of R. Jamil Jonna), Foster and McChesney demonstrated that at the time of the Great Financial Crisis of 2007–09, the top 200 corporations in the United States accounted for about 30 per cent of gross profits in the economy (up from about 13 per cent in 1950), while at the world level the top 500 global corporations received about 40 per cent of total global revenue (up from around 20 per cent in 1960) (Foster, McChesney and Jonna, 2011).

Nevertheless, the main focus of monopoly capital theorists from the 1980s onwards was directed not so much at debates about the status of monopoly capital, but at explaining the onset of economic stagnation, beginning in the mid-1970s, and how financialisation emerged as a countervailing factor, thereby lifting the economy. Key works in this regard were Magdoff and Sweezy's *Stagnation and the Financial Explosion* in 1987, followed by *The Irreversible Crisis* in 1988 (Magdoff and Sweezy, 1987, 1988). In 1997, Sweezy argued that monopolisation and stagnation had led to the emergence of a new layer of contradictions in the system, which he summed up as "the financialisation of the capital accumulation process (Sweezy, 1997)."

Beginning around 2000, theorists in the monopoly capital tradition therefore began to develop the notion of a new phase of monopoly capitalism, or monopoly-finance capital, in which monopolisation, stagnation, and financialisation operated as simultaneous and mutually reinforcing trends. Foster and Fred Magdoff explored this thesis in *The Great Financial Crisis*, published in 2009, shortly after the housing bubble burst. In *The Endless Crisis* in 2012, Foster and McChesney were among the first to argue that with the weakening of financialisation as a result of the crisis of 2007–09, secular stagnation was likely to persist for the indefinite future. Meanwhile, Amin, writing in *The Law of Worldwide Value* in 2011, declared we are living in "the late capitalism of generalised, financialised, and globalised oligopolies (Amin, 2010)." The result of these developments has been a growing interest in the theory of monopoly capital and the insights it provides into the structural crisis of capital in our time. This renewed interest was reflected in the publication in 2016 of a special issue of *Monthly Review* on "*Monopoly Capital* a Half-Century On," with a host of major economic thinkers, including Amin, Kent Klitgaard, Costas Lapavitsas, Michael Meeropol, Ivan Mendieta-Muñoz, Prabhat Patnaik, Jan Toporowski, Mary V. Wrenn, and others.

The growing interest in monopoly capital theory has been further heightened in recent years by the publication in *Monthly Review* in 2012 and 2013 of the two missing chapters of Baran and Sweezy's *Monopoly Capital*; the publication in 2017 of *The Age of Monopoly Capital: Selected Correspondence of Paul A. Baran and Paul M. Sweezy*; and the release of the first volume of Toporowski's long-awaited intellectual biography of Kalecki (Baran and Sweezy, 2012; 2013; Baran and Foster, 2017; Toporowski, 2013).

Concluding an analysis in 2016, Patnaik observed: "Unless some new 'bubble' arises, of which there are no signs, and which too would inevitably collapse, precipitating a new crisis, the world economy will continue to be mired in stagnation. The basic framework of *Monopoly Capital* helps us to understand this predicament better than any other book written since" (Patnaik, 2016).

NOTES

1. This article was initially published in *Monthly Review* 2018. Permission is taken from Monthly Review Press for reprint.
2. On the notion, especially prevalent in the late 1980s and 1990s, that international competition had effectively eliminated monopoly capital, see Brenner (2006), p. 54 and Robert J.S. Ross and Kent C. Trachte, (1990), pp. 38–50.

REFERENCES

Amin, S. (1974), *Accumulation on a World Scale,* New York: Monthly Review Press.

Amin, S. (2010), *The Law of World Wide Value,* New York: Monthly Review Press.

Baran Paul A. (1957), *The Political Economy of Growth,* New York: Monthly Review Press.

Baran Paul A. and Paul M. Sweezy (1966), *Monopoly Capital,* New York: Monthly Review Press.

Baran Paul A. and Paul M. Sweezy (2012), Some Theoretical Implications, *Monthly Review,* Vol. 64, No. 3, pp. 24–59.

Baran Paul A. and Paul M. Sweezy (2013), The Quality of Monopoly Capitalist Society: Culture and Communications, *Monthly Review,* Vol. 65, No. 3, pp. 43-64.

Braran Paul. A. and Paul. M. Sweezy (2013), *The Age of Monopoly Capital: Selected Correspondence of Paul A. Baran and Paul M. Sweezy, 1949–1969,* Nicholas Baran and John Bellamy Foster (eds.), New York: Monthly Review Press.

Braverman, H. (1974), *Labor and Monopoly Capital,* New York: Monthly Review Press.

Brenner, R. (2006), *The Economics of Global Turbulence,* London: Verso.

Cowling, K. (1982), *Monopoly Capitalism,* New York: John Wiley and Sons.

Cowling K. and R. Sugden (1987), *Transnational Monopoly Capitalism,* New York: St. Martin's Press.

Chamberlain, E.H. (1933), *The Theory of Monopolistic Competition,*

Cambridge, MA: Harvard University Press.

Dobb, M. (1947), *Studies in the Development of Capitalism,* New York: International Publishers.

Foster, J.B. (1986), *The Theory of Monopoly Capitalism,* New York: Monthly Review Press.

Foster, J.B. and R.W. McChesney and R. Jamil Jonna (2011), Monopoly and Competition in the Twenty-First Century, *Monthly Review,* Vol. 62, No. 11.

Foster, J.B. and R.W. McChesney, (2012), *The Endless Crisis*, New York: Monthly Review Press.

Guevara, C. (1965), Speech at the Afro-Asian Conference in Algeria, February 24, Available at: http://marxists.org.

Hilferding, R. (1981), *Finance Capital,* London: Routledge and Kegan Paul.

Hymer, S. (1979), *The Multinational Corporation,* Cambridge: Cambridge University Press.

Kalecki, M. (1939), *Essays in the Theory of Economic Fluctuations,* New York: Russell and Russell.

Kalecki, M. (1954), *Theory of Economic Dynamics,* London: George Allen and Unwin.

Kalecki, M. (1990), *Collected Works,* Vol. 1, Oxford: Oxford University Press.

Lenin, V.I. (1939), *Imperialism, the Highest Stage of Capitalism,* New York: International Publishers.

Magdoff, H. (1969), *The Age of Imperialism,* New York: Monthly Review Press.

Magdoff, H. and Paul M. Sweezy (1987), *Stagnation and the Financial Explosion*, New York: Monthly Review Press.

Magdoff, H. and Paul M. Sweezy (1988), *The Irreversible Crisis,* New York: Monthly Review Press.

Mandel, E. (1968), *Marxist Economic Theory,* New York: Monthly Review Press.

Marx, K. (1976), *Capital,* Vol. 1, London: Penguin Books.

Marx, K. (1981), *Capital,* Vol. 3, London: Penguin Books.

O'Connor, J. (1973), *The Fiscal Crisis of the State,* New York: St. Martin's Press.

Patnaik, P. (2016), Monopoly Capital: Then and Now, *Monthly Review,*

Vol. 68, No. 3.

Preobrazhensky, E.A. (1985), *The Decline of Capitalism,* Armonk, NY: M.E. Sharpe.

Robinson, J. (1933), *The Economics of Imperfect Competition,* London: Macmillian.

Ross, Robert J.S. and Kent C. Trachte (1990), *Global Capitalism,* Albany: State University of New York Press.

Schumpeter, J.A. (1942), *Capitalism, Socialism, and Democracy,* New York: Harper.

Steindl, J. (1976), *Maturity and Stagnation in American Capitalism,* New York: Monthly Review Press.

Sweezy, Paul. M. (1942), *The Theory of Capitalist Development,* New York: Oxford University Press.

Sweezy, Paul M. (1997), More (or Less) on Globalization, *Monthly Review,* Vol. 49, No. 4.

Toporowski, J. (2013), *Michał Kalecki, An Intellectual Biography,* Vol. 1, *Rendezvous in Cambridge, 1899–1939,* London: Palgrave Macmillan.

Union for Radical Political Economists (1975), *Radical Perspectives on the Economic Crisis of Monopoly Capital,* New York: URPE.

Veblen, T. (1904), *The Theory of Business Enterprise,* New York: Scribner.

Veblen, T. (1923), *Absentee Ownership and Business Enterprise in Modern Times,* New York: Huebsch.

Weeks, J. (1981), *Capital and Exploitation,* Princeton: Princeton University Press.

12

Late Marx, Luxemburg, and the Conception of 'Accumulation of Capital'[1]

Paul Zarembka

Introduction

Marxist political economy very often refers to the "accumulation of capital" as if it were a transparent concept, one easily understood from Marx's work. Commonly, citing accumulation of capital in a theoretical or empirical analysis suggests a depth of analysis by an author that does not need further explication. It can read with a confidence that "gravity" has in a work of physics. The problem is that, as a concept, it is not clear what accumulation of capital is to mean. In fact, capital is so often referred to as a means of production that, following the classical economists, Marxist political economists do not seem to have broken from Marx's predecessors when mentioning the accumulation of capital. I include Lenin in this characterisation (see Zarembka, 2003).

Marx's multiple-volume work was not called *Capital* in order to refer to means of production. Constant capital, rather, is used to refer to the means of production, measured in value units. The entire work of *Capital* is fundamentally offered to comprehend the social relations of production in capitalism. Class is the fundamental issue. Therefore, his accumulation of capital must be understood with class in mind, not means of production, not constant capital.

Marx himself was a theorist who was constantly evolving, not a person stuck with his earlier thinking. We can recall how late he arrived at "labour power" as an important concept, namely around

1865 (Zarembka, 2020, Chapter II). In this spirit, we can interrogate the concept of accumulation of capital as he used it.

Marx had assumed in *Capital* that he was offering an understanding of a world that was fully capitalist. This continued to be the context for his discussions of accumulation of capital that took place in Volume I and in Volume II. And these discussions suggest, in major part, that more wage-labourers would be involved, in addition to more constant capital. However, when we read his discussions carefully, contradictions emerge. These are discussed in the first two sections of this chapter.

Rosa Luxemburg published her book on the topic in 1913, thirty years after Marx's death. While she did not explicitly interrogate the wording "accumulation of capital", she clearly argued that expansion of wage-labour employment was fundamentally involved. Her main points are elaborated in the following section and then responses by her critics are mentioned subsequently.

Resulting from the preceding discussion, value as a concept may be called into question, or we need to consider how value works in a theoretical environment in which non-capitalist environments are being penetrated by capitalism. After a reflection on Louis Althusser's work, this chapter briefly concludes that Marxist political economy may need some re-examination.

Contradictions within Marx's Conception of Accumulation of Capital

Marx centred his theoretical work in *Capital* within a fully capitalist world. He said that in order to examine the object of our investigation in its integrity, free from all disturbing subsidiary circumstances, we must treat the whole world as one nation, and assume that capitalist production is established everywhere and has possessed itself of every branch of industry. (Marx, 1867, 545, fn. 1)

He wrote this while discussing accumulation of capital, a subject perhaps least expected for such presumption. Several other statements by Marx were made in this regard, notably in Volume II. As a simplifying assumption, who could fault Marx, particularly when we know full well that he knew that the world was much more complex? Still, the presumption is problematic within the internal logic of his work.

Marx's concept of accumulation of capital conflicts with the presumption of a fully capitalist world. His accumulation of capital must be understood to mean an increase in the number of wage labourers and the required means of production. Thus, in a draft of *Capital*, we read 'The process of accumulation is itself an intrinsic feature of the capitalist process of production. It entails the new creation of wage-labourers...' (Marx, 1933, 1061).[2] Then, in Volume I as published, we read:

> A part of the annual surplus-labor must have been applied to the production of additional means of production and subsistence ... Now in order to allow of these elements actually functioning as capital, the capitalist class requires additional labor ... Accumulation of capital is, therefore, increase of the proletariat (Marx, 1867, 544–45, 576).

This requirement, although inadequately appreciated, should be clear enough (for elaboration, see Zarembka 2020, Chapter VI).

Where does the increased supply of labour power come from? In Marx's draft, the answer reads:

> It does this either by extending its rule to sections of the population not previously subject to itself, such as women or children; or else it subjugates a section of the laboring masses that has accrued through the natural growth of population. (Marx, 1933, 1061)

In Volume I, the solution for additional labour power was narrowed as follows: 'the mechanism of capitalist production provides beforehand, by converting the working-class into a class dependent on wages, a class whose ordinary wages suffice, not only for its maintenance, but for its increase' (Marx, 1867, 544). In other words, capital had previously created wage labourers, and now these wage labourers get a bit more than enough for their own subsistence. This may be suggestive of a Malthusian base for population increase. In any case, the incorporation of women and children into the labour force, mentioned in the draft, is neglected in the published work.

Population increase continues to be mentioned by Marx as a major source of additional labour power. In the 19th century, the global population growth rate was only around 0.5 per cent per year. If Marx was considering a country, rather than the whole world, the rate of increase in England was higher, one per cent in the 19th century, but still not enough to rely on for accumulation of capital. Marx's own numerical illustrations of accumulation assume annual population increases of 10 per cent. Another possibility? The increased labour power supply for accumulation of capital could come from continuing penetration of non-capitalist modes, and not merely a creation of wage labourers within population increase. While presumption of a fully capitalist world in *Capital* contradicts such an understanding, proletarianisation of the world was then and is still, in fact, proceeding apace. Thus, *Pagine Marxiste* (November 2004, Year 1, Number 5, p. 5) makes an attempt to record progress, indicating that the global non-agricultural labour force more than quadrupled from 1950 to 2000, representing a 2.9 per cent annual rate of growth, due in part to population growth (about 1.7 per cent annually) and in part to the 'process of proletarianisation, linked to the disintegration of the peasant social framework and to the shift from the rural to the urban areas'.

Perhaps Marx became quite aware of continuing proletarianisation (not only the proletarianisation resulting from original transition from feudalism to capitalism, i.e. 'primitive accumulation'). Thus, consider somewhat more deeply the unpublished 'Results' section, which was to have been the conclusion of Volume I. The most important theoretical concept in 'Results' was formal and real subsumption of labour to capital, following usage beginning in the *Grundrisse*. By the concept of subsumption, it can be argued that Marx 'clearly wished to imply that as economic relations increasingly took on a capitalist character, their scale increased and this brought them even closer to the world market and their point of culmination' (White, 1996, 191). Yet, by leaving 'Results' out entirely as Volume I went to the publisher, any focus on subsumption was lost. Even references elsewhere within Volume I to subsumption were almost completely stricken by Marx, including references to cooperation, division of labour, and use of machinery as stages of subsumption (White, 1996, 200; one remaining definitional passage for 'subsumption' was eliminated in the French edition). The published Volume I shows that "very little remained of the argument that in its cycle of reproduction capital created its own preconditions on an ever increasing scale" (201).[3]

Marx spent many years after the publication of Volume I studying pre-capitalist societies. His motivation could well be the following:

> Just as Marx was about to publish the first volume of *Das Kapital* he had run into serious problems with the section of his projected work which would deal with the circulation of capital. He had hitherto assumed that capital would spread throughout the world carrying all before it, but he had overlooked the fact that even in his own native Hunsruecken despite the development of capitalism, the older, collective, social and economic system still survived. Capitalism, apparently, did not necessarily erode traditional peasant society, but coexisted with it. Marx removed much of the philosophical underpinnings for his earlier view of capitalist development from the published version of *Das Kapital*, continuing the excisions in the second and French editions, and he embarked on a lengthy empirical investigation of how capital actually began to circulate. He had an excellent example to hand in Russia, which had just embarked on the capitalist road, having abolished serfdom a few years earlier. In 1870 Marx learnt Russian and got down to the serious job of collecting materials on Russian economic development. (White, 2001, 12–13, summarizing a major result of his own 1996 book).

It is mostly forgotten that Marx wrote to Engels in 1870 that the most important work published since Engels' own *Condition of the Working Class in England* was Flerovsky's *Condition of the Working [Peasant] Class in Russia* (published in 1869). Flerovsky's book, like, for example, van Onselen's (1976) a hundred years later, focused on the proletarianisation process, including the role of taxation therein: 'The main reason which compels the [peasant] to resort to the capitalist is to pay his taxes' (translation by White, 1996, 249, who also explains that a 'worker' for Flerovsky is a 'peasant' in our usage; see also Forstater, 2005). It is fair to say that Marx was trying to understand the forms of, and limitations, to capital's penetration. This became a continuing study of his to the end of his life, including extensive correspondence with Russians, which in turn has extensive implications for the manner in which we understand Marx and those after him (see White, 2018).

Marx's Late Theoretical Work: Schemes of Reproduction

We could suspect that the question of penetration of non-capitalist modes of production would become integrated into Marx's late theoretical work. It is not to be so, however, and was left to posterity in Rosa Luxemburg's (1913) work. From Engels' 'Preface' to Volume II we know that Marx was working on the schemes of reproduction as the last of his theoretical work. And from Engels' footnoting within Volume II concerning whether he is drawing upon earlier or later manuscripts of Volume II for his own editing, we can understand where individual passages are drawn from. For Section II of 'Simple Reproduction', for example, we can read Engels' note: 'Mainly from Manuscript II [1870], the Schemes from Manuscript VIII [1878]' (Marx, 1885, 399, fn. 44). For the entire chapter on 'Accumulation', we can read that it is from that last Manuscript VIII. We can thus infer that the schemes themselves date from 1878, i.e. long after Marx's studies of Russia began.

Even in 1878, however, Marx was still considering, from a theoretical point of view, the capitalist world to be complete. Immediately before Part III of Volume II, which includes the schemes, we read, 'Apart from [the capitalist] class, according to our assumption—the general and exclusive domination of capitalist production—there is no other class at all except the working-class' (Marx, 1885, 352, apparently also written in 1878, judging from Engels' 'Preface', p. 5). Also, in the chapter 'Simple Reproduction', we read: 'there are here only two classes: the working-class disposing only of its labour power, and the capitalist class' (p. 425, from the 1878 Manuscript VIII). In other words, the process of proletarianisation remains excluded from Marx's last theoretical work on *Capital*, even after studying Russia.

In beginning his discussion concerning accumulation of additional constant capital for department I, Marx says that 'in order that the transition from simple to extended reproduction may take place, production in department I must be in a position to fabricate fewer elements of constant capital for II and so many the more for I' (500–01). That is, in transition to accumulation, production for workers' consumption (department II) is scaled back as production of means of production (department I) is increased. Total employed labour power is seemingly constant. When he turns to additional variable capital needed for the expanding department I, Marx writes:

> We have explained at great length in *Book* [Volume] *1* that labor-power is always available under the capitalist system of production, and that more labor can be rendered fluent, if necessary, *without increasing the number of laborers or the quantity of labor-power employed.* We therefore need not go into this any further, but shall rather assume that the portion of the newly created money-capital capable of being converted into variable capitals will always find at hand the labor-power into which it is to transform itself. (Marx, 1885, 505)

Marx seems to be referring here to production of relative surplus value, leading to workers being expelled from production as technology develops. Again, total labour power employed seems rather constant. Logically, Marx is almost forced to make such a statement as long as he presumes a fully capitalist world, as simple population increase would be his only other possibility.

Nevertheless, when Marx develops his full schemes of production as accumulation of capital proceeds, both departments I and II are increasing substantially, with the composition of capital in each department being held constant. It reads as if Marx, working out his calculations of schemes of reproduction under accumulation of capital, has come face to face with the fact that, unlike his earlier statement regarding Volume I (cited above with italics), more wage labourers are required, after all.

Marx, in the schemes of accumulation, offers two illustrations, with his second having higher compositions of capital in both departments. The latter, he claims, "presupposes a considerable development of capitalist production and accordingly of the productivity of social labour, a considerable previous increase in the scale of production, and finally a development of all the circumstances which produce a relative surplus-population among the working-class" (Marx, 1885, 518). This could be a lead into incorporating the production of relative surplus value as the engine for sustaining a renewed supply of labour power. However, Marx never pursued this in drafts being prepared for Volume II and does not suggest that as his purpose.

The schemes of reproduction in Marx are a remarkable attempt at posing a new problem for investigation. They sustain the political economy of economists such as Kalecki, whom Kowalik (1990) argues is the main continuity from Marx and Luxemburg. They have even influenced 'mainstream' economics. But they do not help much, at least in Marx's own formulation, in addressing a fundamental problem, the possibility of realising surplus value within a fully capitalist system. Nor do they suggest that Marx was incorporating within his last theoretical work the issue of penetration of capitalism into non-capitalist modes of production.

White, whom we have already introduced, considers Marx's problem in drafting Volume II. He argues that the first draft, begun by Marx in 1865, failed 'to establish any necessary connection between expanded reproduction of capital and the extension of capitalist relations'. Accumulation of capital for Marx was to be "a process which would reproduce its presuppositions, the capitalists and workers on an extended scale." "To be unable to show that capital created its own presuppositions, that it created Civil Society, was a serious difficulty for Marx's overall scheme of capitalist development" (White, 1996, 196).

Marx never came close to resolving this problem. And he could not resolve it as long as he separated theoretical questions regarding accumulation of capital from penetration of non-capitalist forms of production ('primitive accumulation of capital' is another matter altogether; see Zarembka, 2002a and 2020, Chapter V).

Luxemburg on Accumulation

Marx's study of the history of capital's penetration, including its difficulties, had a successor in Luxemburg's interest in the question of penetration of non-capitalist forms of production. Luxemburg's interest is evidenced particularly in her *Introduction to Political Economy*, published posthumously (only half of it found after her murder). In fact, her work used many of the same sources Marx had studied. But she also integrated these questions into her own theoretical work.

Marx's *Capital* and Luxemburg's *Introduction to Political Economy* have distinct beginning points. Marx begins with 'Commodities'. Luxemburg does not get to that till her sixth chapter after 'What is Political Economy?', 'Social Labour', and then three chapters on economic history, including primitive communism, the feudal system, and the medieval city and guilds. In other words, for Luxemburg, the capitalist mode of production arises in an historical context. Luxemburg's conclusions concerning primitive communism's longevity are indicative. While the last form of primitive communism—the Russian commune—had survived because of its adaptability, there is 'only one contact that it cannot tolerate or overcome—contact with European civilisation, i.e. with capitalism. This encounter ...accomplishes what millennia and the most savage Oriental conquerors could not: the dissolution of the whole social structure from this inside' (Luxemburg, 1925, 226). To determine the comparative power of capital to rip these people from all means of production and to thrust these societies into value-producing ones, we cannot just look at capital. We also have to look at the weaknesses of the primitive societies, including, as she does, developments in their specific practices of warfare.[4]

The capitalist mode arising in an historical context indicates that theoretical categories are not only socially conditioned, but socially conditioned within the developing historical setting. Suggestive of a rethinking of fundamental aspects of Marxist theory, we turn to this issue later. Here, we discuss our preliminary, Luxemburg's fundamentally important *The Accumulation of Capital* and subsequent *Anti-Critique*, and their dismissal by very many critics, which has constrained development of Marxist theory.

Confronting the problem of realisation is the deepest contribution which Luxemburg's *The Accumulation of Capital* makes to Marxist political economy: under extended reproduction of capital, what is surplus value used for? It cannot be merely luxury consumption of capitalists as that would be simple reproduction. It cannot be increasing workers' consumption as this is no part of surplus value. The possibility that it could be used for increasing constant capital is more complicated. If the composition of capital stays constant, as in Marx's own reproduction schemes in Volume II, then any increase of constant capital is exactly associated with an increase in variable capital (more workers selling their labour power to capitalists). Could not the composition of capital be continually rising, and could not the increasing constant capital then completely absorb surplus value not used for capitalist consumption, with no extension of the capital–wage labour relation? Yet, a rising composition does not mean more machinery being used per work hour, but rather more value (labour hours) in the production of the machinery used by workers in their work hours. The latter increase is not obvious as there is technological change in the production of machinery, even as we have a common sense that workers are working with more advanced technology today than earlier. Magaline (1975) offers an excellent starting point for analysing the difficulties of this question and should help undermine dogma about the composition rising, thereby realising surplus value. Furthermore, if the composition is characterised as the "materialised" composition of capital $C/(v+s)$ rather than the frequent C/v, the result could be even a stability rather than a rise (see Zarembka, 2015 and 2020, Chapter VIII).

Surplus value can, however, overcome the problem of insufficient markets when used for extending capitalist domination of the world, i.e. having more wage labourers attached to means of production controlled/owned by capitalists. Then surplus value can be realised, albeit outside the circuit of capital.

Critics

There are several factors underlying the dismissal of Luxemburg's work, the upshot of which has been to limit the development of Marxist theory. First, Lenin had said, point blank, that Luxemburg was wrong on the accumulation of capital. While Lenin's own economics had not been carefully criticised by anyone, the success of the Bolshevik Revolution with Lenin as leader provided a imprimatur for his opinions not only on political matters, but also on economics. In fact, Lenin's economics is not all that deep and reflects a Ricardianism that went unnoticed. For example, in 1897 Lenin roundly criticised Sismondi before Marx's own comments on Sismondi appeared in *Theories of Surplus Value*. It turned out that Marx was clearly more appreciative of Sismondi than would be expected by Lenin's judgment (see Zarembka, 2003).

Second, Luxemburg's work received no sympathy from Kautsky, even though Kautsky himself used similar arguments as Luxemburg's when in 1902 he criticised extensively a book by Tugan-Baranowsky. Lack of honest evaluation from Kautsky, or even any evaluation at all, was more damaging, at the time, than the fact of Lenin's dismissal. As editor of *Theories of Surplus Value*, Kautsky could know quite well Marx's thoughts on Sismondi. Furthermore, regarding the editorial board of her party's publication *Vorwaerts*, Luxemburg herself commented:

> With regard to my purely theoretical work about a complicated issue involving abstract scientific analysis, the entire Editorial Board of a political daily paper came forward—although two members, at the most, might have read the book—and as an official body handed down a collective judgment against it. In the process they denied that men like Franz Mehring and S. Karski [Julian Marchlewski] possessed any expertise on questions of political economy. Only those who had torn my book apart were to be designated as 'experts'.

Such a fate has befallen no other party publication as far as I know, and over the decades Social Democratic publishers have certainly not produced all gold and pearls (Luxemburg, 1921, 348).

Note that, according to Froelich (1939, 159), Mehring and Marchlewski greeted her book with 'great enthusiasm'.

Third, the undermining of Luxemburg's work was accelerated by Bukharin's (1924) long discussion, offered five years after her murder. Bukharin's critique played a major role in a process that has led a much later survey of the history of Marxist economics to feel comfortable in concluding of Rosa Luxemburg: 'almost no one has been convinced by her attempt to demonstrate that accumulation is impossible in a closed capitalist system'; 'her theory was wrong' (Howard and King, 1989, 112 and 317). Bukharin's commentary is reviewed in detail in Zarembka (2002b, 11-13).

For example, Bukharin quotes but ignores her when she says that money is something between two other things: 'Between the accumulation of surplus value in commodities and the use of this surplus value to expand production[5] there always lies a decisive leap, the *salto mortale* of commodity production, as Marx calls it: selling for money' (Bukharin, 1924, 192, italics in original). Instead, in a section entitled 'Definition of Accumulation', he refers to her defining 'accumulation as accumulation of money capital' (194, italics in original). Would it not be more correct to interpret Luxemburg to say that 'an amassing of money capital' is a result of a necessity within the accumulation process?

After Bukharin, critiques of Luxemburg's work continued, in one manner or another, in works by Grossmann, Pannekoek, Mattick, Sr., Sweezy, Rosdolsky, Tarbuck, Kuehne, Howard and King, and Dunayevskaya, among others, each of whom is discussed in Zarembka (2002b). Often the critiques are inconsistent, one with another, yet a cult of objection was created which includes those of many political stripes.

Finally, the connection between Luxemburg's work, particularly the third part of *The Accumulation of Capital* and *Introduction to Political Economy*, and Marx's late research into Russian society has gone unnoticed. This neglect has been largely due to extremely tardy publication of Marx's late notes.

Value, When the Context is Wider than Capitalism

Value is, of course, the foundation for Marx's theoretical understanding of the capitalist mode of production. Since his 1847 *Poverty of Philosophy* (Marx, 1847), Marx's economic categories are to be understood as socially conditioned. Having re-examined 'accumulation of capital' in light of Luxemburg, what then is to be the appropriate object of analysis leading to this concept of value: the capital–wage labour relation alone or that relation as well as the penetration of non-capitalist modes of production corresponding to accumulation of capital? The former has been universally presumed, based upon Marx's simplifying assumption that 'capitalist production is everywhere established'. Marx already made this presumption a decade before Volume I, i.e. in 1858 Marx wrote Engels an outline of what he was preparing and included a significant comment concerning value, suggesting his focus to be on post-proletarianisation:

> *Value.* This is reduced entirely to the quantity of labour; time as a measure of value ...Value as such has no other 'material' than labour itself... It already presupposes 1. the destruction of natural communism (in India, etc.); 2. the destruction of all undeveloped, pre-bourgeois modes of production which are not governed in their totality by exchange. Although it is an abstraction, it is an abstraction which can only be assumed on the basis of a particular economic development of society ... (Marx and Engels, 1948, 58).

In the *Grundrisse,* we find: 'The economic concept of value does not occur in antiquity ... [It] is entirely peculiar to the most modern economy, since it is the most abstract expression of capital itself and of the production resting on it' (Marx, 1939-41, 776).

This topic of the conception of value is addressed in Zarembka (2020, Chapter II), while beyond the scope of this chapter.

A Possible Reconsideration of Marxist Political Economy

The deeper issue being raised in this chapter may be epistemological. Althusser's (1965) work, for example, opens up this space for discussion, opens up the question of the theoretical object of *Capital.* Marx, says Althusser, did not undertake to 'historicise' the categories of classical political economy, categories such as value. Rather, Marx produced new concepts appropriate to his own theoretical object, in circumstances in which he had no philosophical concepts available 'to think the determination of the elements of a whole by the structure of the whole' (Althusser, 1965, 187).

Marx was stating this point in order to explain that economic categories need not follow each other in the same manner as history, but rather should be determined, in capitalism, by the structure of bourgeois society. For Althusser, *Darstellung* (representation, *mise en scene*) should be recognised as 'the key epistemological concept of the whole Marxist theory of value, the concept whose object is precisely to designate the mode of presence of the structure in its effects, and therefore to designate structural causality itself' (Althusser, 1965, 188).

Althusser, however, seems completely unaware of any difficulty with the concept of 'accumulation of capital', completely unaware of the problematic character of presuming full capitalism, completely unaware that penetration of non-capitalist modes of production may need to be part of the object of theoretical investigation. While a concept such as 'value' is not to be an historisation of classical political economy's conception, neither is it, according to Althusser, to have the same theoretical object as classical political economy's theoretical object. Yet, does not a clarified understanding of accumulation of capital suggest that we cannot discuss penetration of non-capitalist society by capital without examining what it is that is being penetrated. We cannot examine what is being penetrated without the context, a context which must be historical.

NOTES

1. This chapter appeared, in the main part, in *Confronting Capitalism in the 21st Century: Lessons from Marx's Capital*, edited by Marc Silver, Palgrave Macmillan, 2019, pp. 47-65, copyright retained by the author. However, some modifications have been made, and the argument condensed.
2. This passage is from the draft 'Results of the Immediate Process of Production,' which Marx deleted from Volume I before publication. 'Results' can be considered part of the third, next to last, draft of Volume I. No other material from this third draft has survived, perhaps because the remainder was rolled into the final draft. Why third draft? Consider the *Grundrisse* as a first draft of Marx's life work. Then the second draft can be considered to have been drafted between 1861 and 1863, and includes his work on the history of theories of surplus

value. The third, not yet final, draft was begun in 1863 and completed in 1865, including the only draft ever made of what became Volume 3 under Engels' editorship.

3. After pulling 'Results' from Volume I, there is also no record that Marx later returned to the issue of 'subsumption'.
4. Marx, judging by a number of his interventions on this issue, seemed to think that primitive communism resisted capital more than Luxemburg argued. Examining this disparity is unnecessary for our purposes.
5. We are at a loss how Bukharin could so distort Luxemburg's position by skipping over the sentence reproduced here. He even plays with the words *salto mortale* in his own text, getting into the reader's subconscious that he, Bukharin, has read her: the reader is expected to take his word for the fact that, yes, she really does define accumulation as the amassing of money capital

REFERENCES

Althusser, L. (1970 [1965]), L'object du *Capital*, in L. Althusser, E. Balibar and R. Establet (eds.) *Lire le Capital*, trans. by B. Brewster, The Object of *Capital*, in L. Althusser and E. Balibar (eds.) *Reading Capital*, London: New Left Books, pp. 71-198.

Bukharin, N.I. (1972 [1924]), *Der Imperialismus und die Akkumulation der Kapitals*, trans. by R. Wichman as *Imperialism and the Accumulation of Capital*, New York: Monthly Review Press.

Forstater, M. (2005), Taxation and Primitive Accumulation: The Case of Colonial Africa, in P. Zarembka (ed.), *The Capitalist State and Its Economy; Democracy in Socialism, Research in Political Economy*, Vol. 22, pp. 51-64.

Froelich, P. (1967 [1939]), *Rosa Luxemburg—Gedanke und Tat*, trans. by J. Hoornweg, *Rosa Luxemburg: Her Life and Work*, New York: Monthly Review Press.

Howard, M.C. and J.E. King (1989), *A History of Marxian Economics, Vol. 1: 1883-1929*, London: Macmillan.

Kautsky, K. (2019 [1902]), Krisentheorien, trans. by D. Gaido and D. Scattolini as 'Theories of Crises' [Sections 3, 4 and 5 only] in P. Zarembka (ed.) *Class History and Class Practices in the Periphery of Capitalism, Research in Political Economy*, Vol. 32, pp. 199-224.

Kowalik, T. (1990), Rosa Luxemburg, In J. Eatwell, M. Milgate and P.

Newman (eds.), *Marxian Economics,* London: Macmillan.

Luxemburg, R. (2016 [1913]), Die Akkumulation des Kapitals, trans. by N. Gray as The Accumulation of Capital, In *The Collected Works of Rosa Luxemburg, Volume II, Economic Writings 2,* P. Hudis (ed.), London: Verso Books, pp. 1-342.

—— (2016 [1915]), Die Akkumulation des Kapitals oder Was die Epigonen aus der Marxschen Theorie gemacht haben. Eine Antikritik, trans. by G. Shriver as The Accumulation of Capital, Or, What the Epigones Have Made Out of Marx's Theory An Anti-Critique, In *The Collected Works of Rosa Luxemburg, Volume II, Economic Writings 2,* P. Hudis (ed.), London: Verso Books, pp. 343-449.

—— (2013 [1918]), Introduction to Political Economy, trans. by G. Shriver In *The Collected Works of Rosa Luxemburg, Volume I, Economic Writings 1,* P. Hudis (ed.), London: Verso Books, pp. 89-300.

Magaline, A.D. (an anonymous collective) (1975), Lutte de Classes et Devalorisation du Capital: Contribution a la Critique de Revisionnisme, Maspero, translated in part by P. Zarembka, In *Revitalizing Marxist Theory for Today's Capitalism,* P. Zarembka and R. Desai (eds.), *Research in Political Economy,* Vol. 27, 2011, pp. 255-68.

Marx, K. (1963 [1847]), *Misère de la philosophie*; trans. by the Institute of Marxism Leninism, *The Poverty of Philosophy*, Moscow: International Publishers.

—— (1978 [1867]), *Das Kapital. Band I*; 1st English edition (1887) trans. from the 3rd German edition by S. Moore and E. Aveling, F. Engels (eds.), with 4th German edition (1890) changes included as indicated, *Capital,* Volume I, Lawrence & Wishart, 1974. (For the cited translation of the Appendix to the 1st edition, see Roth and Suchting, 1978, pp. 134–50).

—— (1974 [1885]), *Das Kapital. Band II*; trans. from the second German edition (1893) by Ernest Untermann, *Capital,* Volume II, Lawrence & Wishart.

—— (1977 [1864]), *Resultate des unmittelbaren Produktionsprozesses*; trans. By B. Fowkes, *Results of the Immediate Process of Production, Appendix to Capital,* Volume I, New York: Vintage, pp. 941-1084.

—— (1973 [1857–58]), *Grundrisse*, trans. by M. Nicolaus, New York: Vintage Books.

Marx, K. and Engels, F. (1983 [1948]), *Letters on 'Capital'*, trans. by A. Drummond, New Park Publications.

Roth, M. and Suchting, W. (1978), Introduction by the translators to 'The Value-Form', *Capital and Class*, Vol. 4, pp. 134–50.

Van Onselen, C. (1976), *Chibaro: African Mine Labour in Southern Rhodesia, 1900–1933*, London: Pluto Press.

White, J.D. (1996), *Karl Marx and the Intellectual Origins of Dialectical Materialism*, London: Macmillan.

—— (2001) Nikolai Sieber and Karl Marx, In P. Zarembka (ed.), *Marx's Capital and Capitalism; Markets in a Socialist Alternative, Research in Political Economy*, Vol. 19, pp. 3-16.

—— (2018), *Marx and Russia: The Fate of a Doctrine*, New York: Bloomsbury Academic.

Zarembka, P. (2002a), Primitive Accumulation in Marxism, Historical or Trans-Historical Separation from Means of Production?, *The Commoner*, A Web Journal for Other Values, Debate: on Primitive Accumulation. Online. Available at: www.commoner.org.uk/debzarembka01.pdf, March. Reprinted with amendments, In W. Bonefeld (ed.), *Subverting the Present, Imagining the Future*, New York, 2008, pp. 67–75.

—— (2002b), Rosa Luxemburg's *Accumulation of Capital*: Critics Try to Bury the Message, In J.M. Lehmann (ed.), *Bringing Capitalism Back for Critique by Social Theory, Current Perspectives in Social Theory*, Vol. 21, pp. 3-45.

—— (2003), Lenin as Economist of Production: A Ricardian Step Backwards, *Science & Society*, Vol. 67, No. 3, pp. 276–302.

—— (2015), Materialized Composition of Capital and its Stability in the United States: Findings Stimulated by Paitaridis and Tsoulfidis (2012), *Review of Radical Political Economy*, Vol. 47, No. 1, pp. 106-111.

—— (2020), *Key Elements of Social Theory Revolutionised by Marx*, Brill, forthcoming.

13

Financialisation: There's Something Happening Here[1]

Gerald Epstein

"There's something happening here...But what it is ain't exactly clear..."—"For What It's Worth," Buffalo Springfield, 1966

I. Introduction

For anyone who did not know already, the Great Financial Crisis of 2008 made it completely obvious that finance has become a powerful force in our economy. Unfortunately, among those largely in the dark on the eve of the crisis were most of the mainstream macroeconomics profession as well as many regulators and practitioners operating in the financial market itself. This is because, in the post-war period, the thrust of the mainstream analysis was designed to demonstrate that financial markets were either irrelevant to macroeconomic outcomes, or, by facilitating the efficient allocation of resources, a potent force for efficiency and growth (Taylor, 2010; Crotty, 2009). The idea that finance could cause the virtual meltdown of the global economy was foreign to their theories and far from their minds.[2]

For heterodox economists, by contrast, at least since the work of the late Hyman Minsky, this fact had been well known. In the 1970s, Hyman Minsky introduced the role of financial instability in the inherent dynamics of the economy and by 1992 had introduced the term "financial instability hypothesis" to refer to the inherently contradictory role of borrowing and lending in the course of the business cycle and on economic crises.[3] Over the course of the next several decades, heterodox economists expanded their analyses of finance further. By the 1980s and 1990s, they were acutely aware that the size, nature and scope of finance had begun to grow enormously and that it was having much broader impacts on the economy than simply on the business cycle and economic crises: finance seemed to be changing the whole character of the economy and possibly even society itself. Minsky started writing about the rise of "money manager capitalism" suggesting a whole new phase of capitalism that was characterised, in particular, by the type of financial relationships that dominated the economy. Others also began to identify the very nature of the current form of capitalism with the type of financial relations that were dominant in them. Some went as so far as to argue that these financial relations not only structure our economy, but our very language and culture as well. Gerald F. Davis referred to a "portfolio society", "in which the investment idiom becomes a dominant way of understanding the individual's place in society. Personality and talent become "human capital", homes, families and communities become "social capital" and the guiding principle of financial investment spread by analogy far beyond their original application" (Davis, 2009, 6).

Financialisation" is the latest, and probably most widely used term by analysts trying to "name" and understand this contemporary rise of finance and its powerful role. The term had been developed long before the crisis of 2008 but, understandably, since the crisis hit, it has become even more popular. This vast and rapidly expanding literature on financialisation has a number of important strands. Some of the literature focuses on clarifying the definition of financialisation, and assessing whether it is a dominant cause of the ills confronting capitalism or is just a symptom of other, deeper causes; some ask whether financialisation is a new "phase" of capitalist development, perhaps a new "mode of accumulation", or considers whether it is just one among a number of important developments along with "neo-liberalism", "digitisation" and "globalisation" that are arising in the contemporary world; other literature is focused on less theoretical and more empirical matters, trying to measure the nature and extent of financialisation, however defined, and to describe its institutional and economic dimensions; and still other work is focused on attempting to analyse theoretically and empirically the impact of financialisation on important phenomena such as financial crises, productive investment, productivity growth, wages and income distribution; and finally, other parts of the literature are more policy-oriented, trying to grapple with policies and structural changes than can improve the role that finance plays in the economy.

In the rest of this chapter I present the most widely used definitions of financialisation and introduce the main ideas and debates associated with the concept. In Section III, I discuss the dimensions of financialisation with primary reference to the US but add occasional discussions of financialisation in other countries. Section IV is devoted to discussing the impacts of financialisation on various important aspects of the economy including investment, employment and income distribution. Section V concludes.

To anticipate our main conclusion, it is this: as the famous line from Buffalo Springfield says, with financialisation we know that something important is happening here. We just do not know yet exactly what it is.

II. Financialisation: Definitions and Brief History of the Concept

As discussed by Malcolm Sawyer (2013), the term financialisation goes back at least to the 1990s and probably was originated by Republican political operative and iconoclastic writer Kevin Phillips, who first used the term in his book *Boiling Point* (New York: Random House, 1993) and, a year later, used the term extensively in his *Arrogant Capital* in a chapter entitled the "Financialisation of America". Phillips defined *financialisation as* "a prolonged split between the divergent real and financial economies" (Sawyer, 2013, 5-6).

Scholars have adopted the term, but have proposed numerous other definitions. Sociologist, Greta Krippner, for one, gives an excellent discussion of the history of the term and the pros and cons of various definitions.(Krippner, 2005, 2012) As she summarises the discussion, some writers use the term "financialisation" to mean the ascendancy of "shareholder value" as a mode of corporate governance; some use it to refer to the growing dominance of capital market financial systems over bank-based financial systems; some follow Hilferding's lead and use the term financialisation to refer to the increasing political and economic power of a particular class segment, the rentier class; for some financialisation represents the explosion of financial trading with myriad new financial instruments; finally, for Krippner herself, the term refers to a "pattern of accumulation in which profit-making occurs increasingly through financial channels rather than through trade and commodity production". (Krippner, 2005, 14).[4]

I have defined the term quite broadly and generally as: "the increasing role of financial motives, financial markets, financial actors and financial institutions in the operation of the domestic and international economies." (Epstein, 2005, Introduction). This definition focuses on financialisation as a process, and is quite agnostic on the issue of whether it constitutes a new mode of accumulation or broadly characterises an entire new phase of capitalism. Broad definitions like mine have the advantage of incorporating many features, but have the disadvantage, perhaps, of lacking specificity.

Other analysts have used variations on the term financialisation to refer to more or less the same set of phenomena. Tom Palley has used the term "neoliberal financialisaton" in his writings to emphasise the importance of neoliberalism as part and parcel of the rise of financialisation (Palley, 2013a, 8) Some have not referred to financialisation but to "finance-dominated capitalism" (Hein, 2012; Sen, 2014; Palley, 2013a).

The use of the term "neoliberalism" signals a topic of much discussion and debate in this literature: what is the relationship between financialisation, globalisation and neo-liberalism three forces that virtually all analysts in this area agree have had profound impacts on the evolution of our economy (see Kotz, 2014, Dumenil and Levy, 2005, Lapavitsas, 2013)? The main issue is determining the key driving force in contemporary capitalism, and and distinguishing it from the subsidiary, or less important, forces. This literature, though interesting, is ultimately unresolved: in fact, since these phenomena have all arisen more or less together since the 1980s , it might be impossible, to settle this debate.

Another important debate is on the periodisation of "financialisation". Is it only a recent phenomenon, say, important since the 1980s? Or does it go back at least 5000 years, as Malcolm Sawyer has suggested? (Sawyer, 2013, 6).[5] If it goes back a long time, does it come in waves, perhaps linked with broader waves of production, commerce and technology or is it a relatively independent process driven by government policy such as the degree of financial regulation or liberalisation (see Vercelli, 2013; Arrighi, 1994; Krippner, 2012 and Orhangazi, 2008a, 2008b). Arrighi famously argued that over the course of capitalist history, financialisation tends to become a dominant force when the productive economy is in decline, and when the dominant global power (or "hegemon") is in retreat. Think, for example of the early 20th century when Great Britain was losing power relative to Germany and the US, and the UK economy was stagnating. This was a period also of a great increase in financial speculation and instability. (See also Orhangazi, 2008a and Pollin, 1996).

This historical discussion has also melded into a more contemporary discussion of the causes of financialisation. There is a big debate about whether the current wave of financialisation is due to the liberalisation of financial markets starting in the 1980s, or whether it reflects the reduced profitability and stagnation in the non-financial (the so-called "real") economy. In the latter case, it is argued, financiers are forced to find other ways to make profits, and they turn primarily to dangerous speculation in the financial sphere. In short, the question is whether financialisation is due to changes in the nature and regulation of the financial sphere or is it primarily due to profound structural problems in the non-financial economy, including foreign trade and relative global power.[6]

A related argument is whether the current phase of financialisation is due to the massive increases in income and wealth inequality which has led to the need for massive household borrowing and provided the wealth for rich people to invest.

One policy implication of this debate is that if financialisation is a purely financial problem, it might be easier to "fix" "simply" through financial regulation and financial restructuring; if the problems stem from the "real" economy, wealth distribution and the global distribution of power, then "fixes" might not be so easy, and in particular, might require dramatic changes in the very structure of contemporary capitalism and global political economy.

The final set of debates mentioned here concern the impact of "financialisation" on the economy and on those who inhabit it. Those heterodox economists and sociologists who have analysed "financialisation" have generally taken a quite critical view of the impact of financialisation on the economy. Prior to the GFC, some suggested that finacialisation might provide a viable system of regulation and growth (Boyer, 2000). But most analysts identified a number of key problems associated with financialisation: among these problems cited by these analysts are increases in economic instability, increased short-term orientation, reduced long-term investment in equipment, innovation, infrastructure and human capital and an increase in income and wealth inequality. Still, there is no consensus on the precise dimensions of these problems and to what extent they should be attributed to financialisation or other factors such as neoliberalism, digitisation or globalisation.

These broad issues and debates are fascinating and provide frameworks and agendas for investigating key questions with respect to the dynamics and impacts of financialisation. But, in my view, among the most important contributions made in this literature are in the empirical realm, that is, empirical and historical studies that have looked at the dimensions of financialisation, its key institutional embodiments and dynamics, and at its impacts on key economic, political and social outcomes.

III. Dimensions of Financialisation

If one takes a broad perspective on financialisation, then one can identify many dimensions of it. One is the sheer size and scale of financial markets and can be seen quite clearly in the large growth in the size of the financial sector relative to the rest of the economy over the last several decades. This growth in finance has been a quite general phenomenon in many parts of the world. For the most part, we will focus here on data from the US. The growth of finance relative to the size of the economy since 1980 or so has been nothing short of spectacular. A few pieces of data illustrate this point well. Start with profits of financial institutions. In the United States, financial profits as a share of GDP were around 10 per cent in the 1950s. By the early 2000s, financial profits constituted about 40 per cent of total profits in the US, a historical high. After a sharp decline during the Great Financial Crisis of 2008, financial profits have recovered to above 30 per cent of profits, well above the average for the post-war period.

Naturally, with profits having grown so significantly, the size of the financial sector is likely to have been growing as well. Financial sector assets relative to GDP was less than 200 per cent from 1950 to 1985. By 2008, they had more than doubled to well over 4 times the size of the economy. After a short dip following the GFC, financial sector assets had grown to be almost 500 per cent of GDP by 2015 (Epstein and Montecino, 2015).

Trends in the UK are similar to those in the US, with both the size and the profitability of the financial sector and its profitability growing substantially in the post-war period till the great financial crisis, and resumed growth since that time. Indeed, since the crisis, growth of financial assets in the UK have outpaced those in the US, Germany and Japan, relative to GDP (Lapavitsas, 2013, 205). More generally, the size of the financial sector and financial profits relative to the size of the economy has grown substantially in most European countries over this period. (FESSUD, various).

Another dimension that characterises financialisation in many countries has been an increase in the financial activities and financial orientation of non-financial corporations. De Souza and Epstein (2014) present data on the financial activities of non-financial corporations in six financial centres, the US, UK, France, the Netherlands, Germany and Switzerland. They show that in all the six countries—with the possible exception of France—non-financial corporations significantly reduced their dependence of external borrowing for capital investment. And, indeed, in three of the countries—the UK, Germany and Switzerland—non-financial corporations became net lenders, rather than net borrowers, indicating an increasing role for financial lending as a profit centre for non-financial corporations in these countries. Lapavitsas (2013) showed similar trends for the US, UK, Germany and Japan.

A prime aspect of financialisation that analysts agree has been particularly pernicious has been the vast increase of debt levels in many countries and many sectors (Admati and Hellwig, 2013; Taylor, 2012; Turner, 2013). Debt, or leverage, is an accelerator that enables the financial system to generate a credit bubble, that allows some actors, such as private equity and hedge funds to extract wealth from companies, and that can quicken the pace of economic activity more generally, and it is the accelerator on the way down after the bubble bursts, leading to distress, deflation and bankruptcy. (Minsky, 2008; Fisher, 1933; Jarsulic, 2013)

Playing a key role in the development of financialisation is the role of financial innovation; in fact some authors argue that financial innovation itself is financialisation (Vercelli, 2013). To be sure, financial innovation has played a pivotal role in the development of recent financial practices that contributed significantly to the massive growth in financial activities and that ultimately contributed to the financial crisis (Vercelli, 2013; Jarsulic, 2013; Greenberger, 2013; Stout, 2011; FCIC, 2011). Among these seminal financial innovations have been securitisation and structured financial products such as Asset Backed Securities (ABS); Collateralised Debt Obligations (CD)s); the growth of credit derivatives, such as Credit Default Swaps (CDS) that both facilitated and then became embedded in these structured products themselves; and innovation in wholesale funding such as REPO's and REVERSE REPOs all facilitated by complex utilisation of collateral that greased the wheels of the whole system. These financial innovations have implications that are global in scope. The Bank for International Settlements in Basel, Switzerland reports that the global use and level of trading in these instruments has grown spectacularly over the last several decades (BIS, 2013). This process of financial innovation has clearly helped to drive financialisation, both within countries and globally as well.

Financialisation and Non-Financial Corporations

There are other important dimensions of the increased financial activities related to non-financial corporations. Among the most important are the increased role of financial activities as a determinant of the pay packages of top management of non-financial corporations, including, most importantly, the corporate CEO. Perhaps most important are stock options and other stock-related pay for non-financial corporate management. In the US, where this is especially prevelant, CEOs on average receive 72 per cent of their compensation in the form of stock options and other stock-related pay (Galston and Kamarck, 2015; Lazonick, 2015a, 2015b).

This focus on stock price leads non-financial corporations to use their revenue to buy back stocks in order to raise the stock prices and increase their compensation (Cheng, et al., 2015). Regarding the use of funds, Lazonick refers to the pressure as leading to management policies of "downsize and distribute", a dramatic shift from an earlier strategy or retain and reinvest, by which management would retain profits and re-invest back into the human and technological capital of the firm. (see, e.g. Lazonick 2012, 2015a; Almeida, et al., 2016). The numbers in the case of the US are staggering. Using a sample of 248 companies that have been listed on the S&P 500 since 1981, Lazonick reports that: in 1981, firms used 2 per cent of net income for stock buybacks. Between 1984 and 1993, such purchases averaged 25 per cent of net income, from 1994-2003, 37 per cent; from 2004—2013, they used a full 47 per cent of net income for stock buybacks. (Lazonick, 2015a, 2015b). Particular large, well-known corporations used even a higher percent of their income for buybacks.

This focus on stock price is often seen as a prime example of "share-holder value" ideology, a perspective seen by some as the very essence of "financialisation". (Froud, et al., 2006; Aglietta and Bretton, 2001). Shareholder value ideology, promoted in the mainstream of the economics profession by Michael Jensen, among others, argues that since shareholders own the corporations (are the risk-bearing residual claimants"), that the goal of the corporation management should be to maximise the corporate value for shareholders. Since, they argue, shareholders bear all the risk in the corporation, then this maximisation is the most efficient corporate outcome. Lazonick shows that other stakeholders, like workers and taxpayers, bear as much if not more risk than shareholders (Lazonick, 2013). And Stout shows that shareholders do not really own the corporations, nor do they all share the same values as embodied in the Jensen ideal. (Stout, 2012). Hence, "maximising shareholder value" does not mean maximising share price. But it does often lead to short-term, destructive orientation by management.

This is one of the most discussed examples of the role of modern financial markets in creating more "short-termism", as a major component of "financialisation". By 'short-termism" is meant a short time horizon by economic leaders in making production, investment and financing decisions. This short-termism might lead to under-investment in long gestation but highly productive and profitable (in the long-run) investments, under-investment in labour development, under-investment in research and development activities, and over-investment in activities that generate short run profits but that might generate long-run risks and/or losses. (Graham, et al., 2005; Dallas, 2012). The same kinds of pressures face portfolio managers for pension funds and other institutional investors, leading to a similar focus on short-term returns, sometimes at the risk of longer term investments (Parenteau, 2005)

Evidence of short-termism include the reduced holding period of equities in financial markets, survey evidence that managers will cut profitable long-term investments to reach short-term profit goals, and that investors have higher rates of required returns for longer term investments than is necessary (see Haldane and Davis, 2011).

This short–term oriented behaviour is alleged to affect non-financial corporation management not simply because of the direct incentives facing corporate CEOs, but also because of the pressure from outside investors and financial institutions. These include pension funds and related institutional investors (Parenteau, 2005) and also private equity firms (Appelbaum and Batt, 2014) and hedge funds (Dallas, 2012). These financial institutions use access to debt and financial engineering to extract value in the short run from non-financial corporations, possibly at the expense of investment, tax payers and labour.

In short, this strand of literature suggests that "financialisation" not only affects behaviour in the financial sector itself, but also has profound effects on non-financial corporations as well.

Financialisation and Households

As the Great Financial Crisis of 2008 clearly demonstrated, the process of financialisation has not only caught financial and non-financial institutions into its orbit, but also households as well. After all, the epi-centre of the financial crisis in the United Sates was in the home mortgage market and to some extent one segment of that market, the so-called "sub-prime mortgage market". Costas Lapavitsas (2013) and others have argued that the process of financial incorporation of households led to the "financial expropriation" of these households by financial businesses, and expropriation most clearly and obviously expressed by the massive loss in housing wealth experienced by poor people and minorities in the US as a result of the crisis. (See Taub, 2013 and Engel and McCoy, 2011).

The incorporation of households into the "circuits" of financialisation goes beyond the intensive use of mortgages to buy homes, sometimes, as we saw in 2008, with catastrophic consequences. The use of credit cards and other forms of consumer credit, and the widespread indebtedness of students through student loans, also comprise the webs of connections that households have come to have with the financial markets (Kuttner, 2013; Warren, 2014).

Conclusion

As this section has shown, financialisation has numerous dimensions, and has moved in some countries way beyond the "financial sector" itself. Financial returns, financial motives, widespread use of debt and short-termism, among other aspects, have become crucial, if not dominant, for financial firms, non-financial firms, and households. This growth in finance, which accelerated around 1980 in a number of countries, has taken on significant global dimensions as well.

The question naturally arises, what is the impact of financialisation on the economy and on society?

IV. Impacts of Financialisation

Much of the macroeconomic literature on financialisation concerns, of course, the impact of financialisation on crucial macroeconomic outcomes such as economic growth, investment, productivity growth, employment, stability and income distribution. The massive literature on the great financial crisis has made it pretty clear, that aspects of financialisation, including the huge increase in private debt, the use of securitisation and complex financial products, the widespread use of complex over the counter (OTC) derivatives, and the pernicious fraud and corruption, all contributed to the financial crisis and therefore, quite obviously, undermined stability.

But the impacts of financialisation on other macro-outcomes are less obvious, and less studied. Before discussing particular impacts, it will be helpful to present some broad frameworks that have been proposed to understand the impact of financialisation on macroeconomics. (see Palley, 2013a, 2013b; Hein and Van Treeck, 2010; Skott and Ryoo, 2009).

Macroeconomic Models and Financialisation

Space prevents me from giving a thorough overview of the rapidly expanding heterodox literature on models of financialisation, so I will very briefly discuss one framework here, that of Eckhard Hein. Hein uses a Kaleckian model, in which aggregate demand plays a pivotal role in determining investment and output and income distribution of income between profits, wages and "rentier" or "financial incomes" have a big impact on aggregate demand. Eckhard and van Treeck, for example, identify three prime channels through which financialisation can affect macro variables and outcomes: 1. The objectives of firms and the restrictions that finance places on firm behaviour 2. New opportunities for households' wealth-based and debt-financed consumption, and 3. The distribution of income and wealth between capital and labour, on the one hand, and between management and workers on the other hand.

Hein and van Treeck show that within the Kaleckian framework, that expansive effects may arise under certain conditions, in particular when there are strong wealth effects in firms' investment decisions and in households' consumption decisions. However, they show that even an expansive finance-led economy may build up major financial imbalances, i.e. increasing debt-capital or debt-income ratios, which make such economies prone to financial instability.

Financialisation and Investment

Stockhammer (2004) pioneered the theoretical analysis of the impact of financialised manager motives on investment. He showed that finance oriented management might choose to undertake lower investment levels than managers with less financialised orientations. He presented macro- level econometric investment equations that were consistent with this impact in several OECD countries.

Orhangazi (2008b) uses firm level data to study the impact of financialisation on real capital accumulation in the United States. He used data from a sample of non-financial corporations from 1973 to 2003, and finds a negative relationship between real investment and financialisation. Orhangazi explained his results by exploring two channels of influence of financialisation on real investment: first, increased financial investment and increased financial profit opportunities may have crowded out real investment by changing the incentives of firm managers and directing funds away from real investment. Second, increased payments to the financial markets may have impeded real investment by decreasing available internal funds, shortening the planning horizons of the firm management and increasing uncertainty.

Davis (2013) provided further evidence of the negative impact of financialisation on real investment. She also studied a sample of non-financial firms, showing a significant difference between large and smaller firms in the degree to which they receive financial income as a share of total income. Larger firms appear to be more financialised in this sense. Using a firm-level panel, she investigated econometrically the relationship between financialisation and investment, exploring focusing on the implications of changes in financing behaviour, increasingly entrenched shareholder value norms, and rising firm-level demand volatility for investment by NFCs in the US between 1971 and 2011. Importantly, Davis found that shareholder value norms were associated with lower investment, though this relationship tended to be true primarily of large firms.

These results are consistent with the concerns expressed by heterodox analysts and others that financialisation will tend to reduce real investment.

Employment, Human Capital, R&D and Wages

An increasing chorus of analysts among heterodox economists including William Lazonick (2009, 2013, 2014), Eileen Appelbaum and Rosemary Batt (2014) and iconoclast Andrew Haldane (2011), as well as more mainstream economists (e.g. Galston and Kamarck, 2015) and even political figures such as Hillary Clinton have expressed concern that "short-termism" associated with financialisation may be coming at the expense of investments in human capital, research and development, employment and productivity growth. There is some empirical work that is supportive of these fears. In a set of surveys of corporate managers, Graham, et al (2005) show that many chief financial officers are willing to sacrifice longer term investments in research and development and hold on to value employees in order to meet short-term earnings per share targets. In a panel econometric study, Almeida, et al. (2014) similarly find using firm level data that managers are willing to trade-off investments and employment for stock repurchases that allow them to meet earnings per share forecasts. Appelbaum and Batt (2014) in a survey of econometric studies of private equity firms find that especially large firms that use financial engineering to extract value from target companies, have a negative impact on investment, employment research and development in these companies. In short, there is significant empirical evidence that "short-termism" and other aspects of financial orientation have negative impacts on workers' well-being, productivity and longer-term growth.

And, as many of these studies emphasise, these activities do not maximise shareholder value, but often increase incomes for some managers and shareholders, partly at the expense of other shareholders of the firms not to mention stakeholders, such as workers and taxpayers.

Income Distribution

This raises the issue of the overall impact of financialisation on income distribution. An important issue in this area is where do financial profits come from? (Pollin, 1996). Are they the result of provision of services by finance to the rest of the economy, as is asserted by most mainstream economic theory? Or does much of it come in this era of financialisation from the extraction of income and wealth by finance from workers, tax-payers, debtors and other creditors? Iren Levina proposes that much of financial income comes from access to capital gains in financialised markets and therefore does not necessarily reflect a zero-sum game, as is implied by some who argue that financial returns are extracted rather than result from increased wealth. (Levina, 2014). This issue of the source of financial income is extremely difficult to sort out theoretically and there is no consensus on this topic (see Lapavitsas, 2013).

There has been some empirical work to look at the impact of financialisation on income and wealth distribution. Descriptive analysis in the US indicates that the top earners, the 1 per cent or even .01 per cent of the income distribution get the bulk of their incomes from CEO pay or from finance (Bakija, et al. 2012). Econometric work looking at the relationship between financialisation and inequality is also growing. Tomaskovic-Devey and Lin (2011) present an econometric model indicating that since the 1970s, between 5.8 and 6.6 trillion dollars were transferred to the finance sector from other sectors in the economy, including labour and taxpayers.

Lin and Tomaskovic-Devey (2013), using a sectoral econometric analysis for the US, find that in time-series cross-section data at the industry level, an increasing dependence on financial income, in the long run, is associated with reducing labour's share of income, increasing top executives' share of compensation, and increasing earnings dispersion among workers. They do a counterfactual analysis that suggests that financialisation could account for more than half the decline in labour's share of income, 9.6 per cent of the growth in officers' share of compensation, and 10.2 per cent of the growth in earnings dispersion between 1970 and 2008.

Dunhaupt (2013) finds a negative relationship between financialisation and labour share in a larger set of countries. She uses a time-series cross-section data set of 13 countries over the time period from 1986 till 2007. The results suggest that there is indeed a relationship between increasing dividend and interest payments of non-financial corporations and the decline of the share of wages in national income. Other factors that can be accounted for the decline relate to globalisation and a decrease in the bargaining power of labour.

Financialisation and Economic Growth

As the massive recession stemming from the great financial crisis makes clear, there is no linear relationship between the size and complexity of financial markets and economic growth. Several econometric studies have suggested an inverted U-shaped relationship between the size of the financial sector and economic growth. A larger financial sector raises the rate of economic growth up to a point, but when the financial sector gets too large relative to the size of the economy, economic growth begins to decline (see for example, Cecchetti, et al., 2012; Tomaskovic-Devey, 2015). To the extent that this relationship is true, economists are still searching for the explanation. One argument is that as the financial sector increases in size, because of its relatively high pay levels, it pulls talented and highly educated employees away from other sectors that might contribute more to economic growth and productivity. As a University Professor teaching economics since the 1980s, I can verify that many of my undergraduate students had the dream of going to work on Wall Street. Perhaps some of them could have contributed more elsewhere.

V. Conclusion

There is little doubt that the size and reach of financial activities, markets, motives and institutions has grown enormously in the last thirty years, relative to other aspects of the economy. There is a great deal of historical and empirical evidence that, at least to some extent, this growth has contributed to economic instability, an increase in inequality, and in some cases, to a decline in productive investment and employment relative to what might have occurred otherwise. There is less consensus on whether this constitutes a new epoch, phase, or mode of accumulation or what exactly is causing this shift: is it underlying problems in the "productive core" of the economy, a reaction to broader shifts in the global economy associated with globalisation, technological changes associated with digitisation, or primarily due to financial de-regulation as being part and parcel of neoliberalism?

To some extent, policies or programes aimed at reducing the deleterious consequences of financialisation depend, to some extent at least, on the underlying causes of the negative aspects of financialisation. If the problem primarily stems from issues of financial regulation, then adopting strict financial regulations as suggested by many (see, for example, some of the chapters in Wolfson and Epstein, 2013; or Epstein and Crotty, 2013), imposing a financial transactions tax to reduce short term trading, prohibiting destructive stock buy-backs (Lazonick, 2015a), breaking up the large banks (Johnson and Kwack, 2010), change corporate governance so that corporations take into account the preferences of stake holders, and a host of other reforms could well go a long way to taming financialisation. If, the problems stem largely from the vast and growing inequality of income and wealth and the political power that this inequality buys, then deeper reforms of taxation, wages, and ownership as well as money in politics must be implemented.

If the problem goes deeper to the underlying capitalist dynamics that lead to financialisation, then we are looking at even more fundamental reforms. The state of our knowledge does not allow us to clearly sort out these issues. But, it would not hurt to start someplace, start anyplace. Because, we do know: there is something happening here.

NOTES

1. The earlier version of this paper was published in August 2015 as Working Paper of PERI number 394. The permission is taken from author for reprint. The author thanks Jim Crotty and Bob Pollin for many edifying discussions of these issues and Leila Davis, Iren Levina, Juan Montecino and Joao Paolo de Souza for excellent research assistance and collaboration.
2. Mainstream macroeconomics was not always so ignorant of the important role of finance. In the 1920s and 1930s, economists from many traditions, including Hayek, Fisher, and, of course Keynes, were trying to understand the role of financial institutions and markets in financial booms and busts; and others, including Joseph Schumpeter, were trying to analyse the role of finance in long-run economic growth.
3. Harry Magdoff and Paul Sweezy, sometimes called by short-hand, *The Monthly Review School,* in reference to the Marxist journal they founded and edited for many years, were among the first post-war scholars writing in depth about the important role of dominant finance in the structure of the macroeonomy.
4. See also Costas Lapavitsas (2013) and Ozghur Orhangazi (2008) for important contributions.
5. Sawyer was apparently inspired in this statement by David Graeber's monumental book, *Debt: The First 5000 Years.* London: Melville Press, 2011.
6. Paul Sweezy and Harry Magdoff and the so-called Monthly Review School, were important contributors to this perspective on financialisation.

REFERENCES

Admati, A. and M. Hellwig (2013), *The Bankers' New Clothes,* Princeton: Princeton University Press.

Aglietta, M. and R. Bretton (2001), Financial Systems, Corporate Control and Capital Accumulation, *Economy and Society,* Vol. 30 No. 4, pp. 433-66.

Almeida, H., F. Vyacheslav and M. Kronlund (2016), The Real Effects of

Share Repurchases, *Journal of Financial Economics,* Vol. 119, No. 1, pp. 168-185.

Appelbaum, E. and R. Batt (2014), *Private Equity at Work; When Wall Street Manages Main Street,* New York: Russell Sage Foundation.

Arrighi, G. (1994), *The Long Twentieth Century: Money, Power and the Origins of Our Times*, New York: Verso Books.

Bakija, J., A. Cole and B.T. Heim (2012), Jobs and Income Growth of Top Earners and the Causes of Changing Income Inequality: Evidence from US Tax Return Data, https://web.williams.edu/Economics/wp/BakijaColeHeimJobsIncomeGrowthTopEarners.pdf

Bank for International Settlement (BIS) (2013), Triennial Central Bank Survey of Foreign Exchange and Derivatives Market Activity in 2013, Basel: BIS.

Boyer, R. (2000), Is a Finance-Led Growth Regime a Viable Alternative to Fordism? A Preliminary Analysis, *Economy and Society,* Vol. 29, No. 1, pp. 111-45.

Cheng, Y., J. Harford and T. Zhang (2015), Bonus-Driven Repurchases, *Journal of Financial and Quantitative Analysis*, Vol. 50, No. 3, pp. 447-75.

Cecchetti, S. and E. Kharoubi (2012), Reassessing the Impact of Finance on Growth, BIS Working Paper Series #381.

Crotty, J. (2009), Structural Causes of the Global Financial Crisis: A Critical Assessment of the New Financial Architecture, *Cambridge Journal of Economics,* Vol. 33, No. 4, pp. 563-80.

Crotty, J. and G. Epstein. (2009), Avoiding a Financial Meltdown, *Challenge Magazine*, January/February.

Dallas, Lynne L. (2012), Short-Termism, The Financial Crisis and Corporate Governance, *Journal of Corporation Law*, Vol. 37.

Davis, (G. 2009), *Managed by the Markets*, Oxford: Oxford University Press.

Davis, L. (2013), Financialization and the Non-Financial Corporation: An Investigation of Firm Level Investment Behavior in the US: 1971-2011, Department of Economics Working Paper, Amherst: University of Massachusetts.

De Souza, J. Paulo and G. Epstein (2014), Sectoral Net Lending in Six Financial Center, PERI Working Paper Series.

Dumenil, G. and D. Levy (2005), Costs and Benefits of Neo-liberalism: A

Class Analysis, pp. 46-76, In G. Epstein, (Ed.), *Financialization and the World Economy*, Northampton: Edward Elgar,

Dunhaupt, P. (2013), *The Effect of Financialization on the Labor Share*, Berlin: Institute for International Political Economy.

Epstein, G. and J. Crotty (2013), How Big is Too Big? On the Social Efficiency of the Financial Sector in the United States?, In R. Pollin and Jeannette Wicks-Lim (eds.), *Capitalism on Trial: Explorations in the Tradition of Thomas Weisskopf*, Northampton, Ma: Edward Elgar Press.

Engel, Kathleen C. and Patricia A. McCoy (2011), *The Sub-Prime Virus; Reckless Credit, Regulatory Failure and Next Steps*, New York: Oxford University Press.

Epstein, G. (2005), Introduction, In G. Epstein (ed.), *Financialization and the World Economy*, Northampton: Edward Elgar.

Epstein, G. and J.A. Montecino (2015), Banking From Financial Crisis to Dodd-Frank: Five Years On, How Much Has Changed?, PERI Working Paper.

Epstein, G. and A. Jayadev (2005), The Rise of Rentier Incomes in OECD Countries: Financialization, Central Bank Policy, and Labor Solidarity, In G. Epstein (ed.), *Financialization and the World Economy*, pp. 46-76, Northampton: Edward Elgar.

FESSUD, (2000's), Studies in Financial Systems, various. http://fessud.eu/deliverables/.

Financial Crisis Inquiry Commission (FCIC) (2011), *The Financial Crisis Inquiry Report*, Washington, DC: GPO.

Fisher, I. (1933), The Debt Deflation Theory of Great Depressions, *Econometrica,* Vol. 1, No. 4, pp. 337-57.

Froud, J., J. Sukhdev, A. Leaver and K. Williams (2006), *Financialization and Strategy: Narrative and Numbers*, New York: Routledge.

Galston, William A. and Elaine C. Kamarck (2015), *More Builders and Fewer Traders: A Growth Strategy for the American Economy*, Washington, DC: The Brookings Institution.

Graeber, D. (2011), *Debt: The First 5000 Years*, London: Melville Press.

Graham, John R., Campbell R. Harvey and S. Rajgopal (2005), The Economic Implications of Corporate Financial Reporting, *Journal of Accounting and Economics,* Vol. 40, Nos. 1-3, pp. 3-73.

Greenwood, R. and D. Scharfstein (2013), The Growth of Finance, *The*

Journal of Economic Perspectives, Vol. 27, No. 2, pp. 3-28.

Haldane, A. and R. Davies (2011), *The Short Long, Speech*, London: Bank of England.

Hein, E. (2012), *The Macroeconomics of Finance-Dominated Capitalism-and its Crisis,* Northampton, MA: Edwrd Elgar.

Hein, E. and T. van Treeck (2010), 'Financialisation' in Post-Keynesian Models of Distribution and Growth: A Systematic Review, pp. 277-292, In M. Settereld (ed.), *Handbook of Alternative Theories of Economic Growth*, Northampton: Edward Elgar.

Jarsulic, M. (2013), The Origin of the US Financial Crisis of 2007: How a House-Price Bubble, A Credit Bubble and Regulatory Failure Caused the Greatest Economic Disaster since the Great Depression, pp. 21-46, In Martin H. Wolfson and Gerald A. Epstein (eds.), *The Handbook of the Political Economy of Financial Crises*, New York: Oxford University Press,

Jensen, M. (1986), Agency Cost of Free Cash Flow, Corporate Finance, and Takeovers, *American Economic Review,* Vol. 76, No. 2, pp. 323-329.

Keynes, J. (1936) *The General Theory of Employment, Interest and Money*, London: Macmillan.

Kotz, David M. (2014), *The Rise and Fall of Neo-Liberal Capitalism,* Cambridge: Harvard University Press.

Krippner, G. (2005), The Financialization of the American Economy, *Socio-Economic Review,* Vol. 3, No. 2, pp. 173-208.

Krippner, G. (2012), *Capitalizing on Crisis: The Political Origins of the Rise of Finance*, Cambridge: Harvard University Press.

Kuttner, R. (2013), *Debtor's Prison: The Politics of Austerity vs. Possibility*, New York: Alfred A. Knopf.

Lapavitsas, C. (2013), *Profiting Without Producing; How Finance Exploits Us All,* London: Verso Books.

Lazonick, W. (2009), *Sustainable Prosperity in the New Economy: New Business Organization and High-Tech Employment in the United States*, Kalamazoo: W.E. Upjohn Institute for Employment Research.

Lazonick, W. (2013), From Innovation to Financialization: How Shareholder Value Ideology is Destroying the US Economy, In M. Wolfson and G. Epstein (eds.), *The Handbook of the Political Economy of Financial Crises*, pp. 491-511, Oxford: Oxford University Press.

Lazonick, W. (2014), Profits Without Prosperity, *Harvard Business Review,* September.

Lazonick, W. (2015a), *Stock Buybacks: From Retain-and-Reinvest to Downsize-and Distribute,* Washington, D.C.: Brookings Institution.

Lazonick, W. (2015b), *Buybacks: From Basics to Politics, Air Special Report,* Cambridge, MA: The AIRnet.

Lazonick, W. (2015c), Labor in the Twenty-First Century: The Top 0.1% and the Disappearing Middle-Class, *INET Working Paper,* No. 4, February.

Lazonick, W. and M. O'Sullivan (2000), Maximizing Shareholder Value: A New Ideology for Corporate Governance, *Economy and Society,* Vol. 29, No. 1, pp. 13-35.

Levina, Iren A. (2014), A Puzzling Rise in Financial Profits and the Role of Capital Gain Like Revenue, PERI Working Paper #347, April.

Lin, K. and D. Tomaskovic-Devey (2013), Financialization and US Income Inequality: 1970-2008, *American Journal of Sociology,* Vol. 118, No. 5, pp. 1284-1329.

Milberg, W. and D. Winkler (2013), *Outsourcing Economics: Global Value Chains in Capitalist Development,* Cambridge: Cambridge University Press.

Minsky, H. (1975), *John Maynard Keynes,* New York: McGraw Hill.

Minsky, H.(1992), The Financial Instability Hypothesis, Bard College: Levy Institute, Working Paper, No. 74.

Minsky, H. (2008), *Stabilizing an Unstable Economy,* New York: McGraw Hill.

Orhangazi, Ö. (2008a), *Financialization and the US Economy,* Northampton, MA: Edward Elgar.

Orhangazi, Ö. (2008b), Financialisation and Capital Accumulation in the Non-Financial Corporate Sector, *Cambridge Journal of Economics,* Vol. 32, No. 6, pp. 863-886.

Orhangazi, Ö (2011), Financial vs. 'Real': An Overview of the Contradictory Role and Place of Finance in the Modern Economy, In. P. Zarembka and R. Desai (eds.), *Research in Political Economy,* Vol. 27.

Palley, Thomas I. (2013a.), *Financialization; The Economics of Finance Capital Domination,* New York: Palgrave MacMillan.

Palley, Thomas I. (2013b), Overview: Financialization as Financial Neoliberalism, In *Financialization; The Economics of Finance Capital*

Domination, New York: Palgrave MacMillan, Chapter 1.

Parenteau, Robert W. (2005), The Late 1990s' US Bubble: Financialization in the Extreme, In G.A. Epstein (ed.), *Financialization and the World Economy*, Northampton, MA: Edward Elgar.

Pollin, R. (1996), Contemporary Economic Stagnation in World Historical Perspective, *New Left Review*, Vol. 1, No. 219, pp. 109-18.

Sawyer, M. (2013), What is Financialization?, *International Journal of Political Economy*, Vol. 42, No. 4, pp. 5-18.

Sen, S. (2014), *Dominant Finance and Stagnant Economies*, New Delhi: Oxford University Press.

Skott, P. and S. Ryoo. (2009), Macroeconomic Implications of Financialisation, *Cambridge Journal of Economics*, Vol. 32, No. 6, pp. 827-62.

Stockhammer, E. (2004), Financialisation and the Slowdown of Accumulation, *Cambridge Journal of Economics*, Vol. 28, No. 5, pp. 719-41.

Stout, L. (2011), Derivatives and Legal Origin of the 2008 Credit Crisis, *Harvard Business Law Review*, Vol. 1, pp. 1-38.

Stout, L. (2012), *The Shareholder Value Myth: How Putting Shareholders First Harms Investors, Corporations and the Public*, Berrett-Koehler Publishers.

Taub, J. (2014), *Other People's Houses: How Decades of Bailouts, Captive Regulators, and Toxic Bankers Made Home Mortgage Thrilling Business*, New York: Yale University Press.

Taylor, L. (2010), *Maynard's Revenge: The Collapse of Free Market Macroeconomics*, Cambridge, MA: Harvard University Press.

Taylor, A.M. (2012), *The Great Leveraging*, Bank for International Settlements (BIS).

Tomaskovic-Devey, D. and K. Lin (2011), Income Dynamics, Economic Rents, and the Financialization of the US Economy, *American Sociological Review*, Vol. 76, No. 4, pp. 538-59.

Tomaskovic-Devey, D. and K. Lin and N. Meyers (2015), *Did Financialization Reduce Economic Growth*?, Amherst: University of Massachusetts.

Turner, A. (2013), Debt, Money and Mephistopheles: How Do We Get Out of This Mess?, Washington, D.C.: Group of Thirty, Occasional Paper, No. 87, May.

Vercelli, A. (2013), Financialization in a Long-Run Perspective: An Evolutionary Approach, *International Journal of Political Economy*, Vol. 42, No. 4, pp. 19-46.

Warren, E. (2014), *A Fighting Chance*, New York: Metropolitan Books.

Wolfson, Martin H. and Gerald A. Epstein, (eds.), (2013), *The Handbook of the Political Economy of Financial Crises*, Oxford: Oxford University Press.

Wray, L. Randall (2009), Money Manager Capitalism and the Global Financial Crisis, *Real-World Economics Review*, Vol. 51, pp. 55-69.

14

Reflections on the Classical Theory of Imperialism: Does History Repeat Itself?

Paramjit Singh
Balwinder Singh Tiwana

Introduction

History shows that the major economic crises give way to fundamental transformation in the working of capitalist economic system. However, all capitalist crises are the outcome of some fundamental contradictions. The contradiction between capital and labour is the basic contradiction of capitalism that is inherent within the production process. The other contradiction arises with the competition among the free capitalist producers of the same industry to defeat each other at the marketplace to maximise sale. It ruins the small and less competitive players. The third contradiction is between the national capitalist producers producing different products to expand its size to other spheres of production that results in the concentration and centralisation of capital at national level. The last contradiction takes capitalism into a qualitative new age. It constitutes the contradiction between the national capitalists of one region or a country with the capitalists of another region or a country to grab the world market. This last contradiction is the subject matter of what we call classical theories of imperialism.

The original Marxian theory of imperialism is not given by Marx rather it had been developed between 1902 and 1917. The publication of Hobson's populist version of the critique of imperialism in 1902 led Marxist thinkers to understand the contradictions of industrial capitalism that had developed among major centres of the capitalist world after 1870. It gave rise to the Marxian theory of Imperialism. The original Marxist theory of imperialism comprises writings which include (chronologically) Hilferding (1981) first published in 1910, Luxemburg (2003) in 1913, Bukharin (2010) in 1915 and Lenin (2010) in 1917. However, Kautsky's Ultra-imperialism, that was criticised by Bukharin and Lenin and was declared irrelevant around the First World War period owing to its pessimistic approach, became relevant to some extent to understand the imperialistic nature of capitalism in the post-Second World War era.

Classical theories of imperialism are valued as an epochal reflection that have meticulously investigated the logic of capitalist accumulation during the beginning of the 20th century. It has taken Marx's analysis from a closed capitalist economics system into the world economic system. The key features of classical theories of imperialism are principally directed by the course of territorial expansions in search of new economic spheres of influence. Therefore, sometimes the end of colonial rule is seen to be the end of imperialism as well. However, reality is beyond such myopic conclusions. Historical understanding of the development of capitalism reveals that imperialism is a necessary condition for the sustainability of capitalism and accumulation therein. Therefore, the end of colonialism calls for the Marxist scholars to revisit the classical theories with an objective to understand the current conjecture. Undoubtedly, the classical theories of imperialism which were formulated in the first and second decade of the 20th century are no longer directly applicable to understand the imperialist nature of capitalist accumulation in the 21st century. However, it does not mean that classical work altogether became redundant to understand the imperialistic nature of contemporary capitalism. As Boron (2005, 3-4) remarked that "the fundamental parameters of imperialism delineated in the classical works remain central, even though the 'phenomenology' of imperialism has changed." Now, the challenge for the Marxist theorists of the imperialist world system is to assimilate the profundity of classical account and in its light, address the changes in the mode of surplus extraction in the contemporary phase of imperialism.

In the light of these facts, the present chapter is an attempt to synthesise the classical theories of imperialism in order to build a comprehensive understanding of old and contemporary characteristics of imperialism. For that purpose the chapter is divided into four parts. The first part highlights the misery of classical and post-classical bourgeois economics to understand the real nature and working of capitalism. The second part conceptualises imperialism as the monopoly stage of capitalism. The third part unfolds the relationship between economics and politics that played an important role in strengthening the foundations of imperialism. The fourth part highlights export of capital and colonialisation as an essential character of the late 19th and early 20th century imperialism. The concluding part presents the changing nature of capitalism and its imperialistic characteristics.

Capitalism Beyond Say's Law

Bourgeois economic theory is concerned with commodity production and market system where surplus value is produced and distributed. It presents capitalist accumulation purely as an economic process driven by liberal democratic values, harmony of interests and peace. The peaceful development of production forces and relations results in equitable distribution of total produce and the economy's progress on liberal lines. However, Luxemburg (2003, 432-33) emphasised the other aspect of capitalist economy which is beyond the realm of peaceful competition, the marvels of technology and pure commodity exchange. It is the realm of capital's blustering violence which bourgeois economics regarded more or less incidental to foreign policy and quite independent of the economic sphere of capital. This is the sphere which classical theorists characterise as imperialism.

The fundamental problem with classical and developed classical system presented by the post-classical economics through Walras' general equilibrium approach is that it favours some automatic adjustment mechanism which keeps the capitalist economic system in an equilibrium. In this realm of automatic adjustment, all the markets—product, labour and money—are considered to be mechanically interrelated with each other and always achieve balance between demand and supply forces (in other words, they always remain 'clear'). The classical notion of market clearing is based on the Say's law of market. The central theme of classical economics is distribution of output produced by the employed resources based on the marginal productivity theory of distribution. The driving force of all the markets is aggregate supply and whatever is supplied in each market, creates its own demand. The Ricardian explanation of Say's law states:

> No man produces but with a view to consume or sell and he never sells but with an intention to purchase other commodities, which may be useful for him, or which may contribute to future production. By producing then, he necessarily becomes either the consumer of his own goods or the purchaser or consumer of the goods of some other person... Productions are always brought by productions, or by services; money is the only medium by which exchange is effected (Ricardo, 2006, 201-02).

According to Ricardo's explanation of Say's law, exchange of commodities is transformed into mere barter of products. This is a return not only to the time before capitalist production, but even to the time before simple commodity production. Say's law can hold in pre-capitalist consumption dominant societies, where the barter system dominates or if money exists, it plays only the medium of exchange function. As explained by J.B. Say in *Catechism of Political Economy*, "every producer ask for money in exchange for his product, only for the purpose of employing that money again immediately in the purchase of another product; for we do not consume money, and it is not sought after in an ordinary case to conceal it: thus, when a producer desires to exchange his product for money, he may be considered as already asking for the merchandise which he proposes to buy with this money. It is thus the producers, though they have all of them the air of demanding money for their goods, do in reality demand merchandise for their merchandise" (Say, 1817, 105). This process was presented by Marx through the following two equations.

C—C or C—M—C

The process, presented by Say's law or Ricardo's explanation of it, highlights that in the first circuit the commodity undergoes the process of metamorphosis into money and in the next circuit the process of metamorphosis of money into commodity. It is quite consistent that money is then regarded merely as an intermediary in the exchange of products. This interpretation of capitalist economic system has denied the first condition of capitalist production. The sole purpose of production under capitalism is accumulation of more and more capital in money form. The capitalist production process starts with money with a principal objective of valorisation of capital invested in the form of more money as shown by the following equation.

M—C—M′

The logic of capital accumulation which drives the capitalist economic system depends on realisation of surplus value, the value over and above the value of labour power. In a closed capitalist system, production of surplus value is based on conditions that the wages of workers should be less than the total value produced by them. This extra value above the 'necessary labour time' requires the market for its realisation. One part of this demand is fulfilled by the workers as consumers and the other part is fulfilled by the producers as consumers. It is an established fact that the marginal propensity to consume of the workers is near to one which means they consume whatever they earn. However, marginal propensity of the capitalists is less than one which means they consume less than their income because they keep a part of their income for investment. This reinvestment is based on the condition that all the surplus value extracted during the production process should be realised in the market. The circuit of capital accumulation cannot be complete without the realisation of surplus value. Hence, in a closed economic system the realisation of surplus value is blocked by the problem of the narrow base of consumption. The capitalist crisis due to narrow base of domestic consumption can be postponed through intensification of the domestic market by developing new production units and employing new workers. But wages which in a capital-driven economy always remain less than the marginal productivity again pose a serious barrier to accumulation within the boundaries of a national economy. It gives birth to the problem of overproduction/underconsumption that undermines the classical notion of Say's law (that supply creates its own demand) and therefore falsifies the notion of capitalism as a self-sufficient system.

During the 1870s, in advanced machine-driven capitalist economies, consumption failed to keep pace with production due to distributional changes caused by stagnation of real wages and continuous increase in share of profits. The other qualitative change that undermined the Say's law of market was concentration and centralisation of capital, causing further widening of the gap between consumption and production. Concentration and centralisation of capital displaced the perfect competition driven price mechanism with monopolistic price set up, i.e. prices became downward sticky.

Hence, the time period of the 1870s can be characterised as a turning point in the economic history of capitalism due to structural changes in the working of the system. It undermined the logic of capitalist equilibrium based on Say's law. The growth of large-scale production units on the graveyard of smaller ones intensified the concentration and centralisation of capital. Bukharin (2010, 64) argued,

> The destruction, from top to bottom, of old, conservative, economic forms that was begun with the initial stages of capitalism, has triumphed all along the line. At the same time, however, this 'organic' elimination of weak competitors inside the framework of 'national economies (the ruin of artisanship, the disappearance of intermediary forms, the growth of large-scale production, etc.) is now being superseded by the crucial period of a sharpening struggle among stupendous opponents on the world market.

This gave rise to growth of monopolies at national level: the formation of cartels, syndicates, trusts, etc. This phenomenon took capitalism to a phase that was beyond the scope of classical economics. The new phase of capitalism was driven by the collusion between industrial and bank capital with an objective to tighten the control over the national market and state apparatuses at the first stage and the world market at the final stage.

Imperialism as an Outcome of Monopoly Capital

According to Lenin (2010), "imperialism emerged as the development and direct continuation of the fundamental characteristics of capitalism in general."...."Economically, the main thing in this process is the displacement of capitalist free competition by capitalist monopoly" (p. 87). For Lenin, imperialism is the monopoly stage of capitalism that is an outcome of certain changes in the characteristics of capitalism. Lenin's definition of imperialism includes five basic features:

> (i) the concentration of production and capital has developed to such a high degree that it has created monopolies which play a decisive role in economic life; (ii) the merging of bank capital with industrial capital, and the creation, on the basis of this "finance capital" of a financial oligarchy; (iii) the export of capital as distinguished from the export of commodities acquires exceptional importance; (iv) the formation of international monopolist capitalist combines which share the whole world among themselves, and (v) the territorial division of the whole world among the biggest capitalist powers is completed (p. 88).

Hence, the essence of imperialism is monopoly capital. Imperialism can be defined as a stage in the development of capitalism in which several capitalist countries stand against each other to provide the world market to their industrial produce and surplus capital.

Marx's analysis of capitalism systematically deals with three fractions of accumulation of capital: commercial capital which is also known as merchant capital (M—C—M′), industrial capital (M—C (MoP + LP)—P—C′—M′) and bank capital (M—M′). He did not systematically discuss the capitalist accumulation beyond these stages. Hilferding's contribution to the theory of capitalist development is considered as a valuable supplement to the three volumes of Marx's *Capital* for logical understanding of the latest phase of capitalism after the 1870s. Hilferding's analysis deals with next form of capital accumulation that he named finance capital.

The concentration and centralisation process that was well underway in Britain, other European countries and USA resulted in the cut-throat competition, followed by rapid process of amalgamation and combines. This process resulted in concentration of national wealth in a few hands. The displacement of free competition driven capitalism by monopolies in various spheres of production was a turning point in the history of development of capitalism. The process of concentration and centralisation that worked to eliminate free competition through the formation of cartels and trusts brought bank and industrial capital closer. As Hilferding (1981, 121-127) argued, combined enterprises (cartels) accumulated more competitive strength than their pure counterparts (non-combined enterprises). With the growth of combined enterprises during the late 19th century, pure enterprises perished, as they were "crushed between the high price of raw material and competitive price of final produce." Lenin argued, cartels, far from dissipating in thin air as some transitory phenomenon, had become a fairly permanent nerve centre of economic activities, sweeping one industry after another. Lenin conceived this phenomenon as the principal stage in the history of monopolies and characterised it as follows:

> (i) 1860-70, the highest stage, the apex of development of free competition; monopoly is in the barely discernible, embryonic stage. (ii) After the crisis of 1873, a lengthy period of development of cartels; but there is still the exception. They are not yet durable. They are still a transitory phenomenon. (iii) The boom at the end of the 19th century and the crisis of 1900-03. Cartels become one of the foundations of the whole of economic life. Capitalism has been transformed into imperialism (Lenin, 2010, 25).

Cartels were not the only sole catalysts of economic change. During the period in question, along with cartels, the growth of joint stock companies (JSCs) also modified the form of economic control and organisation of industrial production. The operation of JSCs in the stock market, that of issuing shares and raising equity on the stock exchange, divorced ownership from control. This became the perfect breeding ground for bank capital which could bring firms under its control by buying shares (Hilferding 1981, 121-127). Regarding the importance of bank capital in the emerged form of JSCs production, Lenin (2010, 33) rightly remarked, "we shall have a very insufficient, incomplete and poor notion of the real power and significance of modern monopolies if we do not take into consideration the part played by the banks." As industrial capital entered the confines of concentration, bank capital followed suit: proliferation of banking activities subsequently resulted in the concentration of bank capital. As Lenin (2010, 35) points out,

> the big enterprises and the banks in particular, not only completely absorb the small ones, but also 'annex' them, subordinate them, bring them into their 'own' group or 'concern' (to use a technical term) by acquiring 'holding' in capital, by purchasing or exchanging shares, by a system of credit etc., etc.

This was an important distinguishing feature of the banking capital. The collusion between big banks and industries consolidated the process of monopolisation. Investment credit deepened this association even further. Banks, thus, fastened their grip on JSCs. This became the turning point in the accumulation history of capitalism. The dominance of capital in general translated into dominance of finance capital. Hiferding (1981, 121-127) has defined "finance capital as the capital controlled by banks and employed by industrialists." Lenin (2010, 49) defined this process as "the concentration of production; the monopolies arising there from; the merging or coalescence of the bank with industry." Hence, finance capital that became the dominant form of accumulation was considered to be the turning point in the accumulation history of capitalism. There are two significant features of finance capital that differentiated it from the other forms of capital.

First, finance capital relied on the coalescence of financial capital and industrial capital. During that time, the dominant form of valorisation of capital was not through financial activities but through channels of industrial production. Bukharin (2010, 71-72) pointed out, how bank capital assumed the role of an organiser of industry by various forms of credit, by owning stocks and bonds, and by directly promoting enterprises. The valorisation of capital under the domination of finance capital is presented as below:

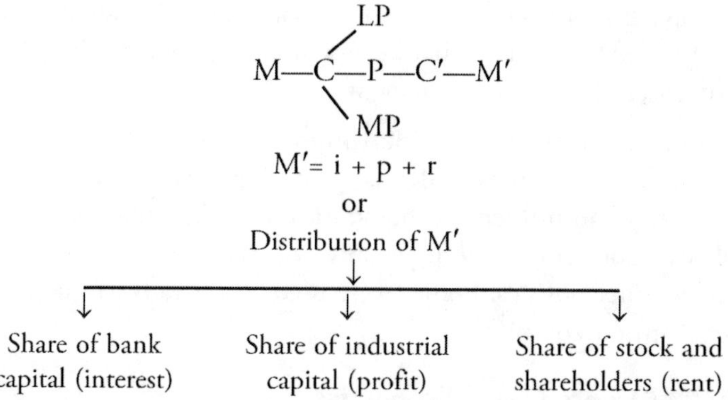

According to the classical analysis of imperialism, the initial M in the above figure illustrating the industrial production process is largely financed by the bank capital for extended reproduction. After the completion of production, the M′ so generated constitutes the share of bank capital, of industrial capital and of rentier class of stock and shareholders. A major part of this M′ is reinvested to expand the sphere of production through the purchase of raw material and employment of new labourers.

Secondly, finance capital of that time was national in character and closely tied to the performance of domestic industry. Major capitalist economies firmly believed that the expansion of national territory was imperative to extend the size of the market for industrial produce. Even under the Keynesian policy regime of apparent restrictions on speculation, financial expansion was allowed more or less in tandem with the production within the national boundaries. Hence, during the beginning of the 20th century, capitalism (particularly industrial and bank capital in metropolises) entered the phase of big monopolies. Since the exploitation of the domestic market was complete, its limited size became an obstacle for capitalist accumulation. The way out was the export of capital from metropolitan to the new territories. However, it does not mean that there were no possibilities for production and employment of capital in metropolitan countries. The export of capital was necessary to explore the possibilities of higher profits. As Marx (1965, 256) writes,

> if capital is sent aboard, this is not done because it absolutely could not be applied at home but because it can be employed at a higher rate of profit in a foreign country.

Export of capital requires political support. The capitalist class (big business, financial elites and aristocrats interested in professional services etc.) had influenced the political class in a manner that the stability of domestic economy is only possible through imperialism. In this manner political bodies were used as a means to impose the imperialism on colonies.

Politics as Concentrated Economics

Capitalism as an economic system is not self-sufficient. It always requires politics and politics of capitalism is ruled by the economically dominant classes. Hence, "political power is nothing but a vehicle for the economic progress. The conditions for the reproduction of capital provide the organic link between two aspects of the accumulation of capital" (Luxemburg, 2003, 433). Regarding the interrelation between economics and politics, Lenin (1965) argued "politics is the most concentrated expression of economics, its generalisation and its culmination." The imperialist project was the product of high economics of that time. As Hobson pointed out, imperialism was the product of private interests and certainly not beneficial for the commonwealth. Imperialism was imposed by privileged groups on the national as a vice policy. The leading British politician saw imperialism as a vice policy. Chamberlin advocated imperialism as a "true, wise and economic policy"… Cecil Rhodes… expressed his imperialist views in 1895 in the following terms:

> I was in the East End of London (working-class quarter) yesterday and attended a meeting of the unemployed. I listened to the wild speeches, which were just a cry for 'bread,' 'bread!' and on my way home I pondered over the scene and I became more than ever convinced of the importance of imperialism….My cherished idea is a solution for the social problem, i.e. in order to save the 40,000,000 inhabitants of

> the United Kingdom from a bloody civil war, we colonial statesmen must acquire new lands to settle the surplus population, to provide new markets for the goods produced in the factories and mines. The Empire, as I have always said, is a bread and butter question, if you want to avoid civil war, you must become imperialists (Quoted by Lenin, 2010, 79).

Hence, imperialism is a political expression of a facilitator for accumulation of capital.

Due to the immense accumulation of capital in old capitalist countries[1] and increased difficulties of surplus extraction/ realisation, imperialism emerged as a wise public policy. The development of capitalism in old capitalist countries during the 1850s and 1860s undermined the classical economics' doctrine of free trade as a means of accumulation. Therefore, the theory of peaceful development of accumulation though free trade lost its relevance with the intensification of the machine economy. As Luxemburg (2003, 430) argued, the very inception of an international system of free trade showed it to be just a passing phase in the history of capitalist accumulation, simply because of a defensive reaction against English free trade by continental European countries and USA.

If we deeply examine the free trade doctrine of classical economics that Britain favoured during the 1850s and 1860s there were reasons for its validity as well as invalidity. Free trade as a doctrine is valid for capitalist countries if it is between capitalist and pre-capitalist nations due to two reasons: (i) It is reasonable to convert the natural or peasant economies into exchange and commercial economies because it ensures capitalist producers to extract surplus. (ii) It is beneficial because it is inherently unequal due to faulty theorisation of specialisation in which pre-capitalist countries should specialise in raw material and capitalist countries in manufacturing goods. The exchange relations in this context are always favourable to the manufacturing producers. It is not beneficial between machine economies due to the equal competitive capacity. The equal competitive capacity inevitably leads towards monopolies and growth of monopolies in this context means international monopolies that will become established at the cost of national industries of some nations.

Hence, the policy of protective tariffs during the last decades of the 19th century became an important tool for equally strong capitalist countries against each other's products that were harmful for their domestic industry. The sentiments of internationalism and universalism which were the outcome of the philosophy of the French Revolution withered away with a powerful revival of capitalist nationalism. Nationalism was used by the growing capitalist nations as an ideological slogan to undermine the free trade doctrine. In order to ensure the profitability of the domestic industry, the political leaders instead of inclining towards liberalism were more interested in protection of the national market. During the late 1870s, protective tariffs became an integral part of the economic policies of young capitalist nations and the old also joined the same (except Britain). The basic building blocks of the pure theory of economic liberalism which were the irreducible atoms of enterprise, the individual or the firm, melt into the air with the rise of bourgeois nationalism and international protectionism.

Table 1: Average Level of Tariff in Europe 1914

Countries	*Tariff (per cent)*	*Countries*	*Tariff (per cent)*
United Kingdom	0	Austria-Hungary, Italy	18
Netherlands	4	France, Sweden	20
Germany	9	Spain	41
Denmark	13	USA (1913)	30

Source: Hobsbawm (1994), 39.

Economic protectionism and competition among the growing industrialised economies turned them into rival economies in which gains were visualised by one nation at the cost of others. It contributed to the higher growth of production and trade between 1880 and 1914 than it had during the free trade decades. Protectionism developed a tendency towards the concentration and centralisation of production at the national level. Along with this, the scientific management of production, technological advancement and transportation revolution transformed the structure of large enterprises.

There was fusion of political and economic interest of the state and national capitalist class as far as international policy was concerned. Political actions were bent to defend the economic interests of certain groups which were economically powerful. "Political rivalries between states and the economic competition between national groups of entrepreneurs fused, thus contributing- as we shall see- both to the phenomenon of imperialism and to the genesis of the First World War. They also led, incidentally, to the growth of industries such as armaments in which the role of the government was decisive" (Hobsbawm, 1994, 54).

Along with protectionism, the other phenomenon that was an integral part of the politics of imperialism was militarism. Nationalism and militarism are not only important in the formation of capitalist society but also important for its maintenance and expansion. History shows that nationalism and militarism play an indispensable role in accumulation history of capitalism. "In the advanced countries, nationalism and militarism cease to serve the purpose of realisation internal unification and freedom on a capitalist foundation".... (Sweezy, 1942, 308). In the advanced stage of capitalism, militarism attains a permanent and important position in society. The outgrowth of old capitalist countries towards imperialist ones required growth of armaments for two reasons: (i) To protect the boarders and strengthen its image as a strong nation within the psychology of countrymen. (ii) As a part of expansionist policy, to grab more non-capitalist territory to secure the capitalist accumulation and surplus realisation through arm power.

Hence, in the age of imperialism that was an outcome of an advanced form of capitalism, the so-called liberal and laissez-faire ideology of the early capitalist state disappeared and its hidden and real character came to the surface. Military state apparatuses which were hidden behind the veil of liberalism appeared on the scene most directly with the intensification of international competition among big finance capitals of advanced capitalist nations. It was visible in many advanced countries of that time. The arms race that began in a modest way in the later part of the 1870s, accelerated in the next decades. British military expenses remained almost stable during the 1870s and 1880s. But these rose from £23.8 million in 1881 to £72.5 million in 1913. The per capita average military expenditure also increased from £0.76 to £1.57 between 1870-79 and 1900-13. All the great powers (see Tables 2 and 3) experienced a many fold increase in military expenditure.

Table 2: Military Expenditure of Great Powers (£ million)

Countries	*1871*	*1881*	*1891*	*1901*	*1913*	*Average 1870-1913*
Britain	22.8	23.8	33.4	121.0	72.5	45.0
Italy	8.50	10.1	15.8	14.8	39.6	14.5
Germany	-	21.8	35.5	49.3	93.4	38.4
Russia	49.2	64.8	78.9	45.2	101.7	68.8
USA	16.3	11.5	15.4	42.1	68.9	27.7
Japan	0.50	2.3	4.0	11.0	22.0	12.0
France	23.9	33.0	37.2	42.5	72.0	37.0
Austria	6.30	7.0	8.9	12.0	25.0	10.0

Source: Hobson (1993), 464-65

The growth of military organisations, the army and the navy was striking during the last decades of the 19th century and the beginning of the 20th century. There was an immense growth of state budget devoted to defence purposes. Tables 2 and 3 illustrate the growth of military expenditure in major countries as percentage of state budgets.

Table 3: Per Capital Military Expenditure in Sterling Equivalent

Countries	*1870-79*	*1880-89*	*1890-99*	*1900-13*	*1870-1913*
Britain	0.76	0.83	0.93	1.57	1.18
Italy	0.32	0.47	0.47	0.60	0.47
Germany	0.44	0.51	0.70	0.99	0.74
Russia	0.66	0.55	0.58	0.54	0.57

USA	0.28	0.21	0.31	0.62	0.42
Japan	0.07	0.08	0.19	0.57	0.29
France	0.70	0.85	0.94	1.25	0.97
Austria	0.35	0.36	0.40	0.58	0.45

Source: Same as Table 2, 466

Hence, militarism was an inevitable outcome of the industrial-military complex of new capitalism. As Bukharin (2010, 127) put it, "armaments are an indispensable attribute of state power, an attribute that has a very definite function in the struggle among state capitalist trusts. Capitalist society is unthinkable without armaments, as it is unthinkable without wars." This is a peculiar feature of capitalist society that when economic conflict among the nations reaches an unusual degree of intensity, it gives birth to a mad orgy of armaments. Thus, the rule of finance capital implies the simultaneous rule of imperialism and militarism. The economic life under the rule of finance capital was driven by the aggressive politics and militarisation of social life. The peace time regimes that are the realm of mainstream economics lose their importance to study the logic of capital accumulation on a global scale. War, nationalism and militarism which are treated as unnatural elements in the neoclassical equilibrium economics and therefore not considered as subjects for study, became real and natural in the imperialistic age of capitalism. Contrary to the mainstream doctrine, one distinguishing feature of Marxian political economy "is the conviction that economic processes must be understood as part of a social organism in which war is at least as typical as peace" (Magdoff, 1970, 237).

"In short, politics and economics cannot be separated in a capitalist society, any more than religion and society in an Islamic one..." (Hobsbawm, 1994, 69). Owing to protection within the European continent and USA during the 1880s along with an objective to monopolise the non-capitalist areas at home and abroad, territorial expansion became the war-cry of capital. The peculiar helplessness of non-capitalist countries can be visualised in the face of competing international capital which aimed to acquire partial or total of these areas as colonies or sphere of interest of metropolitan capital. The immense possession of non-capitalist areas as a basis for operations emerged as a cause as well as ultimate opportunity for imperialist rivalries.

Export of Capital and Colonisation

Growth of production and trade due to economic protectionism between 1880 and 1914 was higher than it had been during the free trade decades. "In 1870 the four main industrial states had produced almost 80 per cent of the total world manufacturing output, but in 1913 they produced 72 per cent of an output which was five times as great" (Hobsbawm, 1994, 43). If we add together the industrial, mining and construction production of four leading nations, in 1913 the USA provided 46 per cent of this total, Germany 23.5 per cent, Britain 19.5 per cent and France 11 per cent (Lewis, 1978, 275). Hence the worry was not depression in production for economists or industrialists; rather it was depression of prices, interest and profits. The most crucial economic factor for imperialism of that time was the influence relating to investment. During the late 19th or beginning of the 20th century, every advanced capitalist nation was trying to export a larger share of its capital outside its own territory to earn higher profits. The actual income earned from the foreign and colonial investment was relatively higher than the income earned by the industrial capital at home. The industrial class which was interested to invest abroad or was not able to find profitable opportunities at home pushed the government to help them to find profitable and secure investment abroad. They used the resources of government to minimise risk on their investment abroad (Hobson, 2017, 52-53).

The expansion of territories during the 1870s had three objectives: (i) to expand the market for the industrial produce, (ii) to export the capital for more profitable employment, and (iii) to export the unemployed workforce from metropolitan countries to the colonies. Therefore, imperialism's rise in the capitalist countries was dictated first by their internal conditions and secondly by the competition to capture the world market.

According to Luxemburg, some important dimensions of

imperialism were to absorb the surplus and maintain the pace of the accumulation process under capitalism. She argued that "the imperialist phase of capitalist accumulation which implies universal competition comprises the industrialisation and capitalist emancipation of the hinterland where capital formerly realised its surplus value. Characteristics of this phase are: lending abroad, railroad constructions, revolutions, and wars." (Luxemburg, 2003, 399). During that time, the flow of trade, capital and labour had two streams: between advanced and emerging countries and between advanced countries and colonies. During the 19th century, all developed regions' trade was around 80 per cent (imports as well as exports). This had meant that trade with colonies was relatively marginal, i.e. about 20 per cent of Europe's trade in the 19th century (Bairoch, 1974). A key aspect of this relationship was highlighted by Hobsbawm. He argued that the relationship between the metropolis and its dependencies was highly asymmetrical. Take for instance, the palpably skewed trade relations between Europe and the underdeveloped regions of Asia, Sub-Saharan Africa and Oceania which were and continued to be highly exploitative. On the other side, trade relations between Europe and young capitalist countries where settlers of European descent thrived—Canada, Australia, South Africa, Argentina, etc—as well as, of course, the USA was equal and development-oriented (Hobsbawm 1994, 73-74).

This gulf between the metropolis and the dependencies was created and widened to accommodate the European emigrants who, according to Lewis (1978, 181), emigrated from Europe in large numbers. Between 1871 and 1915 some 36 million people had emigrated from Europe. It was the biggest mass migration in recorded history, predominatly to the USA, Canada and other temperate regions. This migration in turn was supported by the enormous flow of capital from Europe in the form of public loans for infrastructure and investment. One aspect of the export of capital was visible in terms of public loans for railroad building. As Luxemburg (2003, 401) said,

> ....in the imperialist era, the foreign loan played an outstanding part as a means for young capitalist states to acquire independence." The

> young capitalist states develop under the shadow of old capitalist states. However, old capitalist states "maintain their influence, exercise financial control and exert pressure on the customs, foreign and commercial policy of young capitalist states."

Foreign loans widened the scope for the accumulation of capital by old capitalist countries and at the same time produced the competitive powers or allies for struggle for more non-capitalist territories. Railway building and the loans necessary for it mainly served an important purpose to disintegrate the natural economy, and to spread commodity economy. For instance American railways was largely built with European capital. However, railway construction in Africa and Asia exclusively served the purpose of an imperialist policy, of economic monopolisation and economic subjugation of the backward communities (Luxemburg, 2003, 402). Imperialist policy of rising industrial capitalism used the colonial surplus to fulfil the above objective. As Bagchi (2002, 2229) argued, in the era of the rise of industrial capitalism and its development in Western Europe and the USA, income from colonies played a critical role in boosting investment in Western Europe and allowed enormous amounts of investment to be directed towards sustenance of mass migration of Europeans to the USA, Canada, Australia, New Zealand or South Africa.

The other form of export of capital occurred in terms of foreign direct investment (FDI). Hobsbawm pointed out the asymmetrical relationship in the context of trade between developed capitalism and underdeveloped countries. The same was the case with foreign capital investment. FDI flow from some advanced to other advanced countries was qualitatively different from the FDI flow from advanced to less developed countries. Lenin (2010, 64) argued that "the necessity for exporting capital arises from the fact that in a few countries capitalism has become 'overripe' and capital cannot find a field for profitable investment." The export of capital becomes a means for encouraging the export of commodities. During 1914 the combined share of foreign investment of three great imperial powers (England, France and Germany) was 74.4 per cent of the total foreign investment in the world.

Table 4: Foreign Investment by England, France and Germany

Years	*England*			*France*	*Germany*
	Saving/ GDP (Per cent)	*Foreign invest-ment/ GDP (Per cent)*	*Foreign invest-ment as percentage of savings*	*Foreign in-vestment as percentage of savings*	*Foreign invest-ment as percentage of savings*
1870-79	12.3	4.0	32.5	23.9	10.2
1880-89	12.2	4.7	38.5	5.1	18.8
1890-99	11.0	3.4	30.9	16.5	12.1
1900-04	12.6	3.7	29.4	19.1	8.3
1904-14	13.1	6.5	49.6	17.3	7.5
Net national wealth head overseas in 1914	32.1				
Share of global foreign investment	41.8			19.8	12.8

Source: Daudin, Morys and O'Rourke (2010), 10.

The racial character of imperialism became visible in FDI outflow from imperialist countries. The investment from old capitalist countries was skewed towards Europe and young capitalist countries. As Fei's (1930) calculations highlighted, out of the total publicly issued British capital investment in 1913, the combined share of the USA, Canada and Newfoundland, Australia and New Zealand, Argentina, Brazil and South Africa was 67.77 per cent, whereas the share of non-white colonies, for instance, India and Ceylon, constituted only 11.06 per cent of the total investment. The imperialist racial character of France and Germany is also visible in case of long-term foreign investment. During 1914, out of the total long-term foreign investment of France, 4.89 per cent was in Asia. In case of Germany it was 12.76 per cent in Asia and Africa (including Germany's Asian and African colonies).

Therefore, during 1870-1914, old imperialist countries used the dual policy. Trade, public loans and investment remained biased towards the young capitalist countries to support the mass migration from Europe to new settlements. The non-white geographical locations were considered as an important part of imperialism for extraction of surplus by the imperialist industrial capital due to monopolised foreign trade with these colonies. Along with this, the surplus generated from the non-white colonies, as Bagchi (2002) argued, through invisible earnings which included (but not limited to) home charges, political tribute, monopoly rent, etc., had facilitated European foreign investment to white settlements and helped to improve the wages and standard of living both in the home and the host countries.

Hence, the non-white colonialisation was used as a vice policy by advanced capitalist countries. The use of violent methods which were inevitable in the advanced age of capitalism emerged as the driving force of export of capital. Regarding the violent nature of capitalism, Hilferding (1981, 319) argued,

> When capital first encounters conditions which contradict its need for valorisation, and could only be overcome much too slowly and gradually by purely economic means, it has recourse to the power of the state and uses it for forcible exploitation in order to create the required free wage proletariat. In the early days of capitalism this was the fate of the European peasants and of the Indians of Mexico and Peru, and today the same is happening to the Negroes of Africa. These violent methods are of the essence of colonial policy, without which it would lose its capitalist rationale... The idea of pursuing a colonial policy without having to resort to its violent method is an illusion to be taken no more seriously than that of abolishing the proletariat while maintaining capitalism in existence.

The export of capital in one or the other form, along with internationalisation of cartels was characterised by Lenin as the final partition of the globe—final not in the sense that a repartition is impossible; on the contrary, repartitions are possible and inevitable—but in the sense that the colonial policy of the capitalist countries completed the seizure of unoccupied territories on the planet. Lenin further argued, for the first time the world is completely divided up, so that in the future only redivision is possible i.e. territories can only be passed from one 'owner' to another, instead of passing as ownerless territory to an 'owner' (Lenin, 2010). The passing of territory from one owner to another inevitably resulted in war among the capitalist powers.

Table 5: Colonial Possession of Major Capitalist Countries During 1914 (Area in Million Square Kilometres and Population in Million Inhabitants)

Countries	*Colonies*		*Metropolitan Countries*	
	Area	Population	Area	Population
Great Britain	33.5 (25.02)	393.5 (23.75)	0.3 (0.22)	46.5 (2.81)
Russia	17.4 (13.00)	33.2 (2.00)	5.4 (4.03)	136.2 (8.22)
France	10.6 (7.92)	55.5 (3.35)	0.5 (0.37)	39.6 (2.39)
Germany	2.9 (2.17)	12.3 (0.74)	0.5 (0.37)	64.9 (3.92)
USA	0.3 (0.22)	9.7 (0.58)	9.4 (7.02)	97.0 (5.85)
Japan	0.3 (0.22)	19.2 (1.16)	0.4 ((0.30)	53.0 (3.20)
Total	65.0 (48.54)	522.9 (31.56)	16.5 (12.32)	437.2 (26.38)

Source: Calculated from Lenin (2010), 80
Note: Figures in brackets show percentage.

Hobsbawm (1994, 59) pointed out that

> Between 1876 and 1915 about one-quarter of the globe's land surface was distributed or redistributed as colonies among a half-dozen states. Britain increased its territories by some 4 million square miles, France by some 3.5 millions, Germany acquired more than 1 million... The USA acquired some 100,000, mainly from Spain, Japan and something like the same amount from China, Russia and Korea. Portugal's ancient African colonies expanded by about 300,000 square miles...

Hence, the increased competition at international level to find new outlets for produce and surplus capital gave rise to imperialism. The colonial division of the globe through militarist policies became inevitable during 1914 that led to the First World War.

Concluding Remarks: Does History Repeat Itself?

During the early decades of the 20th century, imperialism had posed a threat to world peace, the outcome of which was the First World War and the conflict had not settled even after. Keynes (1991[1919]) argued that the dreadful material evils that war had produced in Europe were not over, rather they would further extend if we did not seek their proper remedy. After the end of the First World War, the rise of Fascism and Nazism threatened the world peace further. The alliance of these forces with the capitalist class of that time had further intensified the arms race during the inter-war period. The economic consequences of uncontrolled capitalism were visible in the form of the great depression and inter-war anarchy. The anarchy created by the imperialist policy of big capitalist powers led to the Second World War but it also produced decolonialisation. The concept of imperialism, the essence of which was inter-imperialist rivalry, was no longer directly applicable to the post-Second World War capitalism. Kautsky's ultra-imperialism is more suitable to characterise the post-war expansionism of metropolis capitalism. Kautsky (1970, 42) argued that the violent exploitation through force had been replaced by the holly alliance of imperialism where these imperial forces joined hands to exploit the world and hence the character of exploitation had undergone a sea change. Hobson (2017, 278) also had a view parallel to Kautsky's ultra-imperialism. He argued that rapid growth of effective internationalism in the finance and great industrial magnates were destined to control more and more national politics and mute the inter-imperialist rivalry. The era of the Cold War was the era of imperialist alliance run by the international institutions and the USA. During this phase the ideological rivalry between the USA and the Soviet Union was the driving force and instead of direct war between these two powers, proxy wars were fought. During the Cold War period, capitalist countries of the centre avoided the direct means of economic exploitation of Third World countries. This period saw the evolution of indirect means which were exposed by the dependency school led by Paul Sweezy, Paul Baran and Samir Amin. The circuit of capital accumulation shifted from the production sphere to the financial sphere.

The over accumulation of capital by the metropolis capitalists has once again generated the need for new destinations of surplus capital utilisation. Baran and Sweezy (1966) have highlighted new ways of absorption of surplus evolved by capitalism in their work *Monopoly Capital.* Two of the four chapters on absorption of surplus, namely, *Capitalism's Consumption and Investment* and *The Sales Efforts* examine surplus exhaustion within the firm. The latter two, *Civilian Government* and *Militarism and Imperialism* explore how governments help firms exhaust their surplus. However, during the 1970s, capitalism once again faced the crisis of surplus absorption. In order to tackle the situation, the metropolitan capital employed a twofold strategy. First, it deregulated the financial spheres in the home country in order to channelise the surplus produced by the monopoly capital (by both bank and industrial capital) from spheres of production to circulation. Second, it exported surplus capital to pre-capitalist Third World countries. The movement of global capital towards global south has extended the chains of production and value creation across national borders; profoundly transforming the picture of industrial capital in the process. This process has resulted in the emergence of a new phenomenon in the production process known as sub-contracting or arm's length production. Arm's length outsourcing as Smith (2016, 68) defined it "refers to a process where firms outsource part or the entire production process to an independent supplier; independent in the sense that the lead firm owns none of it even though it may control its activities in many ways".... "The outsourcing firm externalises not only commercial risk and low value-added production processes but also externalises direct responsibility for environment pollution, wages and supervision of trade unions... Further, arm's length relationships allow TNCs to offload many of the costs and risks associated with cyclical fluctuations in demand and with much larger disruption in the world market. In the end it is the working masses that pay the higher price in the form of low wages, long hours of work, poor social, employment security and a failure to implement labour standards" (Smith, 2016, 82).

As Amin (2013, 31) pointed out, modern capitalism is not only driven by the monopolistic control over the selected production activities but rather "monopolies now tightly control all the systems of production." Small and medium enterprises of the peripheries are locked into "a network of control and contracts put in place by the international monopolies. Their degree of autonomy has shrunk to the point that they are nothing more than subcontractors of the monopolies" (Amin, 2013, 32). The realisation of centralisation throughout the global north during the last two decades of the 20th century has generalised the control of monopolies over the production system of the whole planet, from Africa to Latin America and Asia. The world today bears witness to a new imperialism—imperialism of rent-seekers, finance capital and monopolies. The rent-seeking class of the global north is financed by the super exploitation of labour in the global south. This new system of imperialist exploitation is driven by two forces: (i) direct and indirect control of monopolies over the southern production system, and (ii) uncontrolled financial speculation on the world scale. This new network of imperialism has brought agriculture and industrial activities of peripheries under the control of international monopoly capital.

The consequences of the crisis of new imperialism became visible after the failure of neoliberal capitalism that can symbolically be understood as the financial crisis of 2008 and widespread unrest around the major centres of global capitalism in the form of the occupy movement of 2011, a reaction against the spectacular rise in inequality. The trend that has developed in world politics after the financial crisis is a symptom of coming anarchy. In order to divert the attention from the catastrophic conditions created by new imperialism, the capitalist class has financed or sponsored a new type of political bodies around the globe—that is of right-wing extremists. On the surface it seems that the new political leadership wants to establish a cultural hegemony. But in reality, the cultural hegemony is a mere tool to create false consciousness in order to divert the attention away from the real contradictions of capitalism.

However, the alliance between right-wing extremism and neoliberal capital has failed to bring the economy back on track. In fact, it has weakened it further. It has taken the world to a situation similar to what it was during the 1870s. Regarding the current conjecture in the history of capitalism it is worth quoting Marx here. Marx made a correction of Hegel's idea that history necessarily repeats itself. Marx argued (2008, 19), "Hegel remarks somewhere that all great events and characters of world history occur, so to speak, twice. He forgot to add: the first time as tragedy, the second time as farce." The re-emergence of nationalism, militarism, protectionism, etc. are symptoms that history is repeating itself and this time not as tragedy but as farce.

The re-emergence of nationalism is seen everywhere. From the election of Donald Trump to Brexit, the nationalist policies of the Japanese Prime Minister Shinzō Abe, Narendra Modi and the Turkish President Recep Tayyip Erdoğan, the success of far-right parties in Italian, German and Austrian elections in 2017 and 2018, nationalism appears to be on the rise globally. Along with this there is a rise of militarism. The world economy's performance remains quite weak since the beginning of the 21st century but the armament industry is flourishing. The total arms sale of the top 100 armament producing companies has increased from $ 286 billion (on constant prices) to $ 420 billion between 2002 and 2018 with the growth of 47 per cent. The total expenditure on armaments in the top 10 countries—USA, China, Saudi Arabia, India, France, Russia, UK, Germany, Japan and South Korea, arranged in descending order—accounted for $ 841 billion in 1991 and increased to $ 1347 billion in 2018. In 2018 military expenditure of these countries accounted for 74 per cent of the world's total. Although there was no direct war between the major imperial powers due to the presence of nuclear weapons, it however, does not mean that there was peace in the recent past and will remain in the near future. During 1946 to 2016, 8.64 million people died in war related conflicts in the world. After the 2008 financial crisis (from 2008 to 2016), the deaths due to war-related conflicts in various parts of the globe were recorded as 549,393.[2]

The growth of protectionism, trade wars and anti-immigrant attitude around the world are outcomes of the widespread economic crisis of new imperialism. Like the First World War that Friedrich Engels had predicted during the 1880s based on his understanding of the developing trends in world politics and military affairs, the crisis driven contemporary capitalism is pushing the state apparatuses, both repressive and ideological, against the working population of the world. The First and Second World War gave the workers of the advanced countries only one choice: that is, to kill fellow workers across the tranches. Once again, the crisis of capitalism has opened the opportunity for fascism to take the centre stage in world politics with the support of big business to divide the working people. However, the contemporary alliance, unlike the alliance between national fascists and national capitalists in earlier times, is operating under the hegemony of global finance capital. This alliance cannot tackle the problem of national unemployment and national crisis as it has happened in the past when strong fascist states had used the capitalist finances to reduce widespread unemployment and underemployment through enhanced military expenditures and government borrowing to build war-related infrastructure. This has opened space for new revolutionary perspectives for Marxists against international finance capital driven imperialism and fascism. This has widened the possibilities for the left on the world scale to think about an international alliance because it is only the left that can lead the people to overcome the existential crises produced by new imperialism.

NOTES

1. The major old capitalist countries of that time were Great Britain, Germany, and France and young capitalist countries included USA, Russia, Australia, Canada, and New Zealand.
2. For data on military and armament expenditure see Stockholm International Peace Research Institute. Available at: https://www.sipri.org/databases/milex

REFERENCES

Amin, S. (2013), *The Implosion of Contemporary Capitalism*, New York: Monthly Review Press.

Bagchi, A.K. (2002), The Other Side of Foreign Investment by Imperial Powers: Transfer of Surplus from Colonies, *Economic and Political Weekly*, Vol. 37, No. 23, pp. 2229-38.

Bairoch, P. (1974), Geographical Structure and Trade Balance of European Foreign Trade from 1800 to 1970, *Journal of European Economic History*, Vol. 3, No. 3, pp. 557-608.

Baran, P. and P.M. Sweezy (1966), *Monopoly Capital: An Essay on the American Economic and Social Order*, New York: Monthly Review Press.

Bieber, F. (2018), Is Nationalism on the Rise? Assessing Global Trends, *Ethnopolitics*, Vol. 17, No.5, pp. 519-40.

Boron, A. (2005), *Empire and Imperialism: A Critical Reading of Michael Hardt and Antonio Negri*, London: Zed Books.

Bukharin, N. (2010 [1915]), *Imperialism and World Economy*, New Delhi: Aakar Books.

Daudin, G., M. Morys, K.H. O'Rourke (2010), Globalisation, 1870-1914, In S. Broadberry and K.H. O'Rourke (eds.), *The Cambridge Economic History of Modern Europe* Vol. 2, Cambridge: Cambridge University Press.

Fei, H. (1930), *Europe: The World's Banker 1870-1914*, New Havana: Yale University Press.

Hilferding, R. (1981 [1910]), *Finance Capital: A Study of the Latest Phase of Capitalist Development*, London: Routledge and Kagan Paul.

Hobsbawm, E. (1994), *The Age of Empire*, London: Abacus Publications.

Hobsbawm, E. (2013), *The Age of Extreme*, London: Abacus Publications.

Hobson, J.A. (2017 [1902]), *Imperialism: A Study*, New Delhi: Aakar Books.

Hobson, J.M. (1993), The Military-Extraction Gap and the Wary Titan: The Fiscal-Sociology of British Defence Policy, 1870-1913, *Journal of European Economic History*, Vol. 22, No. 3, pp. 461-506.

Kautsky, K. (1970 [1914]), Ultra-Imperialism, *New Left Review*, Vol. 59 No. 1, pp. 42-46.

Keynes, J.M. (1991 [1919]), *The Economic Consequences of the Peace*, Palgrave Macmillan.

Lenin, V.I. (2010 [1917]), *Imperialism: The Highest Stage of Capitalism.* Lucknow: Rahul Foundation.

Lenin, V.I. (1965), Once Again on the Trade Unions, The Current Situation and the Mistake of Trotsky and Bukharin, pp. 70-107, In *Collected Works,* Vol. 32, Moscow: Progress Publishers.

Lewis, A.W. (1978), *Growth and Fluctuations 1870-1913*, London: George Allen and Unwin.

Luxemburg, R. (2003 [1913]), *The Accumulation of Capital*, London: Routledge Publishers.

Magdoff, H. (1970), Militarism and Imperialism, *American Economic Review*, Vol. 60, No. 2, pp. 237-42.

Marx, K. (1965), *Capital: A Critique of Political Economy* Vol. III, Moscow: Progress Publishers.

Marx, K. (1990 [1867]), *Capital: A Critique of Political Economy* Vol. I., London: Penguin Books.

Marx, K. (2008 [1852]), *The Eighteenth Brumaire of Louis Bonaparte*, Lucknow: Rahul Foundation.

Ricardo, D. (2006), *Principles of Political Economy and Taxation*, New York: Cosimo Classics.

Say, J.B. (1817), *Catechism of Political Economy*, Philadelphia: M. Carey & Son.

Smith, J. (2016), *Imperialism in the Twenty-First Century*, New York: Monthly Review Press.

Sweezy, P.M. (1942), *Theory of Capitalist Development,* New York: Monthly Review Press, Indian edition (2016), Delhi: Aakar Books.

15

What is Imperialism? Situating Imperialism in Relation to Capitalism and Colonialism

V. Upadhyay

Introduction

What is imperialism, specifically in today's context? This issue is discussed here in the framework of Marxist political economy. Imperialism is also an important subject in other areas such as cultural and literary studies. Those are, however, outside the scope of this chapter.

A recent book by Utsa Patnaik and Prabhat Patnaik, *A Theory of Imperialism* (2017), published by Columbia University Press, claims to formulate a theory of imperialism that has relevance not only for the past, but also in the present era. The authors attempt to refute those Marxist and other writers who today, explicitly 'reject the term "imperialism" insofar as it is taken to mean any systemic tendency for metropolitan capital to dominate the outlying regions in particular.'

The Patnaiks identify 'increasing supply price,' 'the value of money' and 'income deflation' as the three central features of imperialism:

> Imperialism …….. is a coercive relationship exercised by the capitalist sector on the "outside" world to ensure, first, that it obtains the products that it needs from the "outside" world and second, that it does so at non-increasing prices………
>
> …….obtaining goods at non-increasing prices from petty producers located on the tropical landmass, whose products are not producible

> within the capitalist sector that has grown up in the temperate regions of the world.......
>
> The curtailment of local absorption within the periphery of goods produced on the tropical landmass is one way of ensuring that the problem of increasing supply price does not come into play and there is no threat to the value of the currency in the metropolis as capital accumulation occurs there..........
>
> Growing demand for the products of the tropical landmass under these circumstances—in the absence of income deflation imposed on the users of such products to curtail their demand, and above all on the populations of the periphery where such products are produced—will necessarily cause a rise in prices ....and this rise will pose a threat to the value of money.

This book contains a commentary from David Harvey (2017) which is extremely critical of the authors' central argument of 'increasing supply price.' Harvey argues that agricultural products from tropical and subtropical regions are of minimal significance as far as metropolitan capitalism's survival in this age of highly developed and diversified industrial structure is concerned. According to him, a theory of imperialism cannot be sustained on the basis of the dependency of metropolitan capitalism on products from tropical areas.

To quote Harvey:

> The idea that metropolitan capitalism will collapse because of price inflation in the strawberries and blackberries that come from Guatemala in winter and the cut flowers that come from Ecuador or Colombia or that the lack of haricot vert from Kenya in Paris markets will bring the French economy to its knees is farfetched. Some seemingly crucial tropical and subtropical products, such as sugar, are substitutable..........
>
> The dependency of metropolitan capitalism on products from tropical and subtropical regions produced by petty commodity producers is nowhere near as significant as the Patnaiks claim. I cannot imagine that the Indian peasantry is producing much for the metropolitan market, for example........

> Depriving the metropolis of coffee, tea, bananas, cacao, peppers, and spices might provoke revolutionary thoughts in metropolitan populations who are used to such products, but this is hardly a convincing basis for a theory of imperialism. The claim that the agrarian use values extracted from tropical regions are physically critical to metropolitan capitalism does not wash. And the energy and mineral resources taken from tropical regions are not specific to those regions and cannot be analysed in this way.
>
> Unfortunately, the Patnaiks largely ignore the industrialisation occurring on the tropical landmass in favour of their obsession with agricultural production. (pp. 159-61)

One can sense the severity of the criticism. To this, I further add my own criticisms which are related to the two other central themes of the book:

(1) *The Value of Money*: In discussing this issue, the Patnaiks in their book mostly talk about the British pound during the colonial period. There is no reference to the current period, to the dollar. The processes that were relevant in earlier days are of no significance now. If one wants to talk about the rate of inflation in the US today, one would have to talk about factors such as 'the quantitative easing'(where the Fed has bought about $4 trillion worth of securities), imports of cheap Chinese goods, declining prices of IT products, oil prices, fiscal deficit, etc. But the book has none of these.

(2) *Income Deflation:* The book talks about the low incomes or purchasing power of petty producers of agricultural commodities in the tropical areas. In case of India, for example, we blame the policies of the Congress–BJP governments for this situation. Should we shift the blame to some entity called "imperialism"? At one place in the book, they talk about 'austerity measures'. But, here, the reference is to Greece.

So, overall, I argue that it is a weak thesis on imperialism. But the purpose of this chapter is not to produce a book review. Rather, this paper looks at what has caused the production of such a limited analysis.

We look at some other important Marxist works on this theme.

In that context, we look at one paragraph in David Harvey's comment which has invited severe criticism from left/ Marxist writers who accuse him of being an 'imperialism denier'.

According to David Harvey,

> Those of us who think the old categories of imperialism do not work too well in these times do not deny at all the complex flows of value that expand the accumulation of wealth and power in one part of the world at the expense of another. We simply think the flows are more complicated and constantly changing direction. The historical draining of wealth from East to West for more than two centuries has, for example, been largely reversed over the last thirty years. (p. 169)

John Smith (author of the Monthly Review Press book, *Imperialism in the Twenty-First Century*, 2015) is highly critical of Harvey's suggestion that Western countries are now being exploited by some Eastern countries.[1] He says,

> David Harvey, author of the New Imperialism …is an imperialism denier who uses his considerable prestige as a prominent Marxist theoretician to miseducate his readers on the single-most important issue confronting Marxist political economy: the huge drain of value and surplus-value from the global south (in which I include low-wage countries in East Asia) to the imperialist centres, a flow which has greatly increased in scale and importance during the neoliberal era.
>
> …….Harvey's suggestion that the "East" now exploits the "West" repeats almost word for word what he said in his 2014 work, 17 *Contradictions and the End of Capitalism*…..
>
> Harvey's refusal to acknowledge that production outsourcing to low-wage countries signifies a major expansion of direct and indirect super-exploitation of Southern labour by US, European and Japanese multinationals, and his notion that this transformation marks the passing of imperialism not its apogee, has been and remains perhaps the dominant view among those in imperialist countries who call themselves Marxists……

There have been many works on the subject of imperialism in recent years. One major influential work *Empire* is by Hardt and Negri, published in 2000.

Hardt and Negri write,

> ......after the Soviet barriers to the capitalist world market finally collapsed, we have witnessed an irresistible and irreversible globalisation of economic and cultural exchanges. Along with the global market and global order, a new logic and structure of rule—in short, a new form of sovereignty. Empire is the political subject that effectively regulates these global exchanges, the sovereign power that governs the world.......
>
> By "Empire", however, we understand something altogether different from "imperialism". The boundaries defined by the modern system of nation-states were fundamental to European colonialism and economic expansion.... Imperialism was really an extension of the sovereignty of the European nation-states beyond their own boundaries.....In contrast to imperialism, Empire establishes no territorial centre of power and does not rely on fixed boundaries or barriers. It ...... incorporates the entire global realm within its open, expanding frontiers......
>
> Many locate the ultimate authority that rules over the processes of globalisation and the new world order in the United States. ——— Our basic hypothesis——The United States does not, and indeed no nation-state can today, form the centre of an imperialist project. Imperialism is over. No nation will be the world leader in the way modern European nations were. (pp. xii-xiv)

This book is referred to as 'Neo-Marxist' or 'postmodernist.' But this book is similar to *The End of History* by Fukuyama, published in 1992. It looks like a Left version of the same thesis. Look at the authors' own words:

> ....the concept of Empire presents itself not as a historical regime originating in conquest, but rather as an order that effectively suspends history and thereby fixes the existing state of affairs for eternity. From the perspective of Empire, this is the way things will always be and the way they were always meant to be. In other words, Empire presents its rule not as a transitory moment in the movement of history, but as a regime with no temporal boundaries and in this sense outside of history or at the end of history. ....although the practice of Empire is continually bathed in blood, the concept of Empire is always dedicated to peace, a perpetual and universal peace outside history. (pp. xiv-xv)

Such ideas had some relevance during the last decade of the 20th century, but in the early years of the 21st century, these are of no significance. The thesis of *The End of History* has been completely discarded now. *The End of History* phase ended around the middle of the first decade of the 21st century with the onset of the most serious economic financial crisis since the Great Depression.

What is the Marxist Theory of Imperialism? Callinicos (2005) defines imperialism in the following way:

> The Marxist theory of Imperialism is distinctive in that it does not treat empire simply as a transhistorical form of political domination ...... but rather sets modern imperialism in the context of the historical development of the capitalist mode of production. (p.1)

'The Marxist Theory of Imperialism' does not have much to do with Marx.[2] It is largely due to Lenin.[3] In this respect, Lenin's book *Imperialism: the Highest Stage of Capitalism* (1916) has been the most influential work in this field. The book has the following two central themes:

1. Imperialism is the monopoly stage of capitalism.
2. Imperialism became associated with the development of monopolies.

Lenin writes,

> If it were necessary to give the briefest possible definition of imperialism, we should have to say that imperialism is the monopoly stage of capitalism.
>
> ....that capitalism's transition to the stage of monopoly capitalism, to finance capital, is connected with the intensification of the struggle for the partitioning of the world.

Many writers have pointed out the limitations of this analysis—arguing that historical capitalism has always been imperialist. And that, colonialism/imperialism has existed even before capitalism

Lenin did not analyse the impact colonisation had on the colonies. In that sense, it was not a work on colonialism per se. But any evaluation of Lenin's work has to take into account the historical developments taking place in the early part of the 20th century.[4,5,6,7] The task before us right now, however, is to develop an understanding of imperialism in the present context.

To summarise the discussion so far, let us look at the predominant leftist/Marxist framework for the analysis of imperialism:

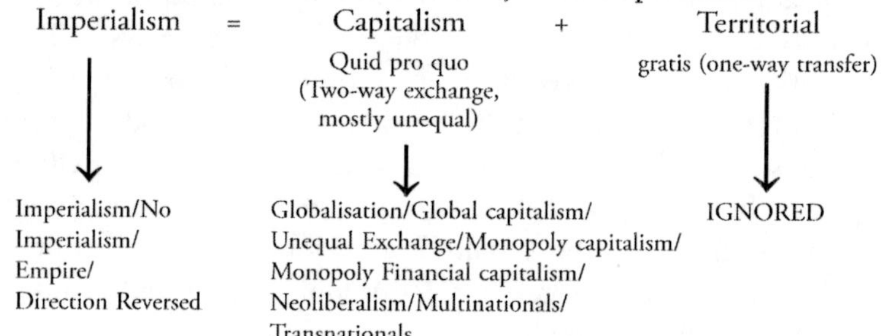

As this framework shows, most left/Marxist thinkers associate imperialism with capitalism. The territorial (i.e. gratis) aspects are generally missing/ ignored in their analysis.

Samir Amin has been writing on this subject for several decades. He defines imperialism in the present context as having two components—economic and political[8]—as given below:

Imperialism of the Triad (US, Europe, Japan)

Economic	Political
Generalised Monopoly Capitalism	Interventions Pre-emptive wars

Although Amin includes political dimension in his framework, the focus of his analysis, however, remains on the economic aspects. His characterisation of the present imperialism as 'imperialism of the Triad' puts Japan in the same category as the US and Europe in the post Second World War period. This implies his emphasis on the economic aspects as, unlike the US and Europe, Japan has not displayed much militaristic aggression in dealing with the countries in the periphery. It is quite evident from his following formulation:

> Another important consequence of this qualitative transformation of contemporary capitalism is the emergence of the collective imperialism of the triad, which takes the place of the historical national imperialisms

> (of the United States, Great Britain, Japan, Germany, France and a few others). (Amin 2015, pp. 30-31)

The foregoing analysis shows that the linking of imperialism with capitalism is the main source of the problematic analysis. This framework may have served a good purpose in the past but it is not capable of understanding the horrifying reality of today where the aggression of the Western powers poses a threat to life itself on the planet. In my opinion, there is thus a need to rescue the term 'imperialism' from the above framework. How that is to be done? Before I talk about my suggestions, let us look at the Patnaiks' book again. The Patnaiks opine that:

> ———Marxist authors in the advanced capitalist countries have produced very little analysis of colonialism. And thus it is not surprising that there is a readiness among them to treat imperialism as no longer relevant........
>
> [About Harvey]—it is clear that he is unfamiliar with the concept of "drain." Indeed the whole of northern academia and even the present day Marxists, with very few exceptions [Paul A. Barran and Andre Gunder Frank and Angus Maddison], have systematically ignored the large literature on the drain available from the South. It refers not just to the direction of capital flows but to the phenomenon of sucking out the surplus of an economy without any quid pro quo...... this "drain" occurred in the form of commodities taken out of these colonies gratis.....
>
> Are there any major continuities between the colonial period and now, continuities that are rooted in the nature of capital....? (pp. 196)

There are three important points here:

1. The authors are looking for some continuity over the period of the last 200 years. As we have seen above, the common thread they discover turns out to be very weak. In fact, too weak to hold the weight of the mighty phenomenon of imperialism.
2. Even the common thread that they discover is not continuous. It has a break of 3-4 decades in the years immediately after the Second World War.

3. Why focus on continuities rooted in the nature of capital? Rather, look at aspects that are beyond the nature of capital, i.e. on gratis. And, here we need to analyse the powerful manifestations, forms or expressions of the phenomenon. And, if forms change, then that change should be analysed. Therefore, we need to redefine 'imperialism' for the present context.

Imperialism Today

Imperialism is not dead: It has yet not been dislodged from the position of captain of the earth ship. Although it is true that Western imperialism faces new unprecedented challenges in the form of emerging multipolarity in world affairs, it however still remains a threat to world peace as ever. The fears posed by Western powers are the reason why the vast majority of global population is unable to choose paths of living of their own choice.

A new definition of imperialism is required in today's context. Most importantly, imperialism needs to be delinked from capitalism. Imperialism today needs to be conceptualised in terms of gratis plus the threats that Western countries pose to the rest of the world or even to the planet itself. The dimensions in which imperialism today manifests itself are: colonial, climate change, dangerous technologies, and economic.

Colonial

After the Second World War, most of the colonies gained independence from direct Western occupation. In South East Asia, colonial occupation, however, continued till the mid-1970s; and in case of Africa, till the mid-1980s. With the dissolution of the Soviet bloc around 1990, the phase of Western hegemony (unipolarity) started with the US becoming the 'sole' superpower. During the early phase of unipolarity, the Western imperialist powers (particularly the USA) generally refrained from pursuing colonial conquests in the Third World countries.

At the beginning of the 21st century, however, Western colonial conquests restarted. The West did not want the window of opportunity provided by the sudden collapse of the Soviet Union to pass. In the early years of the new century, the West resorted to war in Afghanistan and Iraq as a means to maintain its control over global resources (especially petroleum resources). Later, Libya and Syria became the target of Western aggression. Most countries in West Asia, the Middle East and North Africa are facing full-scale was that are interlinked. In all these wars, there is a direct and heavy involvement of Western powers.

Although due to the presence of nuclear weapons, a direct war between the major powers has been prevented, thus far at least. But the absence of direct war between major powers does not imply that there is lack of intention to wage war in these countries. Iran and North Korea are under constant threat of war.

Fear of (imminent) war is gripping all nations, small and large. War fears create a situation where war-preparedness efforts are seeing acceleration everywhere. There is a renewed arms race based on technological sophistication. Prospects for the continuation of arms reduction talks—in any meaningful sense—now appear very bleak, at least in the medium term.

The US is always fighting concurrent wars in many countries. The size of the United States' defence budget is more than $700 billion. The US spends more on defence than China, Russia, Saudi Arabia, India, France, United Kingdom and Japan combined.

Millions of people have been killed or displaced due to war in West Asia, Middle East and North Africa. According to the estimates by UNHCR, the UN Refugee Agency, at the end of 2016 there were 65.6 million people forcibly displaced worldwide. Of these, 22.5 million were classified as refugees.

Climate Change

The climate change phenomenon has acquired life-threating dimensions. Excessive consumption of natural resources, especially of fossil fuels, over a very long period in the West is the major source of our environmental ills. The United States and the European countries have historically been the world's largest emitters of greenhouse gases.

Scientists say that global average temperature must not increase more than 2 degrees Celsius compared to pre- industrial levels. But global average temperature has already recorded increase of more than 1 degree Celsius. 17 of the 18 warmest years since modern record keeping began in the late 19th century have occurred in the 21st century.

The Paris Agreement, signed by 194 states and the European Union, aims at keeping the increase in global average temperature to well below 2^{0} C above pre-industrial levels. This agreement has however been dealt a severe blow by US President Donald Trump's announcement in June 2017 to withdraw his country from the agreement. If this action on the part of the United States leads to dissolution of the agreement, it will have serious adverse implications for the future of humanity as well as for the planet. This threat to the global society is a manifestation of the United States' imperialist power.

Dangerous Technologies

New developments in the areas of warfare technology, biotechnology, artificial intelligence (AI) and surveillance technology, governed by laws of capitalism accumulation with link to high S&T and pursuit of economic growth, threaten the very survival of human life on the planet. These are thus imperialist in character.

Major nuclear powers are now engaged in efforts to modernise their arsenals. New anti-missile technologies and the plans to build low yield nuclear weapons are disturbing the equilibrium that has existed in the post-Second World War period. The United States' new national security strategy displays a "cold war mentality" with an "imperialist character" as it refuses to renounce a unipolar world.

The prospects for the continuation of arms reduction talks after the expiry of the treaties that are presently in force appear quite bleak.

There is now increasing use of artificial intelligence (AI) in development of harmful technologies such as advance weapons/ warfare technology and surveillance technology. In the long run, AI poses an existential threat to the human race. Unregulated and uncontrolled progress in IA could in future result in human extinction. If AI develops into "super-intelligent," surpassing humanity in intelligence, then it is quite possible that it will eventually acquire control over human destiny. In a future scenario, if there is a conflict between humans and super-intelligent AI, the latter can use its enormously superior powers to eliminate the former.

Biotechnology produces genetic modification of existing organism or leads to creation of new ones. Genetically engineered biological agents pose a serious existential risk to the human race. Advancement in biotechnology could lead to modification of humans, altering the very meaning of humanity. Intentional or unintentional release of engineered virus or use of biological weapons could cause damage to existing ecosystems in unforeseen ways.

Economic

One major pillar of America's imperial power is its currency, the dollar. The dollar's present strength is a legacy of the colonial era. Displacing the British pound, the US dollar has been the world's most dominant reserve currency since the Second World War. Most governments and institutions hold their foreign exchange reserves largely in dollars (in the form of US Treasury bills). In international trade transactions/payments and international investments, the US dollar is the most used currency. This makes America a great financial super power. Due to near-universal acceptability of its currency, America continues to exercise enormous control on global economic matters without much challenge from any quarter, at least, yet.

Given that it has a huge influence over the world economy, the United States increasingly resorts to the use of economic sanctions against the targeted countries as a powerful weapon in furtherance of its strategic interests[9]. Recently, the United States has enacted a law, Countering America's Adversaries Through Sanctions Act (CAATSAA) that imposed sanctions on Iran, North Korea and Russia. This law mandates the US administration to punish entities engaging in significant transactions with certain sectors of these countries.

The dollar's continuing dominance in global trade and financial transactions gives the United States tremendous power to hurt its adversaries, as well as those countries that refuse to follow its dictates, through actions such as economic sanctions.

Excluded: Trade and Migration Issues

The world is witnessing a trade war in recent months which is intensifying each passing day. The United States is engaged in a multi-front trade confrontation not only with its traditional allies (Canada, the European Union and Japan) but also its other major trading partners like Mexico and China. The US has imposed tariffs on steel and aluminium imports from Canada, Mexico and the European Union. The main target of US protectionist measures is, however, China whose economic rise the US desperately wants to stop. The US has imposed tariffs on almost all Chinese imports. Not only that, the US government is planning to put restrictions on Chinese investments in 'sensitive' US industries. But protectionist policies, particularly tariffs, hurt not only the targeted countries but also the countries that impose them. Tariff imposition by one country leads to retaliation by its trading partners. Once a country adopts protectionist policies, it soon turns into a 'war of each against all.' As a reaction to US unilateralism, the European Union, Canada, Mexico, China and India have all announced retaliatory measures against American imports. The anti-trade policies/measures are subjects that can be suitably analysed under the heads such as globalisation, global capitalism, and sovereign national policies. These are thus not subjects to be covered under imperialism.

The political landscape in the US and Europe is now witnessing increasing domination of xenophobic ideology. There are now widespread anti-immigration/immigrants sentiments openly espoused not only by extreme right populist fringe groups but also most mainstream, traditional political parties. Anti-immigrant sentiment now cuts across the old left-right political divide. The United States and European Union are taking steps that seek to severely restrict/control immigration. The migration issues, like tariffs and other anti-trade measures, can however, be suitably analysed under the heads such as globalisation, and sovereign national policies. The case of war refugees, as discussed above, is, however, different as it has colonial/imperialist dimensions.

The sketch given below summarises the above discussion on the meaning of imperialism today.

Imperialism Today

Imperialism = Gratis +Threats

Colonial: War (the Middle East, Afghanistan)
Threat of War (Iran, North Korea)
War Preparation (Expenditure)
War Refugees

Climate Change: US withdrawal from the Paris Treaty

Dangerous Technologies

Weapon's Technology (Nuclear, Chemical, Bio, Space)
Bio-technology (GM Technology, Cloning, etc.)
Artificial Intelligence, Mind Control
Surveillance Technology

Economic: Dollar as Reserve Currency
International Payment System
Economic Sanctions

Excluded: Trade, Protectionism, Trade War, Financialisation, Neoliberalism, Globalisation, Foreign Investment, Capital Movement, Government's Fiscal and Monetary Policies, Migration

NOTES

1. See Smith (2017).
2. Marx had written extensively on colonial exploitation with reference to India, Ireland and China. But most of his writings were in the form of comments in response to contemporary events and thus were not part of the core of his theoretical analysis focused on the historical development of capitalism.
3. Lenin's thinking was greatly influenced by Nikolai Bukharin's

Imperialism and World Economy (1915). Lenin had written an introduction for it in December 1915 supporting its main analysis.

4. Rudolf Hilferdig's *Finance Capital (1910)* also had a significant influence on Lenin's work. Hilferdig analysed in details the various forms of concentration and cartelisation of capital. He showed that the banks' increasing influence over industry was the main explanatory factor for economic imperialism and war.
5. Lenin's writings during that period should be seen in the context of the politics of the Second International, an organisation of socialist and labour parties. Most national parties that composed the international supported their respective nations' role in the First World War. Lenin's Bolshevik faction was the only major centre of opposition to the war.
6. Lenin's book is basically a critique of Karl Kautsky's proposition of "ultra- imperialism". Kautsky, regarded as the leading Marxist theoretician at that time, argued that monopolies of various countries could unite to peacefully divide the world. He held out the prospect of "joint exploitation of the world by internationally united finance capital." Lenin argued that the only way of ending imperialist war was the overthrow of the capitalist system through capture of the state power.
7. Lenin had differences with Rosa Luxemberg also on this subject. Rosa Luxemberg in her book *The Accumulation of Capital (1913),* argued that capitalists could not realise profits without having domination over weaker economies. Capitalism's control over non-capitalist areas was necessary in order to access raw materials, markets and cheap labour. Imperialism was thus essential for the dynamics of capitalism. She predicted that encroachment by the capitalist sector would lead to destruction of non-capitalist economies as a result of their absorption into the capitalist sector. Once the process of assimilation of the non-capitalist sector was complete, there will now be no more periphery left to exploit and, as a result, the capitalist system would collapse. Lenin did not agree with such a mechanical notion of history. [See Patnaik, 2008, p. 230].
8. See Amin (2015).
9. With reference to sanctions against Iran, Rudy Giuliani, Trump's personal lawyer, said: "We are the strongest economy in the world...

and if we cut you off then you collapse." (see *The Economic Times*, July 2, 2018).

REFERENCES

Amin, S. (2015), Contemporary Imperialism, *Monthly Review*, Vol. 13. Nos. 4 & 5.

Bukharin, N. (1973 [1915]), *Imperialism and the World Economy*, New York: Monthly Review Press.

Callinicos, A. (2005), Imperialism and Global Political Economy, *International Socialism*, Vol. 2, No. 108.

Hardt, M and A. Negri (2000), *Empire*, Cambridge: Harvard University Press.

Harvey, D. (2017), A Commentary on *A Theory of Imperialism,'* In U. Patnaik and P. Patnaik, *A Theory of Imperialism*, New York: Columbia University Press.

Hilferding, R. (1981 [1910]), *Finance Capital*, London: Routledge and Kegan Paul.

Lenin, V. (2010 [1916]), *Imperialism the Highest State of Capitalism,* New Delhi: People's Publishing House.

Luxemburg, R. (1963 [1913]), *The Accumulation of Capital,* London: Routledge.

Patnaik, P. (2008), *The Value of Money*, New Delhi: Tulika Books.

Patnaik, U. and P. Patnaik. (2017), *A Theory of Imperialism*, New York: Columbia University Press.

Smith, J. (2017), A Critique of David Harvey's Analysis of Imperialism, *MR Online,* August 26.

16

Climate Crisis and the Idea of Degrowth[1]

V. Upadhyay

Global Warming

Global warming is one of the defining issues of our time. The six warmest years in recorded history have been the past six years from 2014 to 2019 and 2010-2019 was the hottest decade ever recorded. Since the mid-20th century, the average temperature of the earth's climate systems has been rising at an unprecedented rate. The climate change crisis caused by rising earth temperature poses an existential threat to life on the planet. In order to safeguard the future of human civilisation as well as the existence of other species, there is an urgent need to find effective ways to deal with the climate crisis.

The major consequences of global warming include, among many others, melting of glaciers and artic ice, thawing of permafrost, extreme weather conditions, extinction of many species, expansion of deserts, and other catastrophic events such as extended draughts and floods. There is a large body of literature that analyses the life-threating consequences of climate change in detail.

The Paris Agreement, negotiated by representatives of 196 state parties and signed in 2016, requires each country to undertake steps to mitigate global warming. Climate scientists warn of disastrous consequences due to climate change if global warming is not kept below 2^0 centigrades compared to pre-industrial levels. According to the Intergovernmental Panel on Climate Change (IPCC), it is imperative to keep global warming below 1.5^0 centigrades compared to pre-industrial levels in order to avoid some irreversible impacts.

But if there is no discernible change in current policies and practices, global warming by the end of the century is certain to be much higher than the 2^0 centigrade level. In fact, as per the predictions of climatologists, 'at current greenhouse gas emission rate, the carbon budget for staying below 1.5^0 centigrades would be exhausted by 2028.' The implementation of the Paris Agreement pledges by countries has lacked a sense of urgency needed to tackle this existential threat.

Conveying his disappointment with the results of the 2019 United Nations Climate Change Conference (COP25), UN Secretary General Antonio Guterres said that "the international community lost an opportunity to show increased ambition on mitigation, adaptation and finance to tackle the climate crisis." The Paris Agreement has been dealt a severe blow by US President Donald Trump's announcement in June 2017 to withdraw the United States from the agreement.

It is now widely recognised that "human influence on climate has been the dominant cause of observed warming since the mid-20th century." The emissions of carbon dioxide largely due to burning of fossil fuels are the main cause of global warming. Other greenhouse gases, such as methane, also contribute to global warming.

High production and consumption levels in the West are the major source of our environment ills. Excessive consumption of natural resources, especially of fossil fuels, in the West (and by rich sections of population in developing countries) now poses grave threats to survival of life on our planet and these threats are immediate rather than distant. As production and consumption levels in the overdeveloped countries are at levels that are environmentally unsustainable, further growth in these countries can only come at enormous cost to the environment.

The Idea of Degrowth

In order to avoid the irreversible damage to our ecology that threatens life on earth, economic growth in industrialised countries would need to be checked. In recent years, a forceful articulation of these ideas has emerged under various names, such as sustainable development, degrowth, anti-developmentalism, alternative development or post-development in Europe and elsewhere. Whereas, there are some who argue that sustainable development requires that long-term growth must be zero or low—equal to the growth rate of 'environmental productivity'.[2] In the industrialised countries, there are others who argue that the ecological crisis that has acquired highly dangerous proportions demands an urgent reduction in production levels in industrialised countries—thus, implying a negative economic growth (degrowth) in these countries.

The declaration of the Second International Conference on Economic Degrowth for Ecological Sustainability and Social Equity held in Barcelona in March 2010, known as 'Degrowth Declaration Barcelona 2010' states that:

> An international elite and a "global middle class" are causing havoc to the environment through conspicuous consumption and the excessive appropriation of human and natural resources. Their consumption patterns lead to further environmental and social damage when imitated by the rest of the society in a vicious circle of status-seeking through the accumulation of material possessions.

During the conference, many new ideas and proposals which are generally absent from mainstream discussions were debated. These include: population and resource consumption; moratoria on infrastructure and resource sanctuaries; promotion of small-scale, self-managed not-for-profit companies; expansion of local commons and establishment of new jurisdictions for global commons; reduction of working hours (work-sharing); introduction of basic income; income ceilings; taxation; discouragement of overconsumption of non-durable goods and under-use of durables by regulation; and abandonment of large-scale infrastructure, such as nuclear plants, dams, incinerators, high speed transportation.

The declaration while advocating degrowth of the world economy also warns of the challenges that the degrowth movement will face in the process of achieving the degrowth objectives:

> A process of degrowth of the world economy is inevitable and will ultimately benefit the environment, but the challenge is how to manage

> the process so that it is socially equitable at national and global scales. This is the challenge of the Degrowth movement, originating in rich countries in Europe and elsewhere, where the change must start from.

This statement of the Degrowth movement cited above makes clear that degrowth is necessary for achieving environmental sustainability. But can degrowth or environmental sustainability be achieved in an iniquitous world? Is degrowth feasible in capitalist society? Can capitalism be made to accommodate ecological concerns? If not, then what has the degrowth movement to say about the alternative social and economic system and about the ways to achieving it?

Degrowth theorists have debated these issues for quite some time now, but they appear to lack a clear vision on these matters as is evident from the works of Serge Latouche, a leading proponent of the degrowth concept. In his 2006 article, "The Globe Downshifted," he writes:

> Eco-compatible capitalism is conceivable in theory, but unrealistic in practice. Capitalism would require a high level of regulation to bring about the reduction of our ecological footprint. The market system, dominated by huge multinational corporations, will never set off down the virtuous path of eco-capitalism of its own accord. It is a system made of anonymous, utilitarian machines for generating dividends. These will not give up their rapacious consumption of resources unless they are forced to do so.......
>
> A society based on economic contraction cannot exist under capitalism. But capitalism is a deceptively simple word for a long, complex history. Getting rid of the capitalists and banning wage labour, currency and private ownership of the means of production would plunge society into chaos. It would bring large-scale terrorism. It would still not be enough to destroy the market mentality. We need to find another way out of development, economism (a belief in the primacy of economic causes or factors) and growth: one that does not mean forsaking the social institutions that have been annexed by the economy (currency, markets, even wages) but reframes them according to different principles. (p. 2)

Latouche does not see the possibility of destruction of capitalism or replacement of capitalist relations with alternative modes of living. Whereas, on the one hand he maintains that capitalism compatible with ecological sustainability can be theoretically imagined but cannot be realised in practice but, on the other hand, he argues for continuation of capitalist relations including wage labour and private ownership of the means of production. He warns that banning of capitalist relations would lead to chaos and possibly large-scale state or social persecution and argues that the politics of class struggle as advocated by Marxists has now lost its potency as a tool of social transformation. His arguments are based on the premise that capitalist institutions and relations are so pervasive and have become so ingrained that these cannot be got rid of. It is, however, difficult to reconcile these arguments with his understanding that capitalism would prove destructive to the planet as it has already proved in relation to society:

> Mechanism for countering power with power, as existed under the Keynes-Fordist regulations of the Social Democratic era, are conceivable and desirable. But the class struggle seems to have broken down. The problem is: capital won. We looked on, powerless if not indifferent, as it swept away everything in its path, including the Western working class. We are currently witnessing the steady commercialisation of everything in the world. Applied to every domain in this way, capitalism cannot help but destroy the planet much as it destroys society, since the very idea of the market depends on unlimited excess and domination. (p. 3)

Socialist theorists find Latouche's views of capitalism full of contradictions. As Foster (2011) puts it:

> ....Latouche's work, which can be viewed as exemplary of the European degrowth project, is beset with contradictions, resulting not from the concept of degrowth per se, but from his attempt to skirt the question of capitalism.....
>
> The ecological struggle, understood in these terms, must aim not merely for degrowth in the abstract but more concretely for deaccumulation—a transition away from a system geared to the accumulation of capital without end.....
>
> As valuable as the degrowth concept is in an ecological sense, it can

> only take genuine meaning as part of a critique of capital accumulation and part of the transition to a sustainable, egalitarian, communal order; one in which the associated producers govern the metabolic relation between nature and society in the interest of successive generations and the earth itself (socialism/communism as Marx defined it).[3, 4] (p. 26)

Capitalism is incompatible with an ecological civilisation for another important reason also. Capitalism by its very nature produces a highly iniquitous society. In such a society with sharp class divisions, the upper class (capitalists) enjoy a very highly disproportionate share of income and wealth generated in the economy which allows them to set their own consumption standards at very high levels. The consumption levels enjoyed by the upper class always remain beyond the reach of the lower classes (the working people): the latter are never able to attain them. This fact notwithstanding, the system succeeds in spreading illusions among the lower classes about the possibility of them catching up with the upper class. This, however, never happens. Even when the lower classes make substantial advances in terms of consumption, as it has happened in the Western world, the gap never narrows as the upper class keeps moving up further ahead. The race goes on, without an end and without any relation with genuine human needs and without any regard to the environment. Magdoff and Yates (2009) explain this logic of the capitalist system in the following words:

> The logic of the system is that we must be perpetually unsatisfied, always wanting more. In a system that guarantees considerable inequity, we are bound to be envious of the consumption of those richer than we are. But every time we think we have reached a higher level of consumption, we see that there are still many richer people above us. And if those below catch up with us, we have to consume more to stay ahead. It could be argued that a consumption-based society would be more acceptable if there were a rough equality of spending power. And this is—and cannot be—the case; capital accumulation will not allow it. We are not and cannot be "slouching towards utopia," to use the inapt phrase of economist J. Bradford DeLong—referring to a utopia of a worldwide majority "middle class" of happy consumers, all buying big-screen televisions and nice automobiles. And does DeLong

> imagine that the world could ecologically support billions of human beings consuming a pace on par with middle class US households? It is estimated that it would take the resources of four worlds like ours to provide the equivalent to what is considered a modestly upscale US consumption pattern for all of the planet's 6.5 billon people. Now, we are certainly not arguing that everyone should be poor or that those currently at the bottom don't need an adequate level of consumption, especially food, clothing, and shelter. But we are saying that the so-called consumer culture that characterises the United States and a few other rich countries is not a model worth fighting for, nor is it ecologically sustainable. (pp. 24-5)

Socialist theorists argue that socialism alone is the answer to the ecological crisis. It is, however, important to note here that socialism, as it has existed historically, has not always been in support of ecology. The relationship between socialism and ecology has seen many twists and turns over time, ranging from integration of ecological concerns in the socialist critique of capitalism during the early phase of Marxist theorisation to a clear state of antagonism between them in the societies that claimed to be socialist, such as the USSR and Eastern Europe before their transition around 1990 and in China today. As Levins (2011) puts it:

> Marxism, since its origin, took a global approach to the position of our species in the world. The plundering of nature by early industrialisation, the metabolic rift between city and countryside, the pollution of the cities and the whole earth, were already known, denounced, and incorporated into the critique of capitalism. The inseparability of humanity and nature was implicit in a dialectical view of life and society.
>
> But socialist movements also resisted ecology. Especially those movements that had abandoned the socialist goal saw jobs as the overwhelming urgency of the male working class, and any notions that might slow down job creation were viewed with hostility......
>
> In the USSR and its allies, an early constitutional commitment to the preservation of nature was undermined by the frantic urgency to expand production under a progressivist notion of modernisation that did not criticise capitalist technology but only its use. With the later

> debasing of Marxism, Soviet pioneering in soil science, evolutionary ecology, and ecosystem, research languished. Brezhnev's touting of 'the scientific-technical revolution' as the solution for the economic stagnation of the USSR also accepted the notion of a single pathway of development of production, which was especially disastrous for agriculture. (p. 32)

Levins argues for infusion of ecology with Marxism, calling it Marxist ecology, which looks out for the species as a whole. Identifying ecology as one of the contemporary sources of enrichment of Marxism, he writes:

> Ecology's contribution to modern Marxism is as a guide to practice and as criticism of the opportunistic sacrifice of the future for immediate urgency....It focuses resistance to capitalist destruction... (p. 33)

Referring to David Harvey's concept of "co-revolutionary movement," Foster (2011) also talks about bringing together various mass movements working towards alternatives to present destructive tendencies. These include: the traditional working-class critique of capital, the critique of imperialism and the critique of ecologically destructive growth.

If capitalism as a mode of production is here to stay in the foreseeable future, as many people believe, could it be reformed to accommodate ecological concerns? Latouche (2006) makes a case in favour of measures suggested by Orthodox economics: internalisation of external diseconomies:

> It would place the costs of our social and environmental problems on the books of the companies responsible for them. Imagine the impact that it would have: if businesses had to accept the costs of the transport, security, unemployment and education that their functioning requires (not to mention the costs of their environmental impact), then our societies would start to function differently. These reformist measures, whose principles were outlined in the early 20th century by the liberal economist Arthur Pigou, would bring about a revolution. (p. 4)

This is nothing, but a stance taken by the environmental economists who adhere to mainstream neoclassical economics. Radical ecologists summarily reject this notion that environmental costs can be internalized in a meaningful way within a capitalist economy framework.

The possibility of use of green technology in critical areas or substitution of green energy sources for fossil fuels to ameliorate ecological dangers is also discounted by radical ecologists. They point out to historical experience that greater efficiency in the use of energy and resources has hardly ever led to conservation. On the contrary, it becomes a push factor for economic growth, causing even greater pressure on the environment. This phenomenon is known as the Jevons Paradox (See Foster, et al., 2010).

The present global economic crisis that started in the West in 2008 has brought miseries to the common people there in the form of high unemployment, poverty and homelessness. It is a usual argument that to overcome these problems, these countries need fast economic growth: Concern for the environment should not acquire primacy in these circumstances.[5] Does this experience of downturn then make the concept of degrowth irrelevant? It should not. If unhindered growth in the West over the past several decades is seen as the source of most of our environmental ills, then a downturn spanning over a period of a few years cannot be viewed as a bad thing. The industrialised countries are already in a state of ecological overshoot, more production in these countries will only cause more environmental destruction.[6] If the aim of degrowth movement is to achieve substantial reduction (up to 30 per cent of current levels, as seen necessary by some to attain environmental sustainability) in the size of economy of Western nations, then a downturn negatively impacting the size of these economies marginally should be seen as an opportunity to experiment the ideas promulgated by degrowth economics. The problems, such as unemployment, poverty and homelessness, in the industrialised countries can be and need to be tackled through distributional measures. Not only equitable sharing of income and wealth, but also of work[7] is the need of the hour. Sharing of work requires shortening of work-time (in parallel with the growth of labour productivity).

As Onaran (2010) puts it, full employment can only be achieved through shorter working times. Ideas such as introduction of basic income, income ceiling and taxation of high incomes at high rates (and of absolutely high incomes at punitive rates and of incomes and wealth of speculators beyond a point at 100 per cent rate) need to be put into practice to protect the working masses from the ill economic effects of the economic crisis. Levels of production in the West are so high that, with equitable distribution, everyone there can easily enjoy a decent level of living. Providing a decent living to everyone in the industrialised world is not the problem: the problem in fact lies somewhere else. As Magdoff and Foster (2010) put it, 'The primary problem is an ancient one and lies not with those who do not have enough for a decent standard of living, but rather with those for whom enough does not exist….A global system organised on the basis of "enough is little" is bound to destroy all around it and itself as well.'

In case of developing countries, especially those with very low per capita incomes, the ideas of degrowth economics cannot be applied mechanically. Condition of most developing countries is far different from the industrialised countries. Most developing countries have been victim of exploitation by Western powers during the long colonial period of over 200 years. These countries suffered almost complete stagnation of their economies due to the impact of Western colonialism. Although some countries have seen a rapid rise in their income levels, at least in aggregate terms (GDP or per capita income) after gaining independence from colonial rule during the post-Second World War period, the condition of most people in developing countries remains as stark as before. Most people in these countries, over three billion (approximately half of humanity), subsisting on less than $2.50 a day (in purchasing power parity terms), lack basic necessities of life, face chronic hunger and grave deprivation. To achieve improvement in the lives of their people, these countries would require economic growth sustained over a fairly long period. This is because the economic problems these people face are too enormous to be tackled by redistributive measures alone.

This, however, does not mean that developing countries have to imitate their Western counterparts as far as the pattern and content of economic growth is concerned, because that would only lead them to the same ruinous path that has been travelled by the industrialised countries.[8] The focus in these countries should not be on economic growth per se, but rather on fulfilment of basic needs of common people, such as access to food, water, healthcare and education as well as providing basic housing amenities and transportation facilities through public transport.[9] This, of course, would require a radical transformation in the social and political structure in these countries.

For centuries now, growth has been the main objective of the world capitalist economy (or, at least, world economy under hegemony of capitalism). 'No-growth capitalism is an oxymoron: when growth ceases, the system is in a state of crisis' (See Magdoff and Foster, 2010).[10, 11] To reorient the world economy towards degrowth would require a phenomenal social and political transformation. It is certainly not a task that can be accomplished easily. As Magdoff (2011) sees it:

> It is inconceivable that capitalism itself will lead directly to an ecological civilisation that provides the basic needs for all people. However, building an ecological civilisation that is socially just will not automatically happen in post-capitalist societies. It will occur only through the concerted action and constant vigilance of an engaged population. (p. 22)

Transition to an ecological society may prove far more problematic than transition to socialism. As per the traditional Marxist theory, the transition to socialism occurs through class-struggle where the working class appropriates the means of production from the control of the capitalist class. In this transition, it is the capitalist class that suffers loss of power. The degrowth transition, on the other hand, demands sacrifice from all, i.e. not only from the capitalist class, but also from the middle classes (and even from the working class in the overdeveloped world). This transition, thus, requires far greater consensus in the society, cutting across the boundaries of class divisions.

NOTES

1. The earlier version of this paper was published in Upadhyay, V. (2016), (ed.), *Essays on Distribution, World Systems, Ecology, and Left Politics*. New Delhi: Daanish Books. This is an extended and revised version.
2. See Onaran (2010).
3. Capitalism is incompatible with a truly ecological civilization because it is a system that must continually expand, promoting consumption beyond human needs, while ignoring the limits of non-renewable resources (the tap) and the earth's waste assimilation capacity (the sink), (Magdoff, 2011).
4. We have now reached a situation where the global capitalist system poses a serious threat to the very survival of human civilisation. As Li (2011) puts it, '(T)he current historical context is fundamentally different from any previous movement in capitalist history. After centuries of relentless capitalist accumulation, the global ecological system is on the verge of collapse and the developing global ecological crisis threatens to destroy human civilisation within the twenty-first century.'
5. '…in terms of the immediate crisis our time that began in 2006, the question of natural limits cannot, on the surface at least, be accorded primacy of place…' (Harvey, 2011, p. 78).
6. With reference to the US economy, Magdoff and Yates (2009) explain this aspect in the following manner: …let us ask ourselves an important question. Is, the roller-coaster ride that capitalism is, what we want? Suppose that, in a few years, somehow things got back to "normal," with the GDP growing at between 2.5 and 3 per cent, with official unemployment between 4 and 5 per cent, with wages growing only enough to keep up with inflation. Suppose even, that we have a better healthcare system than we have now. What then? The "health" of US economy now depends on increasing exploitation at work, supposedly compensated through ever-rising private consumption. What have been the consequences of this? Longer, harder hours have compromised the health and quality of life of workers, reducing their best hours to meaningless drudgery. Rising consumption of more meaningless "stuff" has polluted our planet; it has filled our house with junk we never use; it has forced us to think we need bigger and bigger houses, which in turn has compelled us to move into the suburbs and exurbs, wasting power and water, creating vast expanses

of ugly developments and destroying much of our natural habitat.... The entire system becomes one of making things, throwing them away and making new ones. Waste begetting waste, begetting still more waste.

7. In his 1949 article "Why Socialism?", Albert Einstein had commented: 'Technological progress frequently results in more unemployment rather than in an easing of the burden of work for all.'
8. The current pattern of growth in China is not sustainable over a long horizon. The spectacular growth achieved by China during the last three decades is certain to become unsustainable in the near future. Li (2011) writes: 'The Chinese model of capital accumulation has relied on a set of particular historical factors: the ruthless exploitation of a large cheap labour force; the massive exploitation of natural resources and its consequent degradation of the environment; and a growth model that depends on expanding exports to the markets of core capitalist countries. None of the factors are sustainable beyond the medium term.... As the world's largest energy consumer and carbon dioxide emitter, China is now at the very centre of global ecological contradictions.
9. Wallerstein (2011) calls for categorical rejection of the goal of economic growth and advocates to 'replace it with the goal of maximum decommodification—what the movements of indigenous nations in the Americas are calling buen vivir. This means not only resisting the increased drive to commodification of the last thirty years—of education, of health structures, of the body, of water and air—but decommodifying as well as agricultural and industrial production.' He, however, admits that 'How this is done is not immediately obvious and what it entails we shall only know by experimenting widely with it.'
10. Magdoff and Foster further add: Capitalism's basic driving force and its whole reason for existence is the amassing of profits and wealth through the accumulation (savings and investment) process. It recognises no limits to its own self-expansion—not in the economy as a whole; not in the profits desired by the wealthy; and not in the increasing consumption that people are cajoled into desiring in order to generate greater profits for corporations. The environment exists, not as a place with inherent boundaries within which human beings must live together with earth's other species, but as a realm to be exploited in a process of growing economic expansion....There is no alternative under capitalism to the endless expansion of the "real economy" (i.e.

production), irrespective of actual human needs, consumption, or the environment (pp.7–8).

11. People's Agreement on Climate Change and the Rights of Mother Earth, Cochbamba, Bolivia, April 22, 2010, stated: 'The capitalist system has imposed on us a logic of competition, progress, and limitless growth. The regime of production and consumption seeks profit without limits, separating human beings from nature and imposing a logic of domination upon nature, transforming everything into commodities: water, earth, the human genome, ancestral cultures, biodiversity, justice, ethics, the rights of peoples, and life itself.... Capitalism requires a powerful military industry for its processes of accumulation and imposition of control over territories and natural resources, suppressing the resistance of the peoples. It is an imperialist system of colonisation of the planet.'

REFERENCES

Harvey, D. (2011), *The Enigma of Capital: And the Crises of Capitalism.* UK: Profile Books.

Foster, J.B. (2011), Capitalism and Degrowth—An Impossibility Theorem, *Analytical Monthly Review,* Vol. 8, No. 7.

Foster, J.B., C. Brett and R. York. (2010), Capitalism and the Curse of Energy Efficiency: The Return of the Jevons Paradox, *Analytical Monthly Review,* Vol. 8, No. 10.

Latouche, S. (2006), The Globe Downshifted, *Le Monde Diplomatique* (English Edition).

Levins, R. (2011), Continuing Sources of Marxism: Looking for the Movement as a Whole, *Analytical Monthly Review,* Vol. 8, No. 10.

Li. M. (2011), The Rise of the Working Class and the Future of the Chinese Revolution, *Analytical Monthly Review,* Vol. 9, No. 3.

Magdoff, F. (2011), Ecological Civilization, *Analytical Monthly Review,* Vol. 8, No. 10.

Magdoff, F and J.B. Foster (2010), What Every Environmentalist Needs to Know About Capitalism, *Analytical Monthly Review,* Vol. 7, No. 12.

Magdoff, F. and Michael D. Yates (2009), What Needs to be Done: A Socialist View, *Analytical Monthly Review,* Vol. 7, No. 8.

Onaran, O. (2010), The Crisis of Capitalism in Europe, West and East, *Analytical Monthly Review,* Vol. 8, No. 7.

Wallerstein, I. (2011), Structural Crisis in the World System: Where Do We Go from Here?, *Monthly Review,* Vol. 62, No. 10.

17

Capitalism, Ecology and Eco-Socialism

Pritam Singh

Introduction

This paper is an attempt to contribute to an eco-socialist critique of the widely prevailing theoretical perspectives on capitalism, its crisis and the solutions offered to this crisis. We will focus on examining Keynesianism, monetarism/neo-liberalism, traditional Marxism and the Green perspective. We conclude by arguing that a critical synthesis of Marxian and Green perspectives best captures the most dominant form of the current crisis—the global environmental crisis—of capitalism and offers the most creative way of dealing with this crisis.

Neo-Classical Perspective

From the 1870s till the Great Depression of 1929-33, the neo-classical economic theory had held an almost unquestioned hegemony as an economic doctrine (Bharadwaj 1986). This doctrine preached that a market-based capitalist economy had an inbuilt mechanism to keep the economy in equilibrium. This equilibrium, it was argued, ensured among other things, full employment. Any deviations from this equilibrium, it was argued, got corrected by the forces of supply and demand in the market. This comforting belief or world outlook was rudely shaken by the Great Depression that witnessed major disequilibrium in the labour and product markets. This led to a fundamental crisis of the neo-classical economic doctrine that had for nearly six decades preached the infallibility of the markets.

Neoclassical theorists emphasised scarcity of resources as an important dimension in their theoretical framework, e.g. Jevons writings on the Coal Question highlighting what he thought was the imminent end of coal reserves, but their notion of scarcity was linked to the maximisation objective. It failed to embed the ecological dimension in their analysis of the market economy.

Keynesianism

The crisis of neoclassical economic theory saw the emergence of an alternative economic paradigm of Keynesianism. John Maynard Keynes (1883-1946) developed a critique of neo-classical economic doctrine by arguing that in a situation of economic recession, the state needs to take an active part in giving a stimulus to the economy (Keynes, 1936). A part of this stimulus effort, Keynes believed, was to redistribute income and raise the level of aggregate demand in the economy. His idea that redistribution of income would raise the level of aggregate demand in the economy was based on his insight that low income individuals and groups were more likely to spend any additional rise in their income than what the high income groups were likely to do. Conceptually, this is expressed as: the marginal propensity to consume of low-income groups is higher than that of the high-income groups. The rise of Keynesianism justifying the role of state intervention in a free-market oriented capitalist economy was a significant development in providing theoretical foundations for the desirability of a welfare state. The moral dimension of the welfare state as a protector of the weak and vulnerable had a long history in the British political, religious and social traditions (Fraser, 2009; Thane, 1996; Hennock, 2007; Lowe, 2005) but Keynesianism provided an economic dimension. In the Keynesian framework, the redistributive role of the welfare state was necessary for economic reasons, i.e. for giving an economic stimulus to a depressed economy to move towards economic growth. This economic necessity of the welfare state for economic growth was what propelled Keynesian ideas to widespread acceptance among political leaders and economic policy makers. Keynes's influence on the move towards welfare state policy approach was most dramatic in the UK although he influenced, in varying degrees, the policy paradigms of many other countries especially in the developed capitalist world. Keynes became the godfather of economics in the post war period in developed capitalist economies. The acceptance and wide popularity of Keynesian economics was co-terminus with the acceptance of the desirability of welfare state policies. The need for healthy and educated men for recruitment into the labour force for the expanding industry and that into military during the interwar years were other compelling reasons for expanding the welfare provisions especially relating to health and education (Fraser, 2009, 9-10). According to Derek Fraser,

> "...at a particular stage of capitalist development welfare served industry's needs...businessmen at times could conceive of welfare as sound economic sense" (Fraser, 2009, 9). The National Health Service certainly emerged out of these needs of industry and the military.[1]

Another important politico-economic development after the First World War that had an indirect impact on the strengthening the argument for the Keynesian welfare state was the Bolshevik Revolution in Russia in 1917. The Bolshevik Revolution signalled the first systemic break with capitalism. It gave a tremendous push to the idea that another system that was different from capitalism was possible. The speed with which the Soviet Union was industrialised in the 1930s through central planning frightened political leadership in the developed capitalist economies. Though the Stalinist method of industrialisation was based on forced collectivisation of agriculture, suppression of trade unions and the brutal terror campaign within the Bolshevik party against the critics of Stalinism, the ruling classes in the developed capitalist economies feared that despite the serious flaws of Stalinism, the Soviet success in industrialisation could lead to increasing the popularity of socialism as an alternative to capitalism as an economic system. This fear of attractiveness of socialism seemed even more real especially in the economic circumstance of the early 1930s when the advanced capitalist economies were in the throes of the Great Depression. The Great Depression had created mass unemployment in the industrial working class and the fears of the political leadership in the advanced capitalist countries that socialism as an ideology might become attractive to the working class were not without foundations. The welfare state based on the Keynesian paradigm providing social security to the unemployed and the poor seemed like a way of preventing the unemployed working class from becoming too desperate and militant. Ian Gough (1979, 60, 1997) has argued that the broadening of democracy through universal suffrage and other liberal rights helped to raise working class aspirations and the achievements of welfare improvements were concessions won by the working class. In the context of rising working-class activism, the welfare state perspective inspired by Keynesianism seemed politically necessary too. Perhaps the most notable theoretical and ideological consequence of the multi-fold crises of global capitalism in general and British capitalism in particular during the period of the Great Depression was the undermining of the hegemonic sway of neoclassical economic theory (Foldvary, 1996).

Despite the contribution of the Keynesian framework in bringing to light the structural weakness of neo-classical paradigm's reliance upon market as an automatic stabiliser especially in relation to dealing with recession, this framework too did not have economy-nature relationship centrally embedded into understanding the working of a capitalist economy.

The Decline of the Keynesian Welfare State and Rise of Neoliberal Austerity Paradigm

In the late 1960s/early 1970s and especially after the oil price rise in 1973, the developed capitalist economies were faced with stagflation, i.e. simultaneous existence of inflation accompanied by high degree of unemployment. This phenomenon did not fit in with the Keynesian economic theory which has as one of its central tenets that a certain degree of unemployment keeps wages and hence inflation low, and that it is only with full employment that a high level of inflation can be expected. Monetarist theorists attacked Keynesian theory for its failure to explain this simultaneous existence of high inflation with high degree of unemployment. Monetarist theorists had always been critical of the fiscal policy orientation of Keynesianism but had not succeeded earlier in posing a serious challenge to the theoretical framework of Keynesianism because during the so-called Golden Age of advanced capitalism in the post-war decades, inflation had remained relatively low in spite of high growth rate. The phenomenon of stagflation opened a new and fertile opportunity to the monetarist school of thought to launch a potentially damaging attack on Keynesianism and through that on the idea of the welfare state. Monetarists argued that inflation was due to the excessive level of aggregate money supply which, in turn according to them, was due to the state incurring excessive expenditure. They blamed the fiscal policy inspired by Keynesianism for expanding the role of welfare state intervention that had led to increasing the state expenditure and state indebtedness.

The monetarist attack on the welfare state in particular and the role of state intervention in general implied a support for a free market-oriented model of capitalist economy (Konzelmann, 2014). The monetarists argued that if the role of the state in the economy is decreased to the minimum possible, the free market would automatically make adjustments in the money market and the labour market to bring about a wage rate, level of employment and inflation rate that was necessary for attaining equilibrium in the economy. This mode of argument also implied a criticism of the role of trade unions in exercising the bargaining power of labour in negotiating the level of wages. The trade unions as a social force had been an important part of the architecture of the post-war welfare state. The monetarist attack on trade unions, therefore, tended to undermine an important pillar of support for the welfare state. However, from the viewpoint of the capitalist class as a whole, the role of trade unions in bargaining for social security welfare payments is contradictory in character. On one hand, the welfare payments create a demand for goods and services produced by capital but, on the other, these payments are a deduction from the surplus appropriated by capital. The capitalist class as a whole can, therefore, view trade union struggles for improvements in wages and social security payments positively from one angle (the expansion of market) and negatively from another (reduction of profits).

The free market ideology inherent in the monetarist framework came to be known as neoliberalism. David Harvey has argued that the rise of neoliberalism was not simply due to the perceived failure of Keynesianism in explaining the stagflation crisis of advanced capitalism. He argues that the neoliberal project had been in the making right from the period of the early rise of Keynesianism in the post-war period and that the project had been funded and supported by various US institutions to spread the tentacles of neoliberal ideology (Harvey, 2007). Harvey shows that the main target of neoliberalism was not Keynesianism but, in fact, socialism. The chief theorist of neoliberalism, Fredrick Hayek, was no doubt a rival of Keynes but more than being opposed to Keynes, he was opposed to socialism as a world view and as an alternative economic system to capitalism (Hayek, 1944/1997). Hayek was the most prominent founder of what later came to be known as neoliberalism in the late 1970s and early 1980s (Jones, 2012).

The decline of Keynesianism and the rise of neo-liberalism reached its peak during the regime of Margaret Thatcher as the Prime Minister of a Conservative government that came to power in 1979 in the UK and that of Ronald Reagan as the President of the Republican government that came to power in USA in 1980 (Skidelsky, 1989; Niskanen, 1988; Radice, 2014). Both Thatcher and Reagan were strong critics of the welfare state and ardent supporters of free market capitalism. Piketty (2014) in his much discussed book *Capital in the Twenty-First Century* characterises their rise to power as 'a conservative revolution': 'The growth of capital's share [in national income] accelerated with the victories of Margaret Thatcher in England in 1979 and Ronald Reagan in the United States in 1980, marking the beginning of a conservative revolution" (p. 42).

Marxian Tradition on Global Capitalism, North-South Inequality and Sustainability

Marx and Engels (2002 [1848]) had paid glowing tributes to capitalism in the *Communist Manifesto* for unifying the world market and creating conditions for unlimited progress in technological development and labour productivity. For Marx, capitalism was creating the material foundations for communism: one, by unleashing productive potentialities that could end scarcity and lead to an era of abundance, and two, by creating an international working class which will be the agency to usher in the era of communism, an era of fulfilment of human needs. In visualising communism as an era of fulfilment of human needs, Marx's work did not show critical awareness of the ecological limits to the goal of fulfilment of human needs. Undoubtedly, Marx had brilliant insights on capital-nature relationship in his *Grundrisse* and *Capital* in his remarks on capitalism's use of chemistry in agriculture and consequent destruction of soil fertility which he conceptualised as a metabolic rift. However, Marx's analytical framework had capital-labour relation and not capital-nature relationship as centrally embedded into the framework.

Lenin (1930) in *Imperialism: The Latest/Highest Stage of Capitalism* was less enthusiastic than Marx about the positive implications of expanding capitalism. He viewed export of capital from the advanced industrialised economies to the less industrialised ones as driven by the falling rate of profit in the rich economies and the expected higher rate of profit in the colonies. He saw this search for external markets for capital as the root cause of destructive military conflicts and considered this as the main reason behind the First World War. He looked upon expanding global capitalism as creating permanent conditions for global wars and, therefore, argued for socialist revolution as the solution to this dangerous scenario of wars. Though he was more critical of expanding capitalism than Marx was, he also did not examine the ecological dimensions of the militarist capitalism.

Rosa Luxemburg's (1951) analytical framework which accorded a key importance to consumption in the analysis of the functioning of a capitalist economy had the potential to incorporate ecology. But it merely remained a potential. Ecology did not become integral to Luxemburg's analysis. She argued that capitalist expansion was dependent on creating markets for its products and, therefore, imperialism was an extension of markets beyond the saturated markets of advanced capitalist countries.[2] If for Lenin, the essence of the imperialist stage of capitalism was search by surplus capital in the advanced economies to find investment outlets abroad, for Luxemburg it was search for markets abroad to unload surplus commodities. Luxemburg attributed this incessant search for markets for commodities as the driving force behind imperialist competition and rivalry leading to wars. Her slogan 'barbarism or socialism' was meant to highlight that unless the socialist revolution overthrew capitalism, there was a danger of imperialist wars bringing humanity to a barbaric end. Joan Robinson in an extension of Luxemburg's work theorised military expenditure as an extension of the capitalist market and looked upon this expenditure as essential for the continuous growth of capitalism. Neither Luxemburg nor Robinson looked upon the ecological limits to the expansion of capitalist markets. It is not necessarily wars which could lead humanity to a barbaric end; it could simply be global heating which could lead to an end of the planet earth.[3]

In the post-Second World War period, Paul Baran (1968) and Andre Gunder Frank (1966) produced some of the most influential analysis of global capitalism in which Third World underdevelopment and 'development' of the developed capitalist economies were inter-linked but both had no place for ecology in their theoretical frameworks. For Baran, the process of colonisation led to drain of surplus from the colonies to the metropolitan economies and it was this drain of surplus which had left the colonies in an underdeveloped state and ensured the continuous advancement of capitalism in the developed world. Baran's analysis provided justification for and hopes in the national governments in the Third World. According to this analysis, national governments by using the economic apparatus of planning could stop the drain of their economic surplus to the advanced economies. By using this surplus within their own economies, national governments of the ex-colonies could initiate domestic industrialisation and the process of economic development. Baran's neat analysis gave birth to a whole tradition of radical political economy which abandoned the dominant internalist explanations of Third World underdevelopment and highlighted the externalist dimension to this underdevelopment. However, Baran's diagnosis of the phenomenon of underdevelopment and the prescription for development strategies was not accompanied by an analysis of the implications of these possible developments in the Third World for capitalism as a global system. Nor did his analysis look at the environmental implications of Third World development and underdevelopment.

Andre Gunder Frank's dependency analysis attributed Third World underdevelopment to the integration of the Third World economies into the global capitalist economy. He advocated that Third World countries should delink from the global economy in order to initiate the development process. His emphasis on delinking the underdeveloped economies from the global capitalist economy had the potential to open up new investigations into decentralisation, local economy and local control. These in turn could have opened up new ways of looking at control and utilisation of resources, including natural resources. That potentiality still exists. Frank's work, along with that of Baran, Amin (1976) and Wallerstein (1979), have contributed enormously to highlighting the externalist dimension to Third World development and have provided a powerful critique of internalist schools of thought on underdevelopment, e.g. Rostow's (1960) 'stages of growth' model. However, all of them look upon problems of capitalist underdevelopment and development without bringing into their analysis the dimension of complex interaction between the development process and environment resources.

Bill Warren (1973, 1980) reverted to classical Marxism when he looked upon the imperialist stage of capitalism not as an impediment to Third World development but as the harbinger of development albeit of the capitalist variety. His was the most challenging critique of the neo-Marxist dependency schools of underdevelopment. His analysis was inspired by the success of East Asian capitalism in overcoming underdevelopment through closer integration with the global capitalist economy rather than by delinking from the world economy as had been proposed by Frank. Warren's untimely death prevented the fuller development of his argument which would have brought into sharper focus both the richness of the classical

Marxist treatment of Third World underdevelopment as well as its limitations. The most important limitation of Warren's work as it exists is the complete absence of the examination of the aspects of natural resource constraint and environmental degradation in the process of imperialist expansion of the global economy.

What is worth highlighting from this rather quick overview of the Marxist and neo-Marxist treatments of global capitalism and Third World underdevelopment is that irrespective of whether global capitalism was seen as the engine of progress or retrogression in the Third World, its relationship with nature remained outside this framework.

Green Perspectives on Global Capitalism

Bringing nature into an analysis of the functioning of the economy is the greatest contribution of the Green philosophical, political and economic tradition. Green economic thought views the economic system as a thermo-dynamic system where the economy is a part of nature and nature is a part of the economy (Jacobs, 1993). The thermo-dynamic model of the economy views the economy as a circular flow of matter and money in contrast with the orthodox models (classical, neo-classical, Marxist and Keynesian) which view the economic system as a circular flow merely of money between firms and households in a two-sector model of the economy (government and international sectors can be added to make it a four-sector model without affecting the central argument). The thermo dynamic model is then able to analyse the impact of money flows upon matter (nature) and the consequences of this impact on nature (resource depletion, waste generation and pollution) for the money flows in return. The concept of entropy captures the impact of human economic activities of production, exchange and consumption upon matter (nature). Entropy is the measure of disorderliness and all human economic activities lead to increase in entropy. The increase in entropy is kept in check by nature through the process of reconverting wastes into resources. Sun, earth, land, air, water and space all contribute to this process of absorption of waste generated by human economic activity and to the reconversion of some of this waste into usable resources. Nature's capacity to absorb waste is not unlimited. When the level of waste generation created by human activities exceeds the absorption capacity of nature, it results in pollution. This pollution takes various forms—air pollution, water pollution and land pollution. Pollution, in turn, damages the resources provided by nature for human activities.

The incorporation of nature as embedded into economic analysis enables Green economic analysis to capture the nature-economy relationship in a much deeper way than that done by any orthodox model of economic analysis. This richness of Green economic thought also creates a problem for Green thinking and practice. Because the Greens are ever conscious of the human economic activity upon nature, there is an inherent tendency among the Greens to view economic activities with suspicion. The neoclassical tradition of attempting to price environmental goods, apparently with the aim of reducing their use, is deeply opposed by the Greens in general but deep Greens in particular who view nature as sacred. For the deep Greens, pricing of nature amounts to sacrilege. Many Greens would advocate zero growth partly because of this suspicion of the very method of attempting to price the environment and partly because of the enormous environmental damage that has already taken place. More moderate Greens would subscribe to the perspective of sustainable development, i.e. neither zero growth of the deep Greens nor maximum growth advocated by some neo-classicals. The concept of sustainable development recognises the need for some development and growth but only the kind of growth which is environmentally informed and does not compromise the interests of the future generations. The concept of intergenerational equity is, therefore, central to the concept of sustainable development. Most Greens would also argue that inter-generational equity cannot be achieved without intra-generational equity, i.e. equity between the rich and poor countries.

There is, however, a great deal of ambiguity in the Green economic thought about how to reduce intra-generational equity. There could be two possible routes to reducing intra-generational equity. One route could be by reducing poverty in the Third World either by faster development in the Third World than that in the developed world. The other route could be massive transfer of resources, e.g. by foreign aid from the developed countries to the poor Third World countries. This could also involve major restructuring of the rules and structures of global trade to the advantage of poor economies. The challenge Green economics faces is that once the structures of global flows of labour, commodities, money and capital are brought into the analysis, it requires understanding of the laws of motion of global modes of production and exchange. Most Greens, not all, are reluctant to blame the capitalist nature of the global economy because they fear that blaming capitalism for environmental degradation can be an escape route for those who can pin their hopes on to socialism as a solution to the exploitation of nature. Most Greens are unwilling to accept that merely replacing capitalism by socialism is a solution to the problem of impending environmental disaster facing humanity today. Their unwillingness to accept socialism as a viable alternative is based partly on the experience of countries—USSR, Eastern Europe—which went through a historical phase claimed to be socialist. These countries were as ruthless, perhaps even more, in neglecting/exploiting nature in their quest for faster economic development than capitalist economies are. Greens, therefore, argue that the environmentally damaging implications of economic activities follow from the logic of large-scale production, irrespective of whether these structures of large-scale production are situated in a capitalist economy or a socialist economy. Most Greens are, therefore, supporters of small scale and localised systems of production, exchange and consumption.[4]

Dilemmas of Third World Poverty for Green Economic Perspective on Global Capitalism

Third World poverty generated by global capitalism poses a seemingly irresolvable dilemma for Green economic perspective. Greens in the Western world, like socialists and most liberals, are appalled by Third World poverty from an egalitarian and social justice point of view. They would like to think of ways to reduce or remove poverty. However, most Greens do not recognise the contradictions in their perspective on poverty. Some Western Greens, appalled by mass consumerism in the West, tend to glamorise the Third World poor as close to nature in their low levels of consumption. Some Third World activists like Shiva (1989) also pander to these Western views of the Third World poor. Third World poverty in such accounts becomes a site of Green celebration. It would not be wrong to characterise such celebration as vulgar because this celebration ignores the fact that this poverty means children are either illiterate or studying in schools without any blackboards or even without roofs. This poverty means homelessness and even when they have a roof over their heads, these roofs are so miserable that they get blown away by even a mildly harsh rainstorm or dust storm. Poverty then forces these people to bear the harshness of nature. This poverty also means that children, or even adults, are under-nourished or mal-nourished and when they fall ill, there are inadequate or non-existent medical facilities like doctors, nurses and hospitals. Many more examples of degradation of life that follow from poverty can be provided. Further, glamorisation of poverty amounts to abandoning any egalitarian perspective of reducing or removing poverty.

Some Greens also do not recognise the environmentally damaging consequences of poverty. Poor people in their desperation to survive and reproduce themselves are forced to encroach upon nature in a way that is damaging to nature. Deforestation for clearing land for cultivation and the killing of animals for food and self-survival are just two of the most obvious examples of environmentally damaging consequences of poverty. A study of poor farming communities in Ethiopia, Rwanda and Malawi pointed out that low levels of income and livelihood forced these poor farmers to resort to intensive utilisation of land that resulted in land exhaustion and degradation.[5] Poverty contributes also to high population growth which, in turn, leads to increase in global consumption of natural resources. Increase in consumption of natural resources results in increase in waste, pollution and the consequent impact of pollution on the availability of natural resources.[6]

The Green dilemma regarding poverty gets further confounded if we envision reduction of Third World poverty. If poverty gets reduced in the Third World, it will lead to unprecedented increase in levels of global consumption of natural resources. Even a mild increase in levels of income of the poorest people in just two countries in the Third World , China and India, would result in massive increases in the levels of global consumption of natural resources.[7] Unprecedented levels of generation of waste and emissions of greenhouse gases will follow. This prospect means that either the persistence of Third World poverty which keeps environmental consumption in check is accepted or it is argued that levels of income and consumption in the West are massively reduced. Is it possible to affect a massive reduction in incomes and consumption levels in the rich countries without questioning the logic of the capitalist economic system of production and consumption? It cannot be seriously argued that without a significant regulation of the market mechanism, there is ever any possibility of regulation of the levels and contents of production and consumption. Greens cannot afford to dodge the link between the capitalist nature of the present global economic system and global environmental degradation.

This brings us to the Marxist dilemma about poverty and North-South inequality.

Marxist Dilemma About Global Capitalism, Third World Poverty and Ecological Sustainability

Third World poverty associated with petty commodity production in the informal economy, according to Harriss-White and Harriss (2007), enables global capital to police the ecological limits to its further expansion. Putting it in other words, it could be said that poverty by limiting consumption reduces the ecological limits to capitalist expansion. This view needs to be further probed.

The relationship between Third World poverty caused by global capitalism and environmental degradation is contradictory and poses a dilemma. Poverty may reduce consumption, but poverty also forces poor people to encroach ruthlessly upon nature in order to secure food, survive and reproduce themselves. The dilemma poverty poses vis-à-vis environmental sustainability might be better understood if we pose this question in terms of compatibility versus incompatibility between inter-generational equity and intra-generational equity.

The most commonly accepted definition of sustainability or sustainable development highlights the dimension of inter-generational equity, namely that sustainable development is development that does not compromise the access of future generations to environmental resources at a level—in quality and quantity—that is available to the existing generation. It might be argued, as pointed out earlier, that inter-generational equity, i.e. equity over time cannot be achieved without intra-generational equity, i.e. spatial equity.

Spatial inequality, i.e. inequality between North and South, between advanced capitalist economies and backward capitalist economies, leads to high mass consumption in advanced capitalist economies and to mass poverty in backward capitalist economies. Both lead to environmental degradation and, therefore, impair the possibility of achieving inter-generational equity or sustainability.

We are faced with a further dilemma if we were to argue that intra-generational inequality should be reduced in order to achieve inter-generational equity. Reduction of intra-generational inequality, by whatever means, would lead to reduction in poverty and rise in incomes in backward capitalist economies. Since the marginal propensity to consume of lower income groups is higher, the reduction of poverty will sharply raise the aggregate level of consumption in backward capitalist economies. This will obviously have adverse consequences for the environment both in the present as well as in the future.

The dilemma we are faced thus is that both the persistence of poverty and the reduction of poverty are environmentally damaging though for different reasons. Persistence of poverty causes environmental degradation by forcing poor people to encroach upon natural resources, and reduction of poverty causes environmental degradation by raising levels of consumption.

Resolving the Marxian and Green Dilemmas on Global Capitalism and Poverty

We have discussed the dilemmas Marxian and Green perspectives face regarding the functioning of global capitalism, generation of Third World poverty and the consequences for sustainability. Though these dilemmas originate from different perspectives, yet there are overlapping and common features in both. Faced with these dilemmas, our suggestion is that if a choice has to be made, it should be made in favour of reduction of poverty in backward capitalist economies. This is for two reasons. Firstly, it is for reasons of social and class justice. And the second reason is that reduction of poverty and the rise of consumption in backward capitalist economies creates higher environmental risks for the sustainability of capitalism in advanced capitalist economies. This higher risk may impel the managers of advanced capitalist economies to speed up the search for renewable energy. The increasing realisation in some of the advanced capitalist economies especially in Europe but also in the US about the urgent need to face the challenge of global climate change despite Trump's denial of the challenge could be construed as indicative of this trend. Research and investment into renewable energy is the corner stone of the march towards sustainable future. In the immediate future, embedding sustainability into capitalism might make capitalism more flexible and adaptable. In the long term, capitalism's ever-increasing need for continuously rising levels of higher consumption to keep the engine of accumulation of capital running would erode the compatibility of capitalism with environmental sustainability. However, the embedding of environmentally friendly technologies and processes of production would be conducive to the creation of material foundations for environmentally sustainable alternative to capitalism. An alternative is always shaped by what it is trying to be alternative for. An ecologically oriented capitalism is better than an ecologically destructive capitalism as a precursor to an ecologically oriented alternative to capitalism. The weakness of some Green visions of the future is that they are based on the imagining of compatibility between ecology and capitalism. Marxian perspective has this strength that it does acknowledge the possibility of compatibility between ecology and capitalism in the short or medium term, but it highlights the long-term incompatibility between ecology and capitalism.

To conclude, the development of capitalism in backward capitalist economies has a historically progressive role to play in a way different from the way it was conceived in classical Marxism. The classical Marxism attributed historically progressive role to capitalism in backward capitalist economies because it was believed that increasing penetration of capitalism in these backward economies would break the feudal remnants. This would result, it was believed, in the creation of industrial proletariat—the expected agent of socialist revolution. From the angle of sustainability, the development of capitalism in backward capitalist economies can be considered historically progressive from a different viewpoint than the creation of the industrial working class. The development of capitalism in backward capitalist economies is historically progressive because this will sharpen the ecological limits to global capitalism. This sharpening ecological crisis of global capitalism will necessitate the search for alternatives to capitalism. The dangers of global capitalism for the survival of humanity would contribute to the emergence of global consciousness and solidarity for replacement of capitalism by a system which is ecologically sustainable and socially just—globally and nationally. In one sense, it is immaterial what name is given to this ecologically sustainable and socially just alternative to capitalism. It can be simply called socialism or eco-socialism. More imaginative nomenclature might emerge but what is crucially important is that this scenario creates a meeting ground for Marxian and Green perspectives.

Neither Marxism without incorporating ecology into its perspective nor Green ideology without economic critique of capitalism can provide an answer to the problems of global inequality, poverty and environmental degradation as we face today in 21st century capitalism.

Before we finally conclude, it may be fruitful for further elaboration of the perspective of eco-socialism.

Eco-Socialist Perspective

One major challenge to the reinstatement of expansionary fiscal policy that is being advocated globally to deal with the recession emerging from the Covid-19 crisis is that we are simultaneously faced with a huge and unprecedented ecological crisis. The world economy has reached a stage where to stop global heating and climate change, the goal of accelerated economic growth must be replaced by a more sustainable approach to development (Singh, 2008, 2008a, 2020; Castree, 2010). When the 1929-33 crisis was resolved by the expansionary fiscal policy inspired by Keynesian economic policy, there was neither the theoretical knowledge of the environmental consequences of economic policy nor the material reality of the scale of climate change which is being witnessed now. One line of thought that recognises the enormity of global climate change suggests that instead of the traditional expansionary policy, our present era needs a green expansionary policy or Green Keynesianism. Such a green expansionary or a Green Keynesian policy would entail a drastically changed transport system, energy policy, housing policy and creation of what are called green jobs. Undoubtedly, many of these green policies have positive elements because one could say that green capitalism is better than ungreen and dirty capitalism, but this approach is evasive on the mode of production-environmental destruction link (Singh, 2020). It does not recognise that capitalism is essentially a profit-driven economic system and is therefore inherently destructive of the environment. This profit-driven system is based on exploitation of natural resources (O'Connor, 1998) and continuously needs multiplication of consumer wants to generate the market for the commodities produced by the use of natural resources (Panayotakis, 2011).

A fundamental alternative to environmentally destructive capitalism is the vision of ecological socialism (Singh, 2010, 2010a, 2014, 2020). That vision, on one hand, does not entail the need for a welfare state because the necessity for the welfare state arises out of inequalities in capitalism where the poor and the disadvantaged need to be cared for in some way but, on the other hand, implies welfare for all because there would not be a division between the privileged few and the underprivileged many in the eco-socialist society. However, that goal is a long term one or a medium term one, and in the journey towards that goal, the strengthening of the welfare state is desirable because the idea of the welfare state recognises the institution of community and the collective effort required in responding to some needs of the community. Dearlove and Saunders (1984, 319) have rightly pointed out that "The Welfare State represents a "Trojan horse" within the citadels of capitalism in that it rests firmly on a set of values which are fundamentally opposed to those of capitalism".

Both neoliberal austerity and Keynesian welfare/stimulus stratagems are two different forms of governance of capitalism in response to different phases/cycles of capitalism. The competition between them is only on which one is more efficient, i.e. which one generates higher and maximum possible economic growth. Both are, therefore, anti-ecological. However, from a social equity point of view, the neoliberal austerity paradigm is far more inegalitarian than the Keynesian welfare/stimulus one. Eco-socialism is, therefore, sharply critical of neo-liberal austerity paradigm but has some degrees of affinity with the ecologically modified Keynesian welfare paradigm as a basis for building egalitarian future (Singh, 2020).

Eco-socialism is emerging as a new historically necessary response to the challenges of environmentally destructive growth and increase in poverty both in the developing capitalism economies as well as in the developed capitalist economies. The programme of the Green New Deal is the transitional path to eco-socialism (Singh, 2020).

NOTES

1. I wish to acknowledge that a very fruitful discussion with Liz Perez was helpful on this point.
2. A good articulation of the external market dimension of Luxemburg's theory of imperialism is Patnaik (1972).
3. I have used the word 'global heating' instead of the often used word 'global warming' because global warming seems to suggest a slower and less intense process of rise in global temperature than what is conveyed

by 'global heating'. A consensus has emerged among international climate scientists that if the rise in average global temperature is not kept below 1.5 degrees centigrade by 2030 compared with the average global temperature in the pre-industrial era i.e. before 1850, this will have irreversible changes in the global climate leading to climate catastrophe (See Singh, 2020).

4. For a more nuanced discussion on centralisation versus decentralisation and large-scale production versus small-scale production, see Singh 2010a.
5. Ian Scoones and Camilla Toulmin, *Policies for Soil Fertility Management in Africa*, DFID, London, 1999 cited by Bernstein and Woodhouse (2007), pp. 168-69.
6. Bernstein and Woodhouse (2007, pp. 153-54) refer to a study by Tiffen, Mortimore and Gichuki (1994) which argues apparently in a counter-Malthusian strain that population growth can contribute to environmental recovery. I have not looked at this study, but I am sceptical of such a claim though it is plausible to argue a different point that population increase can lead to increase in land productivity.
7. According to the Chinese State Bureau of Statistics, China's population grew by 8.1 million or 0.6 per cent in 2005 to a total of 1.307 billion (*Financial Times*, March 17, 2006, p. 6). Though the Chinese population size is huge, its rate of population growth is low partly because of the one-child policy imposed by the Chinese state since the 1970s and partly because of the reduction in poverty of some sections of the population as a result of fast economic growth experienced by China in the last few years. The practice of female infanticide has resulted in severe gender imbalance. 'There were 106.3 men for every 100 women', according to the State Bureau of Statistics (FT, ibid.). The practice of female infanticide might have also contributed to the low rate of population growth. This low growth in population might be considered a positive development from the viewpoint of its implications for increase in total level of global consumption. However, due to the absolute level of Chinese population, even a very small increase in the income level of this population implies a massive increase in global consumption. One can argue from a contrary point of view that a low level of absolute population with a very high per capita income and consumption level as in some of the rich capitalist economies may contribute more to total global consumption than a big population with a relatively low per capita income and consumption

level as in some Third World economies. See Singh (2008, 2008a) for further development of the argument on environmental implications of the rising economic powers of BRICS economies.

REFERENCES

Amin, S. (1976), *Imperialism and Unequal Development,* New York: Monthly Review Press.

Baran, P. (1968), *Political Economy of Growth*, New York: Monthly Review Press.

Bernstein, H. and P. Woodhouse (2007), Africa: Eco-Populist Utopias and (Micro-) Capitalist Realities, pp. 147-69, In C. Leys and L. Panitch (eds.), *Socialist Register 2007: Coming to Terms with Nature*, London: Merlin Press.

Bharadwaj, K. (1986), *Classical Political Economy and Rise to Dominance of Supply and Demand Theories*, Delhi: Sangam Books.

Castree, N. (2010), Crisis, Continuity and Change: Neoliberalism, the Left and the Future of Capitalism, *Antipode*, Vol. 41, No.1, pp. 185-213.

Dearlove, J and P. Saunders (1984), *Introduction to British Politics: Analysing a Capitalist Democracy*, Cambridge: Polity Press.

Foldvary, Fred E. (ed.), (1996), *Beyond Neo-Classical Economics: Heterodox Approaches to Economic Theory*, Cheltenham: Edward Elgar.

Frank, Andre G. (1966), *Development of Underdevelopment*, London: New England Press.

Fraser, D. (2009), *The Evolution of the British Welfare State*, London: Palgrave Macmillan. Fourth Edition.

Gough, I. (1979), *The Political Economy of the Welfare State*, London: Macmillan.

Gough, I. (1997), State Expenditure in Advanced Capitalism, *New Left Review* I/92, July-August.

Harriss-White, B. and E. Harriss (2007), 'Unsustainable Capitalism: The Politics of Renewable Energy in the UK', pp. 72-101, In C. Leys and L. Panitch (eds.), *Socialist Register 2007: Coming to Terms with Nature*, London: Merlin Press.

Harvey, D. (2007), *A Brief History of Neoliberalism*, Oxford: Oxford University Press.

Hayek, F. (1944 [1997]), *The Road to Serfdom*, London: Routledge.

Hennock, E.P. (2007), *The Origin of the Welfare State in England and Germany, 1850-1914: Some Policies Compared,* Cambridge: Cambridge University Press.

Jacobs, M. (1993), *Green Economy*, London: Pluto Press.

Keynes, J.M. (2007 [1936]), *The General Theory of Employment, Interest and Money*. London: Macmillan.

Konzelmann, Suzanne J. (2014), The Political Economics of Austerity, *Cambridge Journal of Economics*, Vol. 38, No. 4, pp. 701-41.

Lenin, V.I. (1930), *Imperialism: The Highest Stage of Capitalism,* International Publishers, New York.

Lowe, R. (2005), *The Welfare State in Britain Since 1945*, Basingstoke/New York: Palgrave Macmillan.

Luxemburg, R. (1951), *The Accumulation of Capital* (with an introduction by Joan Robinson), New Haven: Yale University Press.

Marx, K. and F. Engels (2002 [1848]), *Communist Manifesto,* London: Penguin Books.

Niskanen, William A. (1988), *Reaganomics: An Insider's Account of the Policies and the People*, Oxford University Press: Oxford.

O'Connor, J. (1998), *Natural Causes: Essays in Ecological Marxism*, New York: Guildford Press.

Panayotakis, C. (2011), *Remaking Scarcity: From Capitalist Inefficiency to Economic Democracy*, London: Pluto Press.

Patnaik, P. (1972), A Note on External Markets and Capitalist Development, *The Economic Journal*, Vol. 82, No. 328, pp. 1316-323. reprinted in Patnaik (1995), *Whatever Happened to Imperialism and Other Essays*, Tulika, New Delhi.

Piketty, T. (2014), *Capital in the Twenty-First Century*. Cambridge, Massachussets; London, England: Harvard University Press.

Radice, H. (2014), Thatcherism and Alternatives: What Future for British Capitalism? *Capital and Class*, Vol. 38, No. 2, pp. 277-87.

Rostow, W.W. (1960), *Stages of Economic Growth: A Non-Communist Manifesto,* Massachusetts: Cambridge.

Shiva, V. (1989), *Staying Alive*, London: Zed Books.

Singh, P. (2008), 'Shifting Balance', *Himal*, June, Kathmandu.

Singh, P. (2008a), Contemporary Global Capitalism: Multi-pronged Crises, *Economic and Political Weekly*, Vol. 43 No. 41, pp. 36-40.

Singh, P. (2010), Interrogating Marxian, Neo-Classical and Green Perspectives on the Contradictory Implications of Third World/ Asian Development for Global Sustainability, pp. 149-63, In S.S. Gill, L. Singh and R. Marwah (eds.), *Economic and Environmental Sustainability of the Asian Region,* New Delhi: Routledge.

Singh, P. (2010a), Capitalism, Nature and Eco-Socialism, A Review Article on *Coming to Terms with Nature: Socialist Register 2007* edited by Leo Panitch and Colin Leys with Barbara Harriss-White, Elmar Altvater and Greg Albo, *Economic and Political Weekly*, Vol. 45, No. 12, pp. 29-33.

Singh, P. and L.N. Bhusal (2014), Austerity, Welfare State and Eco-Socialism: With Special Reference to the United Kingdom, Economic *and Political Weekly,* Vol. 49, No. 39, pp. 111-18.

Singh, P. (2020), Zeroing in on Responses to Economic Crisis, *The Tribune,* May 2.

Skidelsky, R. (ed.). (1989), *Thatcherism,* Oxford: Basil Blackwell.

Stedman J.D. (2012), *Masters of the Universe: Hayek, Friedman, and the Birth of Neoliberal Politics*, Princeton, N.J. and Oxford: Princeton University Press.

Thane, P. (1996), *Foundations of the Welfare State.* Harlow: Pearson Longman.

Tiffen, M., M. Mortimore and F. Gichuki (1994), *More People, Less Erosion, Environmental Recovery in Kenya,* Chichester: John Wiley.

Tiffen M. and M. Mortimore (1994), 'Malthus Controverted: The Role of Capital and Technology in Growth and Environmental Recovery in Kenya', *World Development*, Vol. 22, No. 7, pp. 997-1010.

Wallerstein, I. (1979), *The Capitalist World Economy*, Cambridge: Cambridge University Press.

Warren, B. (1973), Imperialism and Capitalist Industrialisation, *New Left Review*, 1/81, September-October.

Warren, B. (1980), *Imperialism: Pioneer of Capitalism*, New York and London: Verso Books.

18

Energy, Economic Growth, and Ecological Crisis[1]

Erald Kolasi

Can economic growth continue forever? This relatively simple question has posed some intellectual headaches for modern capitalism. In the *Grundrisse*, Karl Marx argued that capital cannot tolerate any limits, by which he meant that the drive for growth and the search for new markets are both necessary for the political and economic survival of capitalism (Marx, 1973).[2] Viewed in this light, the implications of the question present something of an existential challenge to the current order. Capitalism cannot acknowledge any natural limits to economic growth, for that would mean acknowledging its ultimate demise. To keep up the pretence that capitalism represents a quasi-eternal and invincible system, most political leaders and economists who support the current order have begun reciting a series of elaborate narratives about the relationship between human economies and the natural world.

These narratives all revolve around the central idea that we can decouple economic growth from the material needs of human civilisation. Till the late 20th century, economists generally understood that more economic growth required the use of more energy and materials. But as the postwar compromises between labour and capital began collapsing in the 1970s and 80s, economic theories started to shift in emphasis and direction. Inspired by neoclassical theories, a new generation of economists began to argue that economic growth could continue without the consumption of additional resources from the environment (Solow, 1974). They claimed that we could reach this economic nirvana by doing more with less, investing in clean energy, and developing energy-efficient technologies. In short, they were arguing for nothing less than the long-term sustainability of capitalism, ignoring all the science and evidence piling up along the way.

U.S. primary energy consumption by source and sector, 2017
Total=97.7 quadrillion British thermal units (Btu)

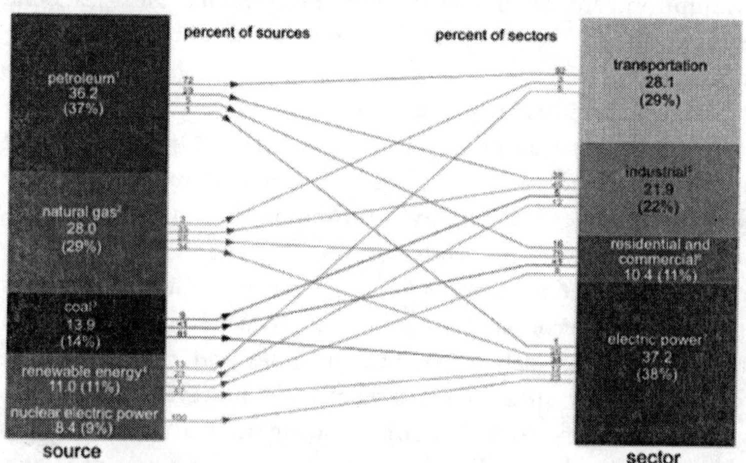

Source: US Primary energy consumption by source and sector, 2017. Energy Information Administration, Annual Energy Outlook for 2018.

At a basic level, pundits and economists generally define decoupling as a process in which the size of the economy expands while resource impacts, usually either carbon emissions or primary energy consumption, decline (Obama, 2017).[3] More specifically, relative decoupling occurs when resource impacts are rising at a slower rate than economic growth. Absolute decoupling occurs when resource impacts are declining in absolute terms, even as the economy keeps expanding (Jackson, 2011). Macroeconomic theories supportive of capitalism measure economic size and activity by calculating the gross domestic product (GDP), which stands for the annual market value of goods and services produced in an economy by adding together gross private investment, consumer spending, government spending, and the trade balance. It should be noted that, although widely accepted by governments and most economists around the world, there are some fundamental scientific problems with using this measure as an accurate barometer of aggregate economic activity.[4]

Divergence between growth in carbon emissions and economic growth, and between economic growth and primary energy consumption, are often conflated in both public and academic discourse about the issue of decoupling, creating all sorts of confusions.[5]

Some economists have also looked at how aggregate demand relates to the consumption of raw materials. Other ideas and concepts related to decoupling regularly circulate in the literature, reflecting the general ambiguity surrounding the issue.

This chapter aims to synthesise and understand these disparate ideas and to offer a comprehensive overview of the relationships between energy, economic growth, and social development. On a practical level, this debate has become fluid and chaotic because wealth and power are at stake. Intellectually, however, many of the arguments amplify confusion by resorting to inaccurate theories and misleading phrases. People often equate the concept of energy consumption with the term energy use, suggesting that they are unaware of important distinctions in how energy accounting works, or even what energy actually means. Many economists think about concepts like energy and efficiency in vastly different ways than physicists, creating ample opportunity for interdisciplinary confusion. This web of definitions and conceptions cries out for some attempt at clarification. Here I explore the nature of the relationship between energy and economic growth, highlighting areas where it makes sense to talk about decoupling while also emphasising some of the fundamental limits and problems of invoking the concept in relation to economics.

The Critical Role of Energetic Conversions

Energy consumption is a complex topic that touches on many different issues about the nature of civilisation. When most governments and organisations talk about energy consumption, they are typically referring to a metric called *primary* energy consumption, which represents the direct use of energy sources without any prior conversions or transformations.[6] Primary consumption includes burning coal at a power plant and distilling crude oil at a refinery. Primary forms of energy are not useful on their own, so they are converted and transformed into secondary forms of energy. For example, we burn coal so we can turn the resulting steam energy into electricity, and we distill crude oil so we can produce gasoline. Coal and crude oil are primary forms of energy while electricity and gasoline are considered secondary forms. The secondary sources can also be converted into other tasks and end uses, collectively known as tertiary sources. However, it must be emphasised that all primary energy sources are themselves the result of earlier conversions and transformations in nature, so they are not so primary after all. For example, the hydrocarbons of the dead plants and animals that make up petroleum are a secondary product of photosynthesis, which requires solar energy and water molecules. This fact hints at an important challenge for the usual methods of energy accounting: the concept of a primary form of energy is theoretically suspect.

There are two common methods of measuring primary energy: the partial-substitution method and the physical-energy content method.[7] Let me explain them with some examples. When a power plant burns through coal, the primary energy simply equals the energy of the coal that goes up in flames. In the case of fossil fuels then, things are pretty easy: just record the amount of stuff that we burn and call that primary energy. But the situation is more complicated for renewable energy sources, such as wind, solar, and hydropower, because nothing was burning while these energy sources generated electricity. Enter the two methods above. In the physical-energy content method, we simply count the electrical energy produced by these sources as primary energy, even though electricity obviously qualifies as a converted form of energy. This is the method used by the International Energy Agency to measure energy consumption for renewables. In the partial-substitution method, we pretend that the produced electricity came from a hypothetical thermal power plant, and then we assume some efficiency for this plant.

For example, if the plant has an efficiency of 20 per cent, then we would multiply the electricity generated by a factor of five. In this case, the primary energy required to produce that electricity is five times larger. The company British Petroleum has adopted this partial-substitution method in its popular global energy reports.[8] The main reason why these differences matter is because they can lead to diverging estimates of energy consumption, especially for nations that rely heavily on renewables.

We can always argue and wonder about which method is more correct, but this line of thinking entirely misses the central theme of the conversation. In reality, beyond the world of statistical accounting, only energetic conversions truly matter. The electrical energy produced by renewables came from dynamical flows in nature, such as sunlight hitting the earth and rivers roaring through dams. The concentration of fossil fuels at their points of processing and refinement required energetic conversions from machines and human labour, which first extracted these fuels and then transported them to a particular location. All this happened before anything was burned and recorded on some logs and charts. Thinking in terms of primary energy consumption obscures the energetic flows and conversions that make all economic activities possible. It also establishes ample opportunities for confusion and misguided results in public discourse. When economists and media outlets show plots of GDP growth diverging from energy consumption, they are actually showing GDP growth diverging from primary energy consumption.[9] They then assume that this alone somehow proves that economic growth has become detached from energy use.

This assumption is highly misleading. To understand why, it helps to review the significance of energy in a broader context beyond economics. We can generally define energy as constrained states of motion that can be exchanged among different physical systems. It can come in many different forms, such as chemical, thermal, kinetic, and potential, to name just a few. The following arguments do not even depend on any particular definition of energy; they just depend on the basic fact that certain forms of energy can be converted into other forms. For example, chemical energy can be transformed into mechanical energy, which is what happens when our car engines burn through fuel and convert the resulting heat energy into the mechanical motion of the wheels. Heat and mechanical energy can also be transformed into electrical energy, like when power plants burn through coal and use the resulting steam energy to drive a generator that produces electricity. Focusing exclusively on primary energy consumption completely ignores and marginalizes these energetic conversions, which should be the central elements of the story.

All conceivable economic transactions, from the exchange of money to the production of commodities, require energetic conversions from various sources. Energy is embedded in all human actions. It does not simply stop counting after we burn through natural resources at some power plant. The flow of energy through the various parts of civilisation facilitates all possible human actions, such as driving to the grocery store, surfing the web, playing video games, watching television shows, and reading romance novels at the beach. In this fundamental sense, economic activities cannot be decoupled from energy use, for that would be like asking economics to step completely outside the laws of physics—a clear absurdity. But this clear absurdity is exactly what certain economic theories imply can actually happen: they artificially detach capital and labour from energetic constraints and effectively sever any and all links between physics and economics (Stern, 2004). Many economists use primary energy consumption as a crutch for how energy impacts economic processes, and in so doing they make it seem like our lives are unfolding in some entirely separate realm from energetic constraints. Instead of focusing exclusively on primary consumption, we should emphasise the importance of what I call aggregate flow, defined as the total sum of all the energy converted through our economic activities. In other words, aggregate flow focuses on the energetic flows and transformations that make civilisation possible. A related quantity of interest is the aggregate flow rate, or AFR, which measures the aggregate flow per unit of time. In general, richer societies have a higher AFR than poorer societies. This means that they can produce and circulate larger amounts of real surplus wealth, in the form of use values. However, an enormous portion of this wealth also takes the form of social, economic, and ecological waste.

In addition to the critical role of conversions, we must emphasise the related importance of energy quality. Not all primary sources of energy are made equal. Some are more efficient than others. Some yield more mechanical work. Others produce more electricity. For example, producing one kilowatt hour of electricity in 2017 required, on average, 7,812 British thermal units (BTUs) of natural gas and 10,465 BTUs of coal.[10] By this measure, natural gas is roughly 25 per cent more efficient than coal at generating the same quantity of electricity. The energy thinker Vaclav Smil identified the power density of an energy source as an important feature for the economic growth and development of civilisation.[11] He defined power density as the energy flux per unit area that could be released in the conversion process of an energy source. Smil has argued that fossil fuels are uniquely important for capitalism because they have higher power densities than other energy sources, such as wind and solar. Larger power densities help generate more production, leading to higher profits by extension. Other measures of energy quality are conceivable, but the basic point is that natural energy sources can have very different uses and attributes. The only way to understand these differences is by looking at the conversions and transformations that follow primary consumption. Failing to take this critical but routinely ignored step makes it seem like all energy sources should be treated equally, as if they all have the same capacities in the process of economic production and consumption.

The Central Flaws in the Neoclassical Theory of Growth

The intellectual foundations of the decoupling narrative derive from neoclassical economic theory, the prevailing paradigm of explanation among orthodox economists that support capitalism. The neoclassical theory is generally plagued by unrealistic assumptions about society, numerous mathematical inconsistencies, and has no predictive power at all.[12] In this piece, however, we focus on the cardinal sin of this intellectual train wreck: its rejection of physics and its ignorance of the natural order. In the 1950s, the economist Robert Solow developed one of the first major models to describe how economic growth happens.[13] In these versions of neoclassical theory, the production inputs of capital and labour combine to produce outputs, or finished goods, that are traded in the economy. Growth in capital leads to more output, but depreciation in capital assets also drags down a portion of that output. The economy eventually reaches a stationary state where growth and depreciation balance each other out and there is no more growth. In order to produce continuous growth, neoclassical theory argues that the economy needs a steady stream of technological progress, defined as a gain in total productivity. This gain implies that productive output can increase while productive inputs are held constant. Solow came up with a mathematical scheme for detecting the impact of this technological growth on changes in GDP. Although his work earned widespread acclaim from other neoclassical thinkers, much of it was based on dubious mathematical results that did not actually validate his claim.[14]

In extensions of Solow's original theory, the productive inputs have typically included capital, labour, and technology. Energy is sometimes subsumed under the three traditional inputs, or it may be treated as a separate input in and of itself. Critically, the production inputs are viewed as largely independent from one another, meaning that they can be substituted as necessary in order to maintain or to boost the maximum level of production. If societies are running short on natural resources, neoclassical theory argues that these shortages can be overcome through technological innovation, efficiency gains, or other forms of substitution. Indeed, neoclassical economists tend to assume that the long-run sustainability of capitalism is materially possible and all we need to do is figure out the social and institutional arrangements that can ensure that sustainability.[15] Solow entertained the idea that the natural world does not provide limits to economic growth on the following grounds: "If it is very easy to substitute other factors for natural resources, then there is in principle no 'problem.' The world can, in effect, get along without natural resources, so exhaustion is just an event, not a catastrophe."[16]

Although his model also showed that competition would eventually result in the exhaustion of natural resources, his statement nicely describes the general attitude that many economists hold about the inevitability of growth under capitalism.

For a highly simplified toy model of what this all means, consider your local pizza store. According to neoclassical theory, the pizza store can maintain or boost current levels of pizza production in the face of any shortfall. A shortage of workers can be overcome by adding more ovens. A shortage of cheese can be overcome through technical improvements that yield more efficient methods of making cheese. A shortage of electricity can be overcome by increasing labour productivity, perhaps by training the workers to make the pizzas faster under the new time constraints. Everything can be replaced. Everything can be substituted, seemingly without end. The ideas and principles just described represent fundamental assumptions in neoclassical economics and they are often used to explain the relationship between energy consumption and economic growth. If there were no hard limits to substitution, then it would be possible for our economies to keep growing even in an ecosphere with declining quantities of natural resources and with highly chaotic, nonlinear ecological consequences that result from the enormous energy losses of capitalist societies. In other words, better technologies and higher efficiencies would always be available to boost production, regardless of any depletions or instabilities in the wider natural world caused by those productivity gains.

To chip away at this elaborate fantasy, it helps to begin with some basic physics. The most fundamental limits to substitution come from thermodynamics, the branch of physics that studies quantities like heat, work, and energy. Thermodynamic limits impose constraints on the maximum efficiency of energy flows through technological systems.[17] Car engines, power plants, and photovoltaic cells are all limited in their capacities to convert one type of energy into another. Technological progress cannot overcome these limits; no car engine can ever be more efficient than an engine running on the Carnot cycle (Jewett and Serway, 2008). In an earlier article for this magazine, I defined the aggregate efficiency of an economic system as the fraction of all primary energy consumption that produces mechanical work and electricity (Kolasi, 2018). I argued that aggregate efficiencies are highly inertial over time because improving them substantially requires enormous investments that would disrupt the reigning economic order.

Once a society has settled into a particular energy structure, changing it much further becomes a daunting task because of elite classes and groups that rely heavily on that structure for their wealth and influence. We can look to the recent experience of Germany for a prominent case study. In 2000, the German government launched its ambitious *Energiewende*, a comprehensive plan to reduce greenhouse gas emissions by shifting energy production towards renewable sources, such as wind and solar (Reed, 2017). For time, the program made some notable achievements. Compared to 1990, greenhouse gas emissions had declined 28 per cent by 2017. That same year, renewables reached a 13 per cent share of primary energy consumption. Although these numbers are impressive, progress has recently come to a standstill. It has become increasingly clear that Germany will not reach the climate targets that it set for 2020. And once we dig into the numbers a bit deeper, even those that look impressive come with huge caveats. For example, the large reduction of carbon emissions since 1990 can be largely attributed to the collapse of heavy industry in East Germany after reunification (Buck, 2018). Over the past eight years, greenhouse gas emissions from Germany have hardly changed. The variabilities associated with wind and solar power have opened up problems related to electricity storage. Prices fluctuate dramatically depending on weather conditions. To compensate for these and other issues, Germany began sabotaging its energy program by constructing a series of new coal power plants when the coal industry pressured Chancellor Angela Merkel's government to relax its policies. The German example offers an important lesson: the necessary substitution of fossil fuels with renewables will never come fast enough under the market logic of capitalism.

Another major limit to substitution comes from the ecological instabilities associated with excessive levels of economic growth.

These instabilities can combine to pump and amplify existing natural phenomena. The amplifier effect works as follows. Economies absorb energy from the natural world and then exploit that energy for cycles of production and consumption. For highly energy-intensive economies, these cycles necessarily yield extensive levels of waste and dissipation, or energy losses that are dumped back out to the environment. These energy losses are not "useless" from the standpoint of physics or ecology. Under the right circumstances, they can power the formation of other natural dynamical systems, including everything from viruses and bacteria to wildfires and hurricanes.[18] These highly chaotic effects associated with energy-intensive economies are largely ignored and dismissed by the neoclassical theory, even though they have often played a central role in the evolution of human history (Bentley, 2013) As a highly dissipative system, capitalism regularly produces very powerful amplifier effects. Collectively, these amplifiers are now creating what Marx called a "metabolic rift" between nature and society, which means that the ecological basis of civilisation is steadily eroding under profit-seeking and energy-intensive development that does not care about replacing what it extracts.[19] The natural world has major tipping points that we should not cross, but indefinite economic growth through substitution virtually guarantees that some of those critical thresholds will be breached, threatening the broader ecosphere that supports human civilisation (Rockström et al., 2009).

Consider another problem. Substitution can occur quite frequently on small and restricted scales of economic activity. A pizza store can always substitute certain ingredients for others. A homeowner can substitute heating fuel for insulation. A company can replace older light bulbs for more efficient lighting in its offices. And even some countries can substitute various forms of wealth for others, at least temporarily. The Pacific island nation of Nauru provides a classic example that highlights the central themes of the debate. In the 20th century, Nauru possessed vast deposits of phosphate, which is highly prized as an agricultural fertiliser. These deposits were extensively mined, depleted, and then traded in global markets, allowing Nauru to reach a sky-high standard of living by 1990 (Kesler, Simon and Simon, 2015). Nauru converted a portion of its earnings from the phosphate trade into a public trust fund, which invested in manufactured capital through financial markets. However, its impressive standard of living collapsed sharply after the phosphate vanished, along with most of the money in the trust fund (Davies and Doherty, 2018). Nauru offers a cautionary tale for the world as a whole. If global civilisation runs out of natural resources, we cannot replace them by investing in commodities through financial markets. People cannot eat money. Substitution in the long run may be possible at the micro level of economic activity, but long-term macro level substitution is downright wishful thinking.

We can better understand the limits to substitution on a global, macroscopic level by considering a specific example: a global economy meeting its electricity needs through the consumption of solar power. There are fundamental limits to the amount of solar energy absorbed by solar panels that can be converted into useful electrical energy. Most commercial photovoltaics convert less than 30 per cent of the solar energy they absorb into electricity; the remaining energy balance is lost as heat and infrared radiation.[20] The theoretical efficiency limits for the most advanced photovoltaic designs are just under 90 per cent, a number that not even the latest labouratory experiments have come close to matching (Vos, De, 1980). But suppose neoclassical theory is right about its eternal commitment to technological progress and that eventually we do manage to produce photovoltaics that are 90 per cent efficient at converting solar energy. Once all theoretical efficiency limits are actually realised, boosting electricity production even further would require the construction of new solar panels, which takes up more land. As the earth has a finite surface area, indefinite growth would not be possible even with the proliferation of renewables. This argument underscores the central point that renewable technologies are important, but they cannot solve the global ecological crisis under the economic regime of capitalism, which is completely reliant on the false promise of eternal growth in production and consumption.

Substituting fossil fuels for renewables while pushing for more growth would still lead to the total ruin of global civilisation in a few centuries.

Economists love to pretend that technological innovation can yield greater "qualitative growth" without any corresponding "quantitative growth" (Worstall, 2014). On the basis of improving knowledge and technological growth, they believe that the monetary value of stuff can keep increasing even as the quantity of stuff itself remains stable. But what they fail to grasp is that technological innovations do not happen magically—they also require energetic conversions. Changes to the production cycle are dependent on the stock of electrical, chemical, and mechanical energy available for research and training. A coder sitting in front of a computer writing a new program needs energy to think and type. The computer itself needs electricity to continue operating. No possible improvement can be made to computer programs without a continuous stream of energetic conversions. Expansions in productivity require energy flows, meaning that all forms of technological change are intertwined with the energetic transformations that facilitate human existence. Technological changes are physically embedded in greater knowledge among people and the development of more productive assets, both of which need energy and material flows to continue operating. Thermodynamic limits also constrain the extent to which these flows can be reduced while sustaining labour and capital. In short, technological changes themselves are subject to hard physical limits, along with the qualitative growth that can be derived from them. Power plants provide one of the most well-known examples of the limits to technological growth. They have been hovering near their peak efficiency ratings for decades and getting them to go much further has proven to be extremely difficult.[21] The failure of breeder reactors for nuclear power plants highlights another prominent technological bust, and plenty of other exotic technologies, like fusion reactors, will inevitably end up in the same category. The bloated profit margins of capitalism depend critically on the energy-intensive basis of its entire existence. Take away that basis and there is no more capitalism.

How Energy and Growth Relate to Emissions

All economic activities, as we have seen, require energy. To better understand what this means, we examine the relationships between energy, growth, and emissions more concretely by looking at the economy of the United States. In recent decades, US economic growth has continued, albeit at a declining rate, even though per-capita primary energy consumption has gone down.[22] In addition, costs associated with primary energy consumption increasingly represent a declining share of US aggregate demand. From these observations, many economists and pundits have concluded that energy use and economic growth have decoupled from one another.[23] But even a quick analysis of the underlying energy shifts in the US economy reveals the falsehood of this narrative. An economy that starts using natural resources with higher energy efficiencies and larger power densities can experience growth even as primary energy consumption declines. Understanding this process would be difficult, perhaps even impossible, if we only looked at primary consumption, which totally ignores conversions. But once we consider that burning a smaller quantity of natural gas, for example, can still yield more electricity than burning a larger amount of coal, then the significance of conversions becomes immediately apparent. Resources with larger power densities can convert more useful energy for economic activities, some of which constitute the basic elements measured by GDP. Economists like David Stern and Robert Kaufmann, among others, have clearly shown that growth in US energy consumption is tightly coupled with growth in aggregate demand once differences in energy quality are factored into the analysis.[24]

The energy crisis of the 1970s motivated the United States to reduce per-capita oil consumption and to focus on efficiency gains by using other natural resources. These efforts resulted in a trajectory of increased natural-gas consumption, which is much cleaner and more efficient as an energy source than coal. Both the switch to natural gas and the increasing proliferation of renewables helped substantially reduce carbon emissions. After peaking in 2005, greenhouse gas emissions in the United States had fallen 14 per cent by 2016 (Hausfather, 2017). But the declines gradually stalled and emissions in 2018 actually increased by more than 3 per cent, the largest rise in 8 years (Plumer, 2019). A hyperactive transportation sector, always critical to economic growth, was the leading culprit behind the latest surge. Recent US experience further reinforces the notion that large-scale reductions in emissions are virtually impossible under an economic system that prioritizes growth above anything else. The unlimited pressure to increase consumption and production can lead to rising emissions even in the context of macro level efficiency gains and technological innovations.

For the world as a whole, a strong positive relationship exists between primary energy consumption and economic growth, and numerous studies on various countries and regions indicate that this relationship is fundamentally causal.[25] Over the last few decades, the rate of global economic growth has started to slow down, mirroring the declining rate of growth in global energy consumption. Some major economies, like those of Japan and the European Union, have already entered periods of stagnation associated with very low growth rates and aging populations. Because these economies are currently dominated by corrupt financial sectors, they are generating uneven growth patterns that mostly enrich wealthy capitalists. By contrast, ordinary people are increasingly drowning in debt so they can finance the cycles and crises of capitalism (Dickler, 2019). Economic progress for the vast majority of society has come to a screeching halt (Desilver, 2018). The global economy may continue to grow at modest rates for the rest of this century, but the signs are already evident that our potential for future growth is limited and constrained by what kinds of energy sources we can collect from the natural world, as well as by the economic irrationalities of today's financialised capitalism.

Capitalism is running out of steam, but not quickly enough to substantially reduce aggregate emissions. Global carbon emissions over the last century have closely followed changes in primary energy consumption. At the start of the decade, optimism about global warming was high. Greenhouse gas emissions flatlined for several years and the upper echelons of the global economy started to believe that economic growth could actually be decoupled from harmful emissions. In 2016, the International Energy Agency triumphantly declared: "Decoupling of global emissions and economic growth confirmed."[26] What a difference two years can make. In 2017, greenhouse gas emissions worldwide saw a sharp spike (Hausfather, 2017). Against a backdrop of increasingly alarming scientific reports about the dangers of global warming, emissions rose again for 2018, at a faster pace than the previous year (Carrington, 2018). Even some advanced economies that had supposedly decoupled growth from pollution witnessed higher carbon emissions in 2018. Detaching emissions from economic growth has turned out to be a vastly more complicated problem than global elites originally believed.

A persistent albatross on this issue is the way that most elites talk about carbon emissions. When governments and organisations measure greenhouse gas emissions, they often do so at the point of manufacture and production. If a US company sets up a factory in India to produce commodities that are then sold to US consumers, the emissions coming from that factory are credited to India, not the United States. This basic process of what is referred to as geographic substitution, where corporations from the capitalist core transfer ecologically destructive manufacturing to developing nations with large pools of cheap labour, has been an important source of the observed divergence between carbon emissions and economic growth in the Western world.[27] In other words, measuring emissions from the point of consumption hardly reveals any decoupling at all. In any case, multinational corporations can only keep shifting production around so much before they run out of places to go. There are limits to geographic substitution as well.

Besides comparing aggregate demand to emissions, another approach for understanding the material foundations of economic growth focuses on the flow of raw materials on their way to the final point of consumption. In a landmark 2012 paper, a group of Australian researchers analysed the aggregate raw materials exchanged among countries through international trade and introduced the concept of the material footprint, defined as the global allocation of used raw material extraction to the final demand of an economy. They concluded that "with every 10 per cent increase in gross domestic product, the average national [material footprint] increases by 6 per cent" (Wiedmann et al., 2013). In their view, "achievements in decoupling in advanced economies are smaller than reported or even nonexistent." They also estimated that roughly 40 per cent of all global raw materials are extracted to facilitate the export of goods and services to other nations, which indicates that reducing the international flows of global capital could be a critical strategy in addressing our intensifying ecological crisis.

For another perspective on why claims about decoupling are premature, consider the following fact: life expectancy in the United States has declined for three consecutive years, the first such sustained decline in a century (Bernstein, 2018). The US economy grew in every one of those years. But the press did not blare the sirens declaring that life expectancy has decoupled from economic growth. Such an admission would raise an unthinkable prospect for the reigning plutocracy: that the lives of common people might actually be getting worse while some billionaires become even richer by selling the rest of us more stuff that does not actually improve our lives. However, when two or three years of mixed and uncertain data suggest that the rise in harmful global emissions has slowed down, the story gets blown out of proportion and becomes a masterful causal narrative about how capitalism can be ecologically sustainable. The collapse of the decoupling delusion offers an important lesson—we should resist the temptation to make grand conclusions about the world when we notice marginal trends over just a few years.

The Accelerating Crisis and the Social Dimension

The early phases of the ecological crisis have already arrived. In 2017, Puerto Rico was struck and heavily damaged by a powerful hurricane lurking over unusually warm waters. That same year, a historic drought in Argentina crippled agricultural exports and triggered a massive recession, which eventually coupled with a currency crisis and forced the country to borrow billions from the International Monetary Fund for the second time in less than two decades (Misculin and Burin, 2018). Severe and unusual droughts in Central America are also disrupting agricultural production and playing a major role in convincing hundreds of thousands of migrants to head north (Wernick, 2019). Major droughts and water shortages in Afghanistan have fuelled widespread resentment against the central government in Kabul and have incited tensions between the country and its neighbours (Jain, 2018). These and thousands of other simultaneous developments are only the opening lines in a multiact play that human civilization will nervously witness and experience over the next few centuries.

Ecological and other left-wing economists have long criticised the dangerous fantasies of neoclassical thinkers. But there is evidence that some elites are also beginning to change their minds on the issue. In 2016, the International Resource Panel concluded that the global consumption of materials since 2000 had grown at a faster rate than global GDP, adding that "global material efficiency, for the first time in a century, has started to decline" (Schandl et al., 2016). In 2017, the chief economist of Norway's Equinor, Eric Waerness, wrote that decoupling economic growth from energy consumption "might be impossible" (Simon, 2017). In 2018, a major report from the International Panel on Climate Change stated that preventing catastrophic levels of global warming would require "rapid, far-reaching, and unprecedented changes in all aspects of society."[28] Antonio Guterres, the Secretary General of the United Nations, told a climate conference in early December 2018 that "we are in deep trouble with climate change" (Dennis and Mooney, 2018). Optimism has finally given way to realism, even if many of these individuals and organisations fail to notice the next required step: a full-blown social, political, and economic confrontation against capitalism.

An analysis of class and society remains critical to understanding the horizon of crisis spearheaded by capitalism. In large part, the ecological crisis is a product of very rich people using and consuming vast amounts of energy. Any proposed solutions to our current existential ills must thoroughly address the class differences responsible for creating them in the first place. Specifically, we must ensure that the transition to an ecological order ends up helping the poor and the working classes while hurting the capitalists, who are mostly responsible for global warming and the planet's other ecological disasters. Western plutocracies have rolled out various market-based taxing and pricing schemes designed to reduce the consumption of fossil fuels, but have been largely oblivious to the fact that these proposals would hurt the livelihood of common people. The proper way to shield the masses during this transition is to establish stronger social control over the production and distribution cycles around fossil fuels and then to impose temporary price controls at the point of consumption. The capitalists lose out on their profits, as they should after having trashed our ecosphere, and the masses do not have to face any sudden sticker shocks.

Under modern capitalism, the class structure of our societies can be broadly divided into three categories: employees, managers, and capitalists. We define capitalists as individuals who earn such large incomes from their assets and companies that they can avoid wage work altogether, if they so choose. In the context of the United States, a rough approximation of a (small) capitalist would be anyone with a net worth greater than $10 million in liquid financial assets—which is not to deny the issue of scale here, with some capitalists having incomes of more than $100 million a year. Of course, plenty of capitalists do engage in wage work, such as CEOs of large multinational corporations. But the point is that, for the lucky capitalists, work is not a necessity; they could maintain their current standard of living without a formal salary. They could easily retire to the Bahamas next week and just live off the income flowing from their assets, such as stocks, equities, real-estate properties, and any companies they may own. However, this option is not available for the vast majority of people in society. Managers and employees both need salaries to survive and to purchase the commodities that enrich the capitalists. In addition, most workers increasingly live a life of debt servitude, in which they owe capitalists lots of money for going to school, buying a home, and using a credit card, among other things. The financial control that capital has over the rest of society also makes it very difficult for workers to demand higher wages and better living conditions. The result is a plutocracy in which a small group of rich people have completely hijacked the political process and thumbed their noses at any demands for democratic change (Formisiano, 2015).

Despite these challenges, the social and ecological imperatives for a new direction are growing rapidly every year. A democratic, ecological, and socialist civilization would substantially limit the commodification of natural resources while also linking the fate of the richest to that of the poorest. It would guarantee these six universals to all people: food, jobs, housing, healthcare, child care, and education. It would restrict and constrain the accretion of wealth. It could do so by imposing wealth taxes on capital and by socializing large parts of the economy, allowing a limited and tightly regulated market to survive. Capitalists all over the world are hoarding vast amounts of financial wealth, which they refuse to invest in the real economy because of low growth rates that offer few opportunities for excessive profits. Governments should seize the vast majority of this wealth and invest it in the improvement of social services, the rebuilding of infrastructure, and the delivery of affordable healthcare. To substantially reduce and permanently control income disparities, society could mandate that the highest salary in any company or organisation be restricted to no more than ten times the lowest salary.

By providing greater resources to the masses, a democratic society would also rescue our families from an escalating list of crises. Capitalism has torn apart the social fabric and crippled modern families by treating workers like cogs in the corporate machinery. More and more families are stressed, depressed, and increasingly feeling alienated from a ruling class that no longer seems to care. An economic system that works for common people would empower families, strengthen relationships, and help children grow into responsible adults. Part of helping families means that society should also invest in rural communities that have been destroyed as jobs and assets flow to wealthy cities. These public investments should include the creation of well-paying jobs, the construction of new clinics and hospitals for easier access to medical services, the delivery of regular cash payments to low-income households, the installation of fiber-optic cables for faster Internet, and infrastructure spending on roads, schools, and homes. Only by providing a critical balance of economic and political concessions to rural areas can we prevent the urban plutocracies from dictating terms to the rest of society. An ecological society would strive to make the allocation of resources between cities and the countryside far more equitable than the one-sided relationship that currently predominates under capitalism.

Our political and business leaders, indoctrinated by capitalist propaganda throughout their lives, have come to believe that economic growth is like a magical elixir capable of curing all evils. For most people in the modern world, it does not seem like an alternative to economic growth, as currently calculated under capitalism, is even conceivable. But imagining and realising these important alternatives may be the only way to spare human civilisation from a looming disaster. Instead of organising our societies and economies around the principle of growth, we should organize them around the principle of sustainable human development, which requires the metabolic stability of the wider ecosphere. By tightly constraining the levels of production and consumption around some dynamic equilibrium and emphasising qualitative human-social relations, as opposed to the cash nexus, we can avoid the periodic bubbles and crises of capitalism while also prolonging the duration of human civilisation. And by distributing more wealth and resources to workers and common people, we can build a fair society untroubled by recurring spasms of political and economic instability. The social and the ecological are inseparable, and together they represent the intensifying political battleground of this millennium. Future generations will judge us harshly if we fail to seize this exceptional moment in history. The impending convergence of crises, from the economic to the ecological, demands nothing less than a new vision for our social order.

NOTES

1. The paper is reprinted with the permission of *Monthly Review* magazine. It was published in *Monthly Review,* Vol. 71, No. 2 [June 2019].

2. Marx writes that "The tendency to create the world market is directly given in the concept of capital itself. Every limit appears as a barrier to be overcome." See Karl Marx (1973).
3. For a prominent example of this line of thinking, see Obama, (2017). Obama writes: "This 'decoupling' of energy sector emissions and economic growth should put to rest the argument that combatting climate change requires accepting lower growth or a lower standard of living."
4. A major issue is the aggregation problem, one of the central weak points in all of macroeconomics. For an excellent, nontechnical introduction to the aggregation problem, see Fix (2019). For a more technical treatment, see J. Felipe and F.M. Fisher (2003): 208–62. The essence of the aggregation problem is the following question: Under what conditions can you add up a bunch of stuff and be certain that you have the right total value? The basic answer is that you can add things up when you have a stable unit of measurement, like mass or energy. In a natural science, like physics, unit stability is a critical requirement for measurement and aggregation. See Gibney (2018) contrast, aggregation is a meaningless concept with unstable units of measurement, such as commodity prices in economics. One cannot define or determine a "real," inflation- adjusted aggregate through unstable units. Many economists find supposedly clever ways to get around this problem. In his famous 1956 paper, Robert Solow flatly declared: "There is only one commodity, output as a whole.... Thus we can speak unambiguously of the community's real income." In other words, he brushed aside the aggregation problem by creating an abstract economy with only one commodity. The flagrant absurdity of this move is par for the course in neoclassical theory, where ridiculous assumptions about the world are more common than breathing oxygen. See Solow (1956).There are other critical concerns with using GDP as a measure of economic value, such as the fact that it does not take into account ecological degradation and vital social services. For more on this line of criticism, see Ward et al., (2017).
5. For a recent example of this conflation, see Moreau (2018) right away by saying: "Decoupling economic growth from energy consumption is a widespread attempt to decarbonise economic activities and increase energy security."
6. See OECD (2001). For a list of things that are included under primary consumption in the United States, see the entry "Primary

Energy Consumption" in the Glossary of the US Energy Information Administration.

7. For an explanation of these methods, see "Statistical Resources" by the International Energy Agency.
8. BP assumes an efficiency rating of 38 per cent for the hypothetical power plant. See British Petroleum (2018), 52.
9. As a quick example, see the charts in Plumer (2014).
10. A BTU is equal to 1,055 joules, the standard unit of energy. A joule is roughly the amount of energy it takes to lift an apple up to your mouth. See Table 8.1, "Average Operating Heat Rate for Selected Energy Sources," *S. Energy Information Administration*, October 22, 2018.
11. For his primary work on the subject, see Smil (2015).
12. The silly assumptions that form the core of neoclassical theory are almost too numerous to recount. One can begin with utility, revealed preferences, and marginal productivity, for just a few metaphysical concepts that must be indirectly inferred from things like prices and wages. The economist Joan Robinson was one of the most brilliant critics of neoclassical economics. For her classic text on the subject, see Robinson (1964). On the mathematical front, neoclassical theory has severe problems related to aggregation and general equilibrium. Refer to endnote 5 for an explanation of the aggregation problem. For the issues surrounding general equilibrium, see Ackerman (2002). Regarding its lack of predictive power, refer to every single dynamic stochastic model that somehow missed the Great Recession back in 2008.
13. See Solow (1956).
14. Solow's conclusions relied on a function known as the Cobb-Douglas production function, which was widely used in economics back then and remains popular to this very day. However, Anwar Shaikh brilliantly tore apart Solow's results in 1974, when he showed that the Cobb-Douglas production function could accurately model data sets for which a production function should not exist. See Shaikh (1974). It turns out that there is a kind of trivial and profound reason for this behaviour. In 2005, Jesus Felipe and J.S.L. McCombie convincingly proved what had been widely suspected by Shaikh and others: that the Cobb-Douglas production function is nothing more than an identity equation, a different way of writing the additive equation capital plus

labor, and reveals absolutely nothing about the neoclassical theory of distribution. See Felipe and McCombie (2005). The Cobb-Douglas function was picking up the factor shares inherent in the empirical data sets, most of which had roughly constant factor shares, because its exponents are the exact same as the factor shares from the identity equation. In sum, the Cobb-Douglas production function is an elaborate way of saying that one equals one.

15. Stern (2004), 40.
16. Solow (1974), 11.
17. Stern (2004), 42.
18. For a comprehensive guide to some recent research on hurricanes and climate change, see Collins and Walsh, eds., (2017). For a review of the role climate change plays in the spread of infectious diseases, see Wu et al. (2016).
19. For more on Marx and his theory of the metabolic rift, see Foster (2000).
20. For an excellent introduction to how photovoltaics work, see "Solar Cell Efficiency," *Energy Education*, June 25, 2018.
21. Stern (2004), 42.
22. See Table 1.7, "Primary Energy Consumption, Energy Expenditures, and Carbon Dioxide Emissions Indicators," *S. Energy Information Administration*, March 26, 2019.
23. For some relatively recent flavours of elite opinion on this topic, see Seitz and Hite (2012), 126. Also look at Saha and Muro (2016).
24. See Stern, "Economic Growth and Energy," 35–51. In an important paper, Kaufmann also documented the structural shifts that occurred within the US energy sector and analysed their impact on economic growth. See Kaufmann (2004).
25. For one of the most influential studies in this field, see Stern (2011). For a review of the statistical relationship between energy use and GDP growth worldwide, see Hannesson, (2009). For a major study on the link between energy and income in certain Asian countries, see Asafu-Adjaye (2000). For a general overview of how energy use has shaped human history, Smil (2017).
26. See "Decoupling of Global Emissions and Economic Growth Confirmed, *International Energy Agency*, March 16, 2016.
27. See Ward et al. (2017).

28. Summary for Policymakers of the IPCC Special Report on Global Warming," Intergovernmental Panel on Climate Change, October 8, 2018.

REFERENCES

Ackerman F. (2002), Still Dead After All These Years: Interpreting the Failure of General Equilibrium, *Journal of Economic Methodology*, Vol. 9, No. 2, pp. 119–39.

Asafu-Adjaye J. (2000), The Relationship Between Energy Consumption, Energy Prices, and Economic Growth: Time Series Evidence from Asian Developing Countries, *Energy Economics*, Vol. 22, No. 6, pp. 615–25.

Bentley, J.H. (2013), Environment Crisis in the World History, *Procedia—Social and Behavioural Sciences*, Vol. 77, pp. 108–15.

Bernstein, L. (2018), S. Life Expectancy Declines Again, a Dismal Trend Not Seen Since World War I, *Washington Post*, November 29.

British Petroleum (2018), *BP Statistical Review of World Energy*, London: British Petroleum.

Buck, T. (2018), Energy Shift Fails to Cut German Carbon, *Financial Times*, October 8.

Carrington, D. (2018), Brutal News: Global Carbon Emissions Jump to All-Time High in 2018, *The Guardian*, December 5.

Collins, J.M. and K. Walsh (eds.), (2017), *Hurricanes and Climate Change*, Vol. 3, New York: Springer.

Davies and B. Doherty (2018), Corruption, Incompetence and a Musical: Nauru's Cursed History, *The Guardian*, September 3.

Desilver, (2018), For Most US Workers, Real Wages Have Barely Budged in Decades, *Pew Research Centre*, August 7.

Dennis, B. and C. Mooney (2018), We Are in Trouble: Global Carbon Emissions Reached a Record High in 2018, *Washington Post*, December 5.

Dickler, D. (2019), Consumer Debt Hits $4 Trillion, *CNBC*, February 21.

Felipe, J. and J.S.L. McCombie (2005), How Sound Are the Foundations of the Aggregate Production Function?, *Eastern Economic Journal* Vol. 31, No. 3, pp. 467–88.

Felipe, J. and F.M. Fisher, (2003), Aggregation in Production Functions: What Applied Economists Should Know, *Metroeconomica*, Vol. 54,

No. 2, pp. 208-62.

Fix, B. (2019), The Aggregation Problem: Implications for Ecological and Biophysical Economics, *Bio Physical Economics and Resource Quality* Vol. 4, No. 1.

Formisiano, R.P. (2015), *Plutocracy in America*, Baltimore: John Hopkins University Press.

Foster, J.B. (2000), *Marx's Ecology*, New York: Monthly Review Press.

Gibney, E. (2018), Largest Overhaul of Scientific Units Since 1875 Wins Approval, *Nature*, November 16.

Hannesson, R. (2009), Energy and GDP Growth, *International Journal of Energy Management*, Vol. 3, No. 2, pp. 157–70.

Hausfather, Z. (2017), Analysis: Global CO2 Emissions Set to Rise 2% in 2017 After Three-Year Plateau, *Carbon Brief*, November 13, 2017.

Hausfather, Z. (2017), Analysis: Why US Carbon Emissions Have Fallen 14% Since 2005, *Carbon Brief*, August 15.

Jackson, T. (2011), *Prosperity without Growth: Economics for a Finite Planet*, Abingdon, UK: Routledge.

Jain, R. (2018), In Parched Afghanistan, Drought Sharpens Water Dispute with Iran, *Reuters*, July 16, 2018.

Jewett, J.W. and R.A. Serway (2008), *Physics for Scientists and Engineers*, Boston: Cengage Learning, p. 618.

Kaufmann, R. (2004), The Mechanisms for Autonomous Energy Efficiency Increases: A Cointegration Analysis of the US Energy/GDP Ratio, *The Energy Journal*, Vol. 25, No. 1, pp. 63–86.

Kesler, S.E., S.C. Simon and A.F. Simon (2015), *Mineral Resources, Economics and the Environment*, Cambridge: Cambridge University Press, p. 302.

Kolasi, E. (2018), The Physics of Capitalism, *Monthly Review*, Vol. 70, No. 1, pp. 29–43.

Marx, K. (1973), *Grundrisse*, London: Penguin Books.

Misculin, N. and G. Burin (2018), How a Year of 'Endless Storms' Battered Argentina's Economy, *Reuters*, December, 20.

Moreau, V. (218), Decoupling Energy Use and Economic Growth: Counter Evidence from Structural Effects and Embodied Energy in Trade, *Applied Energy*, Vol. 215, pp. 54–62.

OECD (2001), Primary Energy Consumption, Organization for Economic Cooperation and Development, November 20.

Obama, B. (2017), The Irreversible Momentum of Clean Energy, *Science*, January 9.

Plumer, B. (2014), Can We Sever the Link Between Energy and Economic Growth?, *Washington Post*, January 17.

Plumer, B. (2019), S. Carbon Emissions Surged in 2018 Even as Coal Plants Closed, *New York Times*, January 8, 2019.

Reed, S. (2017), Germany's Shift to Green Power Stalls, Despite Huge Investments, *New York Times*, October 7.

Robinson, J. (1964), *Economic Philosophy*, Middlesex UK: Penguin.

Rockström J. et al. (2009) A Safe Operating Space for Humanity, *Nature*, Vol. 461, pp. 472–75.

Saha, D. and M. Muro (2016), Growth, Carbon, and Trump: States Are 'Decoupling' Economic Growth from Emissions Growth, *Brookings Institution*, December 8.

Schandl, H., et al. (2016), *Global Material Flows and Resource Productivity*, Paris: International Resource Panel, 40.

Seitz, L. and K.A. Hite (2012), *Global Issues: An Introduction*, Hoboken, NJ: John Wiley & Sons, p. 126.

Shaikh A. (1974), Laws of Production and Laws of Algebra: The Humbug Production Function, *The Review of Economics and Statistics*, Vol. 56, No. 1, pp. 115-20.

Simon, F. (2017), Decoupling Energy from GDP Growth 'Might Be Impossible,' Statoil Says, *Euractiv*, June 15, 2017.

Smil, V. (2015), *Power Density: A Key to Understanding Energy Sources and Uses*, Cambridge: MIT Press.

Smil, V. (2017), *Energy and Civilization*, Cambridge: MIT Press.

Solow, R.M. (1956), A Contribution to the Theory of Economic Growth, *Quarterly Journal of Economics*, Vol. 70, No. 1, pp. 65-94.

Solow, R.M. (1974), The Economics of Resources or the Resources of Economics, *American Economic Review*, Vol. 64, No. 2, pp. 1–14.

Stern, D.I. (2004), Economic Growth and Energy, In C. J. Cleveland (ed.), *Encyclopaedia of Energy*, San Diego: Academic Press, p. 43.

Stern, D.I. (2011), The Role of Energy in Economic Growth, *Crawford School Centre for Climate Economics & Policy Paper*, No. 3.10.

Vos, De A. (1980), Detailed Balance Limit of the Efficiency of Tandem Solar Cells, *Journal of Physics D: Applied Physics*, Vol. 13, No. 5, pp. 839–46.

Ward, J., et al. (2017), The Decoupling Delusion: Rethinking Growth and Sustainability, *The Conversation*, March 12, 2017.

Wernick, A. (2019), Climate Change Is the Overlooked Driver of Central American Migration, *PRI*, February 6.

Worstall, T. (2014), When Physicists Do Economics We Seem Not to Get Economics as the Result, *Forbes*, October 6.

Wiedmann, T.O. et al. (2013), The Material Footprint of Nations, *Proceedings of the National Academy of Sciences*, Vol. 112, No. 20, pp. 6271–76.

Wu, X., et al. (2016), Impact of Climate Change on Human Infectious Diseases: Empirical Evidence and Human Adaption, *Environment International*, Vol. 86, pp. 14–23.

List of Contributors

Anjan Kumar Chakrabarti, Professor, Department of Economics, University of Calcutta, Kolkata, India.

Balwinder Singh Tiwana, Former Professor, Department of Economics, Punjabi University, Patiala, India.

Deepankar Basu, Associate Professor, Department of Economics, University of Massachusetts, Amherst, USA.

Erald Kolasi, PhD in Physics from George Mason University, USA.

Gerald Epstein, Professor and Co-Director, Political Economy Research Institute, Department of Economics, University of Massachusetts, Amherst, USA.

Göran Djurfeldt, Professor, Department of Human Geography, Lund University, Sweden.

Greg Albo, Associate Professor, Department of Political Science, York University, Toronto, Canada.

John B. Foster, Professor, Department of Sociology, University of Oregon, USA and Editor of *Monthly Review*.

Paul Zarembka, Professor, Department of Economics, State University of New York at Buffalo, USA.

Prabhat Patnaik, Professor Emeritus, Centre for Economic Studies and Planning Jawaharlal Nehru University, New Delhi, India.

Pritam Singh, Visiting Scholar, Wolfson College, University of Oxford, Oxford, UK.

Paramjit Singh, Assistant Professor, Department of Economics, Panjab University, Chandigarh, India.

Samir Amin (late), Former Director, Third World Forum, Dakar,

Senegal, West Africa and Co-founder, World Forum for Alternatives, Dakar, Senegal.

Satyaki Roy, Associate Professor, Institute for Studies in Industrial Development, New Delhi, India.

Surinder Kumar, Former Professor of Economics and Former Director, Giri Institute of Development Studies, Lucknow, India.

V. Upadhyay, Adjunct Professor and former Head, Department of Humanities and Social Sciences, Indian Institute of Technology Delhi, India.

About the Editors

V. Upadhyay is Adjunct Professor and former Head, Department of Humanities and Social Sciences, IIT Delhi. He has earlier taught at IIT Kanpur, India; University of New Brunswick, Canada; University of PEI, Canada; McMaster University, Canada; and University of Rajasthan, India. His research interests are in the areas of development economics and political economy. He has published about a hundred research papers in reputed Indian and international journals. He has authored/co-edited several books on the subjects of Indian economy and political economy including *From Statism to Neo-Liberalism: The Development Process in India; Essays on Distribution, World Systems, Ecology, and Left Politics;* and *Plutocracy, Cronyism and Populism: Facets of Neoliberalism in India.* He is an authorised signatory of the Indian Political Economy Association and a member of the Steering Council of the World Association of Political Economy.

Paramjit Singh is an Assistant Professor, Department of Economics, Panjab University, Chandigarh. His research interests are in macroeconomic theory and Marxian political economy. He has more than thirty research publications in reputed national and international journals of political economy to his credit. Dr. Singh is a coordinator of the Indian Political Economy Association.